When should I trave
Where do I go for answ
What's the best and easiest way to plan and book my trip?

frommers.travelocity.com

Frommer's, the travel guide leader, has teamed up with **Travelocity.com**, the leader in online travel, to bring you an in-depth, easy-to-use resource designed to help you plan and book your trip online.

At **frommers.travelocity.com**, you'll find free online updates about your destination from the experts at Frommer's plus the outstanding travel planning and purchasing features of Travelocity.com. Travelocity.com provides reservations capabilities for 95 percent of all airline seats sold, more than 47,000 hotels, and over 50 car rental companies. In addition, Travelocity.com offers more than 2,000 exciting vacation and cruise packages. Travelocity.com puts you in complete control of your travel planning with these and other great features:

Expert travel guidance from Frommer's - over 150 writers reporting from around the world!

Best Fare Finder - an interactive calendar tells you when to travel to get the best airfare

Fare Watcher - we'll track airfare changes to your favorite destinations

Dream Maps - a mapping feature that suggests travel opportunities based on your budget

Shop Safe Guarantee - 24 hours a day / 7 days a week live customer service, and more!

Whether you're traveling on a tight budget, looking for a quick weekend getaway, or planning the trip of a lifetime, Frommer's guides and Travelocity.com will make your travel dreams a reality. You've bought the book, now book the trip!

Travelocity.com
A Sabre Company

Frommer's

Here's what the critics say about Frommer's:

"Amazingly easy to use. Very portable, very complete."
—*Booklist*

♦

"The only mainstream guide to list specific prices. The Walter Cronkite of guidebooks—with all that implies."
—*Travel & Leisure*

♦

"Complete, concise, and filled with useful information."
—*New York Daily News*

♦

"Hotel information is close to encyclopedic."
—*Des Moines Sunday Register*

♦

"Detailed, accurate and easy-to-read information for all price ranges."
—*Glamour Magazine*

Shanghai

1st Edition

by J. D. Brown

IDG Books Worldwide, Inc.
An International Data Group Company
Foster City, CA • Chicago, IL • Indianapolis, IN • New York, NY

ABOUT THE AUTHOR

J. D. Brown has lived and worked in China and has written about China as a literary traveler, a travel writer, and a guidebook author. His work has appeared in such diverse publications as the *New York Times,* the *Washington Post,* the *Michigan Quarterly Review, Islands,* and *National Geographic Traveler.* He is also the author of *Frommer's Beijing* and *Frommer's China: The 50 Most Memorable Trips.* When he is not traveling in the Far East, he lives in Eugene, Oregon.

IDG BOOKS WORLDWIDE, INC.

An International Data Group Company
909 Third Avenue
New York, NY 10022

Find us online at **www.frommers.com**

ISBN 0-02-863672-4
ISSN 1524-4288

Editor: Leslie Shen
Production Editor: Tammy Ahrens
Photo Editor: Richard Fox
Design by Michele Laseau
Cartographer: Roberta Stockwell
Production by IDG Books Indianapolis Production Department

SPECIAL SALES

For general information on IDG Books Worldwide's books in the U.S., please call our Consumer Customer Service department at 1-800-762-2974. For reseller information, including discounts, bulk sales, customized editions, and premium sales, please call our Reseller Customer Service department at 1-800-434-3422.

Manufactured in the United States of America

5   4   3   2   1

Contents

6   Exploring Shanghai 99

7   Shanghai Strolls 133

8   Shopping 150

9   Shanghai After Dark 164

10   Suzhou, Hangzhou & Other Side Trips from Shanghai 177

List of Maps

An Invitation to the Reader

In researching this book, we discovered many wonderful places—hotels, restaurants, shops, and more. We're sure you'll find others. Please tell us about them, so we can share the information with your fellow travelers in upcoming editions. If you were disappointed with a recommendation, we'd love to know that, too. Please write to:

Frommer's Shanghai, 1st Edition
IDG Books Worldwide, Inc.
909 Third Avenue
New York, NY 10022

An Additional Note

Please be advised that travel information is subject to change at any time—and this is especially true of prices. We therefore suggest that you write or call ahead for confirmation when making your travel plans. The authors, editors, and publisher cannot be held responsible for the experiences of readers while traveling. Your safety is important to us, however, so we encourage you to stay alert and be aware of your surroundings. Keep a close eye on cameras, purses, and wallets, all favorite targets of thieves and pickpockets.

What the Symbols Mean

✪ Frommer's Favorites

Our favorite places and experiences—outstanding for quality, value, or both.

The following abbreviations are used for credit cards:

AE	American Express	ER	enRoute
CB	Carte Blanche	JCB	Japan Credit Bank
DC	Diners Club	MC	MasterCard
DISC	Discover	V	Visa
EC	Eurocard		

Find Frommer's Online

www.frommers.com offers up-to-the-minute listings on almost 200 cities around the globe—including the latest bargains and candid, personal articles updated daily by Arthur Frommer himself. No other Web site offers such comprehensive and timely coverage of the world of travel.

The Best of Shanghai

If one simply counts heads, this is the biggest city in the biggest country on Earth. If one simply scans statistics, this is China's capital of commerce, industry, and finance. But numbers don't tell the whole Shanghai story. Shanghai has a colonial past more intense than that of any other city in China, save Hong Kong, and this legacy gives it a dramatic character, visible in the streets today. But the city is not only a museum of East meeting West on Chinese soil. Shanghai has overnight become one of the world's great modern capitals, the one city that best shows what the whole nation is becoming at the dawn of the 21st century. The very pulse of Shanghai is the pulse of Asia's future. Shanghai has not always been much of a delight to tour, but it is now.

During the 1990s, Shanghai was torn apart and rebuilt during the economic boom that shook China to its foundations. One in five of the world's high-lift cranes were at work in the streets of Shanghai, raising tower after glass-and-steel tower in the ruins. Shanghai resembled the largest construction site ever conceived, and it was not always a pretty sight for travelers. But this first great phase of modern reconstruction has passed, and a new, more vital Shanghai has emerged. It is a city that a visitor can comfortably enjoy and explore for the first time since those romantic days of the 1930s, when old Shanghai was a notorious playground for foreign adventurers and a free trade show for overseas taipans and exploiters. The landmarks of Shanghai's colonial period shine through for the first time since the Communists came to power 50 years ago and worked their own duller magic on the cityscape.

Today, there are large neighborhoods of foreign architecture, wonderful for a stroll, where Europeans, especially the French, once resided. Shanghai's great river of commerce, the Huangpu, is lined with a gallery of colonial architecture; known as the Bund, it's grander than any other in the East, and much of it was recently refurbished and is open to the curious visitor. The mansions, garden estates, country clubs, and cathedrals of the Westerners who made their fortunes here a century ago are scattered throughout the city, and there's even a synagogue, dating from the days of an unparalleled Jewish immigration to China. Shanghai's foreign legacy is epitomized by the Peace Hotel on the Bund, the 1929 creation of a

China

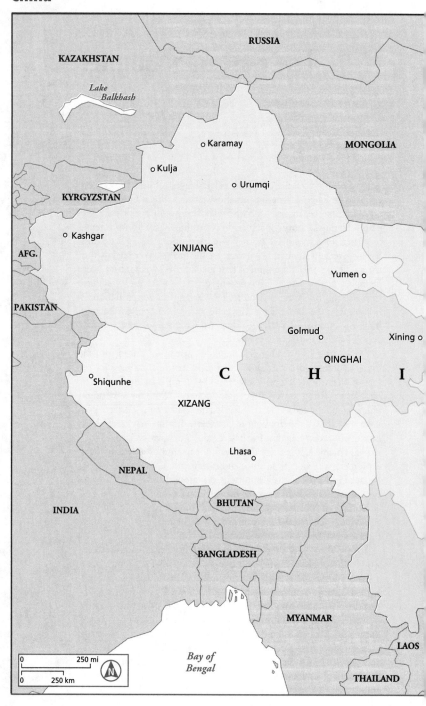

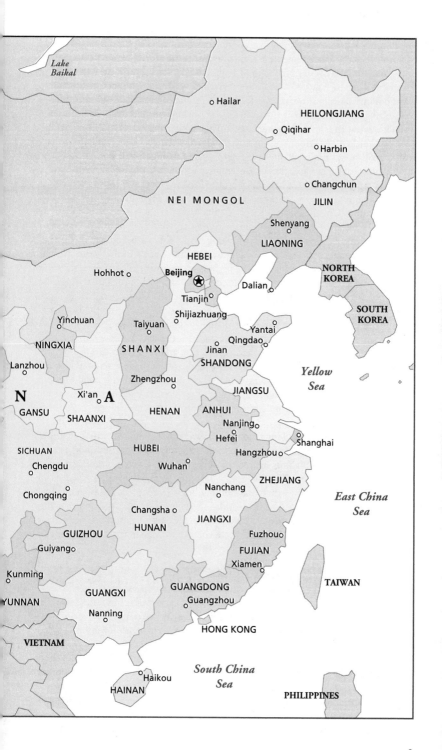

Jewish millionaire, today a masterpiece of Art Deco—a relic of the Jazz Age. These are not the typical monuments of China, but they are typical of Shanghai.

The East has a Western flavor in Shanghai, but at the same time the creations of a strictly Chinese culture have not been erased. A walk through downtown turns up astounding traditional treasures: a teahouse that embodies all that was old China; a classical garden as superb as any in Beijing or Suzhou; an "old town" as quaint and chaotic as any in China; active temples and ancient pagodas; and a museum of Chinese art and artifacts that is universally acclaimed as China's best. Though the pace of new Shanghai rivals that of New York City and its nightlife and cafes now echo the sophistication of Paris, though the architecture and avenues recall 19th-century Europe rather than old Cathay, this is still a Chinese city to the core.

Shanghai is also a city for shoppers (Nanjing Road is the number-one shopping street in all of China), but it is especially the place for those who want to see the future of China. Across the mighty Huangpu River, which served as old Shanghai's eastern border, a truly new Shanghai is taking shape. Known as Pudong, this Shanghai East boasts its own modern attractions: the tallest hotel in the world, China's largest stock exchange, and one of the highest observation decks in Asia, the Pearl of the Orient TV Tower. Not to be outdone, old Shanghai has its own legions of new skyscrapers, too, and a booming collection of fine international restaurants, several of them taking over the rooftops of the colonial gems lining the Bund and the mansions that had gone to seed in Shanghai's French Quarter.

Incredibly crowded, densely packed, Shanghai is the raw center of China's commerce and industry. It has energy and confidence, and it has new dreams. Its polluted rivers are being cleaned up. Greenways and new parks are emerging. Historic neighborhoods, both Chinese and colonial, are being spared the bulldozer and transformed into avenues of shops and cafes. New theaters and cultural centers are attracting top performers from China and abroad.

Shanghai still has a long way to go to become the New York or Paris of China. It is not yet as prosperous as Hong Kong (its nearest rival), nor as international. But the raw complexity of Shanghai is its charm. Sipping a cocktail in a new French restaurant positioned high on the rooftops over the Bund, you can look across the river into the future of China, at the burgeoning Manhattan of skyscrapers in Pudong where a decade ago there was nothing but mud flats, rice fields, and village huts. Only in Shanghai are so many worlds—East and West, past and present—this elevated and pinched together, shoulder to shoulder, like a Picasso mural. This is present-day China on a grand scale, where you can breathe in the exhilaration of a new century for Asia.

1 Frommer's Favorite Shanghai Experiences

- **Dining on Hairy Crab:** The signature dish of Shanghai is absolutely scrumptious, but it is seasonal (autumn), and it is best enjoyed at a big local restaurant, preferably one housed in an old mansion. See chapter 5 for recommended restaurants.
- **Savoring a Sunset on the Bund:** There are now two absolutely romantic spots perched right over the Bund to savor that salute to day's end in style: the outdoor balcony on the 11th floor of the historic Peace Hotel, where the ancient bells of China are played nightly, and the open-air balcony of Shanghai's top international restaurant and lounge, M on the Bund. See chapters 5 and 9.
- **Taking in the Shanghai Museum:** China's finest, most modern, and most memorable museum of historic relics has disappointed almost no visitor since it

opened in the heart of People's Park. Make it a top priority, and allow a few hours more than you think you'll need. See chapter 6.

- **Surveying Shanghai from the Pearl of the Orient TV Tower:** After crossing the Huangpu River from old Shanghai to the new Shanghai (whether by taxi, subway, pedestrian tunnel, or ferry), enjoy the ultimate panorama from the sphere atop Asia's tallest tower. Even the elevator ride is exciting—like a rocket into the clouds. See chapter 6.

- **Cruising the Huangpu River:** A 17-mile (27km) pleasure cruise from the Bund to the mouth of the mighty Yangzi River, past endless wharves, factories, and tankers at anchor, gives substance to Shanghai's claim as China's largest port. Nearly half of China's trade with the outside world travels these same waters. See chapter 6.

- **Mastering the Maze of Yu Garden:** This superb garden estate in the heart of Shanghai's Old Town is a crown jewel of classic Chinese gardens, a lush labyrinth of pavilions, ponds, rockeries, and serene pathways to Old Cathay that never seem to end. See chapter 6.

- **Rediscovering Shanghai's Jewish Past:** In the mid-19th century, Jews from the Mideast helped make Shanghai a great city, and in the mid-20th century, thousands of Jewish refugees flooded the International Settlement north of the Bund. Today, this history can be encountered at the Ohel Moshe Synagogue, where the curator, one Mr. Wang, offers vivid accounts of this little-known but important Jewish ghetto. See chapter 6.

- **Burning Incense in the Temples:** Temples are not Shanghai's strong suit, but there are four worth visiting: the Jade Buddha Temple (with its white jade carvings from Burma); Jing An Temple (the most active); the Confucian Temple (recently restored in Old Town); and Longhua Pagoda (dating from A.D. 977). See chapter 6.

- **Dropping in on a Children's Palace:** Shanghai has several of China's most interesting Children's Palaces (special conservatories for gifted kids), located in virtually unrestored colonial mansions. You can enter the classrooms and watch Shanghai's best and brightest as they learn (primarily music, dance, art, and computers). See chapter 6.

- **Shadow Boxing in the Parks:** Tai chi and other traditional, even more mysterious exercises—as well as Western ballroom dancing—are performed before work every morning in the city parks and on the Bund by thousands of Shanghai residents from age 8 to 80, a sight not to be missed. See chapter 6 for details on Shanghai parks.

- **Drinking Tea in the Perfect Teahouse:** Shanghai's Huxinting (Mid-Lake) Teahouse is the quintessential teahouse in China, often thought to be the original model for the one in the blue-willow plate pattern. Here, at the center of Old Town Shanghai, is the place to pause for a refreshing cup of green tea, just as Queen Elizabeth II did on her visit. See chapter 6.

- **Watching River Traffic from "the Other Bund":** The best place to enjoy the incredible armadas of barges, carriers, fishing boats, naval vessels, sampans, and cruise liners that crowd the Huangpu River is not the Bund, but the new Riverside Promenade on the opposite shore, where the crowds are smaller and the walkway extends all the way to the edge, with the water just a few feet below. It's almost like walking on water. See chapter 6.

- **Mingling with the Masses on the Bund Promenade:** Located on the most widely known street in Asia, the Bund has been converted into a riverside promenade, the ideal place to take a leisurely stroll, watch the barge-and-ship traffic racing to and from the Yangzi delta, and admire on one side the long wall of European colonial architecture from the past and on the other side the rising wall of skyscrapers for the future. The promenade is wide and picturesque, but also crowded with visitors from around the world, including thousands from inside China. This is the first and last place to measure the pulse of China's most vital and increasingly international city, while still staying in touch with the visible monuments of its romantic past. See chapter 7 for details.

- **Admiring the Colonial Architecture of the Bund:** For blocks the river harbor of Shanghai is dominated by the relics of its colonial past, when Europeans and other foreign taipans and adventurers presided over China's richest and most notorious city, raising consulates, banks, trading houses, hotels, private clubs, and the Customs House. These monuments to Shanghai's occupation by foreign financial interests amazingly enough remain, but the new occupants are mostly the Chinese themselves, who are restoring the lavish Western lobbies and interiors of these great buildings to their former splendor, making this Shanghai's finest street museum. See chapter 7.

- **Strolling the French Concession:** This is the most interesting of the colonial districts left in Shanghai, filled with the gorgeous villas, mansions, and apartment houses of the 1920s and 1930s, when the French made their mark in Shanghai. The avenues are being restored, the facades cleaned up, and the great houses with their balconies, private gardens, and carved paneling are opening their doors as upscale (but quite affordable) restaurants. See chapter 7.

- **Antiques Shopping on Shanghai's new "Old Street":** The east-west street that forms the southern border of Old Town—already the top spot for shopping for Chinese treasures—has recently been delightfully restored as a pedestrian lane lined with Ming and Qing Dynasty teahouses and shop houses specializing in antiques. See chapters 7 and 8.

- **Shopping the Nanjing Road Pedestrian Mall:** Nanjing Road was already the most famous and most crowded shopping street in China. With the recent creation of a pedestrian mall here, it is once again a pleasurable place to browse, affording a dramatic mix of modern stores, international boutiques, and cafes with pre–Revolutionary era department stores, office towers, hotels, and traditional silk shops. See chapters 7 and 8.

- **Swinging to Old-Time Jazz in the Peace Hotel:** The nightly performances of New Orleans–style jazz by a Chinese band, with some members who have been playing here since before the Revolution (1949), is the ultimate piece of colonial nostalgia; if the music doesn't grab you, the Peace Hotel lobby and public areas will. This hotel is China's best Art Deco museum. See chapters 7 and 9 for details.

- **Shopping Huaihai Lu and Hengshan Lu:** Shanghai residents and savvy Chinese visitors turn their backs on Nanjing Road (outrageously expensive) and do their upscale shopping and noshing on these two streets, and so can you. Huaihai Lu, which runs parallel to Nanjing Road, is lined with modern shopping malls and small shops; Hengshan Lu has become the city's trendsetter for international cafes and nightspots. See chapter 8.

- **Watching the Acrobats:** A night at a Chinese opera can be tedious, but an acrobatics show is universally appreciated—and Shanghai's dazzling troupes are rightly considered China's very finest at this ancient craft. See chapter 9.

- **Barhopping on Julu Lu:** This street near the Hilton in western Shanghai, along with adjacent streets, including Hengshan Lu, has a greater concentration of new cafes, bars, and nightspots catering to foreigners than any other single district, but you'll need taxis to do proper barhopping across Shanghai. See chapter 9 for a list of the best bars.

- **Toasting the Town from Atop the World's Tallest Hotel:** The view is as good and the drinks, tapas, and spring rolls are infinitely better from the Grand Hyatt's Sky Lounge than from the Pearl of the Orient TV Tower next door. The Cloud Nine Lounge is on the 88th floor of the world's third-highest building; and if you take the back stairs, you can go up still another floor to salute China's biggest city. See chapter 9.

- **Drifting in a Gondola through a Water Village:** The top day trip from Shanghai is to Zhou Zhuang, a traditional "water village" of rice fields, arched bridges, clan houses, and canals, where the local women paddle visitors up and down the main street canal in the Chinese version of Venetian gondolas. See chapter 10 for this and other excursions.

2 Best Hotel Bets

For complete hotel listings, see chapter 4, "Accommodations."

- **Best Hotel for Yesterday:** The legendary Cathay Hotel, now the **Peace Hotel,** 20 Nanjing Dong Lu (☎ **021/6321-6888**), located at Shanghai's most fabled intersection (Nanjing Road and the Bund), is a living museum of Shanghai's Art Deco and colonial past.

- **Best Hotel for Today:** The honor remains with the **Portman Ritz-Carlton,** 1376 Nanjing Xi Lu (☎ **800/241-3333** or 021/6279-8888), owing to its tremendous business and shopping facilities, as well as a recent remodel; right on its heels are the Westin, the Hilton, the Shangri-La, and the Grand Hyatt.

- **Best Hotel for Tomorrow:** The highest hotel in the world, the **Grand Hyatt,** 2 Shiji Da Dao (☎ **800/233-1234** or 021/5049-1234), is also the highest in high-tech amenities and designs. This 21st-century pagoda boasts 60 elevators, 19 escalators, a 57th-floor sky-pool for "swimming in the sky," and a 360° panorama from the cloud tops.

- **Best Hotel on the Bund:** Towering over Nanjing Road at the heart of the new pedestrian mall, the **Hotel Sofitel Hyland,** 505 Nanjing Dong Lu (☎ **800/ 221-4542** or 021/6351-5888), brings a French flair to international accommodations along China's most celebrated shopping avenue.

- **Best View of the Bund:** The nearby Grand Hyatt is higher, but the 28-story **Pudong Shangri-La Hotel,** 33 Fu Cheng Lu (☎ **800/942-5050** or 021/6882-8888), is closer and at just the right elevation for a spectacular view of Shanghai's European architecture across the Huangpu River. The view is even better at night, when this riverfront "colonial scroll" of banks and trading houses is lighted up.

- **Best Hotel for Business:** The **Hilton,** 250 Huashan Lu (☎ **800/445-8667** or 021/6248-0000), Shanghai's first five-star hotel, always tops the poll for foreign business travelers, who value its experienced and efficient service.

- **Best Hotel for Conventions:** The best trappings for MICE (Meetings, Incentives, Conventions, Expositions) travelers can be found at the convenient and friendly **Westin Tai Ping Yang,** 5 Zunyi Nan Lu (☎ **800/WESTIN-1** or 021/6275-8888), an easy walk to the major marketing venues in the Hongqiao Development Zone.

- **Best Hotel Lobby:** The city's most lavish ground floor, stuffed with old-world antiques and European elegance in its Italian and Spanish marble and glass, is right on the Nanjing Road pedestrian mall at the **Grand Nation Hotel,** 719 Nanjing Dong Lu (☎ **021/6350-0000**).

- **Best Hotel for a Cheap Sleep:** Abandon the amenities (except for a private bathroom), pocket the savings, and savor the location of the historic Shanghai **YMCA Hotel,** 123 Xizang Nan Lu (☎ **021/6326-1040**), an easy walk to People's Park, the Shanghai Museum, both Metro lines, and the shopping strips of Nanjing Road and Huaihai Lu.
- **Best Hotel for Film Stars & Movie Fans:** Next door to the chief venue for the Shanghai International Film Festival, the five-star **Holiday Inn Crowne Plaza,** 400 Panyu Lu (☎ **800/465-4329** or 021/6280-8888), fits the bill.
- **Best Boutique Hotel:** Swank and cute, the new **M. P. Boutique Hotel,** 660 Xinhua Lu (☎ **021/6280-1000**), is Shanghai's only European-style boutique hotel, complete with an upscale English pub and restaurant in the old-world lobby.
- **Best World Unto Itself:** This odd category fits to a tee the hotel city-state known as the **Portman Ritz-Carlton,** 1376 Nanjing Xi Lu (☎ **800/241-3333** or 021/6279-8888), which occupies the center of Shanghai Centre and its unparalleled array of conveniences: upscale boutiques, a supermarket, Shanghai's best business center, a cinema, a medical clinic, international airline offices, American Express, and even a Hard Rock Cafe.
- **Best Hotel Room Decor:** Luxury hotel rooms begin to look alike all around the world, but two hotels in Shanghai stand out. The **Grand Hyatt,** 2 Shiji Da Dao, Pudong (☎ **800/233-1234** or 021/5049-1234), has irregularly shaped rooms decorated in Art Deco, traditional Chinese, and high-tech furnishings, including glass counters and sinks. The **Westin Tai Ping Yang,** 5 Zunyi Nan Lu, Changning District (☎ **800/WESTIN-1** or 021/6275-8888), cultivates the Victorian look with an embarrassing wealth of European-style plush amenities and furnishings, giving it the feel of a B&B (except for the extremely comfortable ergonomic desk chairs and bright work lamps).
- **Best Hotel for a Workout:** The health-and-fitness facilities at the **Regal International East Asia Hotel,** 516 Hengshan Lu (☎ **800/222-8888** or 021/6415-5588), don't stop at just the 25-meter lap pool, the aerobics gym, the simulated golf range, and the 12-lane bowling alley; add to that the 10 world-class tennis courts (two indoors), including a center court with spectator seating for 1,200. A more unusual athletic venue is provided for guests at the **Novotel Shanghai Yuan Lin,** 201 Baise Lu (☎ **800/221-4542** or 021/6470-1688), with jogging in the adjacent Botanical Gardens and, in a separate recreation center, table tennis, bowling, and a shooting range.

3 Best Dining Bets

For complete restaurant listings, see chapter 5, "Dining."

- **Best Dining on the Bund:** Shanghai's world-class Mediterranean restaurant, **M on the Bund,** 7th floor, 20 Guangdong Lu (☎ **021/6350-9988**), not only serves impeccable Continental cuisine, but also features a knockout view of the Bund and riverfront from its patio atop a colonial-era trading house.
- **Best Shanghai Cuisine:** Since 1938, **Meilongzhen,** Building 22, 1081 Nanjing Xi Lu (☎ **021/6253-5353**), has served its special chicken in small ceramic crocks and poured tea from pots with foot-long spouts to the delight of those looking for fine Shanghai (and Sichuan) dining in a 1930s setting.

- **Best Setting for Shanghai Cuisine:** For sheer atmosphere, the **Dragon and Phoenix Room,** on the 8th floor of the Art Deco Peace Hotel, 20 Nanjing Dong Lu (☎ 021/6321-6888), can't be topped, with its gaudy, traditional interiors and views of the Bund; the Shanghai crab and eel are good, too.
- **Best Tourist Restaurant:** It's hard to avoid the tour groups that flock to Old Town to eat at the Ming-style pavilion where everyone from Queen Elizabeth to President Clinton also dined, but **Lu Bo Lang,** 115-131 Yu Yuan Lu (☎ 021/6328-0602), does have a quite decent Shanghai menu that makes it worth standing in line.
- **Best Country-Club Dining:** It's not a country-club restaurant: it just looks like one out of Shanghai's colonial past. **Sasha's,** House 11, 9 Dongping Lu (☎ 021/6474-6166), serves European dishes, including roast rack of lamb and fondue, in the garden and from the balconies of a mansion once frequented by the Soongs, Chiang Kai-shek, and even Madame Mao.
- **Best Hotel Dining:** No hotel offers more high-quality choices (or a better view) than the **Grand Hyatt,** in Pudong, 2 Shiji Da Dao (☎ 021/5049-1234), with its Grand Café's international buffets, the Canton's gourmet Cantonese dishes, the Grill's seafood and steaks, Kobachi's yakatori, and Cuchina's Tuscan pastas and pizzas—not to mention the 10 open kitchens that make up the Food Live "food street" on podium level 3.
- **Best Deli:** Stock up big time at the **Bauernstube,** 2nd floor, 5 Zunyi Nan Lu, Westin Tai Ping Yang Hotel (☎ 021/6275-8888), with its large selection of cheeses, sausages, Norwegian salmon, breads, cakes, and roast chicken; or do the same in the **Portman Deli,** Level 1, West Tower, Shanghai Centre (☎ 021/6279-8888).
- **Best People Watching:** The place to be seen is the very chic **Park 97,** 2 Gaolan Lu, in Fuxing Park (☎ 021/6318-0785), the favorite of the modern taipans and sophisticated locals in search of fine Continental cuisine and late-night relaxation.
- **Best Burgers:** For tried-and-true American burgers and fries, the **Hard Rock Cafe,** 1376 Nanjing Xi Lu, Shanghai Centre (☎ 021/6279-8133), is a hard act to follow.
- **Best Coffee Bar:** The lattes and bagels you're looking for are at the Starbucks-like **Espresso Americano,** 105 Shanghai Centre, 1376 Nanjing Xi Lu (☎ 021/6279-8888), with its counter service and outdoor seating.
- **Best Teahouse:** The most famous teahouse in China, its eaves soaring over the pond by Yu Garden, is Shanghai's own **Huxinting** (☎ 021/6373-6950), a welcome haven in the crunch of Old Town shopping and mass tourism.
- **Best Cajun:** Not much competition in this category, but that hasn't stopped **Bourbon Street,** 191 Hengshan Lu (☎ 021/6445-7556), from going all out to bring New Orleans style and sophistication, along with gumbo and jambalaya, to Shanghai.
- **Best Cantonese:** For the second most popular Chinese regional cuisine in town (after Shanghai's own), the two top choices are the long-presiding **Dynasty,** 2099 Yan'an Xi Lu, in the Yangtze New World Hotel by Marriott (☎ 021/6275-0000), and the new **Shang Palace,** 33 Fucheng Lu, in the Pudong Shangri-La Hotel (☎ 021/6882-8888, ext. 22). Both elegant restaurants feature top chefs from Hong Kong.
- **Best French:** The most authentic choice is **Le Bouchon,** 1455 Wuding Xi Lu, Jing An District (☎ 021/6225-7088), a fine little bistro and wine bar where the French owner and French chef focus on one superb entree each evening.

- **Best Indian:** Tough to beat the authentic cuisine, expert service, and dazzling decor at **Tandoor,** 59 Maoming Nan Lu (☎ **021/6472-5494**), considered by many to be Shanghai's top foreign restaurant regardless of cuisine; but the new **Hazara,** 59 Maoming Nan Lu (☎ **021/6472-5494**), is giving Tandoor a strong race.

- **Best Irish Stew:** And the best Irish ale and music, too, are served up nightly at Shanghai's very affable **O'Malley's,** 42 Taojiang Lu (☎ **021/6437-0667**), where even some of the bartenders are from Ireland.

- **Best Italian:** Lots of fine competition here, but the top three are clearly the venerable **Giovanni's,** 5 Zunyi Nan Lu, Westin Tai Ping Yang Hotel (☎ **021/6275-8888**); the flashy **AD,** 3896 Hongmei Lu, Changning District (☎ **021/6262-5620**); and **DaVinci's,** 250 Huashan Lu, Hilton Hotel (☎ **021/6248-0000,** ext. 8622). All are headed by extraordinary Italian chefs.

- **Best Fast Italian:** The less fancy Italian eateries in Shanghai have good food, too, but for a fast-service pizza or pasta with iced coffee or cappuccino, try any of the seven branches of the quick but comfortable **Gino Cafe,** including the outlet near the Peace Hotel at 66 Nanjing Dong Lu (☎ **021/6361-2205**).

- **Best Mexican:** With margaritas from soda fountains and musicians from Guadalajara, the upscale **JJ Mariachi,** 59 Maoming Lu (☎ **021/6472-1778**), is as close to south-of-the-border fun as you'll find in Shanghai.

- **Best Thai:** The Thai craze in Shanghai was touched off by **Irene's Thai,** 263 Tongren Lu (☎ **021/6247-3579**), in 1998, to be followed in short order by Simply Thai, Thai House, Thai Kitchen, and Thaitanium. Irene's is still great, but the best is the most recent to open, the elegant **Lan Na Thai,** 118 Ruijin Er Lu, Ruijin Guest House Building 4 (☎ **021/6466-4328**).

- **Best Vegetarian:** Shanghai's oldest tofu-and-mushroom restaurant, **Gongdelin,** recently moved to the west end of the city's big shopping street, at 445 Nanjing Xi Lu (☎ **021/6327-0218**). It does a land-rush business even though its Chinese menu contains no meat, despite the clever masquerades of its "pork," "eel," and "Peking Duck."

- **Best Vietnamese:** Not only the best, but also the only Vietnamese restaurant in town, **Cochinchina 1883,** 889 Julu Lu (☎ **021/6445-6797**), re-creates a stylish colonial Southeast Asia dining emporium in an old guest house, with an East/West cuisine to match.

Planning a Trip to Shanghai

2

Here are the basics for designing your trip to Shanghai and entering China with the right documents in hand, as well as tips on how to navigate smoothly through the airport and arrive in the city with the fewest hassles.

1 Visitor Information

Foreign travel to the People's Republic of China is handled by an official government agency, **China International Travel Service,** referred to by the initials **CITS.** In Chinese, CITS is called *guoji luxingshe.* CITS can set up international and domestic air flights, train and bus reservations within China, and hotel reservations for Shanghai. It can also provide English-speaking guides and group or individual sightseeing tours through its Shanghai branch offices, which are often located in hotels. **China Travel Service** (CTS) and a host of other government and private travel services also cater to foreign travelers.

CITS OVERSEAS   CITS has opened a few **China National Tourist Offices** (CNTO) abroad to provide tourist information and services. These offices include:

- **In the United States:** 350 Fifth Ave., Suite 6413, New York, NY 10118 (☎ **212/760-9700;** fax 212/760-8809); and 333 W. Broadway, Suite 201, Glendale, CA 91204 (☎ **818/545-7504;** fax 818/545-7506).
- **In the United Kingdom:** 4 Glentworth St., London NW 1 (☎ **0171/935-9427;** fax 0171/487-5842).
- **In Australia:** 44 Market St., Sydney NSW 2000 (☎ **02/9299-4057;** fax 02/9290-1958).

For the locations of CITS and other tourist offices in Shanghai, see "Orientation" in chapter 3, "Getting to Know Shanghai."

SHANGHAI ONLINE   The best way to receive fairly up-to-date information on Shanghai before leaving home is on the Internet. **CITS** maintains two planning and reservations sites at **www. citsusa.com** and at **www.scits.com**. The CITS e-mail address is **info@citsusa.com**. A general source of information for travel in China, including Shanghai, is available at **www.surfchina.com**. The online edition of the local English-language newspaper, *Shanghai Daily,* resides at **www.shanghaidaily.com**, while the online edition of a monthly city magazine (in English) for visitors, *that's Shanghai,* can be viewed at **www.thatsShanghai.com**. Another useful Shanghai Web site is **www.shanghai-ed.com**. A newer site, **www.ctrip.com**, can be used for booking flights and hotels. The **Shanghai Cultural Information & Booking Centre** (☎ **021/6217-2426**) maintains its Web site at **www.culture.sh.cn**.

2 Entry Requirements & Customs

ENTRY REQUIREMENTS

All visitors to Shanghai and the People's Republic of China are required to have a valid **passport** (one that does not expire for at least 6 months after the date of your arrival in China). A special **tourist or business visa** is also required. Tour groups are usually issued a group visa, with the paperwork handled by the travel agency (check with your agent). Visas for individual travelers and businesspeople may be obtained one of two ways: (1) from certain travel agents overseas and in Hong Kong, and (2) from the Chinese embassy or consulate in your country. Unless you are entering China through Hong Kong, where securing a visa from the Hong Kong CTS or local travel agent is quite easy, the safest way to secure a China visa is by doing the paperwork required by the overseas consulate several months ahead of departure. Call, fax, or mail a request for a visa application to the Chinese embassy or consulate in your home country and follow the printed instructions. You will be required to mail a completed visa application form, your valid passport, and payment. Payment depends on the visa you select. A 30-day single-entry tourist visa is the most economical ($30 for U.S. passport holders); 60-day, 90-day, and 6-month visas, permitting single or multiple entries, are also available. In the United States, it takes about 10 days to get your visa once you mail in your application, passport, and payment.

In the United States, the visa office of the Embassy of the People's Republic of China is at Room 110, 2201 Wisconsin Ave., Washington, DC 20007 (☎ **202/338-6688;** fax 202/588-9760).

The consulate general of the People's Republic of China has offices in the following countries:

- **In the United States:** 1450 Laguna St., San Francisco, CA 94115 (☎ **415/674-2900;** fax 415/563-0494); 443 Shatto Place, Los Angeles, CA 90020 (☎ **213/807-8088;** fax 213/380-1961); 520 12th Ave., New York, NY 10036 (☎ **212/868-7752;** fax 212/502-0245); 100 W. Erie St., Chicago, IL 60610 (☎ **312/803-0098;** fax 312/803-0122); and 3417 Montrose Blvd., Houston, TX 77006 (☎ **713/524-4311;** fax 713/524-7656).
- **In Canada:** 515 Patrick St., Ottawa, ON K1N 5H3 (☎ **613/789-9608;** fax 613/789-1414); 240 St. George St., Toronto, ON M5R 2P4 (☎ **416/964-7260;** fax 416/324-6468); and 3380 Granville St., Vancouver, BC V6H 3K3 (☎ **604/736-7492;** fax 604/737-0154).
- **In the United Kingdom:** 31 Portland Place, London W1N 3AG (☎ **0171/631-1430;** fax 0171/436-9178); Denison House, 49 Denison Rd., Rusholme, Manchester M14 5RX (☎ **0161/224-8672;** fax 0161/257-2672); and 43 Station Rd., Edinburgh EH12 7AF (☎ **0131/316-4789;** fax 0131/334-6954).
- **In Ireland:** 40 Ailesbury Rd., Dublin 4, Ireland (☎ **3531/269-1707**).
- **In Australia:** 15 Coronation Dr., Yarralumla, ACT 2600 (☎ **02/6273-4780;** fax 02/6273-4878).
- **In New Zealand:** 2-6 Glenmore St., Wellington (☎ **04/472-1382**).

Visa Application Tip

Americans can download visa application forms and instructions from the Chinese embassy's Web site, at **www.China-embassy.org**.

GETTING A VISA IN HONG KONG   Many U.S., Canadian, Australian, New Zealand, Irish, and British citizens enter China through Hong Kong. Although Hong Kong is now part of China, citizens of these nations are required to have only a valid passport to enter Hong Kong. Visas for entry to the rest of China can be secured at countless travel agencies, including the highly efficient branch of **China Travel Service** (CTS) at 27–33 Nathan Rd., Kowloon (☎ **852/2315-7149;** fax 852/2721-7757), on the second floor of the Alpha Building (entrance on Peking Road).

EXTENDED STAYS   The Foreign Affairs Section of the **Public Security Bureau** (the police), located at 210 Hankou Lu (☎ **021/6321-5380**), 2 blocks south of Nanjing Lu in downtown Shanghai, has the power to extend visas. Those who over-stay are fined about $50 per day.

CUSTOMS

Travelers are allowed to **bring into China** four bottles of alcoholic beverages and three cartons of cigarettes. There is no limit on the amount of foreign currency (although amounts above $10,000 must be declared on a customs form). Guns and dangerous drugs are forbidden. Upon departure, note that antiques purchased in China must have a red wax seal for export. Customs declaration slips must be filled out prior to arrival and departure.

No vaccinations or inoculations are currently required (although an AIDS test certificate is required for those planning to live in China for more than 6 months).

Returning U.S. citizens who have been away for 48 hours or longer are allowed to bring back, once every 30 days, $400 worth of merchandise duty-free. You'll be charged a flat rate of 10% duty on the next $1,000 worth of purchases. Be sure to have your receipts handy. On gifts, the duty-free limit is $100. You cannot bring fresh foodstuffs into the United States; tinned foods, however, are allowed. For more information, contact the **U.S. Customs Service,** 1301 Constitution Ave. (P.O. Box 7407), Washington, DC 20044 (☎ **202/927-6724**), and request the free pamphlet *Know Before You Go.* It's also available on the Web at www. customs.ustreas.gov/travel/kbygo.htm.

U.K. citizens returning from a non-EC country have a customs allowance of 200 cigarettes; 50 cigars; 250 grams of smoking tobacco; 2 liters of still table wine; 1 liter of spirits or strong liqueurs (over 22% volume); 2 liters of fortified wine, sparkling wine, or other liqueurs; 60 cubic centimeters (ml) of perfume; 250 cubic centimeters (ml) of toilet water; and £145 worth of all other goods, including gifts and souvenirs. People under 17 cannot have the tobacco or alcohol allowance. For more information, contact **HM Customs & Excise, Passenger Enquiry Point,** 2nd floor Wayfarer House, Great South West Road, Feltham, Middlesex, TW14 8NP (☎ **0181/910-3744,** or 44/181-910-3744 from outside the U.K.), or con-sult the office's Web site at www.open.gov.uk.

For a clear summary of **Canadian** rules, write for the booklet *I Declare,* issued by **Revenue Canada,** 2265 St. Laurent Blvd., Ottawa K1G 4KE (☎ **613/993-0534**). Canada allows its citizens a $500 exemption, and you're allowed to bring back duty-free 200 cigarettes, 2.2 pounds of tobacco, 40 Imperial ounces of liquor, and 50

Packing for Security

Pickpockets are the bane of many a world's big city, including Shanghai, so be sure to tuck traveler's checks, excess cash, airline tickets, and your ID, particularly your passport, into a concealed pouch or money belt—not into a purse or backpack. Leave photocopies of your passport and traveler's check receipts at your hotel (in a safe-deposit box or room safe) and carry a copy with you.

---

cigars. In addition, you're allowed to mail gifts to Canada from abroad at the rate of C$60 a day, provided the gifts are unsolicited and don't contain alcohol or tobacco (write on the package "Unsolicited gift, under $60 value"). All valuables should be declared on the Y-38 form before departure from Canada, including serial numbers of valuables you already own, such as expensive foreign cameras. *Note:* The $500 exemption can be used only once a year and only after an absence of 7 days.

The duty-free allowance in **Australia** is A$400 or, for those under 18, A$200. Upon returning to Australia, citizens can bring in 250 cigarettes or 250 grams of loose tobacco, plus 1,125 milliliters of alcohol. If you're returning with valuable goods you already own, such as foreign-made cameras, you should file form B263. A helpful brochure, available from Australian consulates or customs offices, is *Know Before You Go.* For more information, contact **Australian Customs Services,** GPO Box 8, Sydney NSW 2001 (☎ 02/9213-2000).

The duty-free allowance for citizens of **New Zealand** is NZ$700. Citizens over age 17 can bring in 200 cigarettes or 50 cigars or 250 grams of tobacco (or a mixture of all three if their combined weight doesn't exceed 250g); plus 4.5 liters of wine and beer, or 1.125 liters of liquor. New Zealand currency does not carry import or export restrictions. Fill out a certificate of export, listing the valuables you are taking out of the country; that way, you can bring them back without paying duty. Most questions are answered in a free pamphlet available at New Zealand consulates and customs offices: *New Zealand Customs Guide for Travellers, Notice no. 4.* For more information, contact **New Zealand Customs,** 50 Anzac Ave., P.O. Box 29, Auckland (☎ 09/359-6655).

3 Money

Chinese currency, the **yuan,** is called **Renminbi** (RMB). The most common denominations of bills are the 100 yuan, 50 yuan, 10 yuan, 5 yuan, 2 yuan, and 1 yuan. In addition, there are smaller bills worth less than 1 yuan in denominations of 5 jiao, 2 jiao, and 1 jiao (10 jiao = 1 yuan). There are even smaller bills and coins, with denominations in fen (100 fen = 10 jiao = 1 yuan). The yuan is commonly called *kwai,* and the jiao is commonly called *mao.*

The current exchange rate is about 8.3 yuan to U.S.$1, making the yuan worth about 12¢. China is still a cash society, so most of your ordinary transactions in shops and cafes require Chinese currency. It is useful to carry a quantity of 10, 2, and 1 yuan notes to pay for taxis, bottled water, admissions, and other small daily purchases. Prices in Shanghai are usually marked with "RMB," but can also be marked with a "Y."

TRAVELER'S CHECKS   Traveler's checks are the easiest and safest way to bring money into China. Traveler's checks, as well as foreign currency, can be converted to RMB at nearly all hotels, many banks, and some restaurants and stores (particularly the Friendship Store). Hotels and banks charge a small fee for conducting

The Chinese Yuan, the U.S. Dollar & the British Pound

For U.S. Readers   At this writing, U.S.$1 = approximately 8.3RMB (or 1RMB = 12¢). This was the rate of exchange used to calculate the U.S. dollar rates given in this book (rounded off). Exchange rates at hotels are usually 8.2RMB per U.S.$1.

For British Readers   The rate of exchange used to calculate the pound values in the accompanying table was £1 = 13RMB (or 1RMB = 8p).

Check the current exchange rates before you arrive and use the following table only as a guide:

RMB	U.S.$	U.K.£	RMB	U.S.$	U.K.£
0.10	0.01	0.01	100	12.00	8.00
0.50	0.06	0.03	150	18.00	11.30
1.00	0.12	0.08	200	24.00	15.10
2.00	0.24	0.15	250	30.00	18.90
3.00	0.36	0.23	300	36.00	22.70
4.00	0.48	0.30	400	48.00	30.25
5.00	0.60	0.38	500	60.00	37.80
6.00	0.72	0.45	600	72.00	45.40
7.00	0.84	0.53	700	84.00	52.90
8.00	0.96	0.60	800	96.00	60.50
9.00	1.08	0.68	900	108.00	68.00
10.00	1.20	0.76	1,000	120.00	75.60
15.00	1.80	1.13	2,000	240.00	151.20
20.00	2.40	1.50	3,000	360.00	226.80
25.00	3.00	1.90	4,000	480.00	302.40
30.00	3.60	2.27	5,000	600.00	378.00
35.00	4.20	2.65	6,000	720.00	453.60
40.00	4.80	3.03	7,000	840.00	529.20
45.00	5.40	3.40	8,000	960.00	604.80
50.00	6.00	3.80	9,000	1,080.00	680.40
75.00	9.00	5.70	10,000	1,200.00	756.00

exchanges, but hotel desks offer convenience and don't charge much more than the banks. Note that the exchange rate for traveler's checks is slightly better than for cash. It is not possible at present to get Chinese currency before you leave home.

You can get traveler's checks at almost any bank. **American Express** offers denominations of $10, $20, $50, $100, $500, and $1,000. You may pay a service charge ranging from 1% to 4%. You can also get American Express traveler's checks over the phone by calling ☎ **800/221-7282;** by using this number, Amex gold and platinum cardholders are exempt from the 1% fee. AAA members can get checks without a fee at most AAA offices.

Visa offers traveler's checks at Citibank locations nationwide, as well as several other banks. The service charge ranges between 1.5% and 2%; checks come in

What Things Cost in Shanghai	U.S.$	U.K.£
Taxi from airport to city center	12.00	8.00
Subway ride	.36	.23
Local telephone call	.06	.03
Double room at the Grand Hyatt (very expensive)	300.00	189.00
Double room at the Shangri-La or Westin (expensive)	240.00	151.20
Double room at the Hilton (expensive/moderate)	180.00	113.40
Double room at the Novotel (moderate)	120.00	75.60
Double room at the YMCA (inexpensive)	64.00	40.40
Lunch for one at The Grape (moderate)	12.00	8.00
Lunch for one at Gino (inexpensive)	4.80	3.05
Dinner for one, without drinks, at M on the Bund (very expensive)	40.00	25.20
Dinner for one, without drinks, at Lan Na Thai (expensive)	18.00	11.30
Dinner for one, without drinks, at Gongdelin (moderate)	12.00	8.00
Dinner for one, without drinks, at Song Yue Lou (inexpensive)	8.00	5.10
Glass of beer	3.50	2.20
Coca-Cola	1.25	.80
Roll of 100 ASA Fujicolor film (36 exposures)	6.00	3.80
Admission to the Shanghai Museum	2.40	1.50
Admission to the Jade Buddha Temple	1.80	1.13
Movie ticket	4.00	2.50
Theater ticket (best seat) to Shanghai Acrobatics	7.20	4.55

denominations of $20, $50, $100, $500, and $1,000. **MasterCard** also offers traveler's checks; call ☎ **800/223-9920** for a location near you.

CREDIT CARDS   In general, it is easiest to exchange traveler's checks for RMB at your hotel and to use a credit card to pay the hotel bill. Most fine restaurants and large stores in Shanghai where tourists go now accept major credit cards, too, but the practice is not as common as in North America and Europe. You can also withdraw cash advances (in RMB) from your American Express, Visa, MasterCard, or Diners Club card at most branches of the Bank of China and at a few select ATMs (although you'll start paying hefty interest on the advance the moment you receive the cash, and you won't get frequent-flyer miles on an airline credit card). You will need your PIN number at an ATM and your passport at a bank when using your credit card for cash withdrawals. If you've forgotten your credit-card PIN or didn't even know you had one, call the phone number on the back of your card and ask the bank to send it to you. It usually takes 5 to 7 business days, although some banks will supply the number over the phone if you tell them your mother's maiden name or pass some other security clearance.

ATMs   Many of Shanghai's ATMs are linked to a network that most likely includes your bank at home. **Cirrus** (☎ **800/424-7787;** www.mastercard.com/atm) and **Plus** (☎ **800/843-7587;** www.visa.com/atms) are the two most popular networks; check the back of your ATM card to see which network your bank belongs to. Before your trip, use the toll-free numbers or Web sites to locate ATMs currently available in Shanghai, or ask your bank for a list of ATMs in Shanghai. Be sure to check the daily withdrawal limit before you depart, and ask whether you need a new personal ID number.

There is an **American Express** cash dispenser installed at Shanghai Centre, 1376 Nanjing Xi Lu.

THEFT   Almost every credit-card company has an emergency toll-free number that you can call if your wallet or purse is stolen. The company may be able to immediately wire you a cash advance off your credit card or deliver an emergency credit card in a day or two. In China, MasterCard holders should call ☎ **10-800-110-7309;** Visa cardholders should call ☎ **10-800-110-2911.** American Express cardholders should visit the Amex office in Shanghai; see "American Express" under "Fast Facts: Shanghai," in chapter 3, for complete information.

If you opt to carry traveler's checks, be sure to keep a record of their serial numbers, separate from the checks, so you're ensured a refund in just such an emergency.

4 When to Go

Shanghai's busiest tourist periods coincide with its mildest weather, in the spring and fall. To avoid the big crowds and still enjoy decent weather, try to visit in late March or early November. Except for the windy, chilly winter months, Shanghai teems with tourists and business travelers, most notably from May through October, when the crowds are largely composed of Chinese shoppers on their summer holidays. July and August are unpleasantly hot and humid months as a rule; locals often sleep on cots on the sidewalks to escape the heat in their small apartments. September and October are the most pleasant months to visit. Whenever you visit, it's best to sightsee on weekdays (the weekends are crowded) and, at popular sites, early in the morning or late in the afternoon.

CLIMATE   Shanghai, located on the 31st parallel north, has a climate comparable to that of the southeastern coast of the United States, except that Shanghai summers are hotter. Spring, from mid-March to mid-May, is mild but increasingly rainy. Summer, from mid-May to mid-September, is humid and quite hot. Winter, from mid-November to mid-March, is chilly, but there is seldom snow and the daytime temperatures are usually above freezing. Autumn, the months of mid-September to mid-October, is the most comfortable season, being neither too hot nor too rainy, although typhoon-propelled rains can hit in September.

Shanghai's Average Temperatures & Rainfall

	Jan	Feb	Mar	Apr	May	June	July	Aug	Sept	Oct	Nov	Dec
Temp. (°F)	40	41	48	58	68	75	82	82	74	66	54	45
Temp. (°C)	5	5	9	15	20	24	28	28	24	19	12	7
Days of Rain	9.0	10.2	13.1	13.5	15.0	13.1	11.4	10.0	11.6	8.4	9.1	8.6

HOLIDAYS   National holidays observed in Shanghai are New Year's Day (Jan 1), Spring Festival/Chinese New Year (first day of the lunar calendar: Jan 24, 2001; Feb 12, 2002; Feb 1, 2003; Jan 22, 2004), Arbor Day (Mar 4), International Working Women's Day (Mar 8), Qing Ming Festival/Grave Sweeping Day (Apr 5, 2001), International Labor Day (a 3-day holiday beginning May 1), Chinese Youth Day (May 4), International Children's Day (June 1), Dragon Boat Festival (June 25, 2001), Founding of the Communist Party Day (July 1), Army Day (Aug 1), Teacher's Day (Sept 10), National Day (a 3-day holiday beginning Oct 1), and Moon Festival/Mid-Autumn Festival (Oct 1, 2001).

Spring Festival, the Chinese New Year, is the most important holiday. Spring Festival can last up to 15 days; temples and parks put on fairs, and the 15th day is marked by the Lantern Festival celebrations. Officially, Spring Festival is a 3-day national holiday, meaning banks, offices, and many workplaces are closed during the first 3 days. **National Day,** a 3-day observance of the founding of the People's Republic of China on October 1, 1949, is the second-most important national holiday. Offices, banks, and many shops are also closed on January 1 and May 1 holidays.

Shanghai Calendar of Events

Festivals and celebrations are not numerous in Shanghai, and many are family affairs, but there are some opportunities to mix with the locals at city parks and other locations at annual public events.

Winter

- **Longhua Temple Bell-Ringing.** On New Year's Eve, crowds gather at Longhua Temple to pray for good fortune as the bell is struck 108 times by visitors and others during a special midnight Buddhist service. Fireworks, dragon and lion dances, folk-art shows, and music continue into the wee hours. December 31.
- **Spring Festival/Chinese New Year.** This is the time when Chinese decorate their homes with red paper (signifying health, wealth, and prosperity), visit friends, settle the year's debts, visit temples, and enjoy family get-togethers. Parks and temples hold outdoor celebrations and markets, the best places for tourists to visit. First day of the lunar calendar: January 24, 2001; February 12, 2002; February 1, 2003.
- **Lantern Festival.** On the 15th day after Chinese New Year, on the first full moon, parks and temples display elaborate and fanciful lanterns, often accompanied by fireworks and folk dances.
- **Guanyin's Birthday.** Held on the 19th day of the second lunar month, about 50 days after Chinese New Year, in honor of the Goddess of Mercy, Guanyin, this is a good opportunity to visit one of the Buddhist temples in Shanghai and join in the celebrations.

Spring

- **Longhua Temple Fair.** Beginning on the third day of the third lunar month (usually in the first week of Apr), this 10-day temple fair, featuring an array of vendors, Buddhist worshippers, and local opera performers, dates from the Ming Dynasty (1368 to 1644).
- **Qing Ming Festival.** Also known as Grave Sweeping Day, held on the 15th day of the third lunar month (usually in Apr), this event honors the dead, although in Shanghai it usually means a mass run on the parks, where kite flying goes into high gear. April 5, 2001; April 5, 2002.
- **International Labor Day.** Nearly everything is closed except hotels, cafes, and some shops, but May Day holds few special celebrations for the tourist. May 1.

Summer

- **International Children's Day.** This holiday holds nothing special for most tourists, but local schoolchildren enjoy themselves on field trips. June 1.

Autumn

- **Mid-Autumn Festival.** Held on the 15th day of the eighth lunar month (late Sept or early Oct), the "Moon Festival" celebrates the harvest moon and revolt

Western Holidays in Shanghai

Christmas has become an increasingly popular holiday in Shanghai, celebrated at hotels and restaurants with large dinner parties. Western **New Year's** has not caught on to the same extent, although Longhua Temple has become *the* place to literally ring in the new year. **Halloween** is celebrated by locals and expatriates at the cafes and discos.

against the Yuan Dynasty. Shanghai residents visit their ancestral homes and eat moon cakes. October 1, 2001.

- **Shanghai Tourism Festival.** This wide-ranging annual festival begins in mid-October and runs well into November. The major shopping streets, parks, and tourist sites take turns hosting special events and performances, and rural areas put on various agricultural festivals. The venues and events change every year. For further information, check with your hotel desk or local tourist newspaper; otherwise, try the Shanghai Cultural Information and Booking Centre (☎ 021/ 6217-2426).

5 Health & Insurance

STAYING HEALTHY   No **vaccinations** are required for entry to China and Shanghai, but be sure your inoculations are up-to-date, particularly for tetanus. Check updated information for travelers to China as provided by your doctor or local or national health agencies.

Probably the two most common ailments upon arrival or shortly after are jet lag and colds. **Colds** can be picked up on the flight over and from exposure to Shanghai air and its citizenry. Since common remedies are not always easy to find, pack an ample supply of cold remedies (tablets and sprays) as well as your preferred pain reliever.

Upset stomach and **diarrhea** are the bane of travelers to third-world countries, which Shanghai still is to some extent. Avoid tap water and street food, and carry the remedies you depend on at home. Such diseases as malaria and hepatitis do exist, but they are no longer considered serious health risks in China's major cities.

Since the flight to Shanghai can be long and crosses many time zones, **jet lag** is a problem (less so if you are flying westward). Take the usual precautions on the flight—avoid alcohol, drink plenty of noncarbonated fluids, walk and exercise as much as space allows. Set your watch to Shanghai time upon departure. Whether or not you can sleep on the way to Shanghai, upon arrival try to coordinate your schedule with the new time zone, putting in a full day and sleeping (as much as possible) through the night. It can require several days to reset your biological clock.

Due to the number of foreign nationals working in Shanghai, several hospitals and clinics have special facilities for treating travelers. The level of service and care is of international caliber. The doctors are expertly trained in Western medicine (although many foreigners try Chinese herbal medicines and other traditional remedies, sometimes with great success). It is recommended, however, that travelers carry sterile syringes, since the hygiene in most health facilities is not always dependable. See "Doctors & Dentists" in the "Fast Facts: Shanghai" section of chapter 3 for a list of facilities catering to foreign visitors.

TRAVEL INSURANCE   Hospitals, clinics, and physicians charge rates nearly on par with those in the West, so check with your health-insurance carrier to see if

---

Travel Tip

Many **prescriptions** can be filled at Shanghai hospitals that cater to foreigners, but since this can be costly and time-consuming, it is best to bring all prescriptions with you. Pack prescription medications in your carry-on luggage. Carry written prescriptions in generic, not name-brand, form, and dispense all prescription medications from their original labeled vials.

If you wear **contact lenses,** pack an extra pair in case you lose one.

---

treatment in China is included in your coverage. Be sure to carry your identification card with you. If you are not covered, consider purchasing a short-term **medical insurance** policy to cover medical and dental emergencies. Most health-insurance companies offer special overseas coverage plans for travelers, as do a number of private insurers (see below).

Emergency medical evacuation is quite expensive ($20,000 or more from Shanghai to the U.S.), so investing in a plan to cover this emergency is also wise.

Trip-cancellation insurance is a good idea if you have paid a large portion of your vacation expenses up front. Trip-cancellation insurance costs approximately 6% to 8% of the total value of your vacation.

If you require additional insurance, try one of the companies listed below, but don't pay for more than you need. For example, if you need only trip-cancellation insurance, don't purchase coverage for lost or stolen property. Rule number one: Check your existing policies before you buy additional coverage. Among the reputable issuers of travel insurance are **Access America,** 6600 W. Broad St., Richmond, VA 23230 (☎ 800/284-8300); **Travel Guard International,** 1145 Clark St., Stevens Point, WI 54481 (☎ 800/826-1300); **Travel Insured International,** Inc., P.O. Box 280568, East Hartford, CT 06128 (☎ 800/243-3174); and **Columbus Travel Insurance,** 279 High St., Croydon CR0 1QH (☎ 0171/375-0011 in London; www2.columbusdirect.com/columbusdirect).

A comprehensive travel insurance plan should provide emergency medical and dental benefits (up to $2,500), emergency medical transportation (evacuation), emergency cash transfers, travel document and ticket replacement assistance, 24-hour multilingual assistance by telephone, and compensation for lost, delayed, and damaged baggage. Additional coverage options include trip-cancellation protection, cash for emergencies, legal coverage, and trip-delay insurance. Trip policies vary widely in price, but fairly comprehensive plans cost from $100 to $200.

6 Tips for Travelers with Special Needs

FOR TRAVELERS WITH DISABILITIES   Despite the fact that China has more citizens with disabilities than any nation on Earth, facilities in Shanghai for travelers with disabilities can best be described as sporadic. Nevertheless, the Chinese have made notable efforts in addressing the needs of people with disabilities (spearheaded for several decades by the son of former supreme leader Deng Xiaoping, who is in a wheelchair as a result of persecution during the cultural revolution). Many Shanghai residents get around via special motorized carts, sections of some major sidewalks are now equipped with "raised dots" to assist the blind, and modern buildings and some major tourist sites have elevators. But the bottom line is that Shanghai is a city of long stairways (even at most subway stations) and crowded, crumbling sidewalks. Even so, travelers with disabilities frequently make their way through the Shanghai obstacle course and enjoy its many sights.

Contact **Mobility International USA,** 45 W. Broadway, Eugene, OR 97405 (☎ **541/343-1284,** voice and TDD; www.miusa.org), for information about special tours to China. Annual membership to Mobility International costs $35, which includes its quarterly newsletter, *Over the Rainbow.* You can also join the **Society for the Advancement of Travel for the Handicapped** (SATH), 347 Fifth Ave., Suite 610, New York, NY 10016 (☎ **212/447-7284;** fax 212/725-8253; www.sath.org), for $45 annually, $30 for seniors and students, to gain access to a vast network of connections in the travel industry. This group provides information sheets on travel destinations and referrals to companies that specialize in tours for travelers with disabilities. Its quarterly magazine, *Open World for Disability and Mature Travel,* is full of good information and resources. A year's subscription is $13 ($21 outside the U.S.).

FOR GAYS & LESBIANS   Shanghai is quite tolerant of gay and lesbian travelers, but dating or sexual involvement with locals of the same sex can be dangerous. In sexual matters, gay or straight, Chinese society is quite puritanical, although walking hand in hand with a same-sex partner won't raise any eyebrows since it is deemed a sign of friendship. Shanghai has a homosexual community, but it is not organized or officially sanctioned in any way. Since foreigners are perceived as "different" from Chinese in the first place, gay and lesbian travelers should experience no discrimination at all in Shanghai. Recently, several nightspots have even become identified with gay, lesbian, and transsexual clienteles.

The **International Gay & Lesbian Travel Association** (IGLTA) (☎ **800/448-8550** or 954/776-2626; fax 954/776-3303; www.iglta.org) links travelers up with the appropriate gay-friendly service organizations or tour specialists. With around 1,200 members, it offers quarterly newsletters, marketing mailings, and a membership directory that's updated quarterly. Membership is open to individuals for $150 yearly, plus a $100 administration fee for new members. Members are kept informed of gay and gay-friendly hoteliers, tour operators, and airline and cruise-line representatives. Contact the IGLTA for a list of its member agencies.

General gay and lesbian travel agencies include **Family Abroad** (☎ **800/999-5500** or 212/459-1800; gay and lesbian), **Above and Beyond Tours** (☎ **800/397-2681;** mainly gay men), and **Yellowbrick Road** (☎ **800/642-2488;** gay and lesbian).

FOR SENIORS   The Chinese respect age far more than their Western counterparts, but don't expect to find a plethora of "senior discounts" at tourist attractions or in stores. If you book a hotel from an international hotel chain overseas, inquire about senior discounts. In Shanghai, brace yourself for tiresome stairways at museums and temples, long walks at all tourist sites, and impatient crowds everywhere at your elbows.

Golden Companions, P.O. Box 5249, Reno, NV 89513 (☎ **702/324-2227**), helps travelers 45 and over find compatible companions through a personal voice-mail service. Contact the company for more information. *The Mature Traveler,* a monthly 12-page newsletter on senior travel, is a valuable resource. It's available by subscription ($30 a year) from GEM Publishing Group, Box 50400, Reno, NV 89513-0400. Another helpful publication is *101 Tips for the Mature Traveler,* available from Grand Circle Travel, 347 Congress St., Suite 3A, Boston, MA 02210 (☎ **800/221-2610** or 617/350-7500; fax 617/346-6700).

FOR FAMILIES   While many children are not delighted with museums and temples, there are plenty of sites to dazzle them in Shanghai. Shanghai residents are family-oriented and friendly toward all children. For Western kids, there are many

Shanghai for Business Travelers

Thousands of foreign businesspeople arrive in Shanghai each year; this city, after all, is China's industrial and financial capital. Business travelers should try to book an international hotel with a large 24-hour business center, located near their work site or relevant local offices. Take plenty of business cards with one side printed in English, the other in Chinese. Many Shanghai-hotel business centers provide this service.

A special **business visa** (the "F" visa) is required for entry into China, and a business visa application must be accompanied by a formal invitation or authorization letter from a Chinese authority or institution, along with a cover letter from your company. For more information on visas, see "Entry Requirements & Customs," earlier in this chapter.

Keys to business success in Shanghai include patience, flexibility, and the cultivation of strong, friendly connections (*guanxi*) with Chinese associates, so read up on China and Chinese business before arrival. There are hundreds of books purporting to unravel the secrets of doing business in China. Two of the best general guides are *Managing in China: An Executive Survival Guide*, by Stephanie Jones (Butterworth-Heinemann, 1997), and *The Business Guide to China*, by Laurence Brahm (Butterworth-Heinemann, 1997).

The **U.S. China Business Council,** 1818 N Street NW, Suite 200, Washington, DC 20036 (☎ **202/429-0340;** fax 202/775-2476), provides business information and consulting; its office in Shanghai is in the West Building of the Jin Jiang Hotel, Room 2331, 59 Maoming Lu (☎ **021/6415-2579;** fax 021/6415-2584).

familiar fast-food and foreign-style eateries, several amusement and theme parks, a natural-history museum and the zoo, indoor playgrounds and toy stores in shopping centers, and plenty of parks for rowing, kite flying, and in-line skating. Many hotels in Shanghai allow young children (usually under 12) to stay free with their parents, and some hotels provide baby-sitting services (usually at an hourly fee). Travelers with infants and small children may well find themselves the center of attention at times, as Shanghai residents are often quite open about talking to and even touching very young visitors from faraway places.

As a rule, there are special discounts for children at museums and attractions, including at amusement parks and the Shanghai Zoo.

Several books on the market offer tips to help you travel with kids. Most concentrate on the United States, but two, *Family Travel* (Lanier Publishing International) and *How to Take Great Trips with Your Kids* (The Harvard Common Press), are full of good advice that can apply to travel anywhere. Another reliable tome, with a worldwide focus, is *Adventuring with Children* (Foghorn Press).

FOR STUDENTS   Student travelers, like visiting seniors, should not expect special rates or other discounts in Shanghai. For students who want to party or exercise, Shanghai has an increasingly interesting nightlife (discos, bars, live music, cinema) and a variety of outdoor and athletic activities, which are supported by an equally active resident population of foreign students studying at Shanghai's universities.

The best resource for students is the **Council on International Educational Exchange,** or CIEE (**www.ciee.org**). It can set you up with an International Student Identity Card (ISIC), and its travel branch, **Council Travel Service** (☎ **800/226-8624;** www.counciltravel.com), is the biggest student travel agency in the world. It can get you discounts on plane tickets and the like.

FOR SINGLE TRAVELERS   The common difficulties that solo travelers, male or female, encounter in Shanghai are their own feelings of loneliness and isolation and the need to fend off a variety of touts met in the streets, at tourist sites, or even in hotel lobbies. These freelancing entrepreneurs have a variety of come-ons, usually involving the purchase of whatever they are really selling (artwork, souvenirs). Sometimes, of course, the Chinese are simply trying to be friendly or practice their English. Sexual harassment cases involving foreign visitors are quite rare. Single travelers are an inviting target for "street merchants," however, and Shanghai is less annoying and far more fun when traveling in a small group. Restaurants are more interesting when you dine with companions, too.

7 Getting There

More than 20 international airlines, from Aeroflot to Virgin Atlantic, serve Shanghai. Since it can be a long trip (10 hr. from London, 11 hr. from San Francisco, 13 hr. from Sydney, 15 hr. from New York—longer with stopovers and connections), consider such factors as airline mileage programs, onboard service, routing, and ticket costs. Leading airlines serving Shanghai from North America, the United Kingdom, Australia, and New Zealand include the following:

- **Air China** (☎ 310/335-0088; www.airchina.com.cn), China's largest airline, offers flights from 28 countries, including four flights weekly from San Francisco, three flights weekly from Los Angeles, two flights weekly from Sydney, and two flights weekly from Vancouver, often at exceptional prices. Its Shanghai office is at 600 Huashan Lu (☎ 021/6327-7888).
- **All Nippon Airways** (☎ 800/235-9262; www.ana.co.jp) flies nonstop daily from Osaka and Tokyo (trip time: 4 hr.). The Shanghai office is at Room 208, West Tower, Shanghai Centre, 1376 Nanjing Xi Lu (☎ 021/6279-7000).
- **Canadian Airlines International** (☎ 800/426-7000; www.cdnair.ca) flies daily from Vancouver. Its Shanghai office is at Suite 702, Central Plaza 227, Huangpi Bei Lu (☎ 021/6375-8899).
- **China Eastern Airlines** (☎ 818/583-1500; www.cea.online.sh.cn), one of China's largest airlines, provides twice-weekly service from Chicago, daily service from Los Angeles, and thrice-weekly service from Sydney. In Shanghai, go to 200 Yan'an Lu (☎ 021/6247-2255 for international, or 021/6247-5953 for domestic).
- **China Southern Airlines** (☎ 888-338-8988; www.cs-air.com), China-owned and managed, has branched out to offer inexpensive international flights from the United States and Europe. Its Shanghai office is at 1926 Yan'an Xi Lu (☎ 021/6219-0343).
- **Dragonair** (☎ 800/223-2742; www.dragonair.com), partly owned by Cathay Pacific Airlines, offers the best flight from Hong Kong (trip time: 2$^{1}\!/_2$ hr.). Its office in Shanghai is at Room 202, West Tower, Shanghai Centre, 1376 Nanjing Xi Lu (☎ 021/6279-8099).
- **Japan Airlines** (☎ 800/525-3663; www.jal.co.jp) flies nonstop from Tokyo (trip time: 3 hr., 40 min.). The Shanghai office is at Room 201, Ruijin Building, 250 Maoming Nan Lu (☎ 021/6472-3000).

- **Korean Air** (☎ 800/438-5000; www.koreanair.com) flies nonstop from Seoul (trip time: 2 hr.). Its Shanghai office is located at 2099 Yan'an Xi Lu (☎ 021/6275-6000).
- **Northwest Airlines** (☎ 800/447-4747; www.nwa.com) flies four times weekly from both San Francisco and Los Angeles, with direct flights via Tokyo from other cities. Northwest code-shares some flights to Shanghai with Air China. In Shanghai, go to Suite 207, East Podium, Shanghai Centre, 1376 Nanjing Xi Lu (☎ 021/6279-8088).
- **Qantas Airways** (☎ 800/227-4500 in North America, 13 13 13 in Australia; www.qantas.com) flies nonstop from Sydney three times a week (trip time: 13 hr.). Its Shanghai office is at Suite 203A, West Wing, Shanghai Centre, 1376 Nanjing Xi Lu (☎ 021/6279-8660).
- **Singapore Airlines** (☎ 800/742-3333; www.singaporeair.com) flies nonstop daily from Singapore (trip time: 6 hr.). The Shanghai office is located at Room 606-608, Kerry Center, 1515 Nanjing Xi Lu (☎ 021/6289-1000).
- **Swiss Air** (☎ 800/221-4750; www.swissair.com) flies to Zurich three times weekly. Its office in Shanghai is at Room 1104, Central Plaza, 227 Huangpi Bei Lu (☎ 021/6375-8211).
- **United Airlines** (☎ 800/538-2929; www.ual.com) has daily direct service from San Francisco, Los Angeles, Chicago, and New York City gateways via Tokyo. In Shanghai, go to Room 204, West Tower, Shanghai Centre, 1376 Nanjing Xi Lu (☎ 021/6279-8009).
- **Virgin Atlantic** (☎ 800/862-8621 in North America, 01293/511-581 in the U.K.; www.virgin-atlantic.com) has direct service twice a week from London. The Shanghai office is at Suite 221, 12 Zhongshan Dong Yi Lu (☎ 021/5353-4600).

Other international airlines serving Shanghai are **Air France,** Room 1301, Novel Plaza, 128 Nanjing Xi Lu (☎ 021/6360-6688); **Ansett Australia,** Unit E, 19th Floor, 918 Huaihai Zhong Lu (☎ 021/6415-5210); **Austrian Airlines,** Room 1103, Central Plaza, 227 Huangpi Bei Lu (☎ 021/6375-9051); **Lufthansa Airlines,** Shanghai Hilton, 250 Huashan Lu (☎ 021/6248-1100); **Malaysia Airlines,** Suite 209, East Wing, Shanghai Centre, 1376 Nanjing Xi Lu (☎ 021/6279-8607); **Royal Dutch Airlines/KLM,** Suite 207, East Podium, Shanghai Centre, 1376 Nanjing Xi Lu (☎ 021/6279-8088); and **Thai Airways,** Room 201, West Tower, Shanghai Centre, 1376 Nanjing Xi Lu (☎ 021/6248-7766).

FINDING THE BEST AIRFARES Full-fare, unrestricted air tickets to Shanghai are expensive. Some of the finest, most luxurious cabin service in the world is conducted on this route, particularly in first- and business-class sections, and if travel comfort is a concern, it might be worth spending the extra money (or airline club miles) for an upgrade. Economy class is crowded on most flights and the seats are narrow (although the food and drink can be of reasonably good quality). The rub

Flight Facts

Remember that a nonstop flight is quickest. Direct flights often require at least one stopover along the way. This can mean a change of planes, which will add hours to a Shanghai trip. Itineraries that involve "code sharing" (in which airlines cooperate in ticketing) can mean that a passenger must change airlines en route as well. Nevertheless, roundabout routes can also be less expensive than nonstop service.

Cyber Deals for Net Surfers

It's possible to get some great deals on airfares, hotels, and car rentals via the Internet. Grab your mouse and surf before you take off—you could save a bundle on your trip. The Web sites highlighted below are worth checking out, especially since all services are free.

- **Arthur Frommer's Budget Travel** (**www.frommers.com**). Home of the Encyclopedia of Travel and *Arthur Frommer's Budget Travel* magazine and daily newsletter, this site offers detailed information on 200 cities and islands around the world, as well as up-to-the-minute ways to save dramatically on flights, hotels, rental cars, and cruises. Book an entire vacation online and research your destination before you leave. Consult the message board to set up "hospitality exchanges" in other countries, to talk with other travelers who have visited a hotel you're considering, or to direct questions to Arthur Frommer himself. The newsletter is updated daily to keep you abreast of the latest-breaking ways to save, to publicize new hot spots and best buys, and to present veteran readers with fresh, ever-changing approaches to travel.

- **Microsoft Expedia** (**www.expedia.com**). The best part of this multipurpose travel site is the Fare Tracker: Sign up for the service, and once a week you'll receive an e-mail with the best airfare deals from your hometown to up to three destinations. The site's Travel Agent will steer you to bargains on hotels and car rentals, and with the help of hotel and airline seat pinpointers, you can book everything right online. This site is even useful once you're booked. Before you depart, log on for maps and up-to-date travel information, including weather reports and foreign exchange rates.

- **Travelocity** (**www.travelocity.com**). This is one of the best travel sites out there, especially for finding cheap airfares. In addition to its Personal Fare Watcher, which notifies you via e-mail of the lowest airfares for up to five different destinations, Travelocity will track the three lowest fares for any routes on any dates in minutes. You can book a flight right then and there, and if you need a rental car or hotel, Travelocity will find you the best deal via the SABRE computer reservations system (another huge travel agent database). Click on Last Minute Deals for the latest travel bargains, including a link to H.O.T. Coupons (www.hotcoupons.com), where you can print out electronic coupons for travel in North America.

- **The Trip** (**www.thetrip.com**). This site is geared toward the business traveler, but vacationers-to-be can also use its exceptionally powerful fare-finding engine, which will e-mail you every week with the best city-to-city airfare deals for as many as 10 routes. The Trip uses the Internet Travel Network, another reputable travel agent database, to book hotels and restaurants.

is that a first-class round-trip seat can cost more than $5,000, and a business-class seat over $2,500. Full fare for economy class usually runs from $1,500 to $2,000.

There are several ways to save hundreds, even thousands, of dollars on a Shanghai flight. First, if you plan ahead, you can book a less expensive **APEX** (Advance Purchase Excursion Fares) ticket. APEX tickets have various restrictions, depending on the airline; they usually must be purchased several weeks or more in advance and are often nonrefundable. Prices are lower in the winter, and weekend flights cost more than weekday flights. Nevertheless, an advance-purchase round-trip ticket in economy class on a major airline, such as United, can be $1,200 or less, depending on how competitive airfares to Asia happen to be at the time.

To save even more, shop around. Check the travel sections of major newspapers, particularly those on the West Coast. Dozens of travel agents, consolidators, and so-called "bucket shops" advertise deeply discounted tickets, for sometimes as low as $800. These tickets, which consolidators usually purchase in blocks from the airlines, carry just about every restriction imaginable and are normally valid on only a few specific dates, but they are great bargains. Their small boxed ads usually run in the Sunday travel section at the bottom of the page. Before you pay, however, ask for a confirmation number from the consolidator and then call the airline itself to confirm your seat. Be prepared to book your ticket with a different consolidator—there are many to choose from—if the airline can't confirm your reservation. Also be aware that these tickets are usually nonrefundable or rigged with stiff cancellation penalties, often as high as 50% to 75% of the ticket price.

Council Travel (☎ 800/226-8624; www.counciltravel.com) and **STA Travel** (☎ 800/781-4040; www.sta.travel.com) cater especially to young travelers, but their bargain-basement prices are available to people of all ages. **Travel Bargains** (☎ 800/AIR-FARE; www.1800airfare.com) was formerly owned by TWA but now offers the deepest discounts on many other airlines, with a 4-day advance purchase. Other reliable consolidators include **1-800-FLY-CHEAP** (www.1800flycheap.com) and **TFI Tours International** (☎ 800/745-8000 or 212/736-1140), which serves as a clearinghouse for unused seats. "Rebators" such as **Travel Avenue** (☎ 800/333-3335 or 312/876-1116) and the **Smart Traveller** (☎ 800/448-3338 or 305/448-3338) rebate part of their commissions to you.

Certain airlines, especially those based in Asia, offer low fares from North America and Europe, but be aware that they cannot fly nonstop to Shanghai; a stopover in their home country is required on the way. Korean Air, for example, flies to Shanghai from North America, but first stops in Seoul, lengthening the long trip by hours; in addition, foreign-based airlines depart only from major gateway cities, which can necessitate adding on an expensive and time-consuming connecting flight.

The newest way to shop for cheap fares is via the Internet. It is now possible to book an international flight entirely online. Many travel sites and the airlines themselves routinely advertise special Internet fares, so don't hesitate to browse for electronic bargains. (See "Cyber Deals for Net Surfers," above.)

8 Booking a Tour Versus Traveling on Your Own

Whether you decide to visit Shanghai independently or on a group tour depends on your experience and goals. Seasoned travelers, especially those who have visited other third-world destinations, or who want to experience Shanghai in some depth, can comfortably explore the city on their own. Touring Shanghai without a net requires time, energy, resourcefulness, and a sense of adventure.

If time is short, however, and your intent is to sample Shanghai's leading treasures in comfort, with a minimum of hassles, a group tour is the answer. Strolling the Bund, visiting Yu Yuan Garden, shopping on Nanjing Road, and viewing the Shanghai Museum are memorable experiences that group tours can deliver effectively. The crucial difference lies in the depth of the experience. The busy dawn-to-twilight group tour simply cannot allow more than an hour or two at even the major sites, barely enough time to snap a picture and get a general sense of the place.

Dozens of tour operators in North America, Europe, Australia, New Zealand, and Hong Kong offer excellent group tours that include a few days in Shanghai. Some of the largest operators are **Globus** (☎ 800/221-0090), **Maupintour** (☎ 800/225-4266), **Pacific Delight Tours** (☎ 800/221-7179), **Travcoa** (☎ 800/992-2003), and **United Vacations** (☎ 800/328-6877). You can speak to the operators directly or use a travel agent.

For a group tour that explores Shanghai in more depth, contact **Helen Wong's Tours,** Level 18, Town Hall House, 456 Kent St., Sydney, NSW Australia (☎ 02/9267-7833; fax 02/9267-7717; www.helenwongstours.com). Helen Wong offers 4-day tours of Shanghai; she has also pioneered special group packages of 10 days or more that are devoted exclusively to the Shanghai experience.

Between joining a group tour and traveling completely independently, there is a wide middle ground. Travel agents, including **China International Travel Service** (CITS) and **China Travel Service** (CTS) in Shanghai, Hong Kong, and overseas (see "Visitor Information," above), can book the essentials for independent-minded travelers who want to customize their trips. Hotel reservations, car-and-driver hires, airport transfers, personalized day tours with English-speaking guides, and other matters can be set up long before departure or upon arrival, although the price can exceed that of a group tour if too many pieces are ordered this way. **Personal guides** can be hired for the entire duration of a stay, which is a luxurious way to see the capital—and often a great way to gain an insider's view. Independent packages can be engineered by tour operators who specialize in China, such as **Asian Pacific Adventures** (☎ 213/935-3156), **Geographic Expeditions** (☎ 800/777-8183), and **Orient Flexi-Pax** (☎ 800/545-5540).

Another option is to come to Shanghai on a group tour that focuses on a special theme. If you are especially interested in Chinese cooking, acupuncture, shopping, architecture, education, tai chi, traditional medicine, art, or another topic, search magazines, newspapers, and the Internet for a small overseas group tour that meets your interest. Such tours are usually one-time offerings, however, led by experts in the field, so finding them requires research and some luck. **Thematic tours** not only provide an opportunity to explore an interest in some depth, but also open doors that remain closed to independent travelers. Some of these tours also include a day or two of general sightseeing, taking in the Shanghai Museum, Nanjing Road, and the Bund.

Fully **independent travel** in Shanghai, on the other hand, depends on your energy, resourcefulness, and ability to act as your own tour guide and travel agent. It is easy to book the basics (flight, hotel) on your own. Beyond that point, you can rely on information in this guidebook—which I've field-tested—to find a wide variety of major sites and hidden delights. The Chinese language will present occasional difficulties, of course, but a good hotel staff (the concierges and bellhops, foremost) can help foreign travelers get around. Shanghai hotels also maintain tour desks, should you tire of being on your own or find that reaching a remote site stretches your tactical skills to the breaking point. One tactic I've often employed when arriving in a strange Chinese city for the first time is to book a group tour at my hotel, using it as an introduction. Then, if what I've seen is intriguing, I return to the site on my own, properly oriented and prepared to deepen the experience.

3 Getting to Know Shanghai

The alien language and initial strangeness of China's largest city can intimidate as well as exhilarate any foreign visitor. This chapter deals with the practical matters you'll need to know about the city. Its facts, tips, and overviews are designed to help you demystify Shanghai's layout, unlock its facilities, and decipher some of the mysterious signs in its streets.

1 Orientation

ARRIVING
BY PLANE

Shanghai has an old airport to the west, **Hongqiao International Airport,** and a new airport to the east, **Pudong International Airport,** which began operations in late 1999. Use of the new Pudong airport has been gradual; so far, it has been regularly served by only a few international carriers. Be sure to find out which of these two airports is handling your departure flight.

Shanghai's **Hongqiao International Airport** (☎ 021/ 6253-6530) is 12 miles (19km) west of the city center. This airport handles most domestic and many international flights. You will receive health and customs declaration forms during your flight; fill them out before arrival and have your passport on hand. It usually takes about 20 minutes to pass through the checkpoints and to retrieve luggage at the carousels. The Arrival Hall is chaotic and crowded. Go to the left, where the walls are lined with hotel counters, and either confirm your hotel transfer or register to get aboard your hotel's shuttle. If you are part of a group tour, you should be met by a local guide. Otherwise, you will be the target of roving taxi drivers and their advance men who will try every verbal stratagem to suck you into an overpriced taxi. Ignore these touts, whatever they promise. Try to exchange a small amount of money at the Bank of China counters in the Arrival Hall (its exchange rates are good). Located in the International Arrival Hall, the **Tourist Service Center** (☎ 021/6268-8899) is open daily from 10am to 9:30pm; it provides maps and information in English. Airport bellmen do not exist at present, so you'll have to haul your own luggage through the masses.

The **Pudong International Airport** is about 18 miles (30km) east of downtown Shanghai. Until the new expressway is extended to the airport (along with the subway), transfers will take more than an hour. The new airport, designed by French architect Paul Andreu, is stunningly high-tech, with deep-blue ceilings and skylights, four identical modules running parallel to the runways, and lakes and gardens surrounding the complex. Its shopping arcades are among Shanghai's best, and the customs and immigration facilities are straight-forward and efficient. It is designed to handle up to 60 million passengers a year. United Airlines was the first international carrier to move from the old airport to Pudong, inaugurating direct San Francisco–Shanghai flights on April 1, 2000, but not all international carriers have followed United's lead.

GETTING INTO TOWN   There are three options for reaching the city from either airport, ranked here by convenience:

Hotel Shuttles   Hotel buses and limousines have service desks along the wall near the main terminal entrance in the Hongqiao Airport. Line up at your hotel counter for help. Someone will make sure that you get on the right hotel bus when it arrives. (When you make advance hotel reservations, be sure to include a request for shut-tle service from the airport, if it is offered, since your name will then appear on the list at the airport counter.) The new Pudong International Airport also has a few hotel counters, but most hotels do not yet offer free shuttle service.

Airport Taxis   The legitimate taxis are lined up in a long queue just outside the Hongqiao Airport's Arrival Hall, to the right at the curb. Join the line. Taxis should charge 60RMB to 100RMB ($7 to $12), depending on the location of your hotel; the drive should take 20 to 40 minutes. Taxis also line up outside the new Pudong International Airport. Touts are not a serious problem here, but that could change. Taxis charge about 120RMB ($14) for the 1-hour or longer trip to hotels in Pudong; the charge is more for hotels in downtown Shanghai and in the western districts.

Most Shanghai taxi drivers are honest, but be sure the meter is on. If it is not, shout "Da biao"; if that doesn't work, select another taxi. Most meters are equipped to print out a receipt. If you haven't been able to change money at the bank counter in the airport, don't panic: many taxi drivers accept foreign currency, and if they don't, they'll wait while you change money at your hotel. A tip should consist of a small bit of change (no more than a few RMB).

Airport Buses   The airport shuttle bus run by **China Eastern Airlines** lines up to the left outside the main terminal of the Hongqiao Airport. The charge is just 3RMB (35¢). The bus stops at a downtown terminal at 200 Yan'an Xi Lu, not far

Departing Shanghai

When you return to either of the Shanghai airports, be sure you have enough RMB in hand to pay the **international departure tax** (90RMB/$11) or the **domestic departure tax** (50RMB/$6). Credit cards and foreign currencies are not accepted for payment of this tax. Go to one of the clearly marked departure-tax counters just inside the departure hall. Be sure to arrive at least 2 hours early, since departures require more time than arrivals, and check-in counters often close 30 to 45 minutes before flight departure times. There are several levels of security to clear, and the lines at airline check-in counters can be long. You'll need to fill out a departure form as well. There are exchange counters near the shopping areas, where you can convert your remaining RMB to your home currency (usually an impossible transaction to take care of once home).

Shanghai

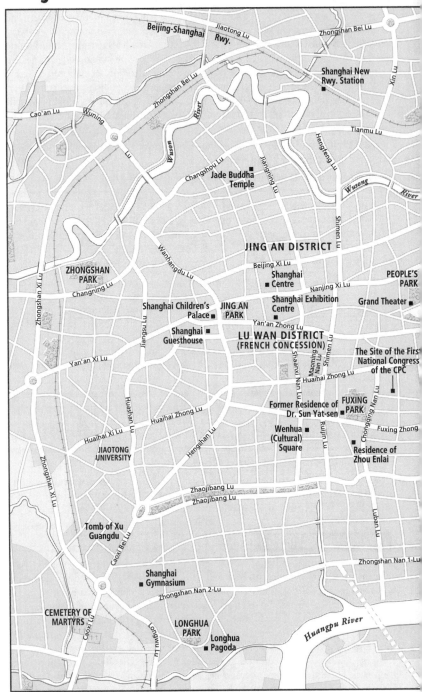

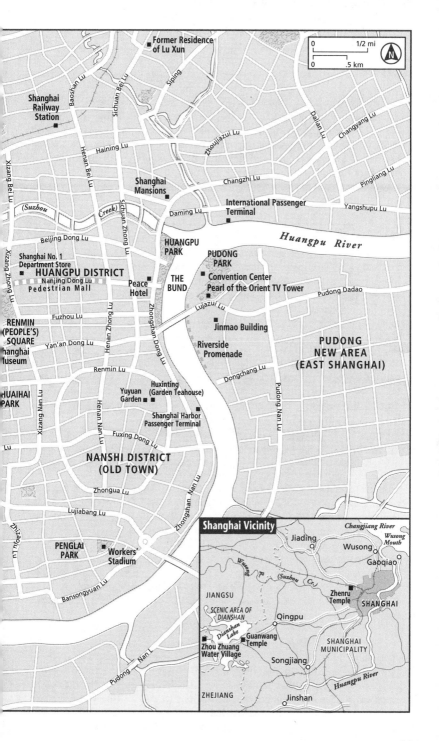

Shanghai Railway Station

Former Residence of Lu Xun

Shanghai Mansions

Shanghai No. 1 Department Store

HUANGPU DISTRICT

Nanjing Dong Lu
Pedestrian Mall

Peace Hotel

RENMIN (PEOPLE'S) SQUARE

Shanghai Museum

HUAIHAI PARK

HUANGPU PARK

THE BUND

International Passenger Terminal

Huangpu River

PUDONG PARK

Convention Center
Pearl of the Orient TV Tower

Pudong Dadao

Jinmao Building

Riverside Promenade

PUDONG NEW AREA (EAST SHANGHAI)

Huxinting (Garden Teahouse)
Yuyuan Garden

Shanghai Harbor Passenger Terminal

NANSHI DISTRICT (OLD TOWN)

Zhongua Lu

Lujiabang Lu

PENGLAI PARK

Workers' Stadium

Streets labeled: Baoshan Lu, Sichuan Bei Lu, Siping, Haining Lu, Henan Bei Lu, Zhoujiazui Lu, Changzhi Lu, Dalian Lu, Changyang Lu, Pingliang Lu, Yangshupu Lu, Daming Lu, Sichuan Zhong Lu, (Suzhou Creek), Beijing Dong Lu, Xizang Bei Lu, Xizang Zhong Lu, Fuzhou Lu, Henan Zhong Lu, Zhongshan Dong Lu, Lujiazui Lu, Yan'an Dong Lu, Renmin Lu, Dongchang Lu, Pudong Nan Lu, Guang Nan Lu, Henan Nan Lu, Fuxing Dong Lu, Zhongshan Nan Lu, Bansongyuan Lu, Zhizao Lu, Pudong Nan Lu

0 1/2 mi
0 .5 km

Shanghai Vicinity

Changjiang River
Wusong Mouth

Jiading
Wusong
Gaoqiao

JIANGSU

Wusong R. (Suzhou Cr.)

Zhenru Temple

SHANGHAI

SCENIC AREA OF DIANSHAN

Qingpu

Dianshan Lake

Guanwang Temple
Zhou Zhuang Water Village

Songjiang

SHANGHAI MUNICIPALITY

Huangpu River

ZHEJIANG

Jinshan

from the Shanghai Centre, but still 2 miles (3km) from the Bund and Huangpu River. You may need to hail a taxi from here to reach your final destination.

BY TRAIN

If you are arriving by train from a mainland Chinese city or from Hong Kong (via the new 29-hour deluxe super train, No. 99), you will have completed your immigration and customs procedures before disembarking. The **Shanghai Train Station** (☎ 021/6317-9234) is massive but modern (there are metal detectors at all entrances), and there's a counter dispensing tourist information in English. You will have to hail a taxi at the queues outside the terminal to reach your hotel (unless your hotel has agreed to pick you up here).

BY SHIP

There are three main passenger piers on the Huangpu River. Arrivals from Hong Kong and Japan usually dock at the **International Passenger Terminal** on Waihongqiao Lu, not far north of the Bund. Ships connecting Shanghai to Qingdao, Guangzhou, Dalian, and other seaports in China usually tie up at the **Gongping Lu Passenger Terminal,** 50 Gongping Lu, which is several miles north of the Bund. Passenger ships cruising the Yangzi River usually dock at **Shiliupu Passenger Terminal,** 111 Zhongshan Dong Er Lu, a short walk from the southern end of the Bund promenade. If you arrive as an independent traveler by ship, you will have to hail a taxi at the passenger terminal to reach your hotel.

VISITOR INFORMATION

Shanghai's official tourist bureau for foreign visitors, **China International Travel Service,** better known as **CITS** (☎ 021/6321-7200), has its main offices at 2 Jinling Dong Lu (on the first floor of the Guangming Building, across the street from the southern end of the Bund promenade). I've used this office with some success, but a more helpful branch is located near the Shanghai Centre, 2 miles west of the Bund, at 1277 Beijing Xi Lu (☎ 021/6289-7827 or 021/6289-8899; fax 021/6289-7838; www.scits.com). CITS can provide maps and information, book tours and tickets, and arrange for English-speaking guides and drivers. Your hotel desk, concierge, or tour counter can render the same services.

Major nongovernmental tourist agencies include **Shanghai Spring International Travel Service,** 1556 Dingxi Lu (☎ 021/6251-5777; fax 021/6252-3734; www.china-sss.com), and the **Jin Jiang Optional Tours Center,** near the Jin Jiang and Garden hotels at 191 Changle Lu (☎ 021/6445-9525; fax 021/6472-0184). The Jin Jiang provides inexpensive group tours, private guide services, cars for hire, hotel reservations, river cruise and entertainment tickets, and other services in an efficient manner.

The official **Tourism Hotline** (☎ 021/6439-0630) can be helpful, but even better is the 24-hour **Tourist Information Line** (☎ 021/6252-0000), maintained by Spring International Travel Service.

The best sources for current information about Shanghai events, shopping, restaurants, and nightlife are the free English-language newspapers and magazines distributed to hotels, shops, and cafes around town. *Shanghai Daily* (**www.shanghaidaily.com**) is an English-language daily newspaper devoted to covering the city in depth. *Shanghai Star* (**www.shanghai-star.com.cn**) is an English-language supplement published by the *China Daily* on Tuesdays and Fridays, while *that's Shanghai* (**www.thatsShanghai.com**) is a glossy monthly magazine with an extensive events calendar, features, and lots of useful ads. Also helpful are the

Making Sense of Shanghai Street Names

Unfortunately, Shanghai's main streets, as well as innumerable smaller streets and alleys that intersect them, are mouthfuls to pronounce and difficult to remember at first, but after a few trips through the city, they begin to sort themselves out. One reason that the street names in *pinyin* (see appendix B) seem so long is that they incorporate the characters for north or south, street or avenue, all running together in the street name. Zhongshan East First Street is written in pinyin as Zhongshan Dong Yi Lu. Common items in street names and their English translations are as follows:

Bei = North	*Jie* = Street	*Yi* = First
Nan = South	*Dajie* = Avenue	*Er* = Second
Dong = East	*Lu* = Road	*San* = Third
Xi = West		
Zhong = Central		

monthly *Shanghai Talk,* the bimonthly *Welcome to China: Shanghai, Travel Shanghai* (produced by the Shanghai Municipal Tourism Administration for foreign visitors), and the weekly *Shanghai Now.*

CITY LAYOUT

Shanghai, with the largest urban population in China (about 13 million), is divided by the Huangpu River into Shanghai West (Puxi) and Shanghai East (Pudong). **Downtown Shanghai** still occupies the west side of the river, but on the other side, to the east, there's a new Shanghai being built. Known as the **Pudong New Area,** this eastward extension of old Shanghai into the new century is epitomized by skyscraping monuments to modernism, from the Pearl of the Orient TV Tower to the 88-story Jin Mao Building, which now houses the highest hotel in the world.

Shanghai's grid of streets and parks has long had a Western imprint. Following the first Opium War in 1842, Shanghai became a Treaty Port, and the British, French, Germans, Americans, and other foreign powers occupied the city, establishing and remodeling their own concessions. Colonial Shanghai is especially visible downtown, along the western shore of the Huangpu River where the **Bund** and the Bund promenade stretch north and south. The Bund contains that remarkable strip of colonial banks, offices, and clubs that forms Shanghai's classic skyline, a museum of architecture marching up and down Zhongshan Lu.

For any traveler, the Bund is the center of the city; from here, downtown opens to the west like a fan. The Peace Hotel with its pyramid dome marks the start of **Nanjing Road** (Nanjing Lu), China's number-one shopping avenue, which runs due west from the Bund for several miles. Southwest of the Bund is the historic Nanshi District, Shanghai's **Old Town.** Thoroughly Chinese rather than colonial, Old Town is the location of Yu Garden and the Huxinting Teahouse, two of Shanghai's most striking treasures.

A mile or so west of the Bund and south of Nanjing Lu, Shanghai's **French Concession** begins, another historic area with its own colonial architecture and attractions. Then, farther west still, beyond the Inner Ring Road that wraps around downtown Shanghai and the French Concession, is the **Hongqiao Development Zone,** where modern commercial and industrial development was concentrated beginning in the 1980s. The Hongqiao area continues west past the Shanghai Zoo to the Hongqiao International Airport.

While sightseeing is concentrated in downtown Shanghai and the French Concession, **north Shanghai** has a scattering of interesting sights, including the Jade Buddha Temple, the Lu Xun Museum, and the Ohel Moshe Synagogue, while **south Shanghai** is home to Longhua Pagoda, Xujiahui Cathedral, Shanghai Botanical Garden, and the trendy cafes and shops of Hengshan Lu. Even the Pudong New Area across the river, east of the Bund, can boast of a delightful riverside park, the city's highest observation decks, and swanky hotels, restaurants, and lounges.

Traveling from district to district in Shanghai used to consume hours, but the recent completion of two major east-west arteries—the elevated Yan'an Expressway and the subway's Metro Line 2—through the massively congested downtown has dramatically reduced commuting time. Even Pudong is no longer out of the way; it is directly connected to downtown Shanghai by the new subway line, two huge bridges, and two tunnels (one for cars, one for pedestrians).

Shanghai is a big city, one of the biggest on Earth, but it is easy to get around on your own. Each of its major districts, from the Bund to the French Concession, is compact enough for a leisurely stroll. And taxis are so plentiful that whenever you tire, your hotel is usually within a 30-minute drive (even less if a subway station is nearby). At the same time, the streets are longer than they look on the map and more crowded than at home—so losing your way, especially on backstreets, is not that unusual.

Main Streets

The main east-west street through downtown Shanghai is **Nanjing Road.** The portion running west from the Bund, through the pedestrian mall to People's Park (Renmin Yuan), is known officially as **Nanjing Dong Lu;** it continues west as **Nanjing Xi Lu.** The Bund (the downtown embankment on the west shore of the Huangpu River) and its promenade run parallel to **Zhongshan Road** (known officially at this point as Zhongshan Dong Yi Lu).

Several major streets run west through downtown Shanghai from the Bund. **Renmin Lu** leads to the northern entrance of Old Town (at Henan Nan Lu) and continues westward as **Huaihai Zhong Lu,** Shanghai's second-most-famous shopping street. **Yan'an Road** (Yan'an Lu) runs west through the downtown corridor and eventually all the way to the airport (after changing its name to **Hongqiao Lu**). The newly elevated expressway above this street, the **Yan'an Viaduct,** is the quickest way to drive across downtown Shanghai; as it nears the Bund, this new expressway dips into the **Yan'an Dong Lu Tunnel,** resurfacing on the east side of the river in Pudong. It used to take an hour to drive from the Hongqiao District through downtown to Pudong, but the Yan'an Viaduct has cut the travel time to 20 minutes.

In downtown Shanghai, the general rule is that streets named for Chinese cities run east-west, while those named for provinces and regions run north-south. The Nanjing Road pedestrian mall is bordered by **Henan Lu** to the east and **Xizang Lu** to the west. Xizang Lu is a major north-west street, since it marks the dividing line between the east and west sectors of Nanjing Road and borders People's Park and People's Square, the site of the Shanghai Museum, the Grand Theater, and the central subway station for both Metro lines.

In the French Concession, the major avenues (**Nanjing Xi Lu, Yan'an Zhong Lu, Huaihai Zhong Lu,** and **Fuxing Zhong Lu**) are extensions of the east-west streets that run through downtown to the Bund. The most scenic north-south streets in the French Concession are **Yandang Lu** and **Sinan Lu** near Fuxing Park, and **Ruijin Lu** and **Maoming Lu** near the historic Jin Jiang Hotel. At the western end of the French Concession, the graceful and trendy avenue of **Hengshan Lu** runs south toward the Xujiahui Cathedral, Shanghai's largest.

Downtown Shanghai, the French Concession, and even large portions of north and south Shanghai, as well as the Pudong New Area, are surrounded by the **Inner Ring Road,** which bears the road name **Zhongshan** along much of its route; it is an elevated expressway for much of its length. The Inner Ring Road is bisected by the **North-South Elevated Road,** which runs above **Chengdu Bei Lu,** the first major street west of People's Square, a rough dividing line between downtown and the French Concession. A second, even more vast ring road is under construction to join the two airports of east and west Shanghai.

FINDING AN ADDRESS

Even though the main streets are laid out in gridlike fashion in downtown Shanghai, it is possible to get lost. The blocks, which appear short and simple on any map, are in reality extremely long. What looks like a 10-minute stroll can stretch to an hour on foot. Moreover, the main streets are constantly intersected by other, sometimes very substantial streets that can be mistakenly identified. The trick is to locate a street sign. Nearly all of Shanghai's big streets have signs on poles (near intersections) that give the name in Chinese characters and in *pinyin,* which is the alphabetical rendering of those characters (used on maps and throughout this book). The street signs can be obscured by the general chaos of the cityscape, by buses and traffic, and by their location, which may be as much as half a block from the actual intersection. Since one big block of buildings can be indistinguishable from the next, architectural landmarks are often few and far between. In the French Concession, Old Town, and other neighborhoods, the grid breaks down and streets and lanes begin running in seemingly random directions, creating complex intersections. You have to be flexible and patient to navigate Shanghai's neighborhoods.

Actual street addresses can be even more difficult to discover, even on major buildings, and often don't exist at all. Part of the problem is cultural, as Shanghai people did not rely in the past on maps or numeric addresses, but rather on intimate familiarity with the neighborhood. Fortunately, most cafes and shops that cater to foreigners now post their addresses; parks, temples, and other large tourist sites can usually be spotted by their traditional gates and the congregation of street vendors and taxis near their entrances; and architectural landmarks, such as the Pearl of the Orient TV Tower, Shanghai Centre, the Peace Hotel, and other tall structures, can serve to orient those who are lost.

MAPS

City maps (*ditu*) are indispensable and are available from hotel desks. Street vendors sell maps as well, although they may be Chinese-only. The best city map you can purchase at home, the *Shanghai Regional Map,* published by Periplus Editions, is also sold in Shanghai, but it is falling out of date. More current and updated frequently is the *Shanghai Tourist Map,* issued by the Shanghai Municipal Tourism

Which Way Do I Go?

If finding an address proves impossible, ask a local. Even if they do not speak English, they might be able to locate it on your map and point you in the right direction. In moments of complete disorientation, you can also hail a cab to beam you back to your hotel. If there are no taxis around, keep your eyes open for a hotel where taxis congregate.

The Streets of Old Shanghai

Up until the establishment of the People's Republic of China in 1949, many of Shanghai's streets bore foreign names, bequeathed to the city by colonial overlords. Here's a partial list of old and new:

Current Street Name	Former Street Name
Fuxing Zhong Lu	Route Lafayette
Henan Lu	Homan Road
Hengshan Lu	Avenue Petain
Huaihai Zhong Lu	Avenue Joffre
Maoming Bei Lu	Moulmien Road
Maoming Nan Lu	Route Cardinal Mercier
Nanjing Dong Lu	Nanking Road
Nanjing Xi Lu	Bubbling Well Road
Renmin Lu	Boulevard des Deux Republiques
Ruijin Er Lu	Route Pere Robert
Ruijin Yi Lu	Route des Soeurs
Sinan Lu	Rue Masenet
Tianshan Lu	Lincoln Avenue
Xizang Nan Lu	Boulevard de Montiguy
Yan'an Dong Lu	Avenue Edward VII
Yan'an Xi Lu	Great Western Road
Yan'an Zhong Lu	Avenue Foch West
Zhongshan Bei Yi Lu	the Bund

Administration and distributed free to hotels. The most useful Shanghai maps are "trilingual," with street and place names rendered in English, pinyin, and Chinese characters. While no map is perfect, and none can keep up with the daily onslaught of new construction (hotels, shops, restaurants) in this booming city, with this guidebook and a trilingual map in hand, you're set to explore Shanghai.

Neighborhoods in Brief

The Shanghai municipality consists of 15 districts, four counties, and the Pudong New Area. It covers an area of 2,448 square miles (6,341km2), with its urban area measuring 1,020 square miles (2,643km2). The seven main urban districts, running from east to west, are as follows:

Pudong New Area The Pudong New Area (nicknamed "East Shanghai") was formerly a backwater beginning on the east bank of the Huangpu River, directly across from the Bund and downtown Shanghai. Its rapid urbanization began in 1990. It is now the site of modern economic monuments (Pearl of the Orient TV Tower, Jin Mao Building), the Shanghai stock exchange, Asia's largest department store, a riverside promenade, and the new Pudong International Airport.

Huangpu District (Downtown Shanghai)   The city center of old Shanghai lies in a compact sector west of the Huangpu River and south of Suzhou Creek. It extends west to Chengdu Bei Lu (the North-South Elevated Highway) along Nanjing Road and encompasses the Bund, People's Square, and the Shanghai Museum.

Nanshi District (Old Town)   Immediately south of downtown and the Bund, between the Huangpu River and Xizang Nan Lu, this area includes the old Chinese city with its traditional shopping, Yu Garden, and the Confucian Temple.

Hongkou District (Northeast Shanghai)   Immediately north of downtown Shanghai, across Suzhou Creek, this residential sector along the upper Huangpu River was part of the International Concession in colonial days. Today, it contains the Ohel Moshe Synagogue and the Lu Xun Museum.

Luwan District (French Concession)   Beginning at People's Square (Xizang Lu) and continuing west to Shaanxi Nan Lu, this historic district was the domain of the French colonial community (up until 1949). The French left their mark on the residential architecture, which boasts such sights as Fuxing Park, the Jin Jiang Hotel, the shops along Huaihai Zhong Lu, and the former residence of Sun Yat-sen.

Jing An District (Northwest Shanghai)   North of the French Concession, this district has its share of colonial architecture, too, as well as the modern Shanghai Centre. Two of the city's top Buddhist shrines, Jing An Temple and the Jade Buddha Temple, are located here.

Xuhui District (Southwest Shanghai)   West of the French Concession and south along Hengshan Lu, this area is one of Shanghai's top addresses for cafes, bars, and shops. Sights include the Xujiahui Cathedral, the Longhua Pagoda, the Shanghai Botanical Garden, and the former residence of Soong Chingling.

Changning District (Hongqiao Development Zone)   Starting at Huaihai Xi Lu, directly west of the Xuhui and Jing'an districts, this corridor of new international economic ventures extends far west of downtown, past Gubei New Town and the Shanghai Zoo, to the Hongqiao Airport.

2 Getting Around

Given the size of Shanghai and the overcrowded condition of its public buses, the taxis and the subway become indispensable for any visitor. Fortunately, both are relatively inexpensive. An adventurous alternative is to travel as many Shanghai residents do, by bicycle.

BY SUBWAY

The Shanghai subway (*ditie*) is the fastest way to cover longer distances, and it's incredibly inexpensive: 3RMB (35¢) per ride up to 12 stops. Operating daily from 5am to 11pm, the subway now has two lines. **Metro Line 1,** the red line with 18 stops, opened in 1994 and winds north-south from the Shanghai Railway Station through the French Concession (Huangpu Nan, Shaanxi Nan, Changshu stations) and down Hengshan Lu (Hengshan Station) past Shanghai Stadium; its central downtown stop is at People's Square (Renmin People's Plaza Station), near Nanjing Road West, over a mile from the Bund. **Metro Line 2,** the green line which began limited operation at the end of 1999, connects with Metro Line 1 at People's Square and runs east-west under Nanjing Road across the river to Pudong.

The new Metro Line 2 is still in its first phase. Its 12 stations, stretching 10 miles (16km) from Zhongshan Park in the west to Longyang Lu in Pudong, a 35-minute run, have elevator access and toilets installed at platform level. When it is up to steam, this line will provide service in both directions as often as every 2 minutes (vs. every 6 minutes on Metro Line 1) during peak hours. Metro Line 1 currently handles 400,000 passengers a day; Metro Line 2 is expected to accommodate up to 600,000. Metro Line 2 will eventually be extended eastward and westward to connect to Shanghai's airports, but this won't happen until at least 2005. Convenient stations for visitors using the new Metro Line 2 include stops at the Pearl of the Orient TV Tower in Pudong (Lujiazui Station), the Nanjing Road pedestrian mall (Henan Station), People's Square (Renmin People's Plaza Station) near the Shanghai Museum, and Jing'an Park near Shanghai Centre and the Hilton (Jing'an Station).

NAVIGATING THE SUBWAY   Using the Metro is easy. Buy an electronic ticket at the ticket window or machines in the station, slip it through the slot at the gate, and take it with you on the ride. Every platform looks the same, with trains running each direction on opposite sides. The station name, in Chinese and pinyin, is posted on pillars facing the tracks. Maps on tunnel walls indicate the next station on the route. Maps of the complete Metro system are posted in each station and over each door inside the subway cars (in Chinese characters and pinyin). In addition, a recording (usually quite audible), first in Chinese, then in English, announces each upcoming stop. It's simple to navigate with all these aids, but should you find yourself going the wrong way, simply exit at the next station, cross the platform, and board the train running the opposite direction. The cars are clean and are seldom jam-packed, except on Sundays and during rush hours.

BY TAXI

With 40,000 taxis in the streets, this is the most common means visitors use to get around Shanghai. (Those 40,000 taxis, by the way, are all scheduled to be converted to run on less-polluting natural gas by the year 2002). There are small, older taxis, without air-conditioning, which charge slightly less, but the larger, more comfortable taxis, mostly Santana sedans (built in the local Shanghai factory by Volkswagen), are your best bet. They congregate at leading hotels, but can be hailed from street corners (just raise an arm and drop it slowly to flag one down). The charge is 10RMB ($1.20) for the first kilometer (0.62 miles), 2RMB (25¢) for each additional kilometer. Cabbies also tack on a surcharge to cover the tolls for crossing bridges and tunnels to Pudong (15RMB/$1.80 for the tunnel, 10RMB/$1.20 for the bridges). Expect to pay about 20RMB to 35RMB ($2.40 to $4.20) for most excursions in the city and up to 60RMB ($7.20) for longer cross-town jaunts. Credit cards aren't accepted by most cabs. Tip 2RMB to 5RMB (25¢ to 60¢).

Finding the Subway

To find a subway entrance, study your map to see which intersection is nearest the station. There are usually several entrances, although they are not always located on the corner. The stations are usually raised white concrete boxes with the name of the stop emblazoned in pinyin. Look for a large sign with the letter M written in a fancy script that resembles a cluster of mountain peaks. If you can't find the sign, look for a large bicycle park on the sidewalk. Anywhere you see people entering and walking down a wide set of stairs from the sidewalk is probably a Metro Line entrance (except for a few street underpasses).

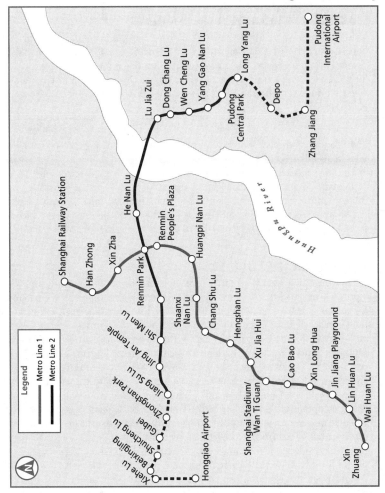

Shanghai Subway

Always insist on using the taxi meter; any negotiated price is a rip-off. Be sure the meter is at zero when you set off. If the meter is not on, say "Qing da biao!" To stop, shout "Ting che!" Carry smaller bills to pay the driver (nothing over a 50RMB note). Receipts can be handwritten upon request (say "Fa piao"), although most taxis are equipped with meters that print out a receipt. To make a taxi service complaint, call ☎ 021/6321-6611.

BY BUS

Public buses (*gong gong qi che*) charge just 1RMB (12¢) per ride, or 2RMB (25¢) if air-conditioned, but they are more difficult to use and less comfortable than taxis or the Metro. Tickets are sold onboard by a roving conductor. To figure out which bus number will get you to your destination, ask for help at your hotel. Buses 20 and 37, for example, run between People's Square and the Bund; Bus 16 connects the Jade Buddha Temple to Old Town; Bus 65 travels from the Bund to the Shanghai Railway Station. Be prepared to stand and be cramped during your expedition,

---

Taxi Tip: Breaking the Language Barrier

Most taxi drivers speak little or no English. If you speak little or no Chinese, get your hotel desk clerk or bellhop to write your destination (and your hotel name and address) on a slip of paper when you set out. Most hotels now provide printed cards for taxi travel, with a blank space to fill in your destination. Many hotels also issue you a slip of paper with the your taxi's ID number on it, in case you have a complaint later.

---

and take care with backpacks and purses, as these are inviting targets for thieves, who frequently target foreigners on public buses.

For more adventurous travelers, Shanghai also operates 10 special no-frills sightseeing buses (numbered 1 through 10) that all depart on regular schedules (every 30 to 60 min.) during daylight hours from **Shanghai Stadium,** stopping at various leading tourist and shopping sites throughout the city (including Pudong and outlying counties). Call ☎ **021/6464-8536** for exact itineraries, schedules, and ticket fees.

BY JIN JIANG CITY TOUR BUS

One of the easiest ways to get around Shanghai is via the Jin Jiang City Tour Bus, a privately operated fleet of three red-and-white buses that runs a great circle route for visitors. The bus affords a quick overview of downtown Shanghai, and it can be used in place of a taxi if the stops happen to match your sightseeing plans. Tickets are 18RMB ($2.15) per person, sold by the bus conductor or at the **Jin Jiang Optional Tours Center,** 191 Changle Lu, across from the Jin Jiang Hotel (☎ **021/ 6445-9525**). Tickets are good for the entire day of issue; passengers can get off at any of the scheduled sightseeing spots along the route and reboard a later bus. Passengers are given a timetable (in English) when boarding. The conductor gives a brief description of what to see before each stop (in Chinese and English). The schedule does vary somewhat, depending on the season, so visit the Jin Jiang tour center or call ☎ **021/6270-1667** for current information.

The bus loads beside the entrance to the Garden Hotel, across Maoming Lu from the Jin Jiang Hotel in the French Concession (nearest Metro station: Shaanxi Nan, 2 blocks south). A circuit of the city takes 1 hour and 45 minutes. These buses are amazingly punctual, given the dense traffic. The first bus leaves at 9am; the last, at 4:15pm, with departures every 45 minutes in the morning, every hour in the afternoon. From the Garden Hotel, the stops in order are: (1) People's Square (south side of the Shanghai Museum); (2) Pearl of the Orient TV Tower, Pudong (southwest of the main entrance); (3) Yaohan Department Store, Pudong (alongside Times Square shopping center); (4) Nanpu Bridge (city bus station); (5) Yu Garden (north entrance to Old Town); (6) the Bund (across Zhongshan Lu from the Peace Hotel); then back to (7) People's Square and (8) the Garden Hotel. Stops are not well marked, so you must remember where you were let out (usually at a busy bus stop) if you plan to reboard at the same spot.

BY BICYCLE

It may look intimidating and downright dangerous, but joining Shanghai's seven million bike riders is not so difficult. The main principles to remember: Ride at a leisurely pace, stay with the flow, and use the designated bike lanes on the big streets. A bicycle is the best way to cover larger portions of Shanghai, especially its backstreets, at your own pace. Some hotels and bike shops rent good bicycles (usually newer mountain bikes) for 10RMB to 20RMB ($1.20 to $2.40) per hour, with better rates for a half or full day. Be sure the brakes are in good working order—you'll need them—and the tires are fully inflated. Should you have a flat or need a repair, there are sidewalk bicycle mechanics on nearly every block, and they charge ridiculously low rates (1RMB or 2RMB/12¢ to 24¢). You'll also need a bicycle lock; sometimes it is built into the back tire. When you reach your destination or need to stop and explore on foot, look for a forest of bikes parked at a major intersection or near a park, attraction, or major store. These are bike parks. Wheel your bike over, lock it next to the others, and pay an attendant, who will give you a paper receipt. Parking costs are no more than a few *mao* (a few cents).

BY BRIDGE, BOAT & TUNNEL

Crossing the Huangpu River has become an increasingly frequent occurrence for Shanghai visitors as the Pudong New Area on the east side of the river flexes its financial and touristic muscle. Pudong's Riverside Avenue alone attracts up to 20,000 visitors a day; Pudong reported 3.69 million tourists in just the first 6 months of 1999. To shift these thousands of daily visitors between east and west Shanghai, there are six basic routes. Two are by bridge: the 2.3-mile-long (3.7km), harp-string–shaped **Nanpu Bridge,** the first to connect Pudong to city center (1991), now handles 45,000 vehicles a day, while the 4.75-mile-long (7.6km) **Yangpu Bridge** (1993) handles 50,000 vehicles a day and boasts the longest bridge span of its type in the world (1,975 ft./602m).

A third route, the cheapest, is by water, via the **passenger ferry** that ordinary workers favor. The ferry terminals have been moved south recently, to the southern end of the Bund on the west shore (tickets are 0.8RMB/10¢) and to the southern end of Riverside Avenue at Dongchang Lu on the east shore (no ticket required from Pudong).

Three more routes across the river are via **tunnels:** the Yan'an Dong Lu Tunnel is plied by motor vehicles; the new Metro Line 2 is filled with German-made subway cars; and the very new "Sightseeing Tunnel of the Huangpu River," with its moving sidewalk, is crammed with pedestrians. All these tunnels are heavily used and appear to be entirely safe, although a foreign engineer who assisted in their construction once remarked, perhaps jokingly, that should a cargo ship happen to sink at just the right point in the Huangpu, a colossal collapse could result.

ON FOOT

The best way to see Shanghai's sights and experience life at street level is on foot. The streets can be almost impossibly crowded at times, but they are always fascinating to stroll—and sometimes dangerous as well. Shanghai residents, who drive on the right side of the road, do not give pedestrians the right-of-way; and at red lights, vehicles seldom stop when making a right turn, whether pedestrians are in the crosswalk or not. Let the street-crosser beware. Walking in downtown Shanghai is rather like walking in Manhattan, with the addition of millions of bicycles that don't always give way, either. In fact, sidewalks in many parts of the city seem to have become the preferred avenues of bicycles, motor scooters, and even full-blown roaring motorcycles. This is illegal, but the police ignore motorized sidewalk traffic, meaning that pedestrians must be extremely alert to avoid becoming road kill, even when keeping to the sidewalks. Drivers always rush to fill an empty space or avenue, wherever they can find one.

Car Rentals

There are plenty of car-rental outlets in Shanghai, but don't plan on picking your SUV up at the airport or anywhere else. Tourists are forbidden to rent cars (or motorcycles or scooters) in China because a Chinese driver's license is required (available only to foreigners with an official residency permit). Of course, major hotels are only too happy to rent chauffeured sedans to their foreign guests by the hour, day, or week, at rates that would make Mr. Avis or Ms. Hertz blush.

Fast Facts: Shanghai

If you don't find what you're looking for in these listings, try the 24-hour **Tourist Information Line** (☎ 021/6252-0000) or inquire at your hotel desk.

Airport   See "Arriving" under "Orientation," at the beginning of this chapter.

American Express   Holders of an American Express card can make inquiries about currency exchange, emergency card replacement, personal-check cashing, and 24-hour ATM access at Room 206, Shanghai Centre, 1376 Nanjing Xi Lu (☎ 021/6279-8082; fax 021/6279-7183). Office hours are Monday to Friday from 9am to 5:30pm and Saturday from 9am to noon. Note that tickets, bookings, and tours are not handled directly by American Express's Shanghai office.

Baby-Sitters   Most four- and five-star hotels can provide baby-sitting services if you give them advance notice. Prices vary, but average about 42RMB ($5) per hour.

Banks   Convenient **Bank of China** branches for currency exchange and credit-card cash withdrawals are located on the Bund at 23 Zhongshan Dong Yi Lu (☎ 021/6329-1979), at 1221 Nanjing Xi Lu (☎ 021/6247-1700), at 2168 Yan'an Xi Lu (☎ 021/6278-5060), at 1207 Huaihai Zhong Lu (☎ 021/6437-8753), and at 2550 Hongqiao Lu (☎ 021/6268-8866). Business hours are Monday to Friday from 9am to noon and 1 to 5pm, and Saturday from 9am to noon.

Many foreign banks maintain offices in Shanghai, including the **Australia & New Zealand Banking Group Ltd.,** 10th floor, Novel Plaza, 116-128 Nanjing Xi Lu (☎ 021/6350-9599); **Bank of America,** Room 104-107A, Union Building, 100 Yan'an Dong Lu (☎ 021/6329-2828); and **Citibank,** 5th floor, Union Building, 100 Yan'an Dong Lu (☎ 021/6328-9661), but none of these handle currency exchange. The most convenient place to exchange currency is at your hotel, where the rates are similar to those at the Bank of China.

Beauty Salons/Hairdressers   Most hotels have on-site upscale hairdressers and Western beauty salons for men and women, with prices somewhat lower than those in Western cities.

Shanghai is a very stylish city, offering plenty of private beauty salons as well. The **Withme Beauty Salon,** Room 208, 20 Donghu Lu (☎ 021/5404-9551), for example, advertises face-lifts and wrinkle reductions. A typical upscale private hairdresser, complete with cappuccino, is the **Yuppies' Hair and Beauty Salon,** 2nd floor, 819 Huaihai Zhong Lu (☎ 021/6473-0156, or cellular 13701911061), open daily from 10am to midnight. A cut and perm here runs about 415RMB ($50). (On the latest *Shanghai Official Tourist Map,* published by the Shanghai Municipal Tourism Administrative Commission, this salon is named "Hujiang Harecut.") Numerous sidewalk barbers give old-fashioned dollar haircuts, often with a head massage thrown in; look along the Huaihai Zhong Lu shopping avenue.

Bookstores   Shanghai's **City of Books,** with two locations, one on the Nanjing Road pedestrian mall at 345 Nanjing Dong Lu (☎ **021/6322-1557**), the other at 465 Fuzhou Lu (☎ **021/6352-2222**), is the city's newest, most modern complex, with a huge collection of books and magazines (in English and Chinese), CDs, DVDs, its own Internet cafe, and a Web site (www.bookmall.com.cn). City of Books is Shanghai's answer to the Borders and Barnes & Noble superstores in the United States.

The city's biggest bookstore is actually the much more staid **Xinhua Bookstore,** 701 Huaihai Zhong Lu (☎ **021/6358-2464**); the Xinhua Bookstore branch on the pedestrian mall at 345 Nanjing Dong Lu (☎ **021/6351-7246**), open daily from 9:30am to 9pm, has a better selection of English-language books than the mother store.

Among other traditional outlets, the **Shanghai Foreign Language Bookstore,** 390 Fuzhou Lu (☎ **021/6322-3200**), once the city's premier bookstore, still carries one of the best selections of maps and English-language books. **Old China Hand Reading Room,** in the French Concession at 27 Shaoxing Lu (☎ **021/6473-2526**), doubles as an arty coffeehouse; open daily from 10am to 11pm. The **Friendship Store,** 40 Beijing Dong Lu (☎ **021/5308-0600**), and the **Shanghai Museum,** 201 Renmin Da Dao (☎ **021/6372-3500**), have good selections of books on Shanghai and Chinese art and culture, as do the gift shops and kiosks in major hotels (which carry foreign newspapers as well).

Business Hours   Since China adopted the 5-day work week in 1995, most banks and government offices are open Monday to Friday from 9am to 5pm, although some still close during the lunch hour (from about noon to 1:30pm), and some have Saturday hours as well. Bank branches and CITS tour desks in hotels often keep longer hours and are usually open Saturday mornings. Shops and department stores are open every day, typically from 9am to 7pm or later. Most hotels keep their money-exchange desks open 24 hours every day. Most temples and parks are open daily from sunrise to sunset. Other tourist sites are typically open daily from 9am to 5pm, although some, such as museums, may close for a day or two during the week (but are open on weekends). Restaurants outside of hotels are generally open at least during these hours daily: 6 to 9am, 11:30am to 2pm, and 5 to 9:30pm. Restaurants catering to foreigners may stay open later, while bars (which often have cafes) don't close until the very wee hours.

Camera Repair/Film   Kodak, Fuji, and other imported films can be purchased all over Shanghai, at hotel kiosks, megamalls, shopping plazas, and camera stores. Prices are on par with those in the West. There are 1-hour and next-day film processing outlets in hotels and shopping centers, too. For reliable camera repair, film, and batteries, try **Guanlong Photographic Equipment Company,** 180 Nanjing Dong Lu (☎ **021/6329-0414**). The new **Kodak Image Center** in the Carrefour supermarket, 560 Quyang Lu, Gubei New Town, offers film developing and cameras.

Climate   See "When to Go," in chapter 2.

Computers   Shanghai lags behind Western cities in installing data ports and modular plugs in hotel rooms, but it is quickly catching up. Hotel business centers offer computer (PC) rentals with up-to-date software, Internet access, and e-mail capabilities.

Consulates   The consulates of most countries are located in or near Shanghai Centre, 1376 Nanjing Xi Lu, several miles west of the city center. The consulates are open from Monday to Friday only, and often close for lunch (from noon to 1pm). Visa and passport sections are open only at certain times of the day, so call in advance.

The Consulate General of the **United States** is at 1469 Huaihai Zhong Lu (☎ **021/6433-6880;** fax 021/6433-4122). The **Canadian** Consulate General is at Suite 604, West Tower, Shanghai American International Centre, 1376 Nanjing Xi Lu (☎ **021/6279-8400;** fax 021/6279-8401). The **New Zealand** Consulate General is at 15A Qihua Tower, 1375 Huaihai Zhong Lu (☎ **021/ 6471-1108;** fax 021/6431-0226). The Consulate General of **Australia** is at 17 Fuxing Xi Lu (☎ **021/6433-4604;** fax 021/6437-6669). The **British** Consulate General is at Suite 301, Shanghai Centre, 1376 Nanjing Xi Lu (☎ **021/ 6279-7650;** fax 021/6279-7651).

Couriers   International parcel and courier services in Shanghai include **FedEx,** 10th floor, Aetna Building, 107 Zunyi Lu (☎ **021/6275-0808**); **DHL-Sinotrans,** 303 Jinian Lu (☎ **021/6536-2900**); and **UPS,** Unit 304A, Hotel Equatorial, 65 Yan'an Xi Lu (☎ **021/6248-6060**). Pickup and delivery can usually be arranged by your hotel.

Credit Cards   See "Money," in chapter 2, for details. American Express, Visa, MasterCard, and Japan Credit Bank are accepted at most hotels, hotel restaurants, and a growing number of stores and restaurants outside of hotels. Diners Club is accepted at many accommodations, but the Eurocard is accepted at only a few of the top hotels. The Discover card seems to be accepted almost nowhere in Shanghai.

Currency   See "Money," in chapter 2, for an explanation of Renminbi (RMB) and conversion rates.

Currency Exchange   Certain branches of the Bank of China (see "Banks," above) and other banks can convert your traveler's checks and national currencies to RMB. The rate is fixed by a government agency. Hotel desks offer currency exchange, usually on a 24-hour basis, at rates nearly as good as those offered by the banks. A passport is required. There are no private offices or kiosks offering currency-exchange services.

Customs   See "Entry Requirements & Customs," in chapter 2.

Doctors & Dentists   Shanghai has the most advanced medical treatment and facilities in China. Hotels can refer foreign guests to dentists and doctors versed in Western medicine; they also usually have in-house or on-call doctors, and some maintain small health clinics.

The following medical clinics and hospitals specialize in treating foreigners and provide international-standard services. **World Link Medical and Dental Centers,** Suite 203, Shanghai Centre, 1376 Nanjing Xi Lu (☎ **021/ 6279-7688**), and Unit 30, Mandarine City, 788 Hong Xu Lu, Hongqiao District (☎ **021/6405-5788**), have 24-hour emergency services, offer Western dental care, and maintain a Web site (www.worldlink-shanghai.com). **New Pioneer International Medical Centre** (NPIMC), 2nd floor, Ge Ru Building, 910 Hengshan Lu, Xujiahui District (☎ **021/6469-3898**), is staffed by Western-trained expatriate doctors and dentists, maintains a laboratory and pharmacy, and offers ambulance and evacuation services.

The **Huashan Hospital,** Wulumuqi Zhong Lu, Jing'an District (☎ **021/ 6248-9999,** ext. 1921), has a special foreigners' clinic on the 19th floor. The **First People's Hospital International Medical Care Center** (IMCC), 585 Jiulong Lu, Downtown Shanghai (☎ **021/6324-3852** or 021/6324-0090), is located near the Bund and offers 24-hour medical emergency assistance. The **Ninth People's Hospital,** 639 Zhizaoju Lu (☎ **021/6377-4831** or 021/6313-8341), has a Western (Canadian-managed) dental clinic on the seventh floor.

The **Drs. Anderson & Partners General Medical Clinic,** 10th floor, D block, New Century Plaza, Hongqiao District (☎ **021/6270-3263**), located near the Westin Hotel, offers Western medical care to the expatriate community. The representative office of **AEA International** (SOS Alarm Centre), 2606 Shartex Plaza, 88 Zunyi Nan Lu (☎ **021/6295-8277**), provides medical evacuation and repatriation throughout China on a 24-hour basis; for emergency medical evacuation, call ☎ **021/6295-0099.**

Documents   See "Entry Requirements & Customs," in chapter 2. Carry your passport at all times, and keep a photocopy of your passport in a separate place as well.

Drugstores   See "Pharmacies," below.

Earthquakes   Shanghai is not located in a particularly earthquake-prone zone. The last big one was in 1624, although a 6.2 quake in the Yellow Sea in 1984 caused some Shanghai residents to jump out of windows in fear. Twenty stations measure tilting, budging, and other seismic activity around Shanghai. New buildings can withstand quakes in the 7.0 range and above. Regional earthquakes over the last 20 years (centered in the East China Sea) have been in the 5.0-to-6.2 range.

Electricity   The electricity in Shanghai is 220 volts, alternating current (AC), 50 cycles. Outlets come in a variety of configurations. Be prepared to supply your own transformers and modem adapters. Hotels do supply a range of standard adapters. The most common adapters are the narrow round two-pin, the slanted two-prong, and the three-prong types.

Emergencies   The emergency phone numbers in Shanghai are ☎ **110** for police, ☎ **119** for fire, and ☎ **120** for ambulance.

Holidays   See "When to Go," in chapter 2.

Hospitals   Consult the hospitals listed under "Doctors & Dentists," above; those hospitals and clinics cater to the expatriate community and foreign visitors.

Information   See "Visitor Information," above and in chapter 2. There are three official **Tourist Information Centers** (also called Consultant Service for Tourists) in Shanghai, with English-language speakers, located at the Hongqiao Airport, International Arrival Hall (☎ **021/6268-8899,** ext. 56750), open daily from 10am to 9:30pm; at the People's Square Metro Station, Main Hall (☎ **021/6438-1693**), open daily from 8:30am to 5pm; and at the Yu Yuan Commercial Building, Yayi Jewelry Store, Old Town Shanghai (☎ **021/ 6355-4909**), open daily from 8:30am to 9pm.

Internet Access   While lagging well behind the West in Internet communications, the business centers at major Shanghai hotels now provide online access and e-mail services, including PC rentals employing familiar English-language

Internet Cafes

Since the first server was introduced in China in 1994, Internet use has boomed and Internet cafes are springing up everywhere. Some of the more established are **Shanghai East Laser Computer Bookstore,** 2nd floor, 190 Hubei Lu (☎ 021/6361-4082), located near Fuzhou Lu, open daily from 9am to 8:30pm (closes at 6pm on Sun); **3C+T,** off Huaihai Lu at 238 Shaanxi Nan (☎ 021/6473-0439), open Monday to Thursday from 10am to midnight, Friday to Sunday from 10am to 2am (its initials stand for "computer, communications, and coffee plus training"); **InfoHighway,** in the French Concession at 181 Ruijin Er Lu (☎ 021/6415-5009), open daily from 9am to 6pm and charging just 5RMB (60¢) per hour; **Jing Xi Internet Bar,** 549 Beijing Xi Lu (☎ 021/6218-0203), open 24 hours daily; and the **Shanghai Library,** 1550 Huaihai Zhong Lu (☎ 021/6445-5555), located in a small office on the ground floor west of the main entrance, open daily from 9am to 6pm and always packed with Chinese students. The Shanghai Library and most of the other Internet cafes listed above levy low user rates, from 6RMB to 15RMB (70¢ to $1.80) per hour for workstations, with nominal charges for sending and receiving e-mail. Hotel Internet fees are generally three to six times higher.

software programs. Charges for computer rentals and e-mail can be put on your hotel bill and paid for with a credit card. In-room Internet access and e-mail using your laptop has become increasingly common in Shanghai's top luxury hotels. An alternative is to use the facilities at a growing number of independent Internet cafes around the city (see below).

Laundry & Dry Cleaning   Launderettes and Laundromats have not made a mark in Shanghai. Your hotel will provide full laundry and dry-cleaning services, often same-day service, with prices depending on the rating of the hotel.

Liquor Laws   The drinking age in Shanghai is 18. Bars keep irregular closing hours, some not shutting down until 4am or later. Supermarkets and some hotel shops sell imported and domestic beer, wine, and spirits.

Shanghai residents don't drink much except on special occasions. Many Chinese believe that Westerners are big drinkers, whatever the occasion or hour of the day. At a banquet or hosted dinner, follow your Chinese host's lead in drinking and toasting, but don't try to keep up if you're having too much, as some Chinese are prodigious drinkers.

Lost Property   First, contact the site where you think you lost an item. Then report the loss to your hotel staff for their suggestions and assistance in calling around town. Items lost in taxis are sometimes returned to your hotel.

Luggage Storage   The train stations have left-luggage counters, but the Metro stations and airports do not. Hotels provide storage (often for a small daily fee) at their bell desks.

Mail   Most hotels sell postage stamps and will mail your letters and parcels. A few hotels even have small post offices. Overseas letters and postcards require 5 to 10 days for delivery. Overseas airmail rates are 4.20RMB (50¢) for a postcard, 5.20RMB (60¢) for an aerogramme, and 6.40RMB (75¢) for a letter (up to 20g or 0.5 oz.). The main **International Post Office,** open from 7am to 10pm daily, is located at 276 Beisuzhou Lu (☎ 021/6324-0069), at the intersection of Sichuan Bei Lu, in downtown Shanghai just north of Suzhou Creek; international parcels are sent from a desk in the same building, but its entrance is actually around the corner at 395 Tiantong Lu. For private couriers offering overseas express mail and parcel service, see "Couriers," above.

Money   See "Money," in chapter 2.

Newspapers & Magazines   The official *China Daily* English-language newspaper appears Monday to Friday, with a special edition on Saturday. It's available free at hotel desks. As the national newspaper, *China Daily* gives versions of national and world news within Communist party guidelines, although there is some self-criticism and its feature articles can be quirky. Monthly editions of English-language magazines and newspapers produced for travelers and expatriates in Shanghai, available at hotels and restaurants around town, include *Shanghai Daily, Shanghai Star, that's Shanghai, Shanghai Talk, Shanghai Travel,* and *Shanghai Now.* Foreign magazines and newspapers, including *USA Today, International Herald Tribune, South China Morning Post,* and Asian editions of the *Wall Street Journal, Newsweek,* and *Time,* are available at kiosks in all international hotels.

Pharmacies   There are no 24-hour drugstores in Shanghai. Hotel kiosks, modern department stores, and supermarkets are stocked with some Western amenities (cough drops, toothpaste, shampoo, beauty aids), but bring your own pain and cold remedies, as these are more difficult to find. The best outlet for Westerners is **Watson's Drug Store,** with locations at Shanghai Centre, 1376 Nanjing Lu (☎ **021/6279-8382**), and at 789 Huaihai Zhong Lu (☎ **021/6474-4775**); both are open daily from 9am to 10pm.

Prescriptions can be filled at **New Pioneer International Medical Centre** (NPIMC), 2nd floor, Ge Ru Building, 910 Hengshan Lu, Xujiahui District (☎ **021/6469-3898**), and **World Link Medical and Dental Centers,** Suite 203, Shanghai Centre, 1376 Nanjing Xi Lu (☎ **021/6279-7688**). Chinese medicines are dispensed at the **Shanghai No. 1 Pharmacy,** 616 Nanjing Dong Lu (☎ **021/6322-4567**), which is open daily from 9am to 10pm.

Police   The Shanghai police force is known as the **Public Security Bureau** (PSB). The main office is downtown at 210 Hankou Lu (☎ **021/6321-5380**). The emergency telephone number for the police is ☎ **110.**

Post Office   See "Mail," above.

Rest Rooms   For hygienic rest rooms, rely on the big hotels. Thousands of public rest rooms are located in the streets, parks, restaurants, department stores, and major tourist sites of Shanghai, but these are seldom clean and do not provide tissues or soap as a rule, although the rest rooms in the newest shopping plazas, fast-food outlets, and deluxe restaurants catering to foreigners are cleaner than average. The public rest rooms in the streets charge a small fee (0.5RMB/6¢ or less), but seldom provide Western-style facilities or private booths, relying instead on squat toilets (porcelain "holes in the floor"), open troughs, and rusty spigots. Tourists often come armed with their own tissues and even a can of spray disinfectant. Look for WC signs at intersections, pointing the way to these facilities. Be prepared to rough it if you are off the beaten track (often meaning anywhere outside a major hotel).

Safety   Shanghai is one of the safest cities in the world for foreign travelers, but as the city modernizes and Westernizes, the crime rate rises. Pickpockets and thieves do exist. At crowded public tourist sites, keep an eye on purses, wallets, and cameras. Always store valuables in a concealed safety pouch. Backpacks and fanny packs are targets on buses, on the subway, and in markets. Use hotel safe-deposit boxes or room safes, and do not open your door to strangers. Violent crimes and cases of sexual harassment against foreign visitors are quite rare, but do occur, so use common sense. Travel with others when possible, rebuff strangers in the streets, and avoid unlighted streets after dark. Beggars are common on Shanghai streets, as are touts hawking merchandise. Idlers who speak a little English may pose as "friends" and try to engage you in conversation in the street. While they are not thieves, as a rule, they are after more than friendship (usually some of your money, often turned over in the form of an outrageously expensive restaurant bill); they should be rebuffed quickly. Don't give strangers your hotel name or phone number, unless you want to be bothered later.

Shoe Repair   Street-side vendors repair shoes and other leather goods for a small fee; most hotels provide the same service.

Smoking   China has more smokers than any other nation, an estimated 350 million, accounting for one of every three cigarettes consumed worldwide. About 70% of the men smoke. Recent anti-smoking campaigns have led to laws banning smoking on all forms of public transport (including taxis) and in waiting rooms and terminals. The ban is spreading to some public buildings. Fines can be levied, but enforcement is sporadic. Hotels provide no-smoking rooms and floors, and many restaurants have begun to set aside no-smoking tables and sections. At present, expect to encounter more smoking in public places in China than in the West.

Taxes   Most hotels levy a 15% tax on rooms (including a city tax), and many restaurants and bars place a 15% service charge on bills. There is no sales tax. The other common tax tourists face is the international departure tax at the airport, currently 90RMB ($11), payable only in Chinese currency in the departure hall before checking in.

Taxis   See "Getting Around," above.

Telephone & Fax   The **country code** for China is **86.** The **city code** for Shanghai is **021.** If you are calling a Shanghai number from outside the city but within China, dial the city code (021) and then the number. If you are calling Shanghai from abroad, drop the first zero.

Local calls in Shanghai require no city code; just dial the eight-digit Shanghai number (or the three-digit emergency number for fire, police, and ambulance). Calls from Shanghai to other locations in China require that you dial the full domestic city code (which always starts with **0**).

To call Shanghai from the United States, dial 011 (the international access code) plus 86 (the country code for China) plus 21 (the city code for Shanghai minus the initial zero) plus the eight-digit Shanghai number.

To make an international direct dial (IDD) call from Shanghai (which you can do from most Shanghai hotel rooms), dial the international access code (**00**) plus the country code for the country you are calling plus the area code and the local phone number. The country code for the United States and Canada is **1;** for the United Kingdom, **44;** for Australia, **61;** and for New Zealand, **64.** To call the United States from Shanghai, for example, dial 00 plus 1 plus the U.S. area code plus the U.S. phone number. If you have questions, speak with the hotel operator or an international operator (☎ **116**).

You can also use your **calling card** (AT&T, MCI, or Sprint, for example) to make international (but not domestic) calls from Shanghai. The local access number for **AT&T** is **10-811;** for **MCI, 10-812;** and for **Sprint, 10-813.** Check with your hotel for the local access numbers for other companies. The directions for placing an international calling-card call vary from company to company, so check with your long-distance carrier before you leave home.

Most Shanghai hotels provide **fax services.** Faxes are an efficient way to communicate overseas (and within Shanghai and China). The charges for faxing overseas are dropping but are still relatively high, owing to the higher rates imposed on international communications by China. Additional hotel charges are usually imposed on faxes as well.

Television & Radio   **Chinese Central Television** operates six stations (CCTV 1, 2, 3, 4, 6, and 8), while **Shanghai Television** (STV) offers three stations, including OTV and cable channel 2. Nearly all programs are in the Chinese language. The hotels, however, provide a spectrum of Western-language satellite stations and international networks. Hong Kong-based Star TV has an English-language channel. Most hotels offer music video stations (such as MTV), CNN, and NHK (Japan), and some offer CNBC, BBC, ESPN, and other channels from the United States, Europe, Australia, and even India. The large hotels offer more than 20 Chinese and international choices. Most hotels offer in-room movie channels or HBO (an Asian version); some offer both.

There are two **radio stations** with substantial English-language programming, FM 101.7 and FM 103.7.

Thomas Cook   There is a Thomas Cook Liaison Office at China Travel Service, 881 Yan'an Zhong Lu (☎ **021/6247-6390;** fax 021/6247-6390).

Time Zone   Shanghai (and all of China) is 8 hours ahead of Greenwich mean time (GMT plus 8), meaning it is 13 hours ahead of New York, 14 hours ahead of Chicago, and 16 hours ahead of Los Angeles. Shanghai does not use daylight saving time, so subtract 1 hour from the above times in the summer. Because China is on the other side of the international date line, you lose 1 day when traveling west from the United States, but you gain it back upon return (across the Pacific).

Tipping   This practice is still officially forbidden in the People's Republic of China, and no tipping is necessary. In reality, however, Shanghai hotel bellhops routinely receive 10RMB or $1 per bag; rest-room attendants, 1RMB or 2RMB (10¢ or 25¢) per visit; taxi drivers, the change from a fare (1RMB/10¢ to 5RMB/60¢); guides on day tours from hotels, 10RMB to 20RMB ($1.20 to $2.40); and waiters (where no service charge is added), hairdressers, and other service personnel, 10% of the bill.

Useful Telephone Numbers   **Spring International Travel Service** maintains a 24-hour hot line for tourist inquiries in English and Chinese (☎ **021/6252-0000**). For the **current time** in Shanghai, dial ☎ **117.**

Water   Water from the tap is not safe for drinking (or for brushing teeth), even in the best hotels. The water available in hotel rooms in flasks, thermoses, or plastic bottles has been boiled and is safe to drink. Clean bottled water (including imported brands) can be purchased almost everywhere, even from street vendors, for 10RMB to 40RMB ($1.20 to $4.80) per liter.

Weather   The *China Daily* newspaper, Chinese TV news programs, and some hotel bulletin boards furnish the next day's forecast. You can also dial Shanghai's weather number (☎ **121**).

4 Accommodations

With many international chain hotels in port, Shanghai offers excellent accommodations, but few bargains. Even the budget hotels (there are no hostels, motels, or B&Bs in Shanghai) charge more than elsewhere in China, with the exception of Hong Kong and Beijing. Rates are highest from May through October.

The Sheraton, Hilton, and Holiday Inn introduced Western management and services to Shanghai in the late 1980s, paving the way for other foreign groups. These high-end ventures are managed by foreign staff, with the exception of the Sheraton Hua Ting, which has dropped the Sheraton name and is now under local management. The two biggest names in locally managed hotels are Jin Jiang and Hua Ting (which recently merged); they offer a variety of hotels, including some rated at the top (four- and five-star).

The Chinese government ranks hotels on a star system. **Five-star hotels** have the complete facilities and services of any international luxury hotel. **Four-star hotels** come close, often lacking only a few technical requirements (such as a large swimming pool or other amenities). Both levels are popular choices for Western travelers, providing English-speaking staff and clean, luxurious accommodations. **Three-star hotels** are almost always Chinese-managed and provide less consistent services, fewer amenities, and more basic rooms, with a reduced dedication to upkeep and maintenance. Some three-star hotels are still adequate for the budget traveler who expects merely a decent place to spend the night. Few of the three-star hotels have experienced English-speaking staffs, however, and most have limited facilities that can best be described as drab or run-down.

Acceptable **budget hotels** are almost nonexistent in Shanghai. Most Western travelers (and tour groups) select from more expensive four- and five-star accommodations. Hotels rated as two-star or below cater to the more rugged backpacking traveler who is not fussy; some offer dormitories and shared bathrooms. There are many hotels without star ratings; the government does not allow these to accept foreign travelers.

HOW TO CHOOSE THE LOCATION THAT'S RIGHT FOR YOU

On the face of it, one would think that the most desirable hotel location would be in **Huangpu,** the district that encompasses the city center, the Bund, and Nanjing Road East, but there are few good hotels here. One can easily walk to some of the major sites and shops from city-center hotels, but taxis have a hard time getting in and out of the heart of the city. Thus, the bulk of Shanghai's better hotels are located west of city center, but still within (long) walking distance.

The **Luwan District (French Concession)** and adjacent **Jing An District (Northwest Shanghai),** both located a few miles west of city center, have the best selection of hotels. A walk to the Bund takes up to an hour; by the Metro or a cab, a few minutes. Taxi rides are required to reach most of the attractions and restaurants from hotels located farther to the west, in the sprawling **Changning District (Hongqiao Development Zone).** There is no subway service from here, but there are many fine hotels in this area, since much of the foreign investment and convention business is still centered near the older airport.

To the east of city center, just across the Huangpu River, the **Pudong New Area** now offers several of Shanghai's best new hotels, and its subway link to downtown (Metro Line 2) has brought it much closer to the action for visitors. Pudong itself has less to offer visitors, but it can readily serve as a base for leisure as well as business travelers.

It's fair to say, then, that no one of the major hotel locations has a complete lock on convenience for the traveler. Few hotels suffer significantly by their locations, since the main tourist sites are scattered around the sprawling city. Hotels located nearest city center, however, including those in the Luwan (French Concession) and Jin An districts, have the most to see in their immediate neighborhoods, while hotels in the Pudong, Changning (Hongqiao), and **Xuhui** (southwest of the French Concession) districts rank close behind.

HOW TO GET THE BEST ROOM FOR THE BEST RATE

The room rates listed in this guide are rack rates. The **rack rate** is the maximum rate charged by a hotel for a room. You'd get that rate if you walked in off the street and asked for a room for the night. Hardly anybody pays these prices, however, and there are ways around them. Don't be afraid to bargain. Always ask politely whether a room less expensive than the first one mentioned is available. Rack rates change with the season (they're lowest from mid-Nov to mid-Mar) and are subject to competition, which is fierce in Shanghai.

Many four- and five-star hotels in Shanghai give travel agents discounts in exchange for steering business their way, so if you're shy about bargaining, an agent may be better equipped to negotiate discounts for you. Book your hotel overseas in advance when possible, through a travel agent, the hotel chain, or a reservations service.

Reservations services work as consolidators, buying up or reserving rooms in bulk, and then dealing them out to customers at a profit. Most of them offer online reservations services as well. A few of the more reputable providers are: **Accommodations Express** (☎ 800/950-4685; www.accommodationsxpress.com), **Hotel Reservations Network** (☎ 800/96-HOTEL; www.180096HOTEL.com), **Quikbook** (☎ 800/789-9887, includes fax-on-demand service; www.quikbook.com), and **Room Exchange** (☎ 800/846-7000 in the U.S., 800/486-7000 in Canada). Online, try booking your hotel through **Arthur Frommer's Budget Travel** (**www.frommers.com**) and save up to 50% on the cost of your room. **Microsoft Expedia** (**www.expedia.com**) features a "Travel Agent" that can also direct you to affordable lodgings.

Shanghai Accommodations

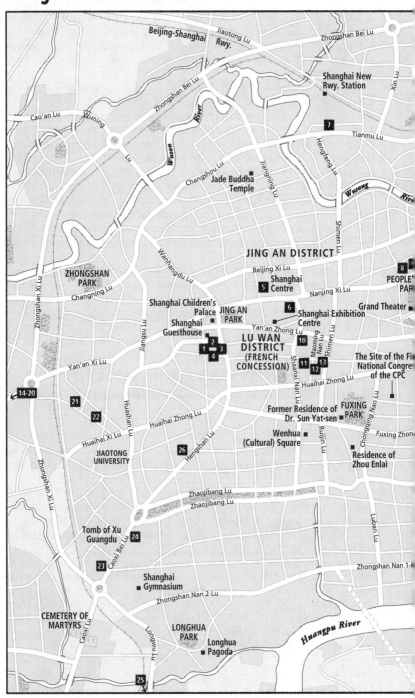

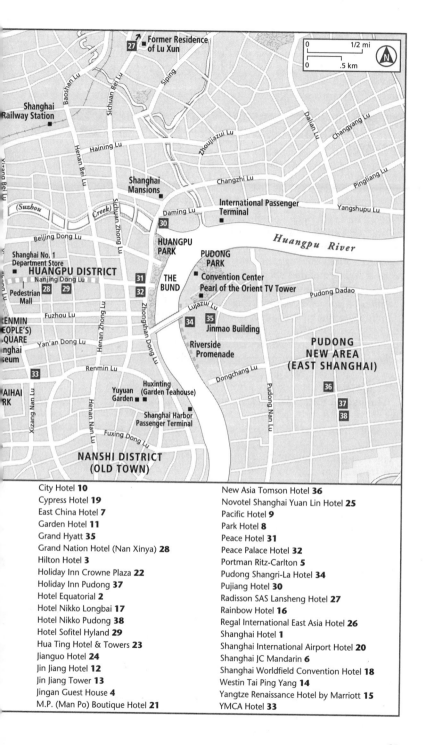

The hotel listings in this chapter are arranged first by location, then by price category. Rates do not include a service charge of 15% per night and a city development tax of $1 to $2 per night. All rooms include private bathroom, satellite television with foreign channels, and nonpotable tap water (unless otherwise noted). Hotel names are rendered first in English, then in pinyin.

1 Huangpu District (Downtown Shanghai)

EXPENSIVE

✪ **Grand Nation Hotel (Nan Xinya).** 700 Jiujiang Lu (northern entrance at 719 Nanjing Dong Lu), Shanghai 200001. ☎ **021/6350-0000.** Fax 021/6350-6666. www. tourinfo.sh.cn. 300 units. A/C MINIBAR TV TEL. 1,066RMB ($130) double. Children under 12 stay free in parents' room. AE, DC, JCB, MC, V. Subway: Henan.

Opened on the Nanjing Road pedestrian mall in 1998 by a local millionaire who fell in love with European art, the Grand Nation has the most lavish lobby in Shanghai, ripping with old-world elegance. The Italian and Spanish marble, art-glass decorations, stained-glass skylights, bird's-eye maple panels and wainscoting, and plush carpets of the public areas continue into the guest rooms, which are small but extremely plush, with marble bathrooms. Rooms, located on the 7th through 20th floors, all face an enormous atrium, which is festooned with Greek statuary. This hotel would be at home in Las Vegas. At present, it is little known even in Shanghai (the owner is considering changing its name). While an excellent deal for the money, the service level lags far behind the facilities, despite the presence of some fine Chinese staff members in higher positions. There are few international guests, beyond overseas Chinese, but there's no more elegant place to stay along Nanjing Road.

Dining: The seventh-floor Athena Atrium, at the bottom of the 13-story atrium, serves Western dishes. The Suyu is a Sichuan restaurant. The hotel's Chinese name comes from its Xinya Cantonese Restaurant in the lobby (Xinya being famous for more than 140 years as a producer of moon cakes). The Xinya, also called the Great Nation Seafood Restaurant, is a complex of cylindrical glass aquariums, home to the live seafood (which includes sharks).

Amenities: Small health club with a few new exercise machines, sauna, massage, billiards, mahjong, business center (no PCs yet), conference rooms, tour desk, beauty salon, shops, newsstand, 24-hour room service, same-day laundry and dry cleaning, newspaper delivery, concierge.

✪ **Hotel Sofitel Hyland (Hailun Binguan).** 505 Nanjing Dong Lu (on Nanjing Rd. pedestrian mall), Shanghai 200001. ☎ **800/221-4542** in the U.S. and Canada, 1300-65-65-65 in Australia, 0800-444-422 in New Zealand, 44/181-283-4500 in the U.K., or 021/6351-5888. Fax 021/6351-4088. www.hotelweb.fr. 400 units. A/C MINIBAR TV TEL. 1,394RMB ($170) double. Children under 12 stay free in parents' room. AE, DC, JCB, MC, V. Subway: Henan.

The best hotel in the district, this Accor-managed 30-story tower in the heart of the pedestrian sector of Nanjing Road can't be surpassed for its city-center location. Opened in 1993, its guest rooms were renovated in 1998. The rooms themselves are quite small, furnished in light brown tones, but well equipped with coffeemakers, hair dryers, two phones, and slippers and robes. Sofitel Club rooms (on floors 22 through 29) are just 82RMB ($10) more and include a Western buffet breakfast. Entrance from Nanjing Road is via stairs and an elevator to the second-floor lobby. There's a European, even French feel to the hotel. Service is efficient, if brusque.

Dining: The fourth-floor Brasserie serves Continental and Asian buffets from 6am to midnight. The Brauhaus pub features its own microbrews and international menu (see chapter 5, "Dining," for a review). The fifth-floor Hai Yur Tang offers noodles and Hong Kong–style dim sum for breakfast, lunch, and dinner. The third-floor Hai Yu Lan Ge restaurant specializes in Shanghai fare for lunch and dinner (see chapter 5, "Dining"). The Sky Lounge, up on the 30th floor, has great views, drinks, and a fine Sunday brunch from 11:30am to 3pm (see "Family-Friendly Restaurants," in chapter 5). A small take-out bakery is located in the lobby on the second floor.

Amenities: Good health club with the latest exercise machines (open from 6am to 11pm), Jacuzzi, sauna, bicycle rental, 24-hour business center (e-mail, PC rental, library), conference rooms, tour desk, concierge, beauty salon, gift shops, newsstand, 24-hour room service, same-day laundry and dry cleaning, newspaper delivery, baby-sitting, airport shuttle.

Park Hotel (Guoji Fandian). 170 Nanjing Xi Lu (near People's Park, a mile/1.6km west of the Bund), Shanghai 200003. ☎ **021/6327-5225.** Fax 021/6327-6958. www.jjusa.com. 208 units. A/C MINIBAR TV TEL. 1,230RMB ($150) double. Children under 12 stay free in parents' room. AE, DC, JCB, MC, V. Subway: Renmin People's Plaza.

Another historic hotel, almost as old as the Peace Hotel, the 20-story Park opened in 1934, later becoming Chairman Mao's favorite in Shanghai. It was once touted as the tallest building in Asia. Today, it retains its past elegance in a nicely restored Art Deco lobby. The guest rooms, which were all modernized in 1997, come equipped with safes, hot pots, hair dryers, and compact bathrooms. The locally managed hotel offers relatively few amenities, and the service level is merely adequate, but its three main restaurants (which serve many tour groups) offer Continental, Cantonese, and Shanghai fare and are well regarded. (See chapter 5, "Dining," for a review of the Feng Zhe Lou restaurant.)

Amenities include a health club, sauna, mahjong room, business center (e-mail, PC rental), conference rooms, tour desk, beauty salon, shopping arcade, concierge, 24-hour room service, same-day laundry and dry cleaning, newspaper delivery, massage, and baby-sitting. The shuttle to the airport is free.

✪ Peace Hotel (Heping Fandian). 20 Nanjing Dong Lu (on the Bund), Shanghai 200002. ☎ **021/6321-6888.** Fax 021/6329-0300. www.shanghaipeacehotel.com. 279 units. A/C MINIBAR TV TEL. 1,312RMB ($160) double. AE, DC, JCB, MC, V. Subway: Henan.

The most historic of Shanghai's hotels, the Peace was built in 1929 by colonial millionaire Victor Sassoon. Known in its heyday as the Cathay Hotel, it was famous throughout Asia. Noël Coward wrote *Private Lives* while staying here in 1930, and Steven Spielberg filmed scenes here for his film *Empire of the Sun.* Now managed by Shanghai's Jin Jiang Group, the hotel offers spacious guest rooms with large closets and high ceilings; some retain their old furnishings and trim, but most were modernized in 1997 and have lost their charm. Some designated no-smoking rooms are available. The two top floors (10 and 11) retain their "Nine Nations" deluxe suites, each furnished in the decor of a foreign nation (the U.S., France, England, Italy, Turkey) and priced at 4,264RMB ($520) per night. The public areas are splendid and romantic (the lobby is an Art Deco masterpiece), the location on Nanjing Road and the Bund is tops, but the amenities and service barely rise to the four-star level.

Dining/Diversions: The Dragon and Phoenix Room (see chapter 5, "Dining") offers a superb view of the Bund, an ornate interior, and a good selection of Chinese and Shanghai dishes. The new Shanghai Night Bar, on the 11th floor, has indoor and outdoor seating, wonderful views, and drinks and snacks. The Old Jazz Bar, in the lobby, is the oldest jazz club in town and a favorite nightspot, featuring Shanghai's oldest jazz musicians.

Amenities: Health club with some exercise machines, sauna, massage, billiards, game room, small business center (e-mail, PC rental), conference rooms, tour desk, beauty salon, souvenir shop, newsstand, concierge, 24-hour room service, same-day laundry and dry cleaning, newspaper delivery, nightly turndown, baby-sitting. The hotel offers an airport shuttle bus, and taxis are flagged down by the bellhops at the front door.

Peace Palace Hotel (Heping Gugong Fandian). 23 Nanjing Dong Lu (west side of the Bund), Shanghai 200001. ☎ **021/6329-1888.** Fax 021/6329-7979. 108 units. A/C MINI-BAR TV TEL. 1,312RMB ($160) double. AE, DC, JCB, MC, V. Subway: Henan.

Directly across the street from the famous Peace Hotel, the Peace Palace was built by the same expatriate Jewish taipan (Victor Sassoon) much earlier, in 1906, making it the oldest European-style hotel in Shanghai. It hosted the International Opium Commission in 1909. Although older, the Peace Palace is not quite as glorious in its original furnishings as the Peace Hotel, but its Renaissance mansion-style interiors are still remarkable. The hotel was closed for a long period before 1998, when it reopened after extensive renovations to its rooms. The guest rooms are furnished in Victorian reproductions, complete with curtains and carpets, a nostalgic touch that stops at the fully modernized bathrooms. In-room safes and electric hot pots are among the amenities. The eighth-floor roof garden was recently redone, affording views of the Bund and Huangpu River. The lobby and hallways are ornate, with chandeliers, original moldings, stained glass, and carved wooden columns. Beyond the colonial atmosphere, however, there are few, very few amenities (not even an airport shuttle), and the service is better at the sister hotel across the street, which is also managed by the local Jin Jiang Group.

Dining: The Shanghai Bund Restaurant (formerly the Crane Longevity Hall), on the first floor, is a vivid reminder of the grand colonial restaurants of the past, now serving a long list of Shanghai and Chinese dishes.

Amenities: 24-hour room service, same-day laundry and dry cleaning.

MODERATE

Pacific Hotel (Jinmen Dajiudian). 108 Nanjing Xi Lu (near People's Park, a mile/1.6km west of the Bund), Shanghai 200003. ☎ **021/6327-6226.** Fax 021/6372-3634. www.jjusa.com. 174 units. A/C MINIBAR TV TEL. 451RMB–492RMB ($55–$60) single, 574RMB–984RMB ($70–$120) double. Children under 12 stay free in parents' room. AE, DC, JCB, MC, V. Subway: Renmin People's Plaza.

Next door to the four-star Park Hotel, the three-star, nine-story Pacific Hotel began as the China United Assurance Company in 1926, before becoming the Overseas Chinese Hotel (Huaqiao Fandian). Changing its name once again to the Pacific, it underwent a thorough renovation in the late 1990s, preserving its striking colonial portico and small but ornate lobby, with coffered ceilings and carved columns in early Italian Renaissance style. The modern guest rooms, with hot-water thermoses instead of coffeemakers, are compact; the televisions receive satellite broadcasts, but most stations are Chinese, as are most of the guests. The Jin Jiang Group of Shanghai provides the management. While services and amenities are average or below, the location and room rates are good.

Rome Hall, on the lobby level, is an elegant dining area, with polished wood floors, white plaster coffered ceilings, wooden paneling, and formal place settings. The fare is Chinese and Shanghainese. The hotel also has smaller restaurants serving

Western, Fujian, Chaozhou, and Cantonese cuisines. Amenities include a small business center (e-mail, PC rental), tour desk, shopping arcade, concierge, 24-hour room service, same-day laundry and dry cleaning, and free airport shuttle.

INEXPENSIVE

✪ **YMCA Hotel (Qian Nian Hui Binguan).** 123 Xizang Nan Lu (south of People's Park, north of Huaihai Zhong Lu), Shanghai 200021. ☎ **021/6326-1040.** Fax 021/6320-1957. www.ymcahotel.com or www.jjusa.com. 150 private rms (with bathroom) plus 20 dorm beds. A/C MINIBAR TV TEL. 525RMB ($64) double. Children under 12 stay free in parents' room. AE, DC, JCB, MC, V. Subway: People's Park Plaza.

This historic 11-story brick building, built in 1929, really was the YMCA in colonial times; it is now a budget hotel managed by the local Jin Jiang Group. The lobby, a few steps down from the street, sparkles, although the rooms, while modernized, are drab and not well maintained. Each private unit has a small TV on the desk, a coffee table with two chairs, and a thermos with hot water. Also available are dorm rooms, each with two wooden bunk beds and clean sheets, for 123RMB ($15) per person (with shared bathroom facilities). The lobby does have a sundries shop and 24-hour Western cafe with drinks and snacks. The staff are friendly, but speak limited English. This is one of the best of the budget hotels in Shanghai and boasts a convenient location for the independent traveler.

There's a Chinese restaurant on the ninth floor serving seafood and Cantonese and Shanghainese dishes. The 24-hour lobby cafe, with Western drinks and snacks (ice cream, cake, sandwiches), is pleasant. Other amenities include a small business center (e-mail, PC rental), conference rooms, 24-hour room service, next-day laundry and dry cleaning, variety shop, in-room massage, karaoke rooms, and satellite TV.

2 Luwan District (French Concession)

VERY EXPENSIVE

Garden Hotel (Hua Yuan Fandian). 58 Maoming Nan Lu (1 block north of Huaihai Zhong Lu), Shanghai 200020. ☎ **212/755-0733** in the U.S., 0171/353-4994 in the U.K., or 021/6415-1111. Fax 021/6415-8866. www.gardenhotelshanghai.com. 500 units. A/C MINIBAR TV TEL. 1,968RMB ($240) double. AE, DC, JCB, MC, V. Subway: Shaanxi Nan Lu.

Built in 1990 on the site of the 1920s French Club and Cercle Sportif, the Garden Hotel has preserved the Art Deco features of the original structure in its west lobby and ballroom, as well as the old garden to the south. This Japanese-managed (Hotel Okura), 34-story tower is impeccably maintained and elegant throughout. The guest rooms, renovated in 1998, are of average size, with writing desks, in-room safes, hot-water pots, data plugs for laptops, and robes and slippers. The white-marble bathrooms contain phones, scales, hair dryers, and potable tap water. The facilities are extensive and first-rate. The language ability of the staff is indicated by the number of dots—blue dots for English, red dots for Japanese—on their uniforms (one dot = basic, two dots = average, three dots = excellent). This luxury hotel in the heart of the French Concession is favored by Japanese travelers and some Westerners.

Dining: The Rose Café (first floor, street entrance) serves Western food from 6am to midnight. Yamazato (second floor) offers Japanese breakfast, lunch, and dinner, and is open from 7am to 10pm. Bai Yu Lan, also on the second floor, specializes in Chinese fare for lunch and dinner. The 33rd-floor Continental Room provides an elegant setting for European dining from 7am to 10pm.

Amenities: 25-meter swimming pool with retractable roof, health club, Jacuzzi, lighted outdoor tennis courts, garden jogging course, business center (e-mail, PC rental, offices, library), conference rooms, beauty salon, newsstand, shopping arcade, florist, concierge, 24-hour room service, same-day laundry and dry cleaning, newspaper delivery, nightly turndown, twice-daily maid service, free airport shuttle.

EXPENSIVE

Jin Jiang Hotel (Jin Jiang Fandian). 59 Maoming Nan Lu (1 block north of Huaihai Zhong Lu), Shanghai 200020. ☎ **021/6258-2582.** Fax 021/6472-5588. www.jinjianghotelshanghai.com. 515 units. A/C MINIBAR TV TEL. 1,476RMB ($180) double. AE, DC, JCB, MC, V. Subway: Shaanxi Nan Lu.

The most famous hotel in the French Concession, the Jin Jiang Hotel opened its doors in 1929 as the Cathay Mansions. It is remembered as the location for the signing of the Shanghai Communiqué by President Nixon in 1972, reestablishing U.S.–China relations. The complex includes three major edifices: the 1929 North Building, now called Castle Mansions; the central Grosvenor House (1931), with its facade an imitation of the Barclay-Vesey Building in New York City, recently redone as a five-star all-suite deluxe hotel; and the old South Building, an aging three-star facility with worn rooms at 820RMB ($100) per night. The North Building, remodeled in 1999, retains its European Gothic style; it offers 193 rooms and five no-smoking floors, plus separate tubs and showers in the bathrooms. The Grosvenor House contains 26 suites with kitchens, each costing 6,560RMB ($800) a night, along with a Presidential Suite housing Chairman Mao's desk (with a concealed compartment on the right side for a pistol) and easy chair. Except for the South Building, the historic Jin Jiang has begun a new chapter as a deluxe five-star, Chinese-managed modern hotel. Its location, in the very heart of the French Concession, is convenient; its service is striving to meet top international standards. Most guests are from Hong Kong, Southeast Asia, North America, and Europe (in that order).

Dining: The Friendship Restaurant, in the North Building, serves international buffets. The Sichuan Restaurant, also in the North Building, has an excellent local reputation. The food street on the hotel grounds includes fine upscale international restaurants and bars. (See chapter 5, "Dining," for reviews of Hazara, JJ Mariachi, Latina, and Tandoor.)

Amenities: 20-meter indoor swimming pool, health club with new exercise machines, Jacuzzi, sauna, massage, six-lane bowling alley, good business center (open from 6am to midnight), conference rooms, tour desk, beauty salon, shopping street (Chinese crafts, boutiques, excellent bookstore), newsstand, concierge, 24-hour room service, same-day laundry and dry cleaning, newspaper delivery, nightly turndown, free airport shuttle.

Jin Jiang Tower (Xin Jin Jiang). 161 Changle Lu (corner of Ruijin Yi Lu), Shanghai 200020. ☎ **021/6415-1188.** Fax 021/6415-0048. www.jjusa.com. 728 units. A/C MINIBAR TV TEL. 1,640RMB ($200) double. Children under 12 stay free in parents' room. AE, DC, JCB, MC, V. Subway: Shaanxi Nan Lu.

When it opened in 1988, this 43-story circular tower was the first Chinese-managed international luxury hotel in Shanghai. Recent renovations (1999) on most floors have brought it back up to five-star level. The Tower trades on its modernity, not history. Everything about its facilities is contemporary and Western, from its three-story-high marble lobby, with plenty of colored glass, to its guest rooms, which are rather small but equipped with coffeemakers, safes, and hair dryers.

Many tour groups, both Chinese and Western, stay here. The hotel has all the amenities and fairly good service, a good location in the French Concession, lots of shopping, and a free airport shuttle.

Dining: The signature restaurant is the two-tiered Blue Heaven Revolving Restaurant at the top (41st) floor of the round tower; it serves good quality Chinese and Western buffets (see chapter 5, "Dining"). The Tulip Coffee Shop (in the lobby) has a Western menu, the Bamboo Garden offers Chinese choices, and the elegant Bund Restaurant serves French cuisine.

Amenities: Outdoor swimming pool, health club with exercise machines, Jacuzzi, sauna, massage, business center (e-mail, PC rental, offices), conference rooms, good tour desk, beauty salon, shops (Chinese crafts, carpets, silks, jade carvings), newsstand, concierge, 24-hour room service, same-day laundry and dry cleaning, newspaper delivery, nightly turndown, free airport shuttle.

MODERATE

City Hotel (Chen Shi Jiudian). 5-7 Shaanxi Nan Lu (south of Yan'an Zhong Lu), Shanghai 200020. ☎ **021/6255-1133.** Fax 021/6255-02111. 274 units. A/C MINIBAR TV TEL. 902RMB ($110) double. AE, DC, JCB, MC, V. Subway: Shaanxi Nan Lu (5 blocks).

A three-star, 26-floor business hotel that opened in 1990 and is updating its rooms, the City Hotel offers basic accommodations with few amenities and frills. The modern guest rooms are plain and simple, with space enough for a desk, coffee table and chairs, and small TV. The deluxe rooms have safes as well. The small lobby in black and white marble sets the businesslike tone. The staff is helpful, but English-language communication can be a problem. The City Business Apartment Building is going up next door, a sister property aimed at midlevel overseas business groups (mostly Chinese, as are the City Hotel's guests). Located at the extreme northwest edge of the French Concession, its chief appeal is its lower room rates.

The bright Café Vienna serves international buffets, while the Yung Cheng has a Sichuan menu. The Shanghai Restaurant offers local dishes in a plush setting. A lounge and karaoke rooms are located on the top (26th) floor. Also on-site are a business center (e-mail, PC rental, offices) and conference rooms; amenities include 24-hour room service, next-day laundry and dry cleaning, and free airport shuttle.

3 Jing An District (Northwest Shanghai)

VERY EXPENSIVE

✪ **Portman Ritz-Carlton Hotel (Boteman Dajiudian).** 1376 Nanjing Xi Lu (Shanghai Centre), Shanghai 200040. ☎ **800/241-3333** in the U.S. and Canada, 800/241-3333 in Australia and New Zealand, or 021/6279-8888. Fax 021/6279-8800. www.ritzcarlton.com. 564 units. A/C MINIBAR TV TEL. 2,050RMB ($250) double. AE, DC, JCB, MC, V. Subway: Jing An.

Shanghai's top hotel is tenaciously guarding its position with a $30-million renovation. The focal point is the two-story lobby, with its use of fiber-optic lighting and laminated stacked-glass sculptures, Indonesian ebony columns, polished chrome, and marble and limestone walls. The very large guest rooms feature extensive use of Chinese carved doors and moldings; amenities range from duvets, safes, and clocks to two phones and robes and slippers. The executive units (floors 41 through 45) have their own concierge and lounge. No-smoking rooms and two units for travelers with disabilities are also available. Located within Shanghai Centre, the 50-story hotel has direct access to numerous airline offices, the American Express office, a post office, a supermarket, a medical clinic, a drugstore, and Shanghai's most upscale boutiques, not to mention a performing-arts theater and the city's top business center (Bellsouth). To top it off, the service is at a truly international level.

Dining: Summer Pavilion has superb Cantonese lunches and dinners (see chapter 5, "Dining"). The Tea Garden hosts international buffets 24 hours a day. Hanagatami, with a chef from Osaka, has a full kaiseki menu, including a sushi bar and teppanyaki grill. The Lobby Bar serves an afternoon tea. The Ritz-Carlton Bar has Shanghai's first walk-in humidor.

Amenities: Indoor-outdoor 20-meter swimming pool, three-story health club (open until 11pm) with 18 exercise machines and weights, aerobics floor, massage, Jacuzzi, sauna, solarium, two squash courts, racquetball court, tennis court, jogging maps, 24-hour Bellsouth business center (e-mail, PC rental, library), conference rooms, tour desk, shopping arcade, beauty salon, florist, newsstand, concierge, 24-hour room service, same-day laundry and dry cleaning, nightly turndown, newspaper delivery, baby-sitting, World Link Medical Center, free airport shuttle.

Shanghai JC Mandarin (Jing Chang Wen Hua). 1225 Nanjing Xi Lu (1 block east of Shanghai Centre), Shanghai 200040. ☎ **021/6279-1888.** Fax 021/6279-1822. 513 units. A/C MINIBAR TV TEL. 2,050RMB ($250) double. AE, DC, JCB, MC, V. Subway: Jing An.

This lovely five-star, 30-story luxury hotel with international management (Meritus) is in the shadow of the Portman Ritz-Carlton and the Shanghai Centre, but it has much to recommend it, including a special play area for children (a rarity in Shanghai). The lobby has a glorious hand-painted mural of Ming Dynasty admiral Cheng Ho (China's Columbus). The guest rooms, which were renovated in 1999, are large and plush, with safes, coffeemakers, and three telephones. One no-smoking floor and several executive floors are available. With good international service, fine facilities, and a modern Chinese atmosphere, it remains one of Shanghai's best hotels, although it has fewer Western guests than the nearby Portman and Hilton.

Dining: The JC Patisserie serves up an international menu, a take-out deli is located in the lobby, and the Peach Garden offers fine Cantonese fare, from chicken rice to dim sum.

Amenities: Large swimming pool, fitness club, massage, Jacuzzi, sauna, tennis and squash courts, gymnasium, 24-hour business center (e-mail, PC rental), conference rooms, tour desk, beauty salon, shopping arcade, newsstand, concierge, valet, 24-hour room service, same-day laundry and dry cleaning, newspaper delivery, nightly turndown, free airport shuttle.

EXPENSIVE

✪ **Hilton Hotel (Jinan Dajiudian).** 250 Huashan Lu (1 block south of Yan'an Zhong Lu), Shanghai 200040. ☎ **800/445-8667** in the U.S. and Canada, or 021/6248-0000. Fax 021/6248-3848. www.hilton.com. 772 units. A/C MINIBAR TV TEL. 1,476RMB ($180) double. AE, DC, ER, JCB, MC, V. Subway: Jing An.

Shanghai's first foreign-owned hotel (1987), the Hilton still rates at the top of the city's accommodations and is a favorite of Western business travelers (the best in Shanghai, according to readers of the *Asian Wall Street Journal*). The services and facilities are top-notch. Guest rooms, renovated in 1997, including three no-smoking floors and four executive floors (35 through 38), are spacious and bright, with safes, work desks, 17-channel satellite television, three telephones, and robes and slippers. The lobby is opulent and bustling; the desk staff and bellhops speak English well. Within walking distance are Jing An Temple, Shanghai Centre, Julu Lu bar street, and the trendy shops and cafes of Hengshan Lu.

Dining: The Atrium Café has international dining from 6am to midnight. Shanghai Express, in the basement, offers Shanghainese and Cantonese "fast food"

24 hours a day. Da Vinci's serves excellent Italian and California cuisine for dinner. The Teppan Grill has a Japanese menu, Sichuan Court offers Chinese dishes, and Sui Yuan features dim sum and other Cantonese favorites, prepared by Hong Kong chefs. Gourmet Corner is a take-out deli in the lobby, open from 8am to 10pm.

Amenities: Large indoor swimming pool in atrium, Clark Hatch–managed health-and-fitness club, exercise machines, massage, Jacuzzi, sauna, solarium, massage, two indoor squash courts, outdoor tennis court, large 24-hour business center (e-mail, PC rental, library, offices), conference rooms, tour desk, beauty salon, florist, newsstand, drugstore, medical clinic, concierge, valet, 24-hour room service, same-day laundry and dry cleaning, nightly turndown, newspaper delivery, baby-sitting, free airport shuttle.

Hotel Equatorial (Gui Du Da Fandian). 65 Yan'an Xi Lu (south of Jing An Temple, Nanjing Rd. West), Shanghai 200040. ☎ **021/6248-1688.** Fax 021/6248-1773. www.equatorial.com. 509 units. A/C MINIBAR TV TEL. 1,558RMB ($190) double. Children under 18 stay free in parents' room. AE, DC, JCB, MC, V. Subway: Jing An.

This four-star hotel has the facilities of a five-star lodging, with service to match. International management is provided by a Singapore group. The 27-story tower is located just north of the Hilton. Guest rooms, renovated in 1998, are bright and airy, with just enough room for a work desk, coffee table, and two chairs. All units come with an electric hot-water pot, safe, hair dryer, and slippers. Two executive floors (1,804RMB/$220 per room) and one no-smoking floor are available. Fitness facilities are extensive, as is the shopping arcade, which even includes a branch of the Bank of China. Guests are largely from Singapore, Southeast Asia, North America, and Europe (in that order), and the English-speaking staff is helpful.

Dining: There's a cake-and-pastry counter and an international cafe serving buffets in the lobby. The Ranch Steak House uses U.S. beef, while the Golden Phoenix serves excellent Cantonese fare. Kampachi specializes in Japanese teppanyaki.

Amenities: 20-meter indoor swimming pool, fitness center, exercise machines (with a view of the pool), massage, outdoor tennis court, squash court, six-lane bowling alley, Jacuzzi, sauna, business center (e-mail, PC rental, offices), conference rooms, tour desk (CITS), courier service (UPS), beauty salon, florist, bookstore, shopping arcade with grocery store, concierge, valet, 24-hour room service, same-day laundry and dry cleaning, nightly turndown, baby-sitting, Bank of China, free airport shuttle.

Jingan Guest House (Jingan Binguan). 370 Huashan Lu (1 block west of Hilton), Shanghai 200040. ☎ **021/6248-1888.** Fax 021/6248-2657. 230 units. A/C MINIBAR TV TEL. 1,476RMB ($180) double. AE, DC, JCB, MC, V. Subway: Jing An.

This nine-story hotel was originally a German-built guest house in the 1930s, and much of its classic Spanish-style architecture has been preserved in the main building. The West Building (1985), however, lacks character, and its small modern rooms are in need of renovation. The rooms in the main building are attractive, with Moorish touches in their woodwork, carved moldings, and furniture; these units have been modernized as well, and feature safes, coffeemakers, satellite television channels, and hair dryers. The suites are palatial, with fanciful carving and false marble columns. The lobby boasts its original ornate decorations (arched ceilings and passageways, carved wooden doors, polished wood floors); there's also an old garden on the south side. Facilities are limited, and the local Jing Jiang Group staff has some trouble with spoken English, but the hotel has a quiet, old-world feel.

Dining: Lilly Hall, on the ninth floor, is a venerable and beautiful Chinese restaurant with good dishes from Shanghai, Sichuan, and Canton. The Valencia

Western Restaurant, with its Spanish furniture and European wall hangings, offers an international menu.

Amenities: Historic garden, small fitness club with exercise machines, massage, Jacuzzi, sauna, business center (e-mail, PC rental), conference rooms, beauty salon, newsstand, concierge, 24-hour room service, same-day laundry and dry cleaning, free airport shuttle.

MODERATE

Shanghai Hotel (Shanghai Binguan). 505 Wulumuqi Bei Lu (west of the Hilton, south of Yan'an Zhong Lu), Shanghai 200040. ☎ **021/6248-0088.** Fax 021/6248-1056. 540 units. A/C MINIBAR TV TEL. 779RMB ($95) double. AE, DC, JCB, MC, V. Subway: Jing An.

Recently remodeled, this 30-story tower dates from 1983 and is now under the management of the local Hua Ting Group. Most of its guests are Chinese, but it can handle non-Chinese guests as well. For a hotel rated at just three stars, it has some nice touches, if few extra facilities. The lobby and its coffee shop are newly redone with golden columns, black wrought-iron gazebos, and imitation gas lamps. Guest rooms are fully modernized, with blue-tone decor, work desks, and space for two chairs and a coffee table. If this location on the edge of the French Concession, near a subway station and the trendy shops and cafes of Hengshan Lu, proves desirable, but the prices at the adjacent Hilton, Equatorial, and Jingan hotels are too steep, the Shanghai will work.

On-site are Chinese, Japanese, and Western restaurants. Other amenities include a small health-club area with exercise machines, gymnasium, Jacuzzi, sauna, business center, large shopping arcade, post office, 24-hour room service, next-day laundry and dry cleaning, and tour desk.

4 Changning District (Hongqiao Development Zone)

VERY EXPENSIVE

✪ **Holiday Inn Crowne Plaza (Yin Xing Jiari Jiudian).** 400 Panyu Lu (northwest of Huaihai Zhong Lu, off Xinhua Lu), Shanghai 200052. ☎ **800/465-4329** in the U.S. and Canada, 1800/221-066 in Australia, 0800/442-222 in New Zealand, 1800553-155 in Ireland, 0800/897-121 in the U.K., or 021/6280-8888. Fax 021/6280-3353. 534 units. A/C MINIBAR TV TEL. 1,886RMB ($230) double. Children under 19 stay free in parents' room. AE, DC, JCB, MC, V. Nearest subway station, Xujia Hui, is more than 1 mile (1.6km) away.

This 27-story tower, upgraded to a Crowne Plaza in 1993, is an excellent hotel with a less than perfect location, unless you're in town for the international film and TV festival in November. Still, it is in a small, pretty neighborhood, west of Hengshan Lu and the French Concession, and the taxi service to and from the hotel is good. So are the large, high-ceilinged guest rooms, which offer a work desk, safe, coffeemaker, hair dryer, two phones, robe and slippers, and clean marble bathroom. The TVs receive 27 stations from all over the world. Both no-smoking rooms and rooms tailored to travelers with disabilities are available. Western travelers predominate, and the service standards are very high. The free airport shuttle bus also makes downtown trips on weekends.

Dining/Diversions: The Orient Express (in the lobby) has an international buffet (from 5:30am to 10:30pm) and champagne Sunday brunch. The second-floor Fu Rong Zhen is an elegant Sichuan/Cantonese restaurant. Akebone serves shabushabu, sukiyaki, and other Japanese favorites. The Deli is a take-out bakery in the lobby. Charlie's Fun Bar, also in the lobby, is one of Shanghai's most popular hotel pubs.

Amenities: Indoor swimming pool, health club, exercise machines, Jacuzzi, sauna, snooker, squash court, massage, business center (e-mail, PC rental, courier service, ticketing), conference rooms, tour desk (extensive city tour options), beauty salon ("The Mane Event"), shopping arcade (antiques, souvenirs, sundries, film), newsstand, 24-hour room service, twice-daily maid service, turndown service, baby-sitting, same-day laundry and dry cleaning, newspaper delivery, concierge, post office, florist.

✪ **Westin Tai Ping Yang (Tai Ping Yang Da Fandian).** 5 Zunyi Nan Lu (1 block north of Yan'an Xi Lu), Shanghai 200336. ☎ **800/WESTIN-1** in the U.S. and Canada, 1800/803-849 in Australia, 1300/650-707 in Sydney, 01800/409-331 in Ireland, 0800/44-1737 in New Zealand, 0800/282-565 in the U.K., or 021/6275-8888. Fax 021/6275-5420. www.westin-shanghai.com. 578 units. A/C MINIBAR TV TEL. 1,968RMB ($240) double. AE, DC, JCB, MC, V. No subway station nearby.

The best choice in a cluster of good hotels in the heart of the Hongqiao Development Zone, halfway between the airport and downtown, the Westin has been one of Shanghai's top hotels since it opened in 1990. Business travelers love it, not just for the location, but also for the highly efficient service and the plush but homey atmosphere. The luxurious European-style lobby is always lively; Americans and other Westerners make up the majority of guests. The accommodations, which occupy floors 6 though 26, include four no-smoking floors, four executive floors (2,829RMB/$345), and units for travelers with disabilities. The standard and larger "grand" rooms (2,296RMB/$280), renovated in 1999, are decorated rather like plush B&Bs, with rich carpeting, stuffed chairs, large work desks with bright lamps, and the most comfortable office chairs in Shanghai. Other in-room extras range from plants, safes, and data ports to daily fresh fruit, robes, slippers, coffeemakers, hair dryers, and even irons and umbrellas. Rubber duckies hang out in the bathtubs, enhancing the "home away from home" feel. Guests can touch "1" on the phone for express service and information on anything from baby-sitting to laundry. Nothing is missing; you can even reserve a tee time and transport to the nearby Shanghai International Country Club.

Dining: Café Bistro, in the lobby, serves excellent international buffets all day. Emerald Garden's Hong Kong chefs specialize in dim sum and Cantonese dishes. Hanano's has tempura and tatami rooms. The Bauernstube Deli (open from 9:30am to 8pm) has one of the largest selections of take-out in Shanghai. Giovanni's (see chapter 5, "Dining") is one of the best Italian dinner restaurants in the city.

Amenities: Indoor swimming pool, health club with new exercise machines, Jacuzzi, sauna, sundeck, billiards, golf reservations, massage, business center (e-mail, PC rental, courier service, library), conference rooms, beauty salon, large shopping arcade, newsstand, 24-hour room service, same-day laundry and dry cleaning, nightly turndown, newspaper delivery, baby-sitting, free airport shuttle.

EXPENSIVE

✪ **M. P. Boutique Hotel (Man Po Binguan).** 660 Xinhua Lu (west of Holiday Inn Crowne Plaza, east of Zhongshan Xi Lu—the Inner Ring Rd.), Shanghai 200052. ☎ **021/6280-1000.** Fax 021/6280-6606. www.mphotel.com.cn. 76 units. A/C MINIBAR TV TEL. 1,230RMB ($150) double. Children under 12 stay free in parents' room. Rates include breakfast. AE, DC, JCB, MC, V. No subway station nearby.

A new experiment in Shanghai accommodations, this is indeed an elegant Western-style boutique hotel. Open since April 1997, it hasn't seen too many Western guests. The staff is quite friendly, and a few speak some English. The hotel is quite charming and quiet, situated in an out-of-the-way, pretty little residential neighborhood within walking distance of the Westin Hotel and the heart of the Hongqiao Development Zone to the west. The six-story building is a brick-and-granite reproduction of the colonial architecture of the taipan era. Guest rooms are furnished in bright tartan wallpapers, wainscoting, and scalloped curtains, with pleated bedspreads and large armchairs; bathrooms are trimmed in black marble. Intimate and upscale, the M. P. is aiming for a four-star rating.

Dining: Oxford's, in the European-decorated lobby, resembles an old English pub, with a round bar and piano, a salad bar, and a steak grill (see chapter 5, "Dining"). The Sabatini Western Restaurant in the back serves international buffets. The Thai Village Sharksfin Restaurant is highly regarded for its Singapore-style seafood.

Amenities: Small fitness room with German-made exercise machines, billiards, pool table, mahjong, fax and courier services, 24-hour room service, same-day laundry and dry cleaning.

Rainbow Hotel (Hongqiao Binguan). 2000 Yan'an Xi Lu (southeast of Westin Hotel), Shanghai 200051. ☎ 021/6275-3388. Fax 021/6275-3736. 630 units. A/C MINIBAR TV TEL. 1,279RMB ($156) double. AE, DC, JCB, MC, V. No subway station nearby.

Managed by Shanghai's Hua Ting Group, the 31-story Rainbow opened in 1988 and renovated its rooms 10 years later. Rated at four stars, it doesn't have quite the amenities and service levels of the nearby Westin and Marriott (Yangtze Renaissance) hotels, from a Western perspective, but its room rates are lower, and overall, it's a convenient and comfortable place to stay in the Hongqiao area, with plenty to offer. The public spaces are fairly grand: the marble-floored lobby opens up to a mezzanine with shopping, and there's an interior courtyard garden with a small pavilion and goldfish pond. The guest rooms, decorated in gold tones, are small but modern, with a work desk, two chairs and a coffee table, a hot pot, a hair dryer, and a TV with in-house movies and some international satellite stations. Most of the guests are overseas Chinese, but Westerners do stay here and the staff speaks quite a bit of English.

Dining: Choices include the Shanghai Lao Ningbo Restaurant, with local specialties; the Rainbow Food Palace, with Cantonese dim sum; and a Western buffet.

Amenities: Indoor swimming pool, fitness center, exercise machines, gymnasium, sauna, massage, billiards, mahjong, business center (e-mail, PC rental), conference rooms, Asiana Airlines ticket office, tour desk, beauty salon, shopping arcade (souvenirs, sundries), newsstand, post office, 24-hour room service, same-day laundry and dry cleaning, free airport shuttle.

Yangtze Renaissance Hotel by Marriott (Yangzi Jiang Da Jiudian). 2099 Yan'an Xi Lu (next door to Westin Tai Ping Yang Hotel), Shanghai 200336. ☎ **800/321-2211** in the U.S. and Canada, 1800/251-259 in Australia, 0800/441-035 in New Zealand, 0800/221-222 in the U.K., or 021/6275-0000. Fax 021/6275-0750. www.marriott.com. 544 units. A/C MINIBAR TV TEL. 1,525RMB ($186) double. AE, DC, JCB, MC, V. No subway station nearby.

Formerly known as the Yangtze New World Hotel and now under management by Marriott, this 33-story, four-star tower opened in 1991 and is currently renovating all of its rooms. It is known for its catering department and its highly efficient international service; it also boasts more facilities and amenities than most hotels in its category, almost equaling those of the more expensive Westin next door. Before the current renovation, the rooms were on the small side, plain and clean, but they already included data ports, safes, hair dryers, work desks, robes and slippers, and marble bathrooms. There are five executive floors and some no-smoking rooms available. The Yangtze has long held a high reputation in Shanghai, catering dinners for visiting heads of state and numbering among its guests many world leaders. About half of its guests, many of them business travelers, are from North America and Europe.

Dining: The Dynasty, on the second floor, is considered by many the best Cantonese restaurant in Shanghai (see chapter 5, "Dining"). Antonio's (lobby level) serves fine Italian lunches and dinners, while the Chaozhou Garden specializes in southern Chinese fare. The second-floor Food Pavilion dishes up inexpensive Shanghai snacks and dim sum from 7am to midnight. The Graffiti Bar, open from 8pm to 3am, has one of the wildest decors in the city.

Amenities: Small outdoor swimming pool, health club, exercise machines, Jacuzzi, sauna, sundeck, business center (e-mail, PC rental), tour desk, beauty salon, florist, shopping arcade, newsstand, 24-hour room service, same-day laundry and dry cleaning, nightly turndown, newspaper delivery, baby-sitting, concierge, free airport shuttle.

5 Xuhui District (Southwest Shanghai)

VERY EXPENSIVE

Hua Ting Hotel & Towers (Huating Binguan). 1200 Caoxi Bei Lu (near Shanghai Stadium and Inner Ring Rd.), Shanghai 200030. ☎ **021/6439-1000.** Fax 021/6255-0830. www.huating-hotel.com. 1,008 units. A/C MINIBAR TV TEL. 1,763RMB ($215) double. AE, DISC, JCB, MC, V. Subway: Wan Ti Guan.

Opened under Sheraton management in 1986 as the first foreign-managed luxury hotel in Shanghai, the Hua Ting reverted in 1996 to Chinese management, but it has kept its five-star facilities in good repair. Room remodeling began in 1999. Guest rooms are modern and above average in space, each with a work desk, coffee table and chairs, and marble bathroom. No-smoking rooms are available, as are executive floors with 24-hour butler service. Plenty of amenities are on offer, and the red marble lobby is gorgeous, but the five-star rating is too generous to apply to the service, which was better under Sheraton.

Adjacent is the Hua Ting Guest House, which once served as quarters for the hotel staff but is now a three-star budget wing of the main hotel (697RMB/$85 for a double), with far fewer amenities and a less efficient staff. The Hua Ting is far from any sightseeing, but it is very near the subway station (Metro 1). Check with **UTELL** (☎ **800/547-4000** in the U.S. and Canada, 0800/556-555 in the U.K.) to see if a substantial room discount can be arranged.

Dining: Guan Yue Tai is a luxurious Cantonese restaurant on the top (26th) floor. Bai Hua Yuan serves Shanghai specialties, Buon Appetito is an Italian eatery, Kagayaki has Japanese fare, and Ka Fei Ting provides Western buffets. The American-style deli is open 24 hours a day.

Amenities: Large indoor swimming pool, health club, exercise machines, Jacuzzi, sauna, massage, billiards, outdoor lighted tennis courts, squash court, bowling alley, conference rooms, 24-hour business center (e-mail, PC rental, offices), tour desk, beauty salon, shopping arcade, 24-hour room service, same-day laundry and dry cleaning, turndown service, free airport shuttle.

✪ **Regal International East Asia Hotel (Fu Hao Huan Qiu Dong Ya Jiudian).** 516 Hengshan Lu, Shanghai 200030. ☎ **800/222-8888** in the U.S. and Canada, 1800/622-895 in Australia, 0800/590-467 in the U.K., or 021/6415-5588. Fax 021/6445-8899. www.regal-hotels.com. 300 units. A/C MINIBAR TV TEL. 1,804RMB ($220) double. Children under 12 stay free in parents' room. AE, DC, JCB, MC, V. Subway: Heng Shan Lu.

The best luxury lodging in the district, the Regal has all the trappings of a grand hotel, from its expansive white-marble lobby to the best health and fitness facilities in Shanghai. The management team is international (with sister hotels in Hong Kong, New York, Los Angeles, and other world cities). Opened in 1997, the 22-story hotel has fairly large, bright and modern guest rooms with safes, hair dryers, coffeemakers, and robes and slippers—all the amenities of a fine five-star hotel. Also available are no-smoking rooms and executive units (floors 19 through 22). Its Shanghai International Tennis Center offers the city's best facilities, including a center court that seats 1,200 spectators. Located along trendy Hengshan Lu in a consular area (U.S., France, Japan, Australia, Germany), it is still a long walk to the French Concession, but the subway station is just a block away.

Dining: The California Restaurant, in the lobby, serves international buffets from 6am to midnight. The second-floor Jade Coral offers Cantonese, Shanghainese, and Sichuan dishes for lunch and dinner.

Amenities: Indoor 25-meter swimming pool, extensive health-and-fitness facilities, European exercise machines, Jacuzzi, sauna, massage, 10 tennis courts, indoor squash court, aerobics gym, simulated golf machine, 12-lane bowling alley, mahjong, billiards, conference rooms, business center (e-mail, PC rental, IDD phone booths, courier service), concierge, tour desk in business center, beauty salon, shopping arcade, 24-hour room service, same-day laundry and dry cleaning, newspaper delivery, nightly turndown, baby-sitting, free airport shuttle.

EXPENSIVE

Jianguo Hotel (Jianguo Binguan). 439 Caoxi Bei Lu (south of intersection of Hengshan and Hongqiao roads), Shanghai 200030. ☎ **021/6439-9299.** Fax 021/6439-9433. 473 units. A/C MINIBAR TV TEL. 1,279RMB ($156) double. Children under 12 stay free in parents' room. AE, DC, JCB, MC, V. Subway: Xu Jia Hui.

This 23-story, four-star, locally managed hotel, opened in 1991, is undergoing a thorough renovation. At present, the guest rooms are small but well kept, with clean marble bathrooms; they will all be enlarged by 2001. There are some no-smoking units available, along with executive rooms (floors 18 through 23), which list at 1,476RMB ($180) a night. The lobby is a four-story atrium with white-marble walls, and there's a small garden on the roof. Guests are mostly Asian, but the staff speaks some English. The back building boasts Shanghai's largest sauna center, with a women's-only section offering separate saunas, aromatherapy, reflexology, and even breast enlargements. A swimming pool is to be open by 2001.

Dining: The Shanghai Restaurant, in the lobby, serves local specialties. There's also a Cantonese restaurant and an international buffet on the property.

Amenities: Fitness center, sauna center, billiards, snooker, small business center (e-mail, PC rental, office), conference rooms, concierge, tour desk, newsstand, 24-hour room service, same-day laundry and dry cleaning, free airport shuttle.

MODERATE

✪ **Novotel Shanghai Yuan Lin Hotel (Nuo Fute Yuan Lin Binguan).** 201 Baise Lu (next to Shanghai Botanical Garden, west of Longwu Lu), Shanghai 200231. ☎ **800/221-4542** in the U.S. and Canada, 1800/642-244 in Australia, 0800/444-422 in New Zealand, 4471/724-1000 in the U.K., or 021/6470-1688. Fax 021/6470-0008. 324 units. A/C MINIBAR TV TEL. 984RMB ($120) double. Children under 12 stay free in parents' room. AE, JCB, MC, V. No subway station nearby.

Perhaps because it is so far south of the city, this suburban hotel is easily the best three-star international hotel in Shanghai. Its facilities, although aging, and its staff (Accor management) rate an additional star. The guest rooms in the six-story main building are small, plain, and basic, but modern and clean. French names are affixed to restaurants and public areas. The black-and-white marble lobby contains a small indoor garden with a goldfish pool. The property includes a cluster of 40 two-story Western-style villas for long-term guests (mostly expatriates with foreign companies such as Coca-Cola and Volkswagen). There's a backdoor entrance (free admission) to the Shanghai Botanical Garden. The staff is friendly, and the free downtown shuttle connects to the nearest subway station.

Le Lotus serves Cantonese and Shanghainese lunches and dinners, while Le Jardin offers Western buffets and international à la carte choices from 6am to 1am. Amenities include an indoor tiled lap pool, health club, exercise machines, sauna, billiards, darts, two outdoor tennis courts, bowling, table tennis, shooting range, business center (e-mail, PC rental), tour desk, beauty salon, newsstand, 24-hour room service, next-day laundry and dry cleaning, concierge, baby-sitting, and free airport shuttle.

6 Hongkou District (Northeast Shanghai)

EXPENSIVE

Radisson SAS Lansheng Hotel (Lansheng Fandian). 1000 Quyang Lu (off Han Dan Lu, near Inner Circle Rd.), Shanghai 200437. ☎ **800/333-3333** in the U.S. and Canada, 1800/333-333 in Australia, 0800/443-333 in New Zealand, 1800/557-474 in Ireland, 0800/374-411 in London, or 021/6542-8000. Fax 021/6544-8400. www.radisson.com. 417 units. A/C MINIBAR TV TEL. 1,312RMB ($160) double. Children under 12 stay free in parents' room. AE, DC, JCB, MC, V. No subway station nearby.

The only internationally managed hotel for miles, the 22-story Radisson is located well north of downtown, but near Pudong via the elevated Inner Circle Road and about halfway between the two airports. The neighborhood is noisy and not scenic. Still, this hotel provides good service, excellent facilities, and a free shuttle to downtown Shanghai. The guest rooms are large, bright, and well appointed (two telephones, safe, work desk); bathrooms are deluxe, with separate showers and tubs. Although the location is not the best, the facilities and service warrant a full four-star rating.

Dining: The Flamingo serves Continental fare. The Terrace Café features Western and Oriental buffets. Fortune Garden is a very formal Cantonese restaurant. The Food Plaza dishes up local Shanghai snacks.

Amenities: Fitness center, exercise machines, Jacuzzi, sauna, massage, reflexology ("healthy foot program," 41RMB/$5 per treatment), six-lane bowling alley, golf simulator, badminton court, table tennis, billiards, business center (e-mail, PC rental, offices), conference rooms, tour desk, newsstand, souvenir store, concierge, 24-hour room service, same-day laundry and dry cleaning, nightly turndown, newspaper delivery, baby-sitting, free airport shuttle.

MODERATE

East China Hotel (Zhong Ya Fandian). 111 Tianmu Xi Lu (southeast of the Shanghai Railway Station), Zhabei District, Shanghai 200070. ☎ **021/6317-8000.** Fax 021/6317-6678. 250 units. A/C MINIBAR TV TEL. 820RMB ($100) double. AE, JCB, MC, V. Subway: Shanghai Railway Station.

This very modern but poorly maintained hotel is worth staying in only in a pinch. It is handy to the railway station, but the neighborhood is ugly and crowded. The guest rooms are modern, but small and a bit run-down. Its TVs receive no Western stations. A night here won't kill you, and the bathrooms are functional, but there's nothing much to recommend it unless you want something better than a dorm room near the train station. The staff speaks some English.

The lobby restaurant serves international buffets. There are also several Chinese restaurants on-site. Other amenities include a fitness center, sauna, business center, souvenir-and-sundries shop, 24-hour room service, and next-day laundry and dry cleaning.

INEXPENSIVE

Pujiang Hotel (Pujiang Fandian). 15 Huangpu Lu (northeast side of Suzhou Creek, north of the Bund), Shanghai 200080. ☎ **021/6324-6388.** Fax 021/6324-3179. 100 private rms (with bathroom) plus 140 dorm beds. A/C MINIBAR TV TEL. 328RMB ($40) double. AE, DC, ER, JCB, MC, V. No subway station nearby.

A favorite of backpackers (dormitory beds are 66RMB/$8 a night), this one-star hotel is just a short jaunt over the Suzhou Bridge (Waibaidu Qiao) to the north end of the Bund and Nanjing Road. The building is loaded with history and colonial atmosphere. Built in 1860 and reconstructed in late Renaissance style on its present site in 1910, it was known for decades as the Astor House, Shanghai's top turn-of-the-century hotel. The Pujiang's interiors today are those of a ruined mansion, with high ceilings, an immense ballroom, and dark corridors festooned in dusty carved woods and paneling. Guest rooms, which include basic modern bathrooms, have seemingly escaped any real maintenance for decades. Don't expect any amenities here other than a Western cafe, an Internet cafe with PCs, and a tour desk, all catering to young independent travelers.

7 Pudong New Area

VERY EXPENSIVE

✪ **Grand Hyatt (Jin Mao Kai Yue Dajiudian).** 2 Shiji Da Dao (Century Blvd.), 54th floor, Jin Mao Tower (southeast of the Pearl of the Orient TV Tower), Shanghai 200120. ☎ **800/233-1234** in the U.S. and Canada, 1800/131-234 in Australia, 0800/441-234 in New Zealand, 0845/758-1666 in the U.K., or 021/5049-1234. Fax 021/5049-1111. www.hyatt.com. 555 units. A/C MINIBAR TV TEL. 2,460RMB ($300) double. Children under 12 stay free in parents' room. AE, DC, JCB, MC, V. Subway: Lujiazui.

Currently the world's highest hotel, running from the 54th to the 88th floor of the Jin Mao Tower, the new Grand Hyatt offers ultra-luxurious accommodations with the city's highest-priced rooms. The views of the Bund just across the river are astonishing, as are the guest rooms, which combine Art Deco and traditional Chinese motifs with high-tech designs. The irregularly shaped, very spacious floor plans all include walls of glass for the view, beds with duvets and leather-panel headboards, Chinese-designed furniture and Italian-made glass-top desks, touch panels for lighting, and ceramic ice buckets fired in local kilns. The large white-marble bathrooms contain glass counters, glass sinks, stainless-steel fixtures, three-nozzled showers, heated mirrors, and separate tubs with picture windows. Regency Club rooms (floors 79 through 85) are 2,706RMB ($330) per night. Staying here is like being in a five-star space capsule, complete with the world's longest laundry chute (88 floors). The public areas encircle a 33-story cylindrical atrium in the center of this glass-and-chrome rocket ship to Shanghai's future. The multitude of elevators and curving public spaces are dazzling, but confusing at first. Service is top-rate, making this the best new hotel in Shanghai.

Dining/Diversions: Show kitchens and city views typify the many upscale dining options. The Grand Café, in the lobby on the 54th floor, serves exquisite international buffets (see chapter 5, "Dining"). On the 56th floor are three restaurants:

the Grill, with a central rotisserie and seafood grill; Kobachi, with yakitori and a sushi bar; and Cucina, with Tuscan fare. Canton (55th floor) serves Cantonese dishes in an elegant setting (see chapter 5, "Dining"). The Patio (56th floor) is a lounge at the base of the 33-floor spiraling atrium. Bar Twist (53rd floor) is a martini bar; the Piano Bar (53rd floor) is a plush retreat that permits cigars; Cloud 9 (87th floor) serves up tapas and cocktails; and the Skylounge (88th floor) is a good spot for champagne. On the lower podiums of the Jin Mao Tower are Food Live, with 10 open kitchens, serving everything from Shanghai dumplings to Häagen-Dazs ice cream. Pu-J's Entertainment Centre is an opulent nightspot with four "action zones," ranging from jazz to disco.

Amenities: Indoor "sky-pool" (world's highest swimming pool), fitness center, exercise machines, Jacuzzi, sauna, business center (e-mail, PCs with flat screens, offices), conference rooms, tour desk, newsstand, 24-hour room service, nightly turndown, twice-daily maid service, same-day laundry and dry cleaning, butler, concierge, airport shuttle and limousines.

New Asia Tomson Hotel (Xinya Tangchen Dajiudian). 777 Zhangyang Lu (at Dongfang Lu intersection in heart of downtown Pudong), Shanghai 200120. ☎ **800/223-5652** in the U.S. and Canada, 0800/447-555 in New Zealand, 1800/553-549 in Australia, 0800/898-852 in the U.K., or 021/5831-8888. Fax 021/5831-7777. www.nathsha.com. 422 units. A/C MINI-BAR TV TEL. 1,722 ($210) double. Children under 12 stay free in parents' room. AE, DC, JCB, MC, V. Subway: Zhangyang Lu.

Pudong's first international five-star hotel (1996), the Tomson is highlighted by large, elegant guest rooms encircling a 21-story atrium with its own interior garden. All units contain safes, coffeemakers, hair dryers, data ports, and robes and slippers. No-smoking rooms and three executive floors are available. Guests can book a golf package that includes a round at the 18-hole Tomson Golf Course in Pudong (3,198RMB/$390 double, including breakfast and dinner). The facilities and service are excellent, the location ideal for those doing business in Pudong's financial district.

Dining: Among the many fine-dining venues are the third-floor Terrace Café, with an international dinner menu; the second-floor Canton Palace, serving up dim sum and Peking Duck; the 24th-floor Chaozhou Restaurant, offering shark's fin and other Cantonese delicacies; and the Ticino Italian Restaurant.

Amenities: Indoor and outdoor swimming pools, fitness center, exercise machines, Jacuzzi, sauna, massage, billiards, golf course (3 miles/5km away), rooftop tennis court, 24-hour business center (e-mail, PCs, offices), conference rooms, newsstand, shopping arcade, beauty salon, 24-hour room service, same-day laundry and dry cleaning, twice-daily maid service, nightly turndown, baby-sitting, concierge, free airport shuttle.

✪ **Pudong Shangri-La Hotel (Pudong Xiangge Lila Fandian).** 33 Fucheng Lu (southwest of the Pearl of the Orient TV Tower, adjacent to Riverside Ave. on the Huangpu River), Shanghai 200120. ☎ **800/942-5050** in the U.S. and Canada, 0800/442-179 in New Zealand, 1800/222-448 in Australia, 020/8747-8485 in London, or 021/6882-8888. Fax 021/6882-6688. www.shangri-la.com. 612 units. A/C MINIBAR TV TEL. 1,968RMB ($240) double. Children under 18 stay free in parents' room. AE, DC, JCB, MC, V. Subway: Lujiazui.

With the best location in Pudong and a marvelous view of the Bund across the river, especially at night, this new 28-story, five-star Shangri-La, opened in 1998, couldn't be more convenient. It is also quite luxurious, with some of the most spacious rooms in the city, each providing generous counter and closet space, a marble-top work desk, a coffee table, a couch, a safe, a coffeemaker, a data port, duvets, and robes and slippers. Bathrooms are equipped with separate tubs and showers. The

Horizon Club offers executive rooms on floors 20 through 22, at 2,624RMB ($320) per night; standard units with a view of the Bund go for 2,378RMB ($290) per night. The wide lobby faces the Riverside Avenue park on the Huangpu River (free park admission for hotel guests). Most of the guests here are Westerners, and Shangri-La's management is up to its usual high international standards. There is free shuttle service to downtown Shanghai on weekdays.

Dining/Diversions: Shang Palace serves fine Cantonese lunches and dinners in elegant surroundings, with inexpensive buffets on weekends (see chapter 5, "Dining"). Inagiku has a teppanyaki bar. The Garden Café, off the lobby, features international buffets, à la carte selections, and a children's menu 24 hours a day (see "Family-Friendly Restaurants," in chapter 5). The lobby Deli offers take-out snacks and Austrian pastries from 8am to 9pm. B.A.T.S. is a lively bar in the basement.

Amenities: Indoor lap pool, fitness center, new exercise machines, Jacuzzi, sauna, tennis court, jogging along Riverside Avenue park area, large business center (e-mail, PCs, library, lounge, offices), conference rooms, newsstand, sundries shop, 24-hour room service, same-day laundry and dry cleaning, twice-daily maid service, nightly turndown, baby-sitting, concierge, free airport shuttle.

EXPENSIVE

✪ **Holiday Inn Pudong (Pudong Jiari Fandian).** 899 Dongfang Lu (south central Pudong), Shanghai 200122. ☎ **800/465-4329** in the U.S. and Canada, 1800/221-066 in Australia, 0800/442-222 in New Zealand, 1800/553-155 in Ireland, 0800/897-121 in the U.K., or 021/5830-6666. Fax 021/5830-5555. www.hi-pudongsha.com or www.basshotels.com. 320 units. A/C MINIBAR TV TEL. 1,312RMB ($160) double. Children under 12 stay free in parents' room. AE, DC, JCB, MC, V. Subway: Yanggao.

This spanking-new 32-story, four-star Holiday Inn is thoroughly Western. The guest rooms are quite spacious and bright, with bird's-eye maple furniture, work desks, couches, large coffee tables, duvets coffeemakers, hair dryers, and robes and slippers. The white-tiled bathrooms, complete with telephones, are spotless. There are three no-smoking floors (27, 28, and 30), three executive floors (30, 31, and 32), and rooms for travelers with disabilities. The TVs receive 22 channels, including HBO, Cinemax, and CNN. Many of the guests are Westerners, most doing business in Pudong, but with the opening of a Metro Line 2 subway station within walking distance, this Holiday Inn should appeal to tourists as well. This is a comfortable, efficient hotel, an excellent deal for a four-star lodging in Pudong, although it is a bit far from the Huangpu River, shops, and cafes near the Pearl of the Orient TV Tower. On weekends, a free shuttle bus makes runs to downtown Shanghai.

Dining/Diversions: The Exchange, in the lobby, serves international buffets, including a good Western/Asian breakfast. Deli Corner offers sandwiches, cakes, meats, and cheeses from 7am to 10pm. On the second floor, Oscar's Trattoria has Italian dishes, while Xu Ri Xuan serves seafood dishes in Cantonese and local Shanghai style. Reuben's is the third-floor cocktail lounge at the bottom of a high atrium, while Flannagan's Pub, outside the front entrance, has an Irish decor (open from 5pm to 1am).

Amenities: Outdoor heated swimming pool, health club, exercise machines, Jacuzzi, sauna, massage, aerobics, table tennis, mahjong, snooker, business center (e-mail, PC rental), conference rooms, beauty salon, newsstand, 24-hour room service, same-day laundry and dry cleaning, newspaper delivery, nightly turndown, baby-sitting, free airport shuttle.

ⓘ Family-Friendly Hotels

Most of Shanghai's international hotels let children stay free in their parents' room, and many can provide baby-sitting services with advance (4-hr.) notice, but very few offer any special programs or facilities for kids. An exception is the **Shanghai JC Mandarin** (see p. 60), which—in addition to its gym, tennis and squash courts, and year-round swimming pool—features a special supervised children's playroom with electronic games and playground equipment.

Hotel Nikko Pudong (Pudong Re Hong Fandian). 969 Dongfang Lu (south central Pudong), Shanghai 200122. ☎ **800/645-5687** in the U.S. and Canada, 1800/282-502 in the U.K., or 021/6875-8888. Fax 021/6875-8688. 376 units. A/C MINIBAR TV TEL. 1,230RMB ($150) double. Children under 12 stay free in parents' room. AE, DC, JCB, MC, V. Subway: Yanggao.

Just south of the new Holiday Inn Pudong, the Japanese-managed Nikko is even newer (1999). It's located in the 31-story Petroleum Building, but there's nothing industrial about these accommodations, which are both spotless and elegant. Guest rooms, equipped with work desks, coffee tables and chairs, coffeemakers, hair dryers, and robes and slippers, are fairly large, and some no-smoking units are available as well. The majority of guests are from Japan and Western countries, most in Pudong on business. Service and facilities are fully worthy of the four-star rating.

Dining: Café Venus, in the lobby, serves a Continental and Asian buffet. There are three fine choices on the third floor: the Fame Cantonese Restaurant, the Pearl Garden Shanghai Restaurant, and the Yamatoya Japanese Restaurant.

Amenities: Indoor swimming pool, health club, exercise machines, Jacuzzi, sauna, bowling alley, mahjong, billiards, business center (e-mail, PC rental), conference rooms, concierge, tour desk, beauty salon, shopping arcade, newsstand, 24-hour room service, same-day laundry and dry cleaning, nightly turndown, baby-sitting, free airport shuttle.

8 Near the Airport

Cypress Hotel (Longbai Fandian). 2419 Hongqiao Lu (between the zoo and Outer Ring Rd., about 3 miles/5km east of Hongqiao Airport), Shanghai 200335. ☎ **800/223-5652** in the U.S. and Canada, 1800/553-549 in Australia, 0800/447-555 in New Zealand, 0800/898-852 in the U.K., or 021/6268-8868. Fax 021/6268-1878. www.jjusa.com. 149 units. A/C MINIBAR TV TEL. 1,230RMB ($150) double. AE, JCB, MC, V. No subway station nearby.

Set on a large, historic garden estate (the former Shanghai Golf Club), with mature forest groves, arched bridges, and streams, the Cypress is one of the few airport hotels in the world that offers fishing. Although rated at just three stars, its facilities, if not its service staff, are nice enough to deserve an extra star. Guest rooms, which were renovated in 1996, are compact, modern, and clean, with safes, work desks, modem ports, hair dryers, and robes and slippers.

Dining: The hotel's three restaurants feature Chinese, German, and international fare. There's also a patio cafe.

Amenities: Large sports center with indoor swimming pool, exercise machines, Jacuzzi, sauna, bowling, snooker, squash, tennis, massage, mahjong, jogging trails, fishing ponds, business center, conference rooms, tour desk, shopping arcade, newsstand, room service, concierge, next-day laundry and dry cleaning, baby-sitting, free airport shuttle.

Hotel Nikko Longbai (Re Hong Longbai). 2451 Hongqiao Lu (west of zoo, $2^1/_2$ miles/4km east of Hongqiao Airport), Shanghai 200335. ☎ **800/645-5687** in the U.S. and Canada, 1800/282-502 in the U.K., or 021/6268-9111. Fax 021/6268-9333. 385 units. A/C MINIBAR TV TEL. 1,558RMB ($190) double. AE, DC, JCB, MC, V. No subway station nearby.

Just west of the Cypress Hotel, the 11-story, four-star Nikko Longbai is a garden hotel catering to Japanese guests, but the staff speaks English as well. This property is well suited for Western travelers who want to stay near the Hongqiao Airport. The soundproofed rooms are simple, compact, and clean, with bay-window views of the garden grounds; the bathrooms are tiled in white vinyl. The long hallways off the lobby open to serene gardens and lead to a complex of extended-stay apartments. The service and facilities are fairly luxurious, making the hotel a good choice for travelers who need to spend a night near the airport but still want to pay for luxury. There's a free shuttle bus to downtown Shanghai, a 20-minute ride away.

Dining: The Fountain restaurant, in the lobby, has an elegant European decor with white wicker chairs, pink tablecloths, and a grand piano; Japanese, Chinese, and Western dishes are on the menu.

Amenities: Outdoor swimming pool, health club, exercise machines, aerobics, Jacuzzi, sauna, sundeck, massage, outdoor tennis courts, golf driving range, business center (E-mail, PC rental), conference rooms, concierge, tour desk, airline ticket office, beauty salon, florist, shopping arcade, newsstand, grocery store, 24-hour room service, same-day laundry and dry cleaning, nightly turndown, baby-sitting, free airport shuttle.

Shanghai International Airport Hotel (Guoji Jichang Binguan). 2550 Hongqiao Lu (10-min. walk from Hongqiao Airport), Shanghai 200335. ☎ **021/6268-8866.** Fax 021/6268-8393. 304 units. A/C MINIBAR TV TEL. 820RMB ($100) double. AE, DC, JCB, MC, V. No subway station nearby.

The nearest major hotel to the airport, this eight-story, three-star hotel has an efficient Japanese-managed staff and free shuttle service to downtown Shanghai as well as to the Hongqiao Airport. There's no fitness center, but this is meant to be strictly a convenient airport stopover. The guest rooms are cozy, modern, and clean, with coffeemakers and hair dryers. Seven suites are available if you desire more amenities. Flight schedule monitors are mounted in the cheery lobby, which features a skylight, a massive chandelier, and a waterfall, as well as shops and a ticketing office.

Dining: The Kobe-Tei Steak House, on the first floor, specializes in teppanyaki. The big lobby restaurant serves Western, Chinese, and Japanese buffets and à la carte selections from 6am to 11pm.

Amenities: Chess and mahjong rooms, small business center (e-mail, PC rental), conference rooms, tour desk, beauty salon, shopping arcade, newsstand, 24-hour room service, next-day laundry and dry cleaning, free airport shuttle.

Shanghai Worldfield Convention Hotel (Shi Bo Hui Yi Dajiudian). 2106 Hongqiao Lu (entrance on Hongmei Bei Lu, 5 miles/8km from Hongqiao Airport), Shanghai 200335. ☎ **021/6270-3388.** Fax 021/6270-4554. www.conventhotel.com. 357 units. A/C MINIBAR TV TEL. 1,394RMB ($170) double. Children under 12 stay free in parents' room. AE, DC, JCB, MC, V. No subway station nearby.

Shanghai's first convention hotel, the six-story, four-star Worldfield opened in 1995. It is located close to the Shanghai Zoo and Gubei New Town, which has many good restaurants. The main building connects to a four-story convention center with an 800-seat Grand Ballroom, a 618-seat auditorium, a 600-seat convention hall, and 20 function rooms. But you don't have to be here attending a convention to enjoy a fresh, modern hotel that's just a 10-minute drive from the Hongqiao Airport. Guest rooms are fairly spacious, and come equipped with safes, hair dryers, international satellite TV, and data ports for laptop computers. The executive floor has its own gymnasium. The friendly staff speaks some English. There are frequent free shuttle buses to the airport and to nearby business centers in Hongqiao, including Gubei New Town.

Dining: In addition to Japanese and Chinese restaurants, there's a poolside coffee shop off the lobby, serving an international menu.

Amenities: Outdoor 22-meter lap pool with six marked lanes, health club, gym, aerobics, Jacuzzi, sauna, massage, business center (e-mail, PC rental), conference rooms, beauty salon, newsstand, 24-hour room service, same-day laundry and dry cleaning, baby-sitting.

5 Dining

Barely a decade ago, Shanghai visitors had a choice of a few rather expensive hotel restaurants and a few cheaper, less appetizing private cafes. Then a restaurant explosion hit in the prosperous 1990s. Today, a dozen promising, mostly upscale, international restaurants and cafes open every month, too many for even resident foreigners to keep up with. The mansions of the French Concession and the colonial buildings of the Bund are quickly filling up, not with the taipans and bankers of the past, but with stylish new places to eat.

While you could eat your way through China by sampling all the regional Chinese restaurants in Shanghai, the emphasis here is on Shanghai's own renowned cuisine. The most celebrated Shanghai dish is hairy crab, a freshwater delicacy that reaches its prime every fall. The rich crabmeat is generally steamed and dipped in a gingery vinegar sauce, but Drunken Crab is also popular (the crabs are salted away for a week or so and drowned in the local Shaoxing rice wine before cooking). Equally sought after is the eel, stir-fried with garlic and served with a sweet dark sauce. The freshwater shrimp and the West Lake carp (from nearby Hangzhou) are also signature treats. There are plenty of "drunken" dishes (those doused in rice wine) on any Shanghai menu worth its ginger or garlic (favorite Shanghai spices). Sauces tend to be oily, rich, and heavy. Hangzhou's Dragon Well (Long Jin) is the tea of choice.

Most foreign visitors, and even foreign residents, do become homesick for home cooking, or at least for something besides another Chinese meal, no matter how tasty. The boom in Shanghai eateries has brought with it a dramatic increase in Western, Japanese, and Thai restaurants. There are enough American, French, German, and even Mexican options of good quality to satisfy an overseas palate, as well as esteemed establishments serving Thai, Japanese, and Brazilian fare, too. It's possible to visit Shanghai for 2 weeks and eat very well without once using chopsticks on a single Chinese dish.

Shanghai recently ranked 19th in food costs among international cities on the corporate travel index published by *Business Travel News*. Business travelers are said to spend an average of $22 for breakfast, $24 for lunch, and $61 for dinner—a total of $107 a day to eat out. The Shanghai tab for the corporate business traveler lags behind similar dining bills in London, Hong Kong, and Tokyo, but

Hotel Versus Non-Hotel Dining

For visitors, the most pronounced division in Shanghai dining is between the hotel and the street. Shanghai's hotels still boast many of the very best restaurants in town. The quality of their food, the skill of their chefs, the hygiene of their kitchens, and the service of their waiters can be of high caliber. But so are those of several dozen private restaurants. These outsiders consistently offer lower prices, hygienic dining areas, good service, and English-language menus. In addition, smaller cafes outside the hotels are beginning to offer tasty Western dishes at even more economical rates. The international hotels now find themselves quite literally surrounded by private competitors, so that even the visiting foodie's dining experience in Shanghai need no longer be confined to the hotel.

is said to exceed that paid in San Francisco, Vienna, or Paris. Leisure travelers to Shanghai, however, usually spend much less than $100 a day on food. An inexpensive dinner without drinks can easily be had for under 75RMB ($9) per person; a moderately priced dinner for between 75RMB and 125RMB ($9 and $15) per person; and an expensive dinner, between 125RMB and 250RMB ($15 and $30). A very expensive dinner could cost 400RMB ($48) or more per person, depending on how many dishes are ordered. Lunches are considerably cheaper, often half the price of a dinner. With its wide range of dishes, a Chinese meal can be cheaper or far more expensive than the average prices indicate. Top hotels routinely add a 15% service charge to dining bills, although this practice is beginning to lessen as competition heats up with outside restaurants (many of which levy no service charges). Hotel restaurants accept major credit cards, as do a growing number of outside restaurants, but diners should always carry enough RMB to pay for a non-hotel meal.

The restaurants listed below are arranged first by location, then by price. The most popular locations for restaurants catering to visitors, regardless of cuisine, are downtown (Huangpu District) and in the French Concession (Luwan District), but the districts northwest (Jing An), southwest (Xuhui), and west (Changning) of downtown have almost as many establishments catering to the foreign traveler. The Pudong New Area across the river is also building up a list of fine eateries, especially in its top hotels.

1 Restaurants by Cuisine

AMERICAN
Bourbon Street (Xuhui, *VE*)
Malone's (Jing An, *M*)
Tony Roma's (Jing An, *M*)

ASIAN
Cochinchina 1883 (Jing An, *M*)
Irene's Thai (Jing An, *E*)
Lan Na Thai (Luwan, *E*)
Zips (Pudong, *E*)

CANTONESE
Canton (Pudong, *VE*)
Dynasty (Changning, *E*)
Shang Palace (Pudong, *E*)
Summer Pavilion (Jing An, *VE*)

CONTINENTAL/FRENCH
Ashanti (Luwan, *E*)
Blue Heaven Revolving Restaurant (Luwan, *E*)
Casj (Xuhui, *M*)

Key to Abbreviations: *VE* = Very Expensive   *E* = Expensive   *M* = Moderate   *I* = Inexpensive

Shanghai Dining

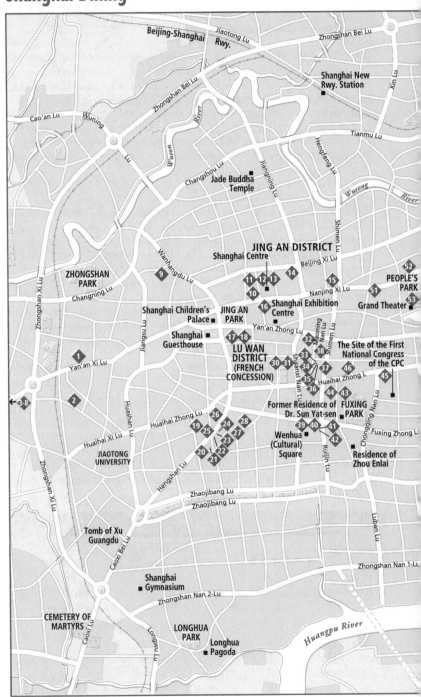

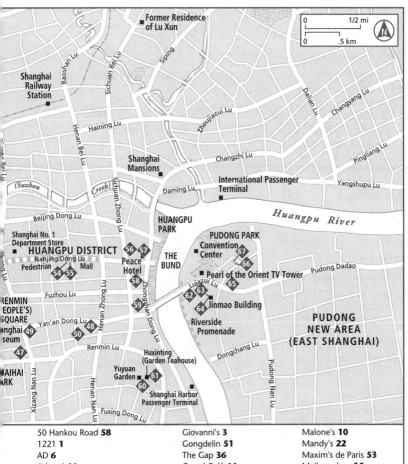

Delifrance (Luwan, *I*)
50 Hankou Road (Huangpu, *E*)
Grand Café (Pudong, *E*)
Kathleen's (Luwan, *M*)
Le Bouchon (Jing An, *E*)
Le Garcon Chinois (Xuhui, *E*)
Mandy's (Xuhui, *M*)
Maxim's de Paris (Huangpu, *E*)
M on the Bund (Huangpu, *VE*)
Park 97 (Luwan, *VE*)
Sasha's (Xuhui, *E*)
Shanghai Drugstore (Luwan, *E*)

DIM SUM

Bi Feng Tang (Jing An, *M*)
Chang An Dumpling (Huangpu, *I*)
Song Yue Lou (Nanshi, *I*)

GERMAN

Brauhaus (Huangpu, *M*)
Judy's Too (Luwan, *M*)
Landhaus (Xuhui, *M*)
Paulaner Brauhaus (Xuhui, *M*)

INDIAN

Hazara (Luwan, *E*)
Tandoor (Luwan, *E*)

IRISH/ENGLISH

Dublin Exchange (Pudong, *E*)
O'Malley's (Xuhui, *M*)
Oxford's (Changning, *M*)

ITALIAN

AD (Changning, *VE*)
Gino Cafe (Huangpu, *I*)
Giovanni's (Changning, *VE*)
Trattoria (Luwan, *M*)

JAPANESE

Itoya (Jing An, *E*)
Jurassic Pub (Luwan, *M*)
Sumo Sushi (Luwan, *I*)
Thousand Taste Noodle Shop
   (Luwan, *I*)

MEXICAN/SOUTH AMERICAN

Badlands (Jing An, *I*)
El Popo's (Changning, *I*)
JJ Mariachi (Luwan, *E*)
Latina (Luwan, *E*)

SHANGHAI

Big Fan (Changning, *M*)
Café 1931 (Luwan, *M*)
Dragon and Phoenix
   (Huangpu, *E*)
Feng Zhe Lou (Huangpu, *E*)
The Gap (Luwan, *M*)
The Grape (Luwan, *M*)
Hai Yu Lan Ge (Huangpu, *M*)
Henry's (Luwan, *E*)
Lu Bo Lang (Nanshi, *E*)
Lulu (Pudong, *M*)
Meilongzhen (Jing An, *E*)
Soho (Changning, *I*)
1221 (Changning, *E*)
Yang's Kitchen (Xuhui, *I*)

STEAK HOUSE

Mr. Stone (Xuhui, *M*)

VEGETARIAN

Gongdelin (Huangpu, *M*)
Jue Lin Shu Shi Chu
   (Huangpu, *M*)

2 Huangpu District (Downtown Shanghai)

VERY EXPENSIVE

✪ **M on the Bund.** 7th floor, 20 Guangdong Lu (half a block west of the Bund). ☎ **021/ 6350-9988.** Reservations required. Main courses 150RMB–400RMB ($18–$48). AE, DC, JCB, MC, V. Daily noon–3pm and 6–11pm. MEDITERRANEAN/CONTINENTAL.

M on the Fringe was such a success in Hong Kong that owner Michelle Garnaut decided to try it on the mainland. The result is a restaurant that has put Shanghai dining on the world map, drawing top international reviews. The various Continental dishes on the changing menu are carefully prepared from the freshest ingredients and served with skill and style. This is in essence a fine modern European restaurant situated on what was the old European banking and trading center of colonial China. M has a gorgeous view, particularly from the spacious rooftop of the building on #5 Zhongshan Dong Yi Lu (the former location of a Japanese shipping firm, built in 1925). The panoramas of the Bund, the busy Huangpu River, and the lighted skyscrapers of Pudong are unsurpassed. The wine list is one of Shanghai's best, too, as is the glittering bar with its cozy chairs and couches. A rattan chair on the open roof, however, is the ideal place from which to sip a nostalgic drink. The three-course weekend brunch at 218RMB ($26) per person is an elegant Shanghai surprise.

EXPENSIVE

✪ **Dragon and Phoenix Room.** In the Peace Hotel, 8th floor, 20 Nanjing Dong Lu (northwest corner of the Bund). ☎ **021/6321-6888.** Reservations required. Main courses 150RMB–350RMB ($18–$42). AE, DC, JCB, MC, V. Daily 11:30am–2:30pm and 5:30–11pm. SHANGHAI/CHINESE.

This classic restaurant in the historic Peace Hotel has an excellent view of the Bund and a gaudy interior in which Art Deco meets extravagant Qing Dynasty ornamentation (red-and-gold columns, ceilings with carved bats and dragons, dark lacquered chairs and tables). Eels swim in the aquariums, traditional musicians entertain in the evenings, and the menu is filled with Shanghai treats, from pork balls to hairy crab. Choices run the gamut of Chinese classics, including Sichuan and Cantonese dishes. The duck dishes are good, as are the fried noodles and the dim sum basket; the real pleasure, however, is in the setting. This is a great restaurant for enjoying the atmosphere of old Shanghai.

Feng Zhe Lou. In the Park Hotel, 2nd floor, 170 Nanjing Xi Lu (north of People's Park). ☎ **021/6327-5225.** Reservations required. Main courses 150RMB–350RMB ($18–$42). AE, DC, JCB, MC, V. Daily 11:30am–2:30pm and 5–8pm. SHANGHAI/CHINESE.

With its large, open seating on polished wooden floors, its marble columns, and its brass trim in a beautifully maintained area of this historic hotel, the Park's premier dining room entertains dozens of foreign tour groups as well as locals in a celebratory mood. Traditional music is played in the evenings, but the hall can become quite noisy. The food comes in big portions; the plates, based on Shanghai and Beijing recipes, are of high quality. The fried yellow fish with pine nuts is popular with locals, but if you're in the mood for Peking duck, you've come to the right place (better duck than in Beijing, some say). The menu is in English, although the wait staff may know little English beyond the names of what is ordered. Don't worry; the food is almost always superb.

50 Hankou Road. 50 Hankou Lu (just east of the Bund). ☎ **021/6323-8383.** Reservations recommended on weekends. Main courses 150RMB–300RMB ($18–$36). AE, DC, JCB, MC, V. Daily 11am–1am. CONTINENTAL.

Occupying a refurbished bank building just off the Bund, this is an elegant but informal spot for Western dining. The decor is mostly Indonesian; wicker chairs, full table settings, and an old brick floor add to the smart but casual atmosphere. The menu features oysters from Australia, liver pâté, and Caesar salads, with European standards ranging from baked escargot to eggplant Milanaise. The grilled steaks and shellfish are superb. Also available are evening specials, which are described on a chalkboard. Set lunches are a relative bargain, starting at 88RMB ($11). The management is from Hong Kong, ensuring attentive service.

Maxim's de Paris. 190-200 Huangpi Bei Lu (west side of Shanghai Grand Theatre in People's Park). ☎ **021/6386-8686,** ext. 2132. Reservations required on weekends. Main courses 150RMB–350RMB ($18–$42). AE, DC, JCB, MC, V. Daily 11am–11pm. FRENCH.

Very reasonably priced by Parisian standards, the French cuisine at Maxim's (a chain owned by Pierre Cardin) is among the best in Shanghai. The decor is decidedly 1920s France, with marble floors, fleur-de-lis sconces, potted plants, and Art Nouveau furniture, making it the perfect location for an elegant dinner before a performance at the adjacent Grand Theatre. The buttery scallop ravioli in a basilic cream sauce is a good choice, although the simple chicken breast stuffed with goat cheese is even tastier. Waiters flambé crêpes suzette at the table for dessert. The wine list is weighted toward French productions, of course. For lunch (when the set business lunch goes for 110RMB/$13), coffee, or dessert, Maxim's offers outside dining in its courtyard, providing a fine place to take a break and enjoy the view across the square to the Shanghai Museum.

MODERATE

Brauhaus. In the Hotel Sofitel Hyland, 2nd floor, 505 Nanjing Dong Lu (on the Nanjing Rd. pedestrian mall). ☎ **021/6351-5888,** ext. 4281. Reservations recommended on weekends. Main courses 75RMB–120RMB ($9–$14). AE, DC, JCB, MC, V. Sun–Thurs 11am–1:30am, Fri–Sat 11am–2:30am. GERMAN.

This large Bavarian-style pub and eating hall is bright and clean, and it commands a fine view through a wall of windows on the Nanjing Road pedestrian mall. The German-style beers, which are brewed in the big tanks next to the long bar, are quite tasty. The menu offers plenty of German favorites, from Wiener schnitzel and bratwurst to sauerkraut and Black Forest cake. The grilled steaks, served with fried potato strips, are hearty and flavorful. Saturdays feature a German buffet with all the beer you can drink for 150RMB ($18). The atmosphere is relaxed and friendly, and the staff, locals in German costume, efficient. This is a comfortable place to hang out in the big booths by the windows, eat hearty German food, drink fresh microbrews, and watch the crowds of Shanghai shoppers below.

✪ **Gongdelin.** 445 Nanjing Xi Lu (south side of Nanjing Xi Lu, between People's Park and Chengdu Bei Lu). ☎ **021/6327-0218.** Reservations recommended on weekends. Main courses 75RMB–200RMB ($9–$24). No credit cards. Daily 6:30–9:30am, 11am–2pm, and 5–9pm. VEGETARIAN CHINESE.

Shanghai's oldest and most famous vegetarian restaurant has been serving up mock duck and other imitation meat entrees for a half century. The decor is nothing to get excited about: basic round tables, white walls, few decorations, and no view. Instead, the food is the claim to fame, the best vegetarian fare in town. Half the fun is in the presentation of these dishes, artfully formed to mimic classic Chinese preparations that normally employ seafood, fowl, and pork. Dinnertime brings in the crowds. There's a take-out counter near the main entrance if you chance by during the day while shopping.

Hai Yu Lan Ge. In the Hotel Sofitel Hyland, 3rd floor, 505 Nanjing Dong Lu (on the Nanjing Rd. pedestrian mall). ☎ **021/6351-5888,** ext. 4395. Reservations recommended on weekends. Main courses 75RMB–120RMB ($9–$14). AE, DC, JCB, MC, V. Daily 11:30am–2:30pm and 5:30–10:30pm. SHANGHAI.

Noted for its authentic Shanghai cooking, the Hai Yu is a clean, casual lunch and dinner spot with a fine view of Nanjing Road. The local specialties are highlighted by dishes featuring freshwater catches and seafood. Especially memorable are the braised fish slices in a wine sauce and the braised river shrimp in the shell with a ginger dip. Traditional music is presented by local musicians from 6:30 to 9:30pm, creating a relaxing atmosphere for an evening of fine Shanghai dining.

Coffee & (Ice) Cream

Through the centuries, the Chinese have drunk tea rather than coffee and treated themselves to fresh fruit rather than ice cream, but in Shanghai, both Western-style coffee bars and ice-cream parlors are common enough. Here's where to go when you need a jolt or a treat:

- **Xiao Xuan Feng Lan Ling Ge,** 132 An Ting Lu, corner of Jianguo Xi Lu off the southern end of Hengshan Lu (☎ 021/6433-7995). This big white house in Xuhui District is perhaps the most stunning in old Shanghai, a mirage from the 1930s (former residence of a city mayor) with an improbable lush green lawn and outdoor swing. Just opened in 1999 and hardly discovered, it is the most romantic of coffeehouses imaginable, with a small bar and cafe inside (open daily from 2pm to 2am).

- ✪ **Espresso Americano,** Shop 105, 1376 Nanjing Xi Lu, west side of Shanghai Centre and Portman Ritz-Carlton Hotel (☎ 021/6279-8888). A Seattle-style coffee bar with pastries, bagels, and a few places to sit inside and out.

- **Planet Café,** 666A Huaihai Zhong Lu at Sinan Lu (☎ 021/5306-4320). This small espresso bar has a few stools at the counter and no snacks, but plenty of espresso (12RMB/$1.45) and cappuccino (18RMB/$2.15) pick-me-ups for your shopping expeditions on Shanghai's favorite avenue.

- **Sole Coffee,** 4 Hengshan Lu (☎ 021/6473-1374). Taiwan-owned, this is a bright, perky clone of Starbucks, located on a fashionable lane west of the French Concession.

- **Java Jive,** 18 Xian Xia Lu (☎ 021/6278-8534). Right next to the Friendship Store, this is a flashy coffee bar with music and foreign magazines.

- **Milano's Ice Cream,** 505 Nanjing Dong Lu (☎ 021/6352-1095). Come here for gourmet ice cream served on the most crowded section of the Nanjing Road pedestrian mall; it's located behind the big picture windows on the ground floor of the Hotel Sofitel Hyland.

- **Swensen's,** 139 Ruijin Yi Lu (☎ 021/5306-5005 or 021/5306-5009). An American ice-cream parlor (with an American snack menu) on one of the French Concession's prettiest streets.

- **Häagen-Dazs,** 2075 Yan'an Lu, Hongqiao area, southeast of the Westin Tai Ping Yang Hotel, open daily from 10am to 11pm (Fri and Sat until midnight). A swank cafe with premium ice creams, frozen yogurts, cakes, coffees, and fruit drinks, all on the expensive side (just like home). There's also a new branch at 558 Huaihai Zhong Lu, west of Yandang Lu, in the French Concession, that keeps the same hours.

Jue Lin Shu Shi Chu. 248 Jinling Dong Lu (at intersection with Fujian Lu). ☎ **021/6326-0115.** Reservations not necessary. Main courses 40RMB–120RMB ($4.80–$14). No credit cards. Daily 6am–7:30pm. VEGETARIAN CHINESE.

Cheaper than the more famous Gongdelin vegetarian restaurant, Jue Lin, located in a run-down three-story corner edifice, serves up excellent dumplings with vegetable fillings, noodle dishes, and vegetable plates, as well as plenty of fascinating non-meat concoctions including "ham" appetizers, fake eel strips, "crab" cakes, a sweet-and-sour "pork" dish (the pork is actually made of mushrooms), and a pretty good mock Peking duck. Always crowded, this is a no-frills local eatery on a busy corner where the attractions are the food and the prices (and perhaps the ground-floor Buddhist shrine).

INEXPENSIVE

Chang An Dumpling. 8 Yunnan Nan Lu (south from Yan'an Zhong Lu, southeast of People's Park). ☎ **021/6328-5156.** Reservations not necessary. Dim sum 10RMB–40RMB ($1.20–$4.80). No credit cards. Daily 24 hours. DIM SUM/BEIJING.

Both sides of this restaurant street south of Yan'an Lu are crammed with dim sum places. The dim sum (steamed pastries) are mostly Beijing (northern Chinese) style. Wheat flower is used to create the steamed buns, which are filled with vegetables or meats (especially pork). If you're in the mood for an authentic Chinese breakfast, lunch, or snack, this is the best street in town. If the menu isn't in English, just point at the item that looks the most interesting. The Chang An offers scores of dumplings with scores of stuffings, and it never closes.

✪ **Gino Cafe.** 2nd floor, 66 Nanjing Dong Lu (half a block from the Bund). ☎ **021/6361-2205.** Reservations not necessary. Main courses 40RMB–75RMB ($4.80–$9). AE, JCB, MC, V. Daily 9am–11pm. ITALIAN.

With superb food for the money, excellent service, a sparkling bistro decor, and the best pan pizza in town, this rates as Shanghai's top fast-food chain. Gino came to Shanghai in 1995 and quickly developed a reputation for its pasta, pizzas, coffees, and desserts. A central kitchen turns out pizzas with semolina in 6- to 13-inch sizes, with such toppings as seafood, curry chicken, beef, vegetarian, and even Hawaiian. The pastas (lasagna, spaghetti, fettuccine) are all priced under 40RMB ($4.80), while the coffee concoctions (cappuccinos, lattes) go for about 20RMB ($2.40). The minestrone soup with garlic bread and the fresh tossed salads cost even less. This is upscale fast food done right.

Among Gino branches to keep in mind for a quick, dependable meal are those in Hongqiao, 22 Xian Xia Lu (☎ **021/6270-4671**), and in Pudong, 501 Zhong Yang Lu, Yaohan Department Store (☎ **021/5830-0809**).

3 Nanshi District (Old Town)

EXPENSIVE

✪ **Lu Bo Lang.** 115-131 Yu Yuan Lu (south shore of teahouse lake). ☎ **021/6328-0602.** Reservations required. Meals 120RMB–250RMB ($14–$30). AE, DC, JCB, MC, V. Daily 7am–10am, 11am–1:45pm, 2–4:30pm, and 5–10pm. SHANGHAI.

This gorgeous, red and white, classical Chinese pavilion with upturned tile eaves soars three stories above the teahouse, pond, and Yu Garden at the heart of the historic Chinese Old Town, and it has been soaring financially ever since world leaders began patronizing it. The walls of the second- and third-floor corridors are plastered with more than 40 portraits of these celebrity patrons, including Queen Elizabeth, Fidel Castro, and President Clinton. The architecture and atmosphere are splendid (imitation Ming Dynasty style, with black tiles and red balustrades), and even the Shanghai dishes aren't too bad, led by the dim sum pastries and the full shark's-fin-and-crab banquet. President Clinton's favorite was the *mei mao su,* an eyebrow-shaped shortcake.

INEXPENSIVE

Song Yue Lou. 23 Bailin Lu (west shore of teahouse lake). ☎ **021/6355-3630.** Reservations not necessary. Meals 40RMB–80RMB ($4.80–$10). No credit cards. Daily 6:30am–8pm. DIM SUM/SHANGHAI.

There's been a two-story pastry restaurant here since about 1910. A decade ago it was called Moslemo; today it seems to be called, in part, "Lake De Delicate Food." By whatever name, you can't miss it, as it runs the whole west shore of the pond at the center of Old Town, affording great views from its smudgy windows. The second floor (a more "formal" dining room) opens at 11am for lunch and dinner. The meal to buy here is simple: dim sum pastries (many of them filled only with vegetable fillings) and tea. There's a picture menu to help in ordering; otherwise, just point or wait for help. The staff is often very friendly. The whole joint is also often jammed to the rafters, just the way a *jiaozi* (steamed dumpling) house is supposed to be.

4 Luwan District (French Concession)

VERY EXPENSIVE

✪ **Park 97.** 2 Gaolan Lu (inside west gate of Fuxing Park). ☎ **021/6318-0785.** Reservations recommended on weekends. Meals 120RMB–350RMB ($14–$42). AE, DC, JCB, MC, V. Mon–Thurs 5pm–2am, Fri–Sun 11am–2am. CONTINENTAL.

One of Shanghai's trendiest restaurants since 1997, the very chic Park 97 is divided into spaces for a cafe, formal dining, a late-night lounge, and an art gallery. The decor is a fashionable blend of Art Deco and high-tech, with French windows on the park. Outside tables do a good business in the summer. Top dishes on the dinner menu include the Caesar salad, coq au vin, salmon and sea scallops, seared tuna, and the pickled pear with goat cheese and black-bean caviar. The wine list offers plenty of European choices and champagnes. Lunch (in the cafe at the entrance, open at 11am daily) is a relative bargain, with pizzas (80RMB/$10), fish-and-chips (95RMB/$11), rib-eye steak (155RMB/$19), and a delicious pan-fried salmon fillet in warm potato salad, carrot spaghetti, and lemon capers (125RMB/$15). The various coffees go for 40RMB ($4.80). Next door (on the south side of the west gate) is Park 97's elaborate new tapas bar, **Lava.**

EXPENSIVE

Ashanti. 16 Gaolan Lu (1 block west of Fuxing Park and Sinan Lu; entrance on west side of church). ☎ **021/5306-1230.** Reservations recommended on weekends. Meals 180RMB–220RMB ($22–$26). AE, DC, JCB, MC, V. Daily 11:30am–2:30pm and 6:30–11:30pm. FRENCH.

Take a vacant Russian Orthodox Church, complete with domes, stained glass, icons, and religious murals; paint the walls peach; hang some avant-garde art; bring over a chef from France; and while you're at it, import plenty of wine from your own estate in South Africa. The result is a very chic French cafe inside a domed Russian church in old Shanghai. There's even a wine bar and three private dining rooms (one in the dome itself). The cafe is small and stylish, but the menu is expansive, with goose liver on sautéed potatoes, beef capriccio in truffle oil (60RMB/$7), and pumpkin mushroom soup (45RMB/$5) among the starters; rack of lamb, lemon-peppered duck breast (98RMB/$12), South China Sea clawless lobster, and ahi with lemongrass risotto (166RMB/$20) among the entrees; and a ginger-and-tamarind crème brûlée (48RMB/$6) among the desserts. The Ashanti-label wines run from 230RMB to 380RMB ($28 to $46) a bottle.

Blue Heaven Revolving Restaurant. In the Jin Jiang Tower Hotel, 41st floor, 161 Changle Lu (corner of Ruijin Yi Lu). ☎ **021/6415-1188,** ext. 84101. Reservations required. Dinner buffet 260RMB ($31), lunch buffet 138RMB ($17). AE, DC, JCB, MC, V. Daily 6–10am, 11:30am–2pm, and 6–10pm. INTERNATIONAL.

A fairly formal, slowly revolving restaurant with excellent views of the French Concession, Blue Heaven sets up an above-average buffet with European dishes predominating over Asian choices. The grilled steaks are particularly fine; the salads, good; the Spanish omelets and French pastries, just okay. Lunch buffets include soft drinks and levy no service charge; dinner drinks cost extra and the 15% service charge is mandatory, as it is in most hotel restaurants. A jazz band entertains nightly from 8pm to closing. The decor (blue carpets, white tablecloths, glittering flecks of starlight) enhances the feel of being in the clouds, happily suspended above the smoggy, feverish metropolis 41 floors below.

✪ **Hazara.** In the Jin Jiang Hotel, 59 Maoming Nan Lu (in the pedestrian lane on the hotel grounds). ☎ **021/6472-5494.** Reservations required. Meals 130RMB–250RMB ($16–$30). AE, DC, JCB, MC, V. Daily 11:30am–2pm and 5:30–10:30pm. INDIAN.

Superb dining in a superb colonial Shanghai setting, Hazara is the city's second great Indian restaurant, newly established on the gorgeous grounds of the historic Ruijin Guest House. Located on the ground floor of a 1930s mansion built by the Mitsui Trading Company, and later a former residence of the fabled Soong family, it couldn't be in a more romantic setting. Chairman Mao is rumored to have stayed under its steep red roof. The restaurant is housed in a courtyard under an orange tent with wooden beams, with intense burners throughout and a stone statue of Ganesh in the back. The interior is very posh, and the dinners are expansive and superbly prepared by Indian and Thai chefs. Hazara is one of two restaurants in the mansion under the umbrella of Faces, which refers to the lounge located with a view of the lawn to the south, a venture by some enterprising owner-managers from Thailand. The service is first-rate.

Henry's. 8 Xinle Lu (corner of Shaanxi Nan Lu). ☎ **021/6473-3448.** Reservations required. Meals 80RMB–210RMB ($10–$25). AE, DC, JCB, MC, V. Daily 11am–11pm. SHANGHAI.

As chic as it gets in Shanghai cafes, Henry's looks every bit like a fashionable French bistro with its simple Art Deco black-and-white decor, elegant table settings, and big picture windows facing the street. The menu, however, is classic Shanghai cuisine, with hairy crab and braised-eel entrees. For foreign visitors, it's the perfect upscale spot to sample the local cuisine without spending a fortune.

✪ **JJ Mariachi.** In the Jin Jiang Hotel, 59 Maoming Nan Lu (in the shopping lane on the hotel grounds). ☎ **021/6472-1778.** Reservations recommended on weekends. Meals 100RMB–200RMB ($12–$24). AE, DC, JCB, MC, V. Daily 11am–2pm and 6pm–2am. MEXICAN.

Opened in 1999, Shanghai's top Mexican restaurant is decorated to the hilt with adobe-style walls, tile floors, leather seats, cast-iron stair railings, and scores of garish south-of-the-border icons and cactus-shaped sconces. Mexican dancers and costumed musicians from Guadalajara perform nightly (dancing lessons are free). The Chinese waiters are decked out in sombreros and bolo ties, and the margaritas are siphoned from a soda fountain. The fajitas are excellent, as are the seafood plates, salsa dips, and cheese fondues. Three-course set dinners are just 98RMB ($12). Top main courses include the enchiladas and the barbecued pork chops with sausage (each 90RMB/$11).

✪ **Lan Na Thai.** 118 Ruijin Er Lu, Building 4, Ruijin Guest House (just south of Fuxing Zhong Lu). ☎ **021/6466-4328.** Reservations recommended on weekends. Meals 120RMB–240RMB ($14–$29). AE, DC, JCB, MC, V. Daily noon–2:30pm and 5:30–11pm. THAI.

Shanghai's best Thai restaurant is a new venture located on the second floor of a beautiful old mansion on the north end of the Ruijin Guest House. Look for signs to Faces, which is the elegant lounge on the main floor. Lan Na Thai is down the corridor toward the two Buddha statues. The chef is from Thailand, as are many of the authentic, fresh ingredients. The service is gracious; the tables overlook the colonial estate and courtyard below. The chicken soup and crab dishes are superb here, as are all the northern Thai selections, including the hot spicy seafood stir-fry (Phad Talay Nim Prik Paow) at 105RMB ($13) and the soft-shell crabs at 115RMB ($14). This is an ideal spot for a relaxing lunch or fine candlelit dinner.

Latina. In the Jin Jiang Hotel, 59 Maoming Nan Lu (in the pedestrian lane on the hotel grounds). ☎ **021/6472-2718.** Reservations recommended on weekends. Set dinners 68RMB–148RMB ($8–$18). AE, DC, JCB, MC, V. Daily 11:30am–3pm and 5pm–midnight. BRAZILIAN.

Barbecue, southern Brazilian style, comes to Shanghai in this swank new restaurant at the Jin Jiang Hotel. Set menus are generous, with oodles of spicy soup, fresh salads, and other side dishes on the buffet tables, accompanied by barbecued meats that run the gamut from chicken hearts to pork ribs, all sliced up at your table by strolling waiters. The steak skewered on a sword is the signature entree. This place is more fun for a group of diners than for one or two looking for a romantic dinner. The prices are exceptionally reasonable, with even cheaper set lunches available. A Brazilian band performs nightly from 6:30 to 10pm.

✪ Tandoor. In the Jin Jiang Hotel, 59 Maoming Nan Lu (in the pedestrian lane on the hotel grounds). ☎ **021/6472-5494.** Reservations required. Meals 130RMB–250RMB ($16–$30). AE, DC, JCB, MC, V. Daily 11:30am–2pm and 5:30–10:30pm. INDIAN.

Shanghai's top Indian restaurant is also one of the city's very best, regardless of cuisine. The management, chefs, and most of the ingredients come directly from India. The decor is elegant, the service extremely gracious and efficient. Classical dancers from India entertain nightly from 6:30 to 10:30pm. Starters include samosas, chutneys, and chicken *chat* (barbecued chicken with lemon juice). Entrees are both vegetarian (*Palak Aloo,* spinach with potatoes) and meat-filled (pork Vindaloo), but the signature dish is a delicious tandoori chicken marinated in yogurt. The bar features a full range of drinks, but meals go best with Masala tea. The buffet lunch is a good deal at 96RMB ($12).

Shanghai Drugstore. 92 Jing Xian Lu (off Maoming Nan Lu). ☎ **021/6256-5321.** Reservations not necessary. Meals 120RMB–210RMB ($14–$25). No credit cards. Daily 6pm–midnight. SPANISH.

This elegant cafe is the creation of world traveler Tomas Chu, who first left Shanghai in 1952. Back home, he has divided up an old warehouse, using carved wooden screens, into an intimate, upscale late-night eatery featuring Spanish wines, silver tableware, glass candelabras, and singing birds in bamboo cages. Typical starters are the fresh melon with ham (48RMB/$6) and a seafood soup (35RMB/$4.20) served cold. The paella goes for 42RMB ($5). The pan-fried sole, usually produced by the owner himself, is 65RMB ($8). Patrons tend to linger late into the evening in this comfortable, quiet, warmly decorated and dimly lit slice of southern Europe.

MODERATE

Café 1931. 112 Maoming Nan Lu (south of Huaihai Lu, near Nanchang Lu). ☎ **021/6472-5264.** Reservations not necessary. Meals 75RMB–120RMB ($9–$14). No credit cards. Daily 2pm–3am. SHANGHAI/ASIAN.

This is a lovely spot to drop in for a Shanghai lunch or a light dinner while strolling through the heart of the French Concession. The interior has been done over in romantic colonial fashion with wooden panels, wall posters of notorious Shanghai, tiny intimate tables, and even an old gramophone in the corner. Waitresses wear the qipao dresses with the slit side, popular in the 1930s. The menu features soups, noodles, and scallions that you roll up into rice pancakes, as well as some Japanese and Thai snacks. The Shanghai dishes are just above average, but the atmosphere is Shanghai past perfect, with candles providing the evening table light.

The Gap. 127 Maoming Nan Lu (north of Huaihai Lu, near Jin Jiang Hotel). ☎ **021/ 6433-9028.** Reservations not necessary. Meals 75RMB–150RMB ($9–$18). AE, DC, JCB, MC, V. Mon–Fri 11am–2am, Sat–Sun 8am–2am. SHANGHAI.

The Gap restaurants in Shanghai are known for their Shanghai dishes, but they are celebrated more for their over-the-top fanciful European decors. The "Film Salon" branch in the French Concession is the most extravagant of these creations; just look for the Red Flag limousine suspended above the main entrance. Cinema is the theme here, and it's entertainment that the Gap provides, with high-powered live dance music, Chinese dancers on stage, bikini-clad waitresses, and fashion shows (from 9:30 to 10pm). The indoor courtyard has artificial stars projected overhead for "outdoor" dining and dancing year-round. The dress code is casual, as is the atmosphere, which attracts mostly locals and other Chinese out to celebrate the evening.

Among five other Gaps are those at 4 Hengshan Lu (☎ **021/6473-8290**), and at 8 Zunyi Nan Lu in the Hongqiao area (☎ **021/6278-2900**).

The Grape. 55 Xinle Lu (2 blocks west of Shaanxi Nan Lu, between Huaihai and Yan'an roads). ☎ **021/6472-0486.** Reservations not necessary. Meals 60RMB–120RMB ($7–$14). No credit cards. Mon–Fri 11am–2am, Sat–Sun 8am–2am. SHANGHAI.

One of the first Shanghai eateries to attract foreign residents, the Grape has opened the doors to its main restaurant right next door to a strange sight indeed: a large domed former Russian Orthodox church now used as a stock exchange; you can see the electronic trading board lit up inside as you walk by. The Grape itself is not a strange place (except for the clusters of plastic grapes, perhaps), but a friendly, down-to-earth cafe serving homemade Shanghai cuisine at reasonable prices. The hot-and-sour soup and garlic chicken wings come highly recommended.

If this location's full, there's another Grape on the same block, on the north side of the street, at 142 Xinle Lu.

✪ Judy's Too. 176 Maoming Nan Lu (south of Fuxing Zhong Lu). ☎ **021/6473-1417.** Reservations not necessary. Meals 75RMB–140RMB ($9–$17). AE, DC, JCB, MC, V. Tues–Sun 6–11pm. GERMAN.

Solid German food, plenty of German beers (Weizen brand), sauerkraut, mashed potatoes, and a late-night party scene have made Judy's highly popular with foreign businesspeople and visitors, especially on Friday and Saturday nights. It's quieter on weekdays and on Sundays, when foreign films are shown starting at 7pm. Snacks (salads, meat loaf, sausages) are served until 2am, when some patrons have been known to take to dancing on the bar. Quieter dinners at economical prices can be secured in the second-floor dining room, which has recently been redecorated in Bavarian cottage style (large wooden tables, window shutters).

Jurassic Pub. 8 Maoming Nan Lu (1 block south of Yan'an Zhong Lu on corner of Julu Lu). ☎ **021/6258-3758.** Reservations not necessary. Meals 40RMB–120RMB ($4.80–$14). AE, DC, JCB, MC, V. Daily 3pm–3am. JAPANESE.

The decor has been dubbed "dinosaur chic," meaning the passageways, dining rooms, furniture, and even the bathroom fixtures are sculpted into replicas of monstrous bones and skins. Diners have a choice of meat dishes, sweet corn pancakes, and other treats, but the teppanyaki grill (upstairs around the central grill) is the real attraction (along with the odd decor and party atmosphere). The main floor contains a bar and dance floor, with live rock music in the evenings. After 10pm, the teppanyaki grill is really jammed with an all-you-can-eat special for just 38RMB ($4.55).

Kathleen's. 207-23 Maoming Nan Lu (1 block south of Fuxing Lu). ☎ **021/6472-5222,** ext. 3049. Reservations not necessary. Meals 45RMB–120RMB ($5–$14). AE, DC, JCB, MC, V. Sun–Thurs 11am–11pm, Sat–Sun 11am–3am. CONTINENTAL.

Sister restaurant to the original cafe in Guangzhou, the new Kathleen's in Shanghai is a bit bolder and more upscale, but the casual atmosphere and low prices have migrated north. The Greek salad, the large burritos, the tasty hamburgers, and the pasta plates with feta cheese and sun-dried tomatoes are familiar favorites. The cheesecake is a fine dessert. Kathleen's serves until very late, making it a far better choice for "home food" than any fast-food chain.

Trattoria. 16 Henan Nan Lu (basement of Central Place at Yan'an Dong Lu). ☎ **021/ 6328-1860.** Reservations not necessary. Meals 80RMB–120RMB ($10–$14). AE, DC, JCB, MC, V. Daily 9am–11pm. ITALIAN.

Near the Natural History Museum in a busy area, this is a good lunch or dinner stop for homemade Italian fare. The stylish interior is resplendent with chrome and fake Greek and Roman statuary. The antipasti buffet is fresh and inviting; so are the pizzas, panini sandwiches, and cakes. The best pasta dish comes with a fine ricotta cheese and grilled portobello mushrooms.

INEXPENSIVE

Delifrance. 381 Huaihai Zhong Lu (Room 125, Shanghai Central Plaza, near Chengdu Lu). ☎ **021/5382-5171.** Reservations not necessary. Meals 28RMB–45RMB ($3.35–$5). No credit cards. Daily 8am–9pm. CONTINENTAL.

This fast-service chain migrated recently from Hong Kong to Beijing and Shanghai. The Shanghai branch is located on the locals' favorite shopping street in a large, upscale shopping center. If decent coffee, deli sandwiches, croissants, and sweet desserts are what you need, this is a better choice than the foreign fast-food chains. Grab a tray, check out the 28RMB ($3.35) baguette-sandwich specials, and take a seat by the window on the mall. The Western breakfast here, at just 18RMB ($2.15), is many times cheaper than what you'll find in the hotels—and a far less packaged affair than at McDonald's.

Sumo Sushi. 668 Huaihai Zhong Lu (near corner of Sinan Lu). ☎ **021/5306-9136.** Reservations not necessary. Meals 28RMB–58RMB ($3.35–$7). No credit cards. Daily 11am–3am. JAPANESE.

A great bargain, with set lunches for 28RMB ($3.35) and set dinners for 38RMB ($4.55). The real deal is à la carte, however, or rather à la carousel, a moving belt from the kitchen along the counter. From 11am to 4pm and from 10pm to closing, you can grab as much as you can stuff in for just 58RMB (under $7). The goodies, which run from sushi to teppanyaki, lack variety, but not quantity or reasonable quality.

Thousand Taste Noodle Shop. 518 Huaihai Zhong Lu (north side, west of Xizang Nan Lu). ☎ **021/6372-5547.** Reservations not necessary. Meals 20RMB–45RMB ($2.40–$5). No credit cards. Daily 11am–2am. JAPANESE.

This spiffy new, Japanese-style fast-food emporium offers oodles of noodles, and some Shanghai dim sum as well. The eatery occupies two stories, with all-glass south walls facing busy Huaihai Road. There are well over 300 of these outlets in

---

⊕ Family-Friendly Restaurants

Many of Shanghai's restaurants are used to serving children, but for foreign visitors and their families, several stand out:

✪ **Hard Rock Cafe,** 1376 Nanjing Xi Lu, at Shanghai Centre/Portman Ritz-Carlton Hotel (☎ 021/6279-8133). The music, decor, and food (American bacon-cheeseburgers, sandwiches, fajitas, fries, and milk shakes) should keep any Western teenager happy. All credit cards are accepted, live bands play rock Monday to Saturday from 10:30pm to 12:30am, and it's open daily from 11:30am to 2am (100RMB/$12 cover after 10pm).

Sky Lounge, Hotel Sofitel Hyland, 30th floor, 505 Nanjing Dong Lu (☎ 021/6351-5888, ext. 4456). Open only on Sunday from 11:30am to 2:30pm, this towering atrium restaurant on the Nanjing Road pedestrian mall has a buffet that keeps adults happy (champagne, caviar, foie gras) and children entertained in their own special playroom. The Sunday buffet is 218RMB ($26), but it's free for children under 130 centimeters (4 ft. 3 in.) tall.

Garden Café, Pudong Shangri-La Hotel, lobby level, 33 Fucheng Lu (☎ 021/6882-8888). If you're on the other side of the river from downtown Shanghai in the Pudong New Area, take the kids here. The plush cafe is within a block or so of two attractions families can enjoy together: the Pearl of the Orient TV Tower and the Riverside Avenue pedestrian promenade. The Garden Café offers a children's menu with Western favorites ("Donald Burger," "Hot Doggie"), and on weekends, it sets up a special kids' buffet table. It's open 24 hours a day.

Asia, but this is the first in Shanghai. Noodles in a bowl start at just 15RMB ($1.80), set meals at 20RMB ($2.40). Order at the counter from a picture book, take a seat by the window, and begin slurping.

5 Jing An District (Northwest Shanghai)

VERY EXPENSIVE

✪ **Summer Pavilion.** In the Portman Ritz-Carlton Hotel (in Shanghai Centre), 2nd floor, 1376 Nanjing Xi Lu. ☎ 021/6279-8888. Reservations required. Main courses 80RMB–340RMB ($10–$41). AE, DC, JCB, MC, V. Daily 11:30am–2:30pm and 5:30–10:30pm. CANTONESE.

Aiming to be Shanghai's premier Cantonese restaurant, the Summer Pavilion certainly has the setting (bright, plush, open dining area with tasteful Chinese gold-and-red trim) and service (expert, attentive) to become just that. The menu is expanding; the Hong Kong chefs are top-notch. This is certainly a superb choice for a grand Chinese dinner or fine lunch. There are tanks of live seafood that can be cooked to your specifications; headlining the menu are shark's fin and abalone. The pork and seafood plates are fresh, tasty, and beautifully presented. You don't have to dress up to enjoy the fare, but many diners do.

EXPENSIVE

✪ **Irene's Thai.** 263 Tongren Lu (2 blocks northwest of Shanghai Centre). ☎ 021/6247-3579. Reservations recommended on weekends. Main courses 120RMB–240RMB ($14–$29). AE, DC, JCB, MC, V. Daily 11am–2pm and 6–11pm. THAI.

This is Shanghai's first modern Thai restaurant (opened in Sept 1998), and it is still one of the best. The interior of this wooden house is exquisite, with decorations imported from Thailand. The ingredients and the executive chef also have Thai origins, ensuring delicious dishes. The salads, in which fruits such as papaya are used, are famous in Shanghai. The best deal is the three-course set lunch (served Mon to Sat), priced at just 68RMB ($8).

Itoya. 128 Shaanxi Bei Lu (2 blocks northeast of Shanghai Centre). ☎ **021/6267-5565.** Reservations required. Main courses 80RMB–240RMB ($10–$29). AE, DC, JCB, MC, V. Daily 11:30am–2pm and 5:30–11pm. JAPANESE.

This branch of a small chain in Shanghai is intimate and stylish. Well known for its seafood and Japanese version of the hot pot, what really packs the place is its all-you-can-eat sushi bar: 98RMB ($12) without drinks, 150RMB ($18) with soft drinks, beer, and sake included.

✪ **Le Bouchon.** 1455 Wuding Xi Lu (near Huashan Lu, northwest of Shanghai Centre). ☎ **021/6225-7088.** Reservations recommended on weekends. Main courses 120RMB–240RMB ($14–$29). AE, DC, JCB, MC, V. Sun–Thurs 5pm–midnight, Fri–Sat 12:30pm–midnight. FRENCH.

A romantic little hideaway created by Maxime Henry of France, this is billed as Shanghai's first French bistro and wine bar. It is very French. Chef Thierry favors a traditional approach: the menu, with only one entree each day, is dictated in part by what's fresh that day at the market. The small menu lists soups, salads, the main course, and desserts; warm bread is set on the table. Goose- and duck-liver salad, a mushroom soup, moist baked salmon, and a chocolate mousse are typical offerings. A three-course set dinner is usually priced at about 150RMB ($18). The wine list is, of course, exclusively French.

✪ **Meilongzhen.** Building 22, 1081 Nanjing Xi Lu (east of Shanghai Centre). ☎ **021/6253-5353.** Reservations recommended on weekends. Main courses 120RMB–240RMB ($14–$29). AE, DC, JCB, MC, V. Daily 11am–1:30pm and 4–10pm. SHANGHAI.

Established in 1938, Meilongzhen is a Shanghai institution, deservedly so for its classic decor and regional cuisine. Occupying the former headquarters of the Chinese Communist party (during the 1930s), it retains the old elegance of the colonial period, with its mahogany and marble furniture, carved wooden paneling, rose wallpaper, and festive Chinese paper lanterns. Many of the dishes on the menu (in English) are derived from Sichuan, but here they are given a regional treatment (in the Huaiyang style, a close neighbor of Yangzhou and Shanghai approaches). The Sichuan duck is wonderful, as is the Meilongzhen Special Chicken, which is served in small ceramic pots. The attentive staff keeps the teacups full, pouring from the traditional long-spouted teapots.

MODERATE

Bi Feng Tang. 1333 Nanjing Xi Lu (1 block west of Shanghai Centre). ☎ **021/6279-0738.** Reservations not necessary. Meals 80RMB–140RMB ($10–$17). AE, DC, JCB, MC, V. Mon–Fri 10am–5am, Sat–Sun 8am–5am. DIM SUM.

The newest branch of this local eatery, known for its dim sum (steamed pastries with vegetable, meat, and seafood fillings), opened here in the summer of 1999. While it has festive indoor dining (with a fishing-village look), it is hugely popular on nice days because of its sidewalk setting: tables under big umbrellas are partitioned off with bamboo fencing, red lanterns are hung out, and the twinkle lights are fired up every night. The dim sum and other Shanghai and Chinese dishes are served until dawn.

✪ **Cochinchina 1883.** Block 11, 889 Julu Lu (southeast of the Hilton Hotel). ☎ **021/ 6445-6797.** Reservations not necessary. Main courses 80RMB–120RMB ($10–$14). AE, DC, JCB, MC, V. Daily 11:30am–2:30pm and 5–11pm. VIETNAMESE.

Shanghai's newest and (at least temporarily) only Vietnamese restaurant opened recently. It aims to present authentic Vietnamese fare with a Shanghai twist. The decor is quite upscale, designed to evoke the early French colonial days of Southeast Asia as it was over a century ago. The large white building, with a front courtyard down an alley off the bar strip on Julu Lu, was previously a guest house for the Chinese Air Force, but that part of its history is no longer visible. The chefs, oddly enough, are from Hong Kong. The food and service, yet to be proven, seem promising; Shanghai has a dearth of fine Asian dining, outside of a very few Thai and Indian restaurants.

Malone's. 255 Tongren Lu (2 blocks northwest of Shanghai Centre). ☎ **021/6247-2400.** Reservations not necessary. Main courses 80RMB–120RMB ($10–$14). AE, DC, JCB, MC, V. Mon–Thurs 11:30am–1am, Fri–Sat 11:30am–2am, Sun 10:30am–midnight. AMERICAN.

Originally part of a chain from Canada (opened in 1994), Malone's is a sports bar and restaurant in the American style. There are dartboards, a pool table, and plenty of TV screens for international sports programs; a happy hour at the big bar from 5 to 8pm; and, on weekends, local dance bands performing from 10pm until closing. The food is an excellent version of American pub grub, with good potato skins, buffalo wings, burgers, fries, sandwiches, and grilled steaks.

Tony Roma's. 1376 Nanjing Xi Lu (west side of Shanghai Centre). ☎ **021/6279-7129.** Reservations recommended on weekends. Main courses 75RMB–120RMB ($9–$14). AE, DC, JCB, MC, V. Daily 11am–11pm. AMERICAN.

Part of a U.S. chain, Tony Roma's has been the place for ribs in Shanghai since 1995. The decor is American, too, with comfortable booths and tables typical of a midrange steak house. In addition to the tasty ribs, this restaurant offers some of the freshest salads in China, including a Thai peanut salad. Portions of all items are generous. Sandwiches and burgers highlight the lunch menu, while onion rings, potato cheese soup, grilled steaks, and, of course, the famous ribs rope in plenty of expatriates and Western travelers for the big dinners.

INEXPENSIVE

Badlands. 895 Julu Lu (3 blocks southeast of the Hilton Hotel). ☎ **021/6466-7788,** ext. 8003. Reservations not necessary. Main courses 40RMB–80RMB ($4.80–$10). AE, JCB, MC, V. Sun–Thurs noon–2am, Fri–Sat noon–5am. MEXICAN.

The best place in Shanghai for cheap (and decent) Mexican food, Badlands has been a favorite stop on the Julu Lu bar street for years. It is really just a hole-in-the-wall with a very friendly, casual crowd of expatriates and young Chinese, but it does have a nice outdoor deck for dining in the summer. The chili, burritos, chimichangas, and buffalo balls (fried cheeses) are all hearty, if hardly gourmet or authentic; prices are half what they are in the better Mexican eateries. Best deal of the week is on "Taco Tuesday" when the tacos go for 10RMB ($1.20) each.

6 Xuhui District (Southwest Shanghai)

VERY EXPENSIVE

✪ **Bourbon Street.** 191 Hengshan Lu (north of Hengshan Lu subway station). ☎ **021/ 6445-7556.** Reservations recommended on weekends. Meals 180RMB–360RMB ($22–$43). AE, DC, JCB, MC, V. Daily 11am–2am. CAJUN.

Shanghai's only Cajun and Creole restaurant, Bourbon Street has brought the French Quarter to the French Concession. The setting is a sparkling new, three-story white colonial mansion (it looks old, of course); the chef comes straight from New Orleans. The spacious interior has dark wood floors and an atrium with a wall of glass looking out on the garden (where there's outdoor seating all summer). The best seating is on the second-floor balcony, painted rose and black, with potted ferns and an iron latticework railing. There's also room for a full bar, pool tables, and a walk-in cigar humidor. The country-style Creole menu offers Louisiana crab cakes (75RMB/$9), a fresh market salad with chicory and mustard sauce, baked oysters (95RMB/$11), gumbo, crawfish étouffée, shrimp Creole (125RMB/$15), and bouillabaisse (190RMB/$$23). A fine dish of red beans and rice is 80RMB ($10). Presentation and service, like the peppery cooking, are exceptional.

EXPENSIVE

Le Garcon Chinois. House 3, 9 Hengshan Lu (down lane between Dongping Lu and Wulumuqi Lu). ☎ **021/6431-3005.** Reservations not necessary. Meals 120RMB–240RMB ($14–$29). No credit cards. Daily 11am–1am. FRENCH.

This new (late 1999) entry on the French bistro scene occupies the first two floors of an old house. In the summer, tables are set out on a small terrace and a patio. There's a deli on the first floor, and the bar and dining room upstairs. Le Garcon Chinois offers some nice dishes in the French nouveau mode. Among the top choices are a New Zealand steak, duck breast in a chopped salad, cheese-baked mussels, and chicken medaillons. The French bread is baked on the premises, as are the pastries. Currently, this is considered a very cool place to hang out in the evenings; the owner plays his saxophone in the cozy bar.

✪ **Sasha's.** House 11, 9 Dongping Lu (intersection with Hengshan Lu). ☎ **021/6474-6166.** Reservations required. Meals 150RMB–300RMB ($18–$36). AE, DC, JCB, MC, V. Daily 11am–11pm. CONTINENTAL.

Beautifully situated behind a wrought-iron fence in a mansion in the Soong family's old compound (and once home to Chiang Kai-shek, then later to Mao's wife), Sasha's brings country-club dining to Shanghai—in summer, the front garden opens with tables under white umbrellas. There are tables on the overhanging balconies and in the back garden, too, when weather permits. The menu is quite good to excellent across the board, with the seafood courses and the roast rack of lamb at the top. The three-course set dinners are 150RMB ($18), or 230RMB ($28) with one glass of imported wine; weekend barbecues go for 150RMB ($18); and business-lunch specials are 99RMB ($12). The newly added fondues on the third floor are priced at 110RMB ($13). This is colonial dining, as nostalgic as it gets these days in otherwise ultra-modern Shanghai.

MODERATE

Casj. 33 Wuxing Lu (northwest of Hengshan Lu, between Kangping Lu and Huaihai Lu). ☎ **021/6466-5608.** Reservations not necessary. Meals 90RMB–150RMB ($11–$18). AE, DC, JCB, MC, V. Daily 11am–11pm. CONTINENTAL.

This intimate little restaurant is a very stylish cafe in a surprisingly stylish neighborhood (reminiscent of certain blocks of Manhattan). The atmosphere is relaxed and refined. The warmly colored curving walls provide space for a contemporary art gallery. The cafe seating is in the front, while the cigar lounge takes up the rear. The French nouveau and fusion dishes are nicely presented, and above average in quality.

Landhaus. 5A Dongping Lu (2 blocks east of Hengshan Lu, southeast side of Puxjin Monument). ☎ **021/6473-7296.** Reservations not necessary. Meals 50RMB–120RMB ($6–$14). No credit cards. Daily 10am–2am. GERMAN.

Housed in a striking two-story wooden house with a fenced front porch and balcony, this comfortably rustic cafe and bar offers up sausages, sauerkraut, schnitzels, and mashed potatoes, as well as some European dishes, at quite reasonable prices. The quality and service are basic, but both are more than would be expected from the low prices. Set lunches are just 40RMB ($4.80), and the evening pasta buffet, served from 6 to 9pm, is an even better deal at 50RMB ($6). In the late, late evening, Landhaus drops its German trappings and turns into an agreeable place for drinks and pop music.

Mandy's. Hengshan Lu (just south of Dongping Lu). ☎ **021/6474-6628.** Reservations not necessary. Meals 90RMB–120RMB ($11–$14). No credit cards. Mon–Fri 2–11pm, Sat–Sun 11am–11pm. CONTINENTAL.

Yet another sparkling new Western-oriented restaurant on fashionable Hengshan Lu, Mandy's is seeking its own niche. The menu features an assortment of European dishes, but nothing stands out except the grilled steaks. The dark wooden paneled dining room upstairs, with its polished wood floors, stained-glass windows, and chandeliers, is a bright, cheery setting for a fine dinner. In summer, the garden puts on an excellent barbecue buffet on Friday and Saturday from 6 to 10pm (88RMB/$11).

Mr. Stone. 2nd floor, 4 Hengshan Lu (at Dongping Lu). ☎ **021/6473-9662.** Reservations not necessary. Main courses 80RMB–120RMB ($10–$14). AE, JCB, MC, V. Daily 11:30am–11:30pm. STEAK HOUSE.

Located on the corner at the north end of Hengshan Lu's densest gallery of trendy Western-style cafes and shops, upstairs from T.G.I.F. (yes, the American chain), this Australian steak house does some of the tastiest beef in town. The steaks, from the United States as well as Australia, are fried to sizzling perfection over heated volcanic stones right at your table. This is a restaurant, obviously, for steak lovers, and for those who like it with plenty of imported Aussie beer.

✪ **O'Malley's.** 42 Taojiang Lu (1 block west of Hengshan Lu). ☎ **021/6437-0667.** Reservations not necessary. Meals 60RMB–100RMB ($7–$12). AE, JCB, MC, V. Daily 11am–2am. IRISH.

Best known as one of Shanghai's top bars and music spots, O'Malley's also sports a menu of Irish, English, and American favorites that include hearty helpings of mashed potatoes and flavorful steaks and burgers, all at fair prices. Service is friendly and efficient. The old two-story mansion has been decorated like a down-and-out Irish pub, with plenty of cozy booths and tables on its main floor and balcony. In summer, the large and private front lawn offers quiet courtyard dining. The beers, naturally, are quite good, as is the Irish dance music that usually runs from 8:30pm to midnight Wednesday to Monday.

Paulaner Brauhaus. 150 Fenyang Lu (2 blocks west of Hengshan Lu, near the Dongping Lu intersection). ☎ **021/6474-5700.** Reservations not necessary. Meals 80RMB–160RMB ($10–$19). AE, JCB, MC, V. Mon–Sat 6pm–2am, Sun 11:30am–midnight. GERMAN.

Shanghai's biggest beer house is a stunning three-story structure isolated from the road by a large green courtyard that serves as a summer beer garden. The yellow-and-white plaster walls with dark-green window trim restore the bright look of this massive 1930s building, which now houses its own German-style brewery. In addition to the home-brewed and imported beers, Paulaner has a large German menu

The Buffet Line

When it comes to chowing down, Shanghai's restaurants know how to put on a buffet; they are usually excellent values. Weekend brunches (mostly held in the big hotels) are not necessarily cheap, but they are sumptuous events and extremely popular among expatriates and Shanghai residents alike. Here's a sampler of some goodbuffets and brunches:

- **Wuninosachi,** 402 Shaanxi Nan Lu, Luwan District (☎ 021/6445-3406). From 5:30 to 11pm, everything (absolutely everything) on the menu of this popular Japanese cafe is available in unlimited quantities for 150RMB ($18). That includes the seafood, tempura, noodles, and dumplings (with fresh ingredients flown in from Japan)—even the sake.

- **Hilton Hotel,** 250 Huashan Lu, Jing An District (☎ 021/6248-3848). The Hilton holds one of Shanghai's very best Sunday brunches (from 11am to 2:30pm) in its two fine lobby restaurants: ✪ Da Vinci's (ext. 8622) and the Atrium (ext. 8616). The fare is international (mostly Western); the price is 210RMB ($25) and well worth it.

- **Holiday Inn Crowne Plaza,** 400 Panyu Lu, Changning District (☎ 021/6280-8888). The same musicians who serenaded American saxophonist (and president) Bill Clinton now entertain us at a great Sunday Jazz Brunch in the lobby-level Orient Express restaurant (ext. 11040) from 11am to 2:30pm. The 178RMB ($21) price includes sparkling wine and Baskin-Robbins ice cream.

- **Pudong Shangri-La Hotel,** 33 Fucheng Lu (☎ 021/6882-8888). Sundays from 3 to 6pm bring on high tea (scones, sounds of Bach) in the lobby lounge (60RMB/$7). Meanwhile, Shang Palace upstairs has its dim sum brunch for just 79RMB ($9), including soft drinks, beer, and dessert (Sat and Sun from 8:30am to 2:30pm).

- **Holiday Inn Pudong,** 899 Dongfang Lu (☎ 021/5830-5555). International theme buffets (the menu changes every month) are held nightly in the Exchange restaurant on the ground floor (128RMB/$15).

- **Hotel Nikko Pudong,** 969 Dongfang Lu (☎ 021/6875-8888, ext. 3839). Here's possibly the cheapest big hotel dim sum buffet line in town, served in the third-floor Fame restaurant Saturday and Sunday from 10am to 4:30pm. The price, which even includes a soft drink, is 48RMB ($6) per person.

that's heavily into sauerkraut and sausages, cabbage and bratwurst. Every Sunday from 11:30am to 4:30pm, the place pulls out all the stops and runs a full German brunch for 140RMB ($17). Evenings, the big hall reverberates to the music of a Filipino dance band (from 6pm to 1:30am, Mon to Sat).

INEXPENSIVE

Yang's Kitchen. Shop 3, 9 Hengshan Lu (south of Dongping Lu, near Mandy's). ☎ 021/6431-3028. Reservations not necessary. Main courses 40RMB–80RMB ($4.80–$10). No credit cards. Daily 5:30–11:30pm. SHANGHAI.

Inside, this small cafe is nothing special at all (certainly not the upscale decor Hengshan Lu is famous for). Outside, there's a small garden for summer dining, but it's the low prices and great food that have brought Yang increasing praise and customers. Open only for dinner, Yang knows what to focus on: a full Shanghai home-style meal, done the right way, with sweet and heavy oil and buttery fresh-water seafood.

7 Changning District (Hongqiao Development Zone)

VERY EXPENSIVE

✪ **AD.** 3896 Hongmei Lu (near Gubei New Town, south of Hongqiao Lu). ☎ **021/6262-5620.** Reservations recommended on weekends. Meals 240RMB–380RMB ($29–$46). AE, DC, JCB, MC, V. Daily 11:30am–2pm and 5–10pm. ITALIAN.

The extravagant marble interiors, with antique furniture, vaulted ceilings, sculpted fireplaces, and imported Italian fabric wallpaper, give AD an operatic atmosphere. This is the very upscale creation of Antonio Donnaloia, former chef at the Westin. It's complete with stainless-steel counters, copper frying pans, an attentive staff attired in Gianni Versace uniforms, and a gourmet menu to match. Top menu choices include seafood soup, risotto, prawns with vegetables, calamari, and a selection of great desserts.

✪ **Giovanni's.** Westin Tai Ping Yang Hotel, 27th floor, 5 Zunyi Nan Lu. ☎ **021/6275-8888.** Reservations required. Meals 240RMB–360RMB ($29–$43). AE, DC, JCB, MC, V. Daily noon–2pm and 6–10:30pm. ITALIAN.

This upscale bistro with the big view is plush yet homey, with top service and cuisine. The opera music suits the fine Italian decor. The calamari is good, the pastas and antipasti are great, and the crème brûlée extraordinary. The fresh-baked breads are delicious, as are the grilled tenderloin (160RMB/$19) and steaks seasoned with herbs (150RMB/$18). This is the place to enjoy imported wine with dinner, and Giovanni's has a superb wine list.

EXPENSIVE

✪ **Dynasty.** Yangtze Renaissance Hotel by Marriott, 2099 Yan'an Xi Lu. ☎ **021/6275-0000.** Reservations required. Meals 160RMB–340RMB ($19–$41). AE, DC, JCB, MC, V. Daily 11am–2:30pm and 5–10:30pm. CANTONESE.

Long regarded as Shanghai's top Cantonese restaurant, Dynasty defends its title with an elegant setting and extensive menu. The dishes are prepared by the same chefs (many from Hong Kong) who routinely cater dinners for visiting heads of state at special banquets and luncheons. The open dining space and the large tables with white tablecloths are thoroughly Cantonese, as is the menu, where you can't go wrong with the fresh seafood dishes (prawns and lobster are good bets) or the dim sum lunch.

✪ **1221.** 1221 Yan'an Xi Lu (between Panyu Lu and Dingxi Lu). ☎ **021/6213-6585.** Reservations recommended on weekends. Meals 100RMB–250RMB ($12–$30). No credit cards. Daily 11am–2pm and 5–11pm. SHANGHAI.

Very chic, very quiet, this is a very popular place among resident foreigners and business travelers for fine Shanghai dining at a reasonable price. The subdued orange-and-white interior sets a casual, upscale mood. The special fragrance tea (with eight ingredients, including fruits and flowers) is poured from long-spouted teapots by a skilled staff. The dishes are Shanghai in origin, but with a touch of East/West fusion cooking. The Drunken Chicken is a signature entree, as are the Lionhead Meatballs (12RMB/$1.45) and the dishes simmered in clay pots, such as the lamb. Interesting choices include the crispy duck, the crispy tofu, the shredded pork with scallions that you roll up with pancakes, and the steamed eel slices served in a large ceramic bowl (128RMB/$15), enough to feed the table. If you have a larger group and want a banquet of sorts, 1221 can oblige with a lavish 12-course onslaught (priced at 250RMB/$30 per person).

MODERATE

Big Fan. 1440 Hongqiao Lu (south down an alley, west of the Inner Ring Rd.). ☎ **021/ 6275-9131,** ext. 268. Reservations recommended on weekends. Meals 80RMB–160RMB ($10–$19). No credit cards. Daily 11:30am–2pm and 5:30–9pm. SHANGHAI.

Located in a 1930s cluster of villas and apartments, the Big Fan has plenty of fans among foreign business travelers and Shanghai residents alike. The house is decorated in posters recalling the old Shanghai of taipans and colonial-era clubs; the dining rooms are cozy, with wooden panels and period furniture. The staff speaks little in the way of English, but the menu has been translated for foreigners, and it is headlined by excellent fresh seafood dishes. This is a place loaded with nostalgic charm, as comfortable as the living room of a foreign banker.

Oxford's. M. P. Boutique Hotel, 660 Xinhua Lu (near Kaixuan Lu). ☎ **021/6280-1000.** Reservations recommended on weekends. Meals 80RMB–120RMB ($10–$14). AE, DC, JCB, MC, V. Daily 10am–9pm. ENGLISH/CONTINENTAL.

The classy European decor seems too fancy for the prices, which are extremely reasonable here. Offerings include set lunches, a high tea, and set dinners priced in the 35RMB-to-90RMB ($4.20-to-$11) range. The set dinner includes unlimited trips to the salad bar, where the fixings are quite fresh. Much of the menu has an English slant, with rabbit, Norfolk pie, fish-and-chips, and even Yorkshire pudding available. Guinness and Boddingtons are on tap in the lobby bar, and grilled-steak dinners start at 120RMB ($14).

INEXPENSIVE

El Popo's. Lane 19, Building 12, Golden Lion Garden, Rong Hua Xi Dao (rear of shopping plaza in Gubei New Town). ☎ **021/6219-8519.** Reservations not necessary. Meals 50RMB–80RMB ($6–$10). AE, JCB, MC, V. Daily 11am–midnight. MEXICAN.

A stylish Tex-Mex restaurant with two eye-popping stories of sombreros, saddle blankets, and matador murals, El Popo's (sometimes called Viva El Popo's) has earned a reputation for relaxed dining and hearty meals. The Mexican-trained Chinese chef has created his own fusion food here (Tex-Mex meets Shanghai), with a solid assortment of burritos, fajitas, and tapas. Tortilla chips come with three kinds of salsa; during happy hour, from 5 to 7pm, tapas are half-price. The best meal deal consists of an enchilada and taco with rice and beans for 44RMB ($5). Hungry hombres head over on Saturday and Sunday for the big buffet (108RMB/$13). The Mexican fare places second behind JJ Mariachi, but the prices are much lower here.

Soho. 2077 Yan'an Xi Lu (alley on southeast side of Friendship Center). ☎ **021/6219-2948.** Reservations recommended on weekends. Meals 25RMB–80RMB ($3–$10). AE, DC, JCB, MC, V. Daily 11am–midnight. SHANGHAI/SICHUAN.

A hip bistro that is every bit a taste of Manhattan's SoHo, including art glass partitions and abstract art on the walls, Soho in Shanghai actually caters more to local yuppies than expatriates. The wide-ranging Chinese menu is in English, even if the waiters (who are quite efficient) speak only Shanghainese. The best seats are on the main floor, near the coffee bar; groups eat in the upstairs balcony. The vegetable dishes and seafood entrees are good choices; so is the chicken with cashews (quite zesty) at just 35RMB ($4.20). A popular choice here is the *subao cuisan,* a dish made of mushroom strips that looks and tastes like barbecued eel.

Pizza to Go or Stay

Sooner or later, Chinese food overload strikes most travelers, and the only antidote seems to be America's favorite Italian hot dish: pizza. Shanghai, with its usual international flair, has plenty of pizza take-outs (with free delivery), some of them cooking up whole pies and slices almost as good as the real thing back home. For instance:

Gino Cafe (see p. 82), with outlets all over the city, has the best little pan pizzas (and best indoor seating) among local pizzerias.

Pizza Italia, 103 Dong Zhu An Bang Lu, west of Shanghai Centre in Jing An District (☎ 021/6226-6137), boasts a genuine Italian brick oven and an Italian chef to stoke it. Slices are 10RMB ($1.20); 12-inchers, 40RMB ($4.80). Open daily from 11am to midnight; counter seating only.

Yellow Submarine, 911 Julu Lu, Jing An District (☎ 021/6415-1666), the "old-timer" (established in 1994), offers 12-inch pies with unlimited toppings for 68RMB ($8). Open daily from 11am to midnight.

Melrose Café, 845 Hengshan Lu, Xuhui District (☎ 021/6431-9802), is the place for slices with cappuccino. Lunch specials include a 6-inch pizza, soup, and soda for 45RMB ($5), but locals favor the Beijing-duck pizza with sliced duck, green onions, and hoisen sauce. Open daily from 10am to 2am (and even later in summer).

8 Pudong New Area

VERY EXPENSIVE

✪ **Canton.** In the Grand Hyatt Hotel, Jin Mao Tower, 55th floor, 2 Shiji Da Dao. ☎ 021/5049-1234. Reservations recommended on weekends. Meals 200RMB–400RMB ($24–$48). AE, DC, JCB, MC, V. Daily 11am–midnight. CANTONESE.

With a 360° view from this grand height, elegant decor, impeccable service, and master chefs from Hong Kong, the Grand Hyatt's Canton is the most luxurious restaurant for haute Cantonese cuisine in Shanghai. The cozy balcony seating is partitioned by gold-leaf glass screens, etched with Chinese calligraphy; the floors employ granite, wood, and brass materials to form traditional patterns; and the ceremonial gates at the entrance are fashioned from hand-chiseled limestone. Table service is stylish as well. The glass plates, hammered-silver bowls, cherry-wood silver-tipped chopsticks, and Art Deco tea glasses are perfect accompaniments to the gracious service and the carefully presented and prepared food. The shark's-fin (65RMB/$8) and bird's-nest soups are superb; the abalone and other seafood dishes are surprisingly delicate; and the dim sum dumplings are filled with delicate rather than brash mixtures of shark's fin, mushrooms, and greens. "Delicate" and "exquisite" are the two words that leap to mind frequently here, where one must sample a number of items, each tiny but divine.

EXPENSIVE

Dublin Exchange. Senmao Building, 2nd floor, 101 Yin Cheng Dong Lu (east of the Pearl of the Orient TV Tower). ☎ 021/6841-2052. Reservations not necessary. Meals 80RMB–210RMB ($10–$25). AE, DC, JCB, MC, V. Mon–Fri 11am–midnight. IRISH.

Recently opened as the sister bar to O'Malley's, the Dublin Exchange is far more upscale, with its stunning dark wooden Irish interior and fine, mostly European menu. The chef is in fact one of Europe's rising stars, and the food from his kitchen beats that found in most any pub in Ireland or England. Here the bar snacks include the "Pick O' Plenty" (a mix of bacon, sausage, and chicken wings with deep-fried cheese and potato wedges, for 80RMB/$10). A typical lunch special, for under $10, consists of ham, potatoes, and sauerkraut. The Guinness and Kilkenny ales on tap are as good as you'll find in China (but still a bit bitter). Main courses are as likely to be seafood and pastas as Irish stew (which makes a tasty full dinner for 130RMB/$16). Live Irish music livens the place up some nights, usually from about 8 to 10pm, but Dublin is still looking for a customer base, catering at present to bankers and other expatriates in Pudong with its popular business lunches, and closing up on weekends.

✪ **Grand Café.** In the Grand Hyatt Hotel, Jin Mao Tower, 54th floor, 2 Shiji Da Dao. ☎ **021/5049-1234.** Reservations recommended on weekends. Meals 120RMB–240RMB ($14.40–$28.80). AE, DC, JCB, MC, V. Daily 24 hours. CONTINENTAL/SHANGHAI.

An Art Deco bistro with the best buffet tables in Shanghai, the Grand Hyatt's Grand Café also offers a view of downtown Shanghai across the river through a wall of glass three stories high. The show kitchen is the heart of the buffet area. On its granite bar are the fixings for a do-it-yourself green salad, a selection of appetizers, imported cheeses and homemade breads, and seafood on ice awaiting your instructions to the cook. The show bar features European aperitifs, iced teas, Swiss hot chocolates, lattes, and fresh-squeezed juice, while the dessert bar is nearly beyond description. Bistro favorites include the salad Niçoise and the pork schnitzel on warm potato salad; Shanghai headliners include steamed dumplings in soup, braised pork with spinach, and fried noodles. The buffet breakfast is priced at 160RMB ($19); the buffet lunch, 168RMB ($20); and the buffet dinner, 188RMB ($23).

✪ **Shang Palace.** In the Pudong Shangri-La Hotel, 2nd floor, 33 Fucheng Lu (south of Pearl of the Orient TV Tower). ☎ **021/6882-8888,** ext. 22. Reservations recommended on weekends. Meals 160RMB–240RMB ($19–$29). AE, DC, JCB, MC, V. Mon–Fri 11:30am–2pm and 5:30–10pm; Sat–Sun 8:30am–2:30pm and 5:30–10pm. CANTONESE.

This is just the place for a fine night of dining on southern Chinese cuisine prepared expertly by Hong Kong chefs and attentively served by a skilled staff. Shang Palace is the signature restaurant of this five-star hotel chain, and the new Pudong branch lives up to its reputation with an extensive menu ranging from sizzling vegetable dishes to excellent seafood, including shark's fin, crab, and lobster choices. The decor is richly Chinese without being gaudy, warm and open yet subdued enough for good conversation over dinner. Some of the best food is Hong Kong–style dim sum dumplings, which are the feature at the special buffets on Saturday and Sunday from 8:30am to 2:30pm, an all-you-can-munch feast for just 79RMB ($9).

Zips. Senmao Building, 46th floor, 101 Yin Cheng Dong Lu (east of the Pearl of the Orient TV Tower). ☎ **021/6431-3300.** Reservations recommended on weekends. Meals 120RMB–240RMB ($14–$29). AE, DC, JCB, MC, V. Mon–Sat 11:30am–2pm and 5:30–8:30pm. SOUTH-EAST ASIAN/CONTINENTAL.

Zips is a hip restaurant with an even hipper view, towering 600 feet above the Huangpu River, with panoramas of downtown Shanghai. The theme of the decor is maritime, with porthole lights in the walls and hardwood partitions in the shape and heft of bulkheads on a Yangzi River steamer. The menu is filled with tasty

Natural Viagra

While there are scores of new Western-style restaurants on the Shanghai scene, their numbers lag far behind the local culinary craze for snake. Recent estimates put the number of snake restaurants in Shanghai at more than 6,000. Most of these serpent bistros are illegal, but this hardly muzzles their popularity. The snake markets that stock these cafes are located in the western suburbs (but it's pretty difficult to hire a CITS guide willing to take foreign visitors to the snake pits). It is hard to find the snake cafes at all if you can't speak and read Chinese, but one of the leading snake pavilions charges $4 a pound for common water snakes, $20 a pound for cobra, and $35 a pound for pit-viper meat (cooked to order). The attraction? A traditional belief that snake (and especially snake blood) increases vitality (not to mention virility).

---

international selections from Malaysia, Italy, and America. It's stylish, but not terribly expensive, and fun; silent movies and old cartoons are projected on one of the warm golden walls. Appetizers, which run about 70RMB ($8), include spring rolls filled with anchovies and mozzarella; main courses, averaging 90RMB to 100RMB ($11 to $12), include teriyaki beef fillets and a lavish grilled-cod-and-jumbo-prawn dish with a Thai-style peanut sauce. While enjoying the view after lunch or dinner, try the decadent crêpes drizzled in chocolate sauce.

MODERATE

Lulu. 2nd floor, 66 Lujiazui Lu. ☎ **021/5882-6679.** Reservations not necessary. Meals 40RMB–120RMB ($4.80–$14). AE, JCB, MC, V. Daily 11:30am–10:30pm. SHANGHAI.

This small, crowded, fashionable cafe is the Pudong favorite for home-cooked Shanghai meals, especially among the city's yuppie residents. It's noisy, smoke-filled, and has a local flavor, so it's not the spot for relaxed dining. The occupants of the seafood tanks at the second-floor entrance end up in some delicious dishes, but Lulu is best known for its shredded pork and scallions wrapped in pancakes, its tofu dishes, and a nice *cai fan* (rice with vegetables scramble).

Exploring Shanghai 6

The sights of Shanghai are spread across a number of districts, so if your time is quite short, it is wise to book a day tour of the highlights through your hotel tour desk. Otherwise, getting around on your own, even via taxi or the subway, can be time-consuming at first. The city is flat, but the blocks are long, and what looks like a 10-minute walk on the map can turn into a much longer march. If time allows, however, it is certainly worthwhile to explore parts of the city on foot, immersing yourself in the life of the streets. Again, your hotel staff can be helpful in showing you on a map how to reach some of the top attractions.

A few of Shanghai's sites require day trips. Visits to the garden city of **Suzhou,** to **Hangzhou**'s West Lake, and to the water village of **Zhou Zhuang** are covered in chapter 10. The many treasures of the city itself—its temples, historic houses, museums, parks, shopping avenues, and colonial neighborhoods—are described in this chapter, with a special focus on Shanghai's four top attractions: the **Bund, Yu Garden** (and **Old Town**), the **Shanghai Museum,** and the **Huangpu River Cruise.**

HOW TO SEE SHANGHAI

There are three basic ways to see the sights: by organized tour, by hired car, and on your own. The organized tours offered at hotel tour desks give quick overviews of major sights in the company of English-speaking guides. They usually cost about 250RMB ($30) for a half-day tour, 500RMB ($60) and up for a full-day tour that includes lunch. This is a good way to cover ground in a hurry, with a minimum of hassles. Private or special theme tours with a guide and transportation can be arranged (at a higher fee) by **China International Travel Service (CITS),** 1277 Beijing Xi Lu (☎ 021/ 6289-7827), or the **Jin Jiang Optional Tours Center,** 191 Changle Lu (☎ 021/6445-9525). CITS maintains convenient branches in many hotels.

A second option is to hire a car for the day through your hotel. There's no guide along, but you can take your time to see as many sights as you can fit in, and at your own pace. This is an expensive option, costing from 800RMB to 1,200RMB ($96 to $180) for a driver and car—it's cheaper if you simply hire a taxi for the day yourself on the streets.

Shanghai Attractions

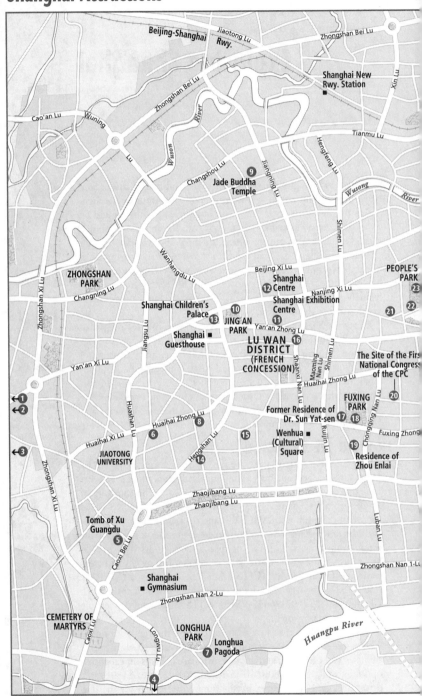

Beijing-Shanghai Rwy.
Jiaotong Lu
Zhongshan Bei Lu

Shanghai New Rwy. Station

Zhongshan Bei Lu

Cao'an Lu
Wuning Lu

Wusong River

Tianmu Lu

Hengfeng Lu

Xin

Changshou Lu
Jianing Lu

9 Jade Buddha Temple

Wusong River

Shimen Lu

Wanhangdu Lu

Beijing Xi Lu

PEOPLE'S PARK

23

ZHONGSHAN PARK

Changning Lu

Shanghai **12** Centre

Nanjing Xi Lu

21 **22**

Shanghai Children's Palace

10

13 JING AN PARK

Shanghai Exhibition Centre **11**

Yan'an Zhong Lu

Zhongshan Xi Lu

Jiangsu Lu

Shanghai ■ Guesthouse

LU WAN DISTRICT (FRENCH CONCESSION)

16

Shaanxi Nan Lu

Maoming Nan Lu

Shimen Lu

The Site of the First National Congress of the CPC

Yan'an Xi Lu

Huashan Lu

Huaihai Zhong Lu

Huaihai Zhong Lu

20

FUXING PARK

Former Residence of Dr. Sun Yat-sen **17** **18**

Chongqing Nan Lu

←1
←2

8

Fuxing Zhong

Huaihai Xi Lu

6

Hengshan Lu

15

Wenhua ■ (Cultural) Square

Ruijin Lu

←3

JIAOTONG UNIVERSITY

14

19 Residence of Zhou Enlai

Zhaojibang Lu
Zhaojibang Lu

Luban Lu

Zhongshan Xi Lu

Tomb of Xu Guangdu
5

Caoxi Bei Lu

Zhongshan Nan 1-Lu

Shanghai ■ Gymnasium

Zhongshan Nan 2-Lu

Huangpu River

CEMETERY OF MARTYRS

Caoxi Lu

Longwu Lu

LONGHUA PARK

7 Longhua Pagoda

4↓

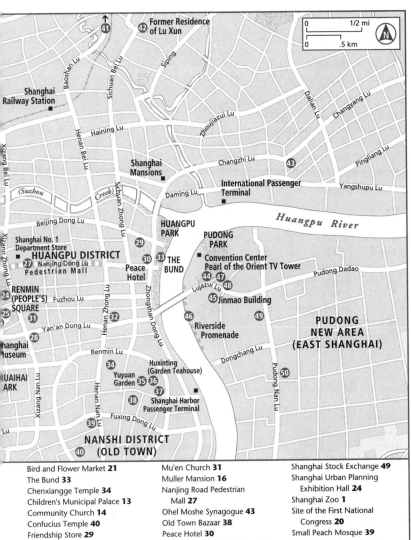

Bird and Flower Market **21**
The Bund **33**
Chenxiangge Temple **34**
Children's Municipal Palace **13**
Community Church **14**
Confucius Temple **40**
Friendship Store **29**
Fuxing Park **18**
Grand Theatre **22**
Great World **28**
Gubei New Town **2**
Huxinting Teahouse **36**
Jade Buddha Temple **9**
Jin Mao Tower **45**
Jing An Temple **10**
Longhua Temple and Pagoda **7**
Lu Xun Park and
 Memorial Hall **42**
Lujiazui Central Green **47**
Lujiazui Development
 Exhibition Room **48**

Mu'en Church **31**
Muller Mansion **16**
Nanjing Road Pedestrian
 Mall **27**
Ohel Moshe Synagogue **43**
Old Town Bazaar **38**
Peace Hotel **30**
Pearl of the Orient TV Tower **44**
People's Park **23**
People's Square **25**
Riverside Promenade **46**
Shanghai Arts and Crafts
 Research Center **15**
Shanghai Botanical Gardens **4**
Shanghai Centre **12**
Shanghai Circus World **41**
Shanghai Exhibition Centre **11**
Shanghai Library **8**
Shanghai Museum **26**
Shanghai Natural History
 Museum **32**

Shanghai Stock Exchange **49**
Shanghai Urban Planning
 Exhibition Hall **24**
Shanghai Zoo **1**
Site of the First National
 Congress **20**
Small Peach Mosque **39**
Soong Ching-ling's Former
 Residence **6**
Sun Yat-sen's Former
 Residence **17**
Temple of the City God **37**
Wangou International
 Cemetery **3**
Xujiahui Cathedral **5**
Yaohan/Nextage Department
 Store **50**
Yu Garden **35**
Zhou's En-lai's Former
 Residence **19**

The last option is to strike out on your own with a map and a plan, using taxis, the subway, and your own two feet. This allows you to see the sights at your own pace at relatively little expense, but you do have to make your own arrangements and pay your own entrance fees.

Suggested Itineraries

Several of the top attractions are within walking distance of one another (**Nanjing Road,** the **Bund, Old Town, Yu Garden**), but others are a considerable distance apart, making group tours by bus almost mandatory to take in everything during a short visit.

If You Have 1 Day

Spend your only day in Shanghai playing tourist, by booking a group tour of the city through your hotel. This will give you a chance to see some of the top attractions (**Yu Garden,** the **Bund,** the **Pearl of the Orient TV Tower** or the **Jin Mao Tower,** the **Jade Buddha Temple,** and perhaps **People's Square**), with a full Shanghai lunch included. If you want to do it on your own by taxi and subway, visit the **Nanjing Road Pedestrian Mall,** the **Bund, Old Town,** and **Yu Garden,** with a tour of the fabulous **Shanghai Museum** in the late afternoon. In the evening, you should have just enough time for dinner in your hotel and an **acrobatics** show, or perhaps a fine meal at **M on the Bund.** Either way, you won't have trouble sleeping.

If You Have 2 Days

Spend your first day with a group city tour booked through your hotel. The second day will give you time to browse **Nanjing Road,** the **Bund,** the **Peace Hotel,** and **Old Town,** where you can enjoy tea and snacks at the **Huxinting Teahouse.** In the afternoon, take a cruise on the **Huangpu River** or stroll the **French Concession,** with stops at some of its attractions (the residences of **Soong Ching-ling** and **Sun Yat-sen, Fuxing Park,** site of the **First Communist Congress,** the **Shanghai Arts and Crafts Research Institute,** the **Jin Jiang Hotel**). Two days should give you time to take in the very top attractions (such as the Bund, Yu Garden, and the Shanghai Museum), with a little time left over for shopping and browsing the historic neighborhoods.

If You Have 3 Days

Three days is the minimum to do much Shanghai sightseeing. It requires 2 days just to take in the top sites listed in the 1- and 2-day itineraries above. On the third day, you should have time to wander farther afield with stops at a **Children's Palace** and one of the religious sites such as the **Ohel Moshe Synagogue,** the **Xujiahui Cathedral,** the **Longhua Pagoda,** or the vibrant **Jing An Temple.** If none of these sites grabs you, consider a full-day guided tour with lunch to the fascinating **Zhou Zhuang** water village, booked through your hotel.

If You Have 4 or More Days

This will give you more time to explore Shanghai's top attractions, although a week would be better. You'll be able to sift through all the big sights and begin to explore those that are off the beaten track. It makes sense to mix group day tours with explorations on your own. Shanghai's shopping streets, riverfront, Old Town, French Concession, and even the Pudong New Area are rewarding areas for a stroll

A Tour of the City by Bus

An efficient, inexpensive alternative to booking a group tour of the city's high-lights from your hotel or a travel agency is the do-it-yourself **Jin Jiang City Tour Bus,** which consists of a privately operated fleet of three red-and-white buses that runs a great circle route through downtown Shanghai and Pudong. Tickets are just 18RMB ($2.15) per person, sold by the bus conductor or at the **Jin Jiang Optional Tours Center,** 191 Changle Lu, across from the Jin Jiang Hotel (☎ **021/6445-9525**). Tickets are good for the full day; passengers can get off at any of the scheduled sightseeing spots along the route and reboard a later bus. Passengers receive a timetable (in English) when boarding, and the conductor gives a brief description of what to see before each stop (in Chinese and English).

The bus route originates beside the entrance to the Garden Hotel, across Maoming Lu from the Jin Jiang Hotel in the French Concession (near the Shaanxi Nan Metro station, 2 blocks south). A circuit of the city takes 1 hour and 45 minutes. The first bus leaves at 9am; the last, at 4:15pm, with departures every 45 minutes in the morning, every hour in the afternoon. You can get off at a sight, pay a visit, and get back on a later bus using the day's ticket. From the Garden Hotel, the stops in order are: (1) the Shanghai Museum at People's Square; (2) Pearl of the Orient TV Tower, Pudong (southwest of main entrance); (3) Yaohan Department Store, Pudong (alongside Times Square shopping center); (4) Nanpu Bridge city bus station; (5) Yu Garden and Old Town; and (6) the Bund. The bus then returns to People's Square and the terminal at the Garden Hotel, completing the circuit. It doesn't stop at all of the major sites—just enough of them to provide an overview of the city in a day.

(see chapter 7 for detailed walking tours). At People's Square, in addition to a mandatory visit to the Shanghai Museum, there are also opportunities for a back-stage tour of the adjacent **Grand Theatre** and the new **Shanghai Urban Planning Exhibition Hall.** Old Town has several temples and a mosque worth exploring. There's also the **Shanghai Zoo,** a **Flower and Bird Market, Lu Xun Park,** the **Great World Center** amusement hall, and the **Shanghai Botanical Gardens.** Much of what gives Shanghai its special quality is the mix of the traditional Chinese with the very modern and the very colonial European, reflected in its fascinating blend of period architecture—something best appreciated at one's leisure in the streets. Even a full week isn't enough time to fully absorb Shanghai's attractions and unusual atmosphere, but it will give you a broad picture of where China has been in the past century and where it is going in the future.

1 The Bund (Wai Tan)

The Bund (which means the Embankment) refers to Shanghai's famous waterfront running along the west shore of the Huangpu River and forming the boundary of old downtown Shanghai. Today, it consists of a marvelous promenade, stretching from Suzhou Creek in the north to Jinling Lu in the south, the perfect platform for strolling along the busy river. Just across the wide avenue (Zhongshan Dong Yi Lu) that parallels the promenade is Shanghai's signature cityscape, a long wall of colonial-era European buildings erected by foreign governments, trading houses, and expatriate millionaires mostly during the prosperous and notorious 1920s and 1930s.

On the other side of the river, casting the shadow of Shanghai's future over its colonial past, are the modern towers of the city's remarkable economic boom: the skyscrapers of the Pudong New Area that include some of Asia's and the world's tallest structures, the high-tech pagodas of the 21st century.

The views along the Bund promenade, a pedestrian-only walkway, are as dramatic as they are complex, with the massive European Customs House and historic Peace Hotel tower on one side and the Tinkertoy spheres of the Pearl of the Orient TV Tower on the other. Even closer are the barges, fishing boats, ocean liners, and cargo ships slipping past one another on the Huangpu River, the channel to the Yangzi River and the Pacific Ocean that has made Shanghai the country's largest port.

ESSENTIALS

The Bund promenade is the artery at the heart of Shanghai. Stretching for 1 mile (1.6km), it is pleasant to stroll, but at any hour it can be crowded by an array of international visitors, Chinese tourists, and plenty of locals, many of whom are here to sell snacks and souvenirs from their carts and stalls. In the very early morning hours, it fills up with local workers intent on practicing tai chi and other traditional exercises; after dark, when the lights come on, it is thronged with foreigners and natives alike who are walking off a dinner or heading for a nightspot. By day, the Bund serves as the path for an invigorating stroll before one branches off on Nanjing Road for shopping, sets off for sightseeing in nearby Old Town and Yu Garden, or crosses the river east to the financial center of Pudong. The promenade is a raised embankment, designed to act as a dike against the Huangpu River, since downtown itself, situated on a soggy delta, is slowly sinking below the river level. It is open round-the-clock and there is no charge for admission. Everything seems to begin or end at the Bund.

EXPLORING THE BUND

The Bund has a few small attractions of its own, in addition to its scenic location at the heart of new and old Shanghai. On its north end, the Suzhou Creek enters the Huangpu beneath the 60-foot-wide iron **Waibaidu Bridge,** built in 1906 to replace the original wooden toll bridge built in 1856 by an English businessman. On the river shore now stands a new granite obelisk, the **Monument to the People's Heroes,** dedicated to the patriotic champions of the past (as defined by the Communist party), beginning in the 1840s. It was erected in 1993 and contains a small historical gallery at its base, the **Bund History Museum,** which contains interesting photographs of the Bund. The museum is open daily from 9am to 5pm; admission is 10RMB ($1.20).

Just south of the monument, at street level, is **Huangpu Park** (open daily from 6am to 7pm in winter, until 10pm in summer; free admission). This is where the British Public Gardens once stood, a notorious park designed by a Scottish gardener that in colonial days was reputed to have a sign posted forbidding entrance by dogs and Chinese. South of here, across from the Peace Hotel, is the entrance to the new **pedestrian tunnel** under the Huangpu, complete with moving sidewalk, that connects downtown Shanghai to the Pudong New Area and the Pearl of the Orient TV Tower.

Farther south down the Bund promenade are scores of vendors, a few restaurants, and excellent overlooks facing the river. Near the southern end of the promenade are offices and docks for passenger ferries that ply the river with sightseers. You'll

The Bund

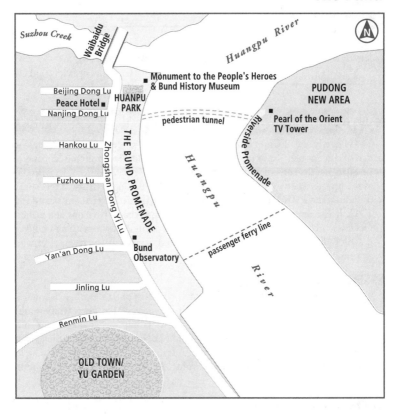

also notice the picturesque **Bund Observatory,** often called the "Shanghai Light-house," a slender round brick tower located on the promenade side of Zhongshan Avenue (at Yan'an Lu) that looks like a nautical pagoda. During the colonial hey-day of the Bund, it served the harbormasters as a control tower for keeping an eye on the junks and clipper ships that clogged the great port. First built in 1884, the observatory was rebuilt in 1907. Then, in 1949, it was moved to the side to make way for the widening of Zhongshan Lu. Up until 1999, it was a charming histori-cal museum (you could climb the cast-iron circular stairway inside to the lookout), but it is currently closed and its future as a museum is uncertain.

At its southern end, the promenade forms the entrance to a modern pyramid-shaped restaurant, and there a pedestrian overpass crosses over at Jinling Lu, lead-ing to Shanghai's Old Town to the southwest.

The chief architectural attractions of the Bund line the west side of Zhongshan Avenue, across from the promenade, where about 50 of the historic European buildings form downtown Shanghai's classic cityscape. The Customs House, British Consulate, private clubs, hotel bars, great trading houses, and international banks have now all been replaced by Chinese tenants, but some of the grand lobbies of the 1920s and 1930s have been skillfully restored, and the **Peace Hotel,** at the corner of Nanjing Road and the Bund, is still serving guests in all its Art Deco splendor. For a complete walking tour to this gallery of European architecture along the Bund, see chapter 7.

Seen from the river, towering above their couchant guardian warships, the semi-skyscrapers of the Bund present, impressively, the façade of a great city.
—Christopher Isherwood, 1937

2 Yu Garden (Yu Yuan)

Yu Garden is one of China's loveliest private classical gardens. Its name means "garden of contentment," and it is indeed a pastoral world apart from modern and hectic Shanghai. Its construction was completed in 1577 by an official, Pan Yunduan, as the private estate for his father, who served in the Ming Dynasty as the Minister of Punishments. The portion known as the Inner Garden (Nei Yuan) was added in 1709. It is a remarkable maze of gorgeous Ming Dynasty pavilions and elaborate rockeries, arched bridges, and goldfish ponds, encircled by a massive, undulating dragon wall. Occupying just 5 acres (2 hectares), it nevertheless seems as expansive as a small town, with room for 30 pavilions.

ESSENTIALS

Yu Garden is located at the heart of Old Town (Nan Shi), a few blocks southwest of the Bund in downtown Shanghai. The main entrance and ticket window are on the north shore of the Huxinting Teahouse pond; the **management office** (☎ 021/6326-0830) is located at 218 Anren Lu, on the east side of the garden.

Hours are daily from 8:30am to 5pm. Admission is 20RMB ($2.40). The least crowded time to visit is in the early morning. Allow 2 hours for a leisurely tour of this site.

EXPLORING YU GARDEN

Strolling through Yu Garden is rather like strolling through a miniature version of the Forbidden City, confusing but enthralling. The traditional layout of the estate has produced several dozen gardens-within-gardens, each partially concealed by white walls but connected to the next sector by arched bridges and curving pathways. From the main entrance, you should head straight into the northwest sector of the garden, and then proceed clockwise to the east along the pavilions on the north wall. Next, turn south along the west wall and continue from hall to hall, ending up in the impressive Inner Garden in the southwest sector. Don't worry too much about getting lost; just keep going and you'll get around most of the estate. The dragon wall that encircles the entire complex shouldn't be counted on as a landmark; it, too, is divided into sections, and acts like a magnificent set of screens, each inner wall ending in the carved head of the dragon. The major sites from the northern entrance clockwise to the east and south are as follows:

THREE EARS OF CORN HALL (SANSUI TANG) This is the first and largest of the garden's grand pavilions. Note that its entrance and windows are decorated with fine carvings of rice, millet, wheat, fruit, and other emblems of a plentiful harvest. The main wall contains an essay on the garden written by its founder, Pan Yunduan.

HALL FOR VIEWING THE GRAND ROCKERY (YANGSHAN TANG) Immediately north of the Three Ears of Corn Hall, this graceful two-story tower serves as the entrance to a marvelous rock garden behind. Its upper story, known as the Chamber for Gathering Rain, provides a fine view of the Grand Rockery.

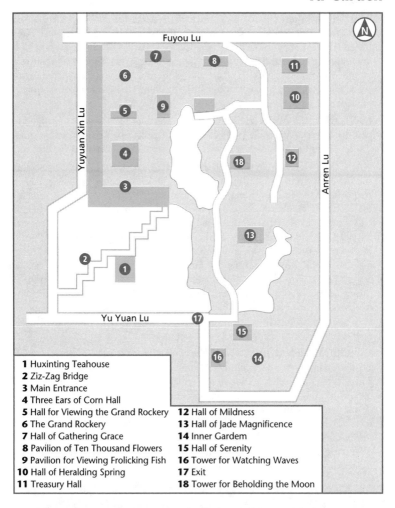

Yu Garden

Fuyou Lu

Yuyuan Xin Lu

Anren Lu

Yu Yuan Lu

1 Huxinting Teahouse
2 Ziz-Zag Bridge
3 Main Entrance
4 Three Ears of Corn Hall
5 Hall for Viewing the Grand Rockery
6 The Grand Rockery
7 Hall of Gathering Grace
8 Pavilion of Ten Thousand Flowers
9 Pavilion for Viewing Frolicking Fish
10 Hall of Heralding Spring
11 Treasury Hall
12 Hall of Mildness
13 Hall of Jade Magnificence
14 Inner Gardem
15 Hall of Serenity
16 Tower for Watching Waves
17 Exit
18 Tower for Beholding the Moon

THE GRAND ROCKERY (DAJIE SHAN)   A pond separates the viewing hall from the rockery. They are connected by the Corridor for Approaching the Best Scenery. The Grand Rockery consists of 2,000 tons of rare yellow stones pasted together with a rice glue and designed by a famous garden artist of the Ming, Zhang Nanyang. The twisted mountainlike sculpture, intended to evoke peaks, ravines, caves, and ridges, stands 46 feet (14m) high. Behind the rockery, at the northwest corner of Yu Garden, is the Hall of Gathering Grace (Cui Xiu Tang); to the east is the Pavilion of Ten Thousand Flowers (Wan Hua Lou), where a 4-century-old gingko stands in the front courtyard. South of these two pavilions, on the east shore of the Grand Rockery, is the tiny Pavilion for Viewing Frolicking Fish (Yu Le Xie) and its ancient wisteria.

HALL OF HERALDING SPRING (DIAN CHUN TANG)   If you continue east from the Grand Rockery and the Pavilion of Ten Thousand Flowers, you will come to two halls in the northwest section of Yu Garden. The northern building is the known as the Treasury Hall. To its south is the Hall of Heralding Spring, the most famous historical building in the garden. It was here in 1853 that the secret "Society of Little Swords" (Xiaodao Hui) plotted to join the peasant-led Taiping Rebellion that aimed to overthrow the Qing Dynasty. The uprising was a bloody one in Shanghai, with the rebels ruling the city for a year before being put to the sword by a combination of Chinese and Western soldiers. Today, there is a small collection of uprising artifacts in this hall, including weapons and coins minted by the rebels.

HALL OF MILDNESS (HEXU TANG)   South of the rebels' old headquarters, past the Tower of Joy, is the Hall of Mildness, worth stepping inside to examine its display of old Qing Dynasty furniture, fashioned by hand from banyan-tree roots.

HALL OF JADE MAGNIFICENCE (YU HUA TANG)   This hall opens into a southern courtyard on the most celebrated stone sculpture in the garden, the **Exquisite Jade (Yu Ling Long),** which was originally procured by an emperor of the Northern Song at the beginning of the 12th century A.D. This honeycombed slab is highly treasured in China as the perfect "Tai Hu" rock, that is, a stone that has been aged and naturally carved by the waters of nearby Tai Lake to achieve its bizarre appearance. Such rocks represent mountain peaks in classical Chinese garden design, and this rock satisfies the three elements of appearance (that it be rough, craggy, and pitted). Water poured into the top of this boulder will spurt out through its numerous holes; incense lighted at its base will swirl outward from its openings. Destined for the emperor, the rock somehow came into the possession of Pan Yunduan, who transported it down the Yangzi and Huangpu rivers (where the boat capsized and divers were dispatched to retrieve it).

INNER GARDEN (NEI YUAN)   The entry gate to the Inner Garden is south of Exquisite Jade Rock and a number of other halls and ponds in the main garden. This is often the quietest section of Yu Garden, particularly in the morning. Its Hall of Serenity (Jing Guan Tang), at the north entrance, and Tower for Watching Waves (Guan Tao Tang) are magnificent. Local artists and calligraphers often use these and other pavilions to display (and sell) their works. The exit from Yu Garden is located just inside the Inner Garden and to your right (west); it turns into the narrow lane of Yu Yuan Lu, which runs past Lo Bu Long restaurant and Huxinting Teahouse on the south shore of the Old Town pond.

3 Shanghai Museum (Shanghai Bowuguan)

Frequently cited as the best museum in China, the Shanghai Museum moved to its present location at People's Plaza in 1996. Its 11 state-of-the-art galleries and three special exhibition halls are arranged on four floors that encircle a spacious cylindrical atrium in the center. The floors are carpeted, the track lighting is bright and focused, the exhibits are tastefully displayed, and the explanatory signs are in English as well as Chinese. The museum draws upon 120,000 historic artifacts, less than in the world-renowned Chinese collections in Beijing, Taipei, and Xi'an, but more than enough to fill the galleries on any given day with outstanding treasures, presented in grand style for an international audience. Foreign visitors to the museum often rank it as Shanghai's very best attraction.

ESSENTIALS

The **Shanghai Museum** is located on the south side of People's Square (Renmin Guang Chang), downtown, west of the Bund, at 201 Renmin Da Dao (☎ 021/ 6372-3500). The entrance is at the top of the stairway on the north side of the

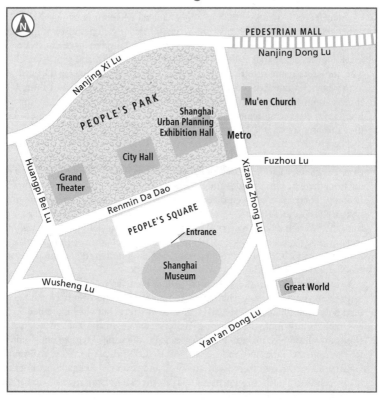

building, facing the three monumental structures that now occupy the north half of the square (Grand Theatre to the west, City Hall in the middle, Shanghai Urban Planning Exhibition Hall to the east). Metro Lines 1 and 2 both have their main stations on the northeast corner of People's Square.

The Shanghai Museum is open Sunday to Friday from 9am to 5pm (no tickets sold after 4pm) and on Saturday from 9am to 10pm (no tickets sold after 9pm). Admission is 20RMB ($2.40), free on Saturday from 5 to 7pm, and 60RMB ($7.20) with an audiophone. The audiophone, which you rent at the counter to your left as you enter the lobby, is highly recommended. It provides a narrative in English of the major exhibits, each of which has a number you can key in to the device. When you press the selected exhibit number, it activates a light beam that highlights the exhibit while the explanatory tape is played.

EXPLORING THE MUSEUM

After buying tickets, proceed into the large, round atrium. You enter each gallery through well-marked doors that encircle the atrium on all four floors. Elevators, escalators, and stairways serve each floor. On the second, third, and fourth floors are small gift shops that sell museum reproductions, books, postcards, and gifts. Two larger gift shops on the ground floor offer even more merchandise. In addition, on the second floor, a fine tearoom with traditional furniture serves cookies, snacks, teas, mineral water, and coffee.

Unlike most museums in China, the Shanghai Museum is arranged by theme rather than by dynasty. The first floor contains major galleries displaying bronzes and stone sculptures. The second floor has wonderful displays of ceramicware. The third floor holds separate galleries for paintings, calligraphy, and seals (the "chops" with the user's name or office, which served ancient China like an ID card). The fourth floor features exhibits of jade, coins, furniture, and minority cultures. The stone-sculpture gallery (first floor) and the jade gallery (fourth floor) are the most impressive, but the museum is also renowned for its holdings of paintings, calligraphy, and bronzes.

The first floor has two extensive displays, the **Bronze Gallery** and the **Sculpture Gallery.** Among the outstanding bronzes are two wine vessels, one in the shape of an ox (*zun*) and the other a traditional pot (*he*) used by the King of Wu, both dating from the Late Spring and Autumn period (770 to 476 B.C.) of the ancient Zhou Dynasty. There's also an even older squarish wine vessel (*lei*) from the late Shang Dynasty (1600 to 1100 B.C.), as well as a typical food vessel on three legs (*ding*) from the Western Zhou Dynasty (1100 to 771 B.C.). The sculptures are even more magnificent, with a kneeling clay figure playing a bamboo flute from the Eastern Han (A.D. 25 to 200) and a Buddhist image of Sakyamuni in stone from the Northern Wei (A.D. 386 to 534).

On the second floor, the **Ceramics Gallery** contains many tricolored figurines from the magnificent Tang Dynasty (A.D. 618 to 907) and delicately painted and fired pots from the Ming Dynasty (A.D. 1368 to 1644) kilns at Jingdezhen.

On the third floor, the **Painting Gallery** contains many ancient original art works on silk scrolls, including landscapes from the Ming Dynasty and Buddhist scrolls from the Tang and Song (A.D. 960 to 1279) dynasties. The **Calligraphy Gallery** shows the various styles of artistic "handwriting" developed in China over many centuries, with specimens as old as the Tang Dynasty. Altogether, the museum owns some 15,000 of these fine scrolls. The **Seal Gallery** displays intricate carved chops in stone used by emperors and their courts to notarize official documents. On this floor there are also displays showing the basic elements of calligraphy, explaining the relationship between Chinese painting and calligraphy, and demonstrating how the artists' tools were used.

The fourth floor has a splendid **Jade Gallery,** with intricately carved jade wine vessels, jewelry, and ornaments, some from quite ancient periods. The **Coin Gallery** has coins that predate the First Emperor's reign (221 to 207 B.C.), as well as gold coins from Persia discovered on the Silk Road. The **Furniture Gallery** contains elaborately carved screens inlaid with jade from the Qing Dynasty (A.D. 1644 to 1911), a six-poster canopy bed from the Ming Dynasty (A.D. 1368 to 1644), and a wonderful folding wooden armchair, also from the Ming. The **Minority Nationalities' Art Gallery** features quite colorful art and ceremonial creations from the more remote reaches of the Chinese empire, most of them dating from the early 20th century.

4 Huangpu River Cruise

The Huangpu River, the undulating, muddy dragon that divides the two Shanghais, east and west, past and future, serves as the city's shipping artery both to the East China Sea and the mouth of the Yangzi River, which the Huangpu joins 18 miles (29km) north of downtown Shanghai. The Bund and its promenade are landmarks of Shanghai's 19th-century struggle to reclaim a waterfront from the bogs of this river, which originates in nearby Tai Lake and the streams that feed it. The

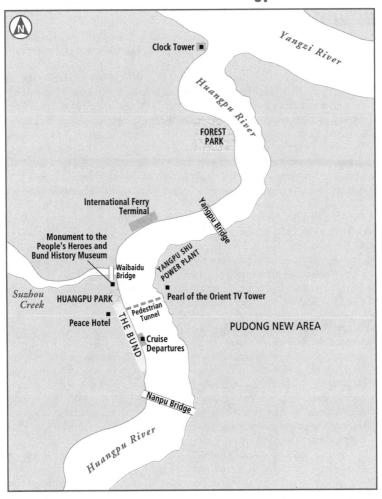

Pudong New Area on the river's opposite (east) shore is evidence in glass and steel of the financial power of the river.

The Huangpu's wharves are the most fascinating in China. The port handles the cargo coming out of the interior from Nanjing, Wuhan, and other Yangzi River ports, including Chongqing, 1,500 miles (2,400km) deep into Sichuan Province, the rice bowl of China. From Shanghai, which produces plenty of industrial and commercial products in its own right, as much as a third of China's trade with the rest of the world is conducted each year—a substantial part of it flowing up and down the Huangpu River. Mile for mile, this is the most important river in China.

Mornings and afternoons, tour boats make the 3$^{1}/_{2}$-hour voyage up the Huangpu to the Yangzi River delta. From the river, you'll have unrivaled views of Shanghai's port facilities, the ships of the world that dock here, and the junks and Chinese barges that clot the narrow river avenue. Unrivaled, too, are the postcard views of Shanghai's celebrated European skyline to the west and the booming cityscape of Pudong to the east.

ESSENTIALS

The main ticket office for cruises is the **Shanghai Huangpu River Cruise Company, Ltd.,** at 229 Zhongshan Dong Er Lu (☎ **021/6374-4461**), located on the southern end of the Bund promenade; it also has a ticket office "under" the promenade at street level (219 Zhongshan Dong Er Lu) and further north up the same street at 153 Zhongshan Dong Er Lu. All are open daily, and the schedule usually includes a full morning cruise (from 9am to 12:30pm) and a full afternoon cruise (from 2 to 5:30pm). Both these full cruises make a complete circuit of the Huangpu to its mouth. This cruise company also offers a night cruise from 7 to 9pm, splendid when the lights are on the Bund and Pudong, but this voyage does not go downriver to the Yangzi. Cruise schedules vary depending on the season, and on weekends additional cruises are sometimes added, so check ahead. Tickets can be purchased at any of the three Bund offices listed here or through your hotel desk. Prices for the full cruise start at 45RMB ($5.40) and top out at 100RMB ($12). Buy the best ticket, since this reserves a comfortable seat with a fine view on the top deck, as well as a small buffet with drinks and local snacks. You can also book shorter river cruises (1 to 2 hr.) at reduced prices. The shorter cruises meander up and down the main waterfront area between the two great suspension bridges to the north and south. The river tour boats are wide double-deckers, about 150 feet long, equipped with a kiosk selling snacks; a bar selling tea, coffee, sodas, and beer; and a buffet dining room. Upper decks are nonsmoking.

CRUISING THE HUANGPU

As soon as you're aboard, stake out a soft chair on the upper deck. You'll be surrounded by picture windows and served hot tea and nuts, but as the ferry pulls away from the dock, you won't be able to resist going out on deck to admire the Shanghai waterfront. The granite offices, banks, consulates, and hotels of Shanghai's past colonial masters form a stately panorama along the Bund, while on the Pudong side, the Pearl of the Orient TV Tower, the Jin Mao Tower, and the new skyscrapers form the tallest and most expensive new building project in the world. There's the river traffic, too, to keep one's eyes from ever resting.

The ship heads north, downstream, passing **Huangpu Park** across from the **Peace Hotel** on the Bund. With its stunning green pyramid roof, it's still the loveliest piece of architecture in Shanghai, east or west. The park borders **Suzhou Creek** at the northern end of the Bund, where a new monumental sculpture to China's revolutionary martyrs soars in ribbons of marble, rising like Shanghai's economic expectations.

Suzhou Creek is spanned by **Waibaidu Bridge,** which once linked the American and British concessions. The Americans staked out the northern shore; the British claimed the downtown waterfront. Sixty feet (18m) wide, with two 171-foot-long (51m) spans, this bridge was regularly crossed by human-powered rickshaws, introduced to Shanghai from Japan by a Frenchman. Trams were soon routed across the bridge, too, as were motorcars, which have been driving the streets of Shanghai since 1901.

Less than a mile north of Suzhou Creek on the west shore is the **International Passenger Terminal,** where luxury cruise ships tie up. The Huangpu River jogs sharply east at this point on its way to the Shanghai shipyards, where cranes and derricks load and unload the daily logjam of freighters. The freighters are stamped with the country names of the world's shipping giants (United States, Japan, Holland, Russia, Norway), and archenemies can often be seen unloading side by side.

Across the river on the eastern shore, vast coal yards crop up, along with petro-leum-storage facilities. At the **Yangshupu Power Plant,** the stacks are tipped with flames night and day. Here one begins to sense fully Shanghai's industrial might. The river seems endless and its industrial ranks—the dry docks, factories, and power plants—equally unlimited, like an army of millions massed on both shores of a worldwide economic battlefield.

The Bund and the Pearl of the Orient TV Tower rapidly fade from view as the Huangpu slowly begins to curve northward again. The ship crosses under **Yangpu Cable Bridge,** which like **Nanpu Cable Bridge** to the south is one of the largest such structures in the world. The Yangpu Bridge is considered the world's first "slant-stretched" bridge and has the longest span in the world, some 1,975 feet (602m). Its total length is almost 5 miles (7.6km), and 50,000 vehicles pass over its six lanes every day.

What overwhelms river passengers even more than the long industrial shoreline is the traffic slinking up and down the waterway. The Huangpu is, on the average, just 600 feet (183m) wide. It is like a superhighway without visible lanes, glutted with gigantic freighters, tugs, tiny sampans and, above all, the undulating trains of unpainted wooden barges, tied together to save fuel, forming serpentine dragons on a serpentine river. Flotillas of these heavily laden barges, their gunwales just above the waterline, usually number a dozen or more. Their open holds are stuffed with coal, lime, brick, produce, scrap metal, and a thousand other commodities in tran-sit. The rear cabins are homes to families who sleep and cook and work and play on the Huangpu. The family bicycle is often parked on-deck. Potted flowers festoon the cabin roofs. Noisy outboard engines, often in teams of four or five, propel these barges from the stern. Laundry lines stretch from cabin roof to prow. Dishes are washed and meals are cooked with water scooped from the brown river. More than 2,000 oceangoing ships compete with the 20,000 barges, fishing junks, and row-boats that stalk the Huangpu every year.

There are also navy gunboats and even an occasional submarine anchored on the shores. A sign in English nailed to the railing of the tour boat deck sternly warns that photographs of military craft and installations are strictly forbidden, but there's seldom anyone aboard to enforce the ordinance.

The Huangpu eventually empties into the mighty Yangzi River at **Wusong Kuo,** where the harbormasters wait beneath a ghostly pale clock tower, its hands frozen. This marks the end of Shanghai's little river and China's largest one as they converge near the Pacific Ocean. The estuary is as vast as an ocean itself, or rather a nether-world of water moving in contrary directions on crisscrossing tides, salted and silted, muddied and fresh. An armada of vessels, large and small, waits in the estu-ary for a sea change, for shipments to be readied, for a turn at the Shanghai docks. On this watery tarmac, the population of boats surpasses that of any man-made marina. The vessels wait and bob up and down, moving nowhere on their anchors as if time itself has stopped.

The tour boats from Shanghai venture only far enough out into this twilight zone of tides and currents to pivot slowly and turn back into the narrowing passageway of the Huangpu. The return trip is more relaxing. The procession of barges, as end-less as silk shops and clothing stores on Shanghai's Nanjing Road, becomes almost routine. The ship eventually sails into Shanghai as countless clipper ships and ocean steamers have over the past 160 years, docking at the foot of a colonial skyline in China's mightiest port on the river that seems to seamlessly knit together Shanghai's past and future.

5 Temples, Churches, Mosques & Synagogues

For visitors, Shanghai's most popular Buddhist shrine is the Jade Buddha Temple. The Longhua Temple is also on the route of some travelers; its pagoda is the most interesting one in the city. The Jing An Temple is small but very lively; the Chenxiangge Temple in Old Town, recently reopened, has a good display of modern Buddhist statuary; and the Confucian Temple, newly renovated, is a peaceful retreat. Shanghai is also home to several active Christian churches and an Islamic mosque where foreign visitors may worship or visit. What really sets religious Shanghai apart, at least in China, is its Jewish legacy, most powerfully evoked by the reopening of the Ohel Moshe Synagogue as a museum and study center.

TEMPLES

Chenxiangge Temple. 29 Chenxiangge Lu, Nanshi District. ☎ **021/6328-7884.** Admission 5RMB (60¢). Daily dawn to sunset. The temple is located 1 block west of Jiujiaochang Lu, the street that forms the western boundary of the Old Town Bazaar.

The grounds first served as the private estate of Pan Yunduan, who built Yu Garden during the Ming Dynasty. Under the succeeding Qing Dynasty rulers, the grounds served as a Buddhist temple, but it was abandoned during the Cultural Revolution (1966 to 1976), becoming a factory. In 1989, restoration began, culminating in its reopening as a Buddhist nunnery and small Old Town tourist attraction in 1994. The centerpiece is an altar with a golden statue of the Buddha. The Buddha's vault is adorned with images of 384 disciples, created since 1990 by a single master craftsman.

Confucius Temple (Wen Miao). Wenmiao Lu, Nanshi District. ☎ **021/6407-3593.** Admission 8RMB (95¢). Daily 8:30am–4:30pm. In the southwest section of the Old Town District, the temple is located on the north side of Wenmiao Lu, 1 block east of Zhongshan Lu.

Built in 1855 on the site of the Zitong Clan Temple, and most recently restored to celebrate the 2,550th birthday of Confucius in 1999 (after serving as a Children's Palace), this temple honoring China's Great Sage is a quiet refuge from the nearby crowded streets of Old Town. The narrow winding lane that leads to it from Henan Lu on the east gives a true picture of urban life in Shanghai. The entrance opens on the courtyard of the newly renovated Dacheng Hall. Inside are statues of Confucius flanked by his two disciples, Mencius and Yanhui, and his two favorite musical instruments, a drum and set of bells. Behind this hall and to the right (northeast) is Zunjin (Scripture Esteeming) Tower, the former library now containing a display of miniature rock gardens in pots. Southward from here, along the eastern corridor of the complex, is Mingling Pavilion, a former lecture hall now housing a gallery of wooden sculptures, along with a pretty goldfish pool with a large "Tai Hu" rock. The final structure, back near the entrance, is Kuixing Ge (Liberal Arts Star Tower). Consecrated to the god of liberal arts, this three-story, 66-foot-high (20m) pagoda is the only original structure left on these tranquil grounds, having been erected in 1855.

✪ Jade Buddha Temple (Yufo Si). 170 Anyuan Lu, Putuo District. ☎ **021/6266-3668.** Admission 15RMB ($1.80). Daily 8–11am and 1–5pm. Located just outside the Jing An District in northwest Shanghai, between Jiangning Lu and Shaanxi Bei Lu.

Shanghai's most popular temple with visitors, the Jade Buddha complex has an exceedingly short history, having been completed in 1918, but it exudes a powerful potion of thick incense, flashy decorations, and a dark, seedy atmosphere that makes it seem centuries older. The architectural style comes from the Song Dynasty

(A.D. 960 to 1279), when swirling eaves were the style; the brilliant yellow walls are of recent origin. This is an active Buddhist monastery today (devoted to the Chan or Zen sect, which originated in China), but the real emphasis appears to be on tourism.

The chief attractions are the painted religious statues, which are stacked high in the three main halls. The Treasure Hall of the Great Hero (Daxiong Baodian) contains golden images of the Buddhas of the past, present, and future, flanked by their 18 followers (*luohans*). The White Jade Buddha, located up a narrow set of old stairs on the second floor of Wentang Hall, is the true treasure. Carved in Burma and brought to Shanghai in 1881 by Huigeng, a Chinese pilgrim, it is twice life-size (weighing 455 lb. and measuring over 6 ft. tall in seated position). In another special pavilion, there's a Sleeping Buddha, also carved from a single slab of Burmese jade and brought to Shanghai by the same benefactor.

Jing An Temple (Jing An Si). 1686 Nanjing Xi Lu, Jing An District. ☎ **021/6248-6366.** Admission 5RMB (60¢). Daily 9am–5pm. Located across the street from Jing An Station (Metro Line 2) on the corner of Huashan Lu.

Always lively and crowded, this small, garishly decorated temple has the longest history of any shrine in Shanghai, about 17 centuries, but its chief antiquities are a Ming Dynasty copper bell (the Hongwu Bell), which weighs in at 3.5 tons, and stone Buddhas from the Northern and Southern States period (A.D. 420 to 589). Although its name means "Palace of Tranquillity," it is hardly the place for quiet meditation these days, nor was it in the past. Before Liberation (1949), this was Shanghai's richest Buddhist monastery, presided over by the Abbott of Bubbling Road, an imposing figure who kept seven mistresses and a White Russian bodyguard. After Liberation, it was converted to a plastics factory before its most recent renovation, in 1999. The three Southern-style main halls, each with their own courtyard, date from the most recent reconstruction (1880).

✪ **Longhua Temple (Longhua Si).** 2853 Longhua Lu, Xuhui District. ☎ **021/6456-6085.** Admission 5RMB (60¢). Daily 7am–5pm. Situated a long, unpleasant walk southeast of the Wan Ti Guan subway station near Shanghai Stadium in south Shanghai, this temple is easiest to reach by taxi.

Shanghai's largest temple is one of its most fascinating, featuring the city's premier pagoda (Longhua Ta). The seven-story, eight-sided, thousand-year-old pagoda is gorgeous, but it is not currently open for visits or climbs. The temple grounds, on the north side of the street, are extensive. Rising eaves, six-sided windows, arched entryways, and square courtyard walls are typical of the charming design. The temple dates from the Song Dynasty (A.D. 960 to 1279); the present halls date from the late Qing, a century ago. The temple is active, its main halls impressive, its courtyards crowded with incense-bearing supplicants. There's a vegetarian restaurant between the third and fourth halls, and the fourth hall, with its three golden Buddhas, is lined with pictures of the deceased for whose souls the monks pray daily. The side halls contain interesting statuary and a workshop of wood-carvers. The temple is famous for its midnight bell-ringing every New Year's Eve, which takes place in the old three-storied Bell Tower near the entrance. This Ming Dynasty tower was renovated twice, in 1566 and 1892; you can strike the Bell Tower's 3.3-ton (3,000kg) bronze bell, cast in 1894, three times by paying the bell monk 10RMB ($1.20).

There is also a Japanese Buddhist Temple, built in the 1930s, at 455 Zhapu Lu, Hongkou District, not active, but often visited by Japanese tourists. The design is unusual, with a series of circular relief sculptures capped by a massive semicircular sculpted lotus.

Temple of the City God (Chenghuang Miao). 1 Yicheng Lu, Nanshi District. ☎ **021/ 6328-4494.** Admission 5RMB (60¢). Daily 8:30am–4pm. Located on the north side of Fang-bang Zhong Lu, just west of Anren Lu, the temple occupies the southeast corner of the Old Town Bazaar in the thick of the pedestrian area, sharing a wall with the Inner Garden of Yu Yuan.

Every Chinese city once had its Temple of the City God, the central shrine for Daoist worship. Shanghai's version dates from the Ming Dynasty, when it was a private garden estate, becoming the main area temple in 1726. Today, it has been extensively restored to serve as a kind of religious amusement park for tourists in the Old Town Bazaar. Its stone arch marks the southeast entrance to this shopping district. Old statues of Lao Zi (founder of Daoism) and Huo Guang (a local military hero) remain, but the altar, with its gold-painted figures, is new. The courtyard was the local setting for lively fairs and markets, a tradition that has recently been reinstituted on Sunday mornings.

MOSQUES & CHURCHES

In addition to the places listed below, there are other cathedrals, churches, mosques, and places of worship in Shanghai. For the locations and times of services, inquire at your hotel.

Community Church (Guoji Tang). 53 Hengshan Lu, Xujiahui District. ☎ **021/ 6437-6576.** Services Sun 7:30am, 10am, and 7pm. North of Hengshan Station (Metro Line 1), east side of Hengshan Lu near Wulumuqi Nan Lu intersection.

Established in 1925 and also called the International Church, this is the best known of Shanghai's Protestant churches among foreign residents and visitors, and the largest in use. The ivy-covered English-style building and grounds are beautiful, fully in keeping with this upscale colonial-style shopping district on the fringes of the French Concession. Special services and a Sunday school for foreign passport holders are currently held at 4pm on Sundays (☎ **021/6406-5394**).

Mu'en Church (Mu'en Tang). 316 Xizang Zhong Lu, Huangpu District. ☎ **021/ 6322-5069.** Located on the east side of People's Square. Services Sun morning (exact times not available).

Formerly known as the Moore Church, it was established in 1887 and expanded in 1931 to seat more than 1,000 worshippers. Since reopening in 1979 after its closure during the Cultural Revolution (1966 to 1976), it has built up a local membership that numbers in the thousands. Originally the Methodist church of Shanghai, this nondenominational church (now known as the Mu'en or Mercy Church) has a Chinese woman serving as its pastor. Two bishops were consecrated here in 1988, the first in China in 3 decades; the same year, the American evangelist Billy Graham preached here.

Small Peach Garden Mosque (Xiao Taoyuan Qingzhen Shi). 52 Xiao Taoyuan Lu, Nanshi District. ☎ **021/6377-5442.** Admission 10RMB ($1.20). Daily sunrise to sunset. Southeast of the intersection of Fuxing Dong Lu and Henan Nan Lu, a few blocks south of the Old Town Bazaar.

Shanghai's largest mosque dates from 1925. Its main prayer hall (facing Mecca to the west) can hold several hundred worshippers (non-Muslims not permitted to enter). The courtyard contains a minaret for calls to prayer.

Shanghai's other mosque that welcomes foreign visitors is the **Song Jiang Mosque** (Song Jiang Qingzhen Si), located in the southwest suburb of Songjiang (☎ **021/5782-3684**). Shanghai's oldest mosque is at 378 Fuyou Lu (built in 1870).

Jewish Shanghai

As China's most international city, Shanghai experienced several waves of Jewish immigration, each leaving its mark. Sephardic Jews were the first to arrive, in the late 1840s, after China was forced to open the port of Shanghai to foreign traders and missionaries. The Sassoons, who emigrated from Baghdad in the mid-19th century, were the first Jewish family to make a fortune in Shanghai. Their business was real estate, and both the Peace Hotel on the Bund and the villa estate next to the zoo (now the Cypress Hotel) were their creations. Silas Hardoon was a later Jewish real-estate baron, but one who also traded in opium; his great estate was razed to make way for the Sino-Soviet Shanghai Exhibition Center on Yan'an Xi Lu (south of the Portman Ritz-Carlton Hotel). The Kadoories, like the Sassoons, amassed their fortune in old Shanghai. They are survived by the "Marble House," the city's most popular and impressive Children's Palace (on Yan'an Xi Lu).

The more recent waves of Jewish emigrants were not to be known for their wealth or extravagance. They were refugees: first White Russian Jews who fled the Bolsheviks in the 1920s; then European Jews fleeing Hitler. The numbers of Jews in pre–World War II Shanghai eventually topped 20,000. In February 1943, the occupying force of the Japanese army forced the Jews of Shanghai into a "Designated Area" within the Hongkou District north of the Bund, where the local synagogue became the center of their material and spiritual life until the end of the war.

Travelers interested in the Jews in Shanghai can still visit that center, the **Ohel Moshe Synagogue (Moshi Huitang),** 62 Chang Yang Lu, Hongkou District (☎ **021/6512-0229** or 021/6541-6312). Built in 1927 by the Ashkenazi Jewish community of Shanghai, it no longer serves as a synagogue, but as a museum devoted to the Jews in Shanghai. Visitors are welcome Monday to Friday from 9am to 4:30pm. The third floor has displays, period photographs, a list of Shanghai Jews, and a small bookstore.

The best way to visit the synagogue is by arranging a tour of Jewish sites through CITS in Shanghai. You will be met at the synagogue by a local Chinese man, Wang Fah Liang, who can recount many stories of how the Chinese and Jewish refugees lived together under Japanese occupation (in a neighborhood bounded on the north by Zhoujiazui Lu, the south by Huimin Lu, the east by Tongbei Lu, and the west by Gongping Lu). Your guide will then take you to nearby **Huoshan Park (Huoshan Gong Yuan),** where there is a memorial to Jewish refugees.

Travelers interested in learning more about the Jewish community in Shanghai, attending Shabbat dinners, or participating in religious services should contact **Rabbi Shalom Greenberg** (☎ **021/6279-7164** or 021/6289-9903; fax 021/6289-9957; e-mail: sjcchina@usa.net or rabbishalom@yahoo.com).

✪ **Xujiahui Cathedral (Xujiahui Da Jiao Tang).** 158 Puxi Lu, Xuhui District. ☎ **021/6439-4298** or 021/6438-2595. Services Sat 7pm, Sun–Fri 5:30, 6, 7, and 8am, with an additional 7pm mass on Sun; open to visitors daily 7:30–11am and 1–4pm. Located on the west side of Caoxi Bei Lu, a few blocks south of Xujiahui Station (Metro Line 1).

Once known as St. Ignatius, this is Shanghai's great cathedral, opened by the Jesuits in 1906. The foundation was laid much earlier, in 1848, as the Jesuits long had a mission in this area of the city. The Gothic cathedral was built next to the birth-place of Xu Guangqi, a pupil of the Jesuits' most famous missionary to China, Matteo Ricci (1553 to 1610). Xu, a librarian and landowner (the district's full name, Xujiahui, means "Xu Family Village"), was baptized Paul. He donated land here to the Jesuits, and is commemorated today by a statue and public park next to the cathedral.

As a missionary center, the cathedral grounds included a library, an orphanage, a college, a publishing house, and its own weather station. Today, it is the city's largest cathedral, with space for more than 2,500 inside. Its twin redbrick spires and gargoyled roof are district landmarks; its vast interior of altars, stone columns, Gothic ceilings, stained-glass windows, and paintings of the Last Supper and Stations of the Cross is yet another chapter in Shanghai's living history of European architecture.

Other major Catholic churches include the **Shanghai Fujia Catholic Church,** 1115 Pudong Lu, Pudong New Area (☎ **021/5885-3172**); the **Dongjiadu Catholic Church,** 185 Dongjiadu Lu, Nanshi District (☎ **021/6378-7214**), the first large cathedral in Shanghai, built in 1853 in the Spanish baroque style, located 2 blocks west of the Huangpu River; and **Christ the King Catholic Church (Junwang Tang),** also called the Good Shepherd Church, 361 Julu Lu, Jing An District (☎ **021/6217-4608**), which holds services in English at 5:30pm on Saturdays and at 10am on Sundays.

Active Protestant places of worship that open their doors to foreign worshippers include the **Shanghai Grace Church of Christianity,** opened in 1910 at 375 Shaanxi Bei Lu, Jing An District (☎ **021/6253-9394** or 021/6258-5598); **Church of St. Joseph,** built in 1860 at 36 Sichuan Nan Lu, Huangpu District (☎ **021/6328-0293**); **Kunshan (Jingling) Church,** built in 1923 at 135 Kunshan Lu, east of Sichuan Bei Lu, Hongkou District (☎ **021/6324-3021**), the place where Chiang Kai-shek wed Soong Mei-ling; and **All Saints Church (Zhusheng Tang),** 425 Fuxing Zhong Lu at Danshui Lu (☎ **021/6385-0906**), a lively church in the French Concession that has just begun holding services again.

6 Parks & Gardens

Shanghai's parks are splendid places for a stroll, combining scenic vistas with people-watching opportunities. They are particularly lively at dawn, when locals gather for their morning exercises (ranging from the shadow-boxing forms of tai ji quan to ballroom dancing). All parks and gardens are gated, with ticket booths charging small admissions at the entrance.

In addition to those listed below, Shanghai has many smaller parks that are chiefly notable today as relaxing oases in the midst of a sprawling urban desert, devoid of natural beauty. **Jing An Park,** 1649 Nanjing Xi Lu (south of Jing An Temple), was completely remodeled in 1999 when the new Jing An Metro Station was created; it is still a fine spot to relax beside the large pond. **Shanghai Park,** located in the triangle formed by Yan'an, Hongqiao, and Yili roads in the Hongqiao Development Zone, is also undergoing a complete renovation. **Guilin Park,** 1 Guilin Lu, Xuhui District, near Shanghai Normal University, is a Suzhou-style classic garden with pavilions, pools, and rockeries, built in 1933 on the private estate of Pockmarked Huang, a Shanghai "godfather" of the notorious Green Gang (*Qing Bang*). **Zhongshan Park,** 780 Chang Ning Lu, Changning District, built in 1914 as Jessfield Park, once contained the campus of St. John's University, Shanghai's first international college; today, it is known for its extensive rose and peony gardens, and as the westernmost stop to date on the Metro Line 2.

You Paid What?

47,000 hotels, 700 airlines, 50 rental car companies. And a few million ways to save money.

Travelocity.com
A Sabre Company

Go Virtually Anywhere.

AOL Keyword: Travel

Will you have enough stories to tell your grandchildren

Yahoo! Travel

Fuxing Park (Fuxing Gongyuan). 2 Gaolan Lu, Luwan District. ☎ **021/6372-0662.**
Admission 5RMB (60¢). Daily 6am to sunset. Located in the French Concession south of Huaihai Zhong Lu, the west entrance is on Gaolan Lu, the north entrance on Yandang Lu, and the
southeast entrance on Chongqing Nan Lu off Fuxing Zhong Lu.

Formerly Gujiazai Garden, a private estate in the French Concession, Fuxing Park
was purchased by foreign residents and opened to the public in 1909. It was popu-
larly known as French Park, styled after a city park in Paris with wide, tree-lined
walks and flowerbeds. There's a large stage in the center of the park, rose gardens to
the east, and, near the north entrance, a statue of Karl Marx and Friedrich Engels
before which Chinese couples often practice their ballroom dancing. The 6,943
trees represent 120 species, creating an urban forest covering 22.7 acres (9.18
hectares) at the heart of Shanghai's busiest shopping district. In the summer, you
can board a quiet old Ferris wheel for a serene view of the rooftops of the French
Concession.

Lujiazui Central Green (Lujiazui Gongyuan). 480 Lujiazui Lu, Pudong New Area. Admission 5RMB (65¢). Daily 6am–8pm. East of the Pearl of the Orient TV Tower and Lujiazui subway station, north of the Jin Mao Tower. Main entrance is on the north side, at Yin Cheng
Dong Lu; ticket booth is half a block east of entrance.

This big new urban park, covering 100,000 square meters, still looks too new and
raw (like Pudong itself), but once the shade trees take over, it should be inviting.
For now, it has the largest, most Westernized green lawn you're likely to see in
China, accented by white magnolias. A large lake in the shape of the Pudong New
Area occupies the center of the park. Tables on the shore, shaded by sail-shaped
canopies, are perfect for picnics, snacks, or drinks (available at a kiosk). The park is
presently so high-tech, it even features a series of in-ground audio speakers spout-
ing out piped-in New Age mood music.

The highlight of the park is the Lujiazui Development Exhibition Room, an
urban-history museum housed in a wonderful colonial mansion. The east side of
the river is not associated with old Shanghai and European communities, but this
courtyard mansion was clearly the estate of a very wealthy foreign taipan. Fashioned
from orange and black brick, this house was built here between 1914 and 1917.
The large windows are trimmed in dark, carved woods; the door panels belong in
a German castle; and the floors retain their original green-marble tiles. The displays, photographs, old maps, and artifacts, meant to tell the story of Pudong's
rapid development, are scant and annotated in Chinese only, but the house itself is
splendid.

People's Park (Renmin Gongyuan). 213 Nanjing Xi Lu, Huangpu District. Admission
5RMB (60¢). Daily 6am–8pm. At Nanjing Rd. West and Xizang Zhong Lu; just west of People's Plaza Station (Metro Lines 1 and 2).

The city's "Central Park" is built on the site of colonial Shanghai's horse-racing
track, once a favorite weekend amusement for the British community. Today, the
30 acres (12 hectares) of trees, ponds, rock gardens, amusement rides, and concrete
are packed with locals and their families. The southern portion of the park, People's
Square (Renmin Guang Chang), which once contained the southern half of the
racetrack, is Shanghai's Tiananmen Square. Opened in 1951 and renovated in
1994, the square has become Shanghai's cultural center, with an underground shopping arcade, the central subway station, the Shanghai Museum, the Grand Theatre,
the 20-story Municipal Hall, and the Shanghai Urban Planning Exhibition Hall.
The square is a popular place with locals who feed the pigeons, gossip on the
benches, teach their kids to fly kites, and attend ballroom-dancing lessons.

✪ **Riverside Promenade (Binjiang Da Dao).** East shoreline, Huangpu River, 2 blocks west of the Pearl of the Orient TV Tower and Lujiazui subway station. Admission 5RMB (60¢). Daily 7am–10pm. Main entrances on either side of Lujiazui Lu.

Pudong's answer to the Bund promenade, Riverside may lack its own colonial European architecture, but it offers a fine view of the Bund at a distance, with the river in the foreground. After dark, when the Bund's buildings are lit up and beacon lights sweep the river lanes, the view is one of the best in Shanghai. The Riverside Promenade also affords marvelous vistas of the Pudong skyline: not only of its towers and skyscrapers, but also of the new Shanghai International Conference Center and its enormous glass domes in the shape of world globes. The very best daylight view (one you can't get from the Bund) is from the Wave-View Platform on the north end of the promenade; here, the river tide sweeps within 3 feet of the platform lip, putting you right on the river.

The Riverside Promenade project began in 1992 on the former site of the Li Xin Shipbuilding Yard. It extends for 1¹/₂ miles (2.4km) along the waterfront, from Dongchang Lu and the river ferry terminal in the south to Taidong Lu in the north. Dancing fountains, black anchors, and enormous three-ring iron rope sculptures evoke a maritime theme. Kiosks are currently the only concessions on the walkway, which is refreshingly uncrowded compared to the Bund promenade on the other side of the river.

✪ **Shanghai Botanical Gardens (Shanghai Zhiwuyuan).** 1111 Longwu Lu, Xuhui District. ☎ **021/6410-2461** or 021/6451-3369. Admission 22RMB ($2.65). Daily 7am–5pm in summer, 8am–4pm in winter. Located on the west side of Longwu Lu, near the Novotel Yuan Lin Hotel, about 1 mile (1.6km) east of Xin Long Hua Station (Metro Line 1).

The city's premier garden opened in 1978 after 4 years of construction and land-scaping. The grounds, covering 200 acres (81 hectares), are divided into spacious sectors, each devoted to magnolias, peonies, azaleas, roses, osmanthus, ferns, bamboo, maples, or conifers. The orchid garden is considered the best in China. At a new area, the "Plant Evolution Section," horticultural experiments are conducted; in a more traditional garden, medicinal plants are grown and harvested. The hallmark section is the "Penjing Bonsai Garden" (requiring a separate 5RMB/60¢ admission), with hundreds of bonsai displayed in a large complex of corridors, courtyards, pools, and rockeries. There is an attached "Rock Penjing" display as well, in which rocks are carved and glued together to form miniature mountains that are placed in trays of water. The extensive garden grounds are punctuated with restaurants and exhibition halls, vendors' stalls, and children's playgrounds.

7 Museums & Mansions

Many of Shanghai's museums and historic residences are housed in the European mansions and estates of colonial Shanghai. The setting is often the chief attraction. While lighting and display are seldom state-of-the-art and English signage can be spotty or nonexistent, simply touring these fine storehouses is fascinating.

Lu Xun Park and Memorial Hall (Lu Xun Gongyuan). 146 Jiangwan Dong Lu, Hongkou District. ☎ **021/5696-2894.** Admission 1RMB (12¢). Daily 6am–8pm. The Memorial Hall, 2288 Sichuan Bei Lu, is open daily 9am–5pm, ☎ 021/6540-2288, admission 5RMB (60¢). The Former Residence of Lu Xun is nearby, at 9 Dalu Xinchun, Shanyin Lu (Xiangde Lu).

Hongkou park, opened in 1905, was renamed for China's best-known 20th-century writer, Lu Xun (1881 to 1936), who lived in the neighborhood from 1927 until his death. Lu Xun's mausoleum occupies a prominent position in the park, next to a new museum devoted to his life, the Lu Xun Memorial Hall. Lu Xun is credited

Shanghai's Culture Street (Wen Hua Jia)

Just a block from Lu Xun Park and Memorial Hall is Duo Lun Lu, recently christened Shanghai's Culture Street (Wen Hua Jia), a new attraction angling off Sichuan Bei Lu in the historic Hangkou District. Hangkou, north of the Bund, was once the American Concession, which merged with the British Concession to form the International Settlement; by the time Lu Xun moved into the neighborhood in the 1930s, the area had become a Japanese enclave. The stately brick homes and shops on this half-mile (0.8km) stretch of the street have been preserved and refurbished, and cars are now banned, making it a fine historic pedestrian mall of bookshops, teahouses, antiques shops, and historic homes. The street is further enhanced by new park benches, bronze statues of famous writers and artists who lived here in the 1930s, and photos of old Shanghai hung from street lamps. Check out the small museum (145 Duo Lun Lu) and the store devoted to Chairman Mao memorabilia (185 Duo Lun Lu).

---

with developing the modern style of Chinese prose. He was also the first to translate science-fiction novels into Chinese. He is hailed as a political revolutionary as well; his tomb is engraved with an inscription penned by Chairman Mao. Lu Xun's bronze statue is in the marble lobby of the museum. The main exhibit room covers about 11,000 square feet (1,000m²) on the second floor and includes galleries displaying his many books and old photographs, as well as furniture from his study, his hat and goatskin gown, and his death mask. Signs are in English.

Muller Mansion. 30 Shaanxi Lu, Jing An District.

Anyone who passes by this extravagant construction in the northwest corner of the French Concession at Yan'an Zhong Lu can't help but wonder what this gigantic gingerbread mansion *is*. It was the home of a Norwegian shipping magnate and horse-racing taipan who decided to build himself a castle of wondrous Gothic steeples and spires, a house of eclectic styles on a grand scale that epitomizes the excesses of colonial Shanghai. Unfortunately, it can only be admired at a distance, as it's the headquarters of the Shanghai Committee of the Chinese Communist Youth League, but one assumes that someday soon it will give into the entrepreneurial pressures of modernization and be converted to a museum-quality shopping center or restaurant, open at last to the curious traveler.

Shanghai History Museum (Shanghai Lishi Bowuguan). 1286 Hongqiao Lu, Changning District. ☎ **021/6275-5595.** Admission 10RMB ($1.20). Daily 9am–3:30pm. Located 2 blocks west of the Inner Ring Rd. (Zhongshan Xi Lu) and south of the Hongqiao Development Zone (Westin Tai Ping Yang Hotel area).

This museum's more than 1,000 rare exhibits tell the story of colonial Shanghai under European dominance from 1860 to 1949—but it was recently closed and its future is uncertain. The same goes for the adjacent Shanghai Money Museum, with its 13,000 coins, some dating back over 5,000 years. The Wanguo International Cemetery is located behind the History Museum, to the south; it contains the Soong Ching-ling Mausoleum, 21 Songyuan Lu (☎ **021/6278-8011**).

Shanghai Urban Planning Exhibition Hall. East side of People's Square, Huangpu District.

Scheduled to open to its exhibits to the public in 2000, this will be one of the world's largest museums dedicated to showcasing urban development. The five-story building, constructed of microlite glass, is 141 feet (43m) high, 10 feet (3m) higher than its sister building at the other end of the block, the Grand Theatre. The retail stores in the underground level (connecting to the subway stations on People's Square) are crafted in the style of 1930s Shanghai. Exhibits include virtual-reality headsets to show the sights, sounds, and smells of the future cityscape of Shanghai (on the second floor), a scale model of the city (third floor), and a film of Shanghai's development since the mid-19th century (fourth floor).

Site of the First National Congress of the Communist Party (Zhonggong Yidahuizhi). 374 Huangpi Nan Lu, Luwan District. ☎ **021/6328-1177.** Admission 3RMB (35¢). Daily 8:30–11am and 1–4pm (closed Mon and Thurs mornings). Located 3 blocks south of Huangpi Nan Lu Station (Metro Line 1); the actual entrance is around the corner at 76 Xingye Lu.

This stunning building of brick and marble contains the room where on July 23, 1921, Mao Zedong and 11 other Chinese revolutionaries organized the Communist party. The original teacups and ashtrays remain on the organizing table. The site also contains other galleries, all well lighted, with explanatory signs in English. Among the artifacts and displays are a Qing Dynasty bronze cannon, swords and daggers used by rebels during the Tai Ping and Small Swords rebellions in 19th-century Shanghai, and a boundary stone used to demarcate the entrance to the British Concession, dated May 8, 1899. The site is the historic anchor of the Taipingqiao Project, an urban-renewal zone covering 128 acres (52 hectares) and costing $3 billion. Hong Kong's Vincent Lo (of the Shui On Group) has undertaken the first phase, the Xin Tian Di (New Heaven and Earth) Project. The entire neighborhood is being transformed into a new Times Square of retail outlets, restaurants, and offices, all constructed in the traditional Shanghai style of stone-faced houses (*shikumen*), such as were built in the city a century ago. The initial phase, designed by Boston-based Wood & Zapata, is scheduled for completion in 2001.

✪ Soong Ching-ling's Former Residence (Song Qingling Guju). 1843 Huaihai Zhong Lu, Luwan District. ☎ **021/6437-6268.** Admission 8RMB (95¢). Daily 9–11am and 1–4:30pm. Located behind the wall on the south side of the street, near Tianping Lu intersection; look for guard box and ticket window at entrance.

Soong Ching-ling (1893 to 1981) is revered throughout China as a loyalist to the Communist cause. Born in Shanghai to a wealthy family, she married the founder of the Chinese Republic, Dr. Sun Yat-sen, in 1915. Her equally famous sister, Soong Mei-ling, married the president of the Republic, Chiang Kai-shek, whom she followed into exile to Taiwan when Mao triumphed in 1949. Soong Ching-ling stayed in China, where she held many important political and cultural posts in the Communist government.

This two-story white residence with green shutters, at the rear of the entry courtyard, served as her residence from 1948 to 1963. The 1920s villa, built by a Greek sea captain in the French Concession, is little changed; the rooms are much as Soong left them, including her upstairs office, her bedroom, and the bedroom of her devoted maid, Li Yan'e (although this floor is often closed to visitors). The original telephone is in the foyer, and also inside the house are books from her college days in Wellesley, Massachusetts; phonograph records; and photos and paintings. The backyard consists of a patio with wicker furniture and a spacious lawn. There are two black sedans in the garage, one presented to Soong by Stalin in 1952.

Sun Yat-sen's Former Residence (Sun Zhongshan Guju). 7 Xiangshan Lu, Luwan District. ☎ **021/6437-2954.** Admission 8RMB (95¢). Daily 9–4:30pm. Located 1 block north of Fuxing Zhong Lu on corner of Sinan Lu, 1 block west of Fuxing Park.

China's Sex Museum

Although seemingly unthinkable in this puritanical empire, where the sale of pornography is still punishable by death, Shanghai has nevertheless become the location of China's first official sex museum. The **Museum of Ancient Chinese Sex Culture** opened discreetly in 1999 on the eighth floor of the old Sincere Building, overlooking the Nanjing Road Pedestrian Mall, 479 Nanjing Dong Lu (☎ **021/6351-4381**). It operates daily from 10am to 9pm, charges a relatively hefty 50RMB ($6) admission, and can be reached only via a special elevator located in an alley on the west side of the building. The creation of Professor Liu Dalin of Shanghai University, the museum displays most of his private collection of more than 1,200 sex artifacts. Professor Liu has shown his collection internationally, and sporadically in China since 1993, but this is the gallery's first permanent home. The new museum, with its own retail store and coffee shop, is divided by topic into 10 sections, each well displayed and annotated in English. The wide array of sexual relics includes ancient tomb paintings, statuary, and erotic devices, including a pottery penis with a woman's head dating back to 2,000 B.C. Among the more unusual exhibits are those devoted to foot binding, furniture designed to enhance lovemaking, "sensual Buddhas" (erotic religious figures), and "trunk bottoms" (explicit china figures placed at the bottom of dowry trunks by parents to instruct prospective brides). The museum's purpose, explains Professor Liu, is "to further abandon sex mystery," although visitors from the West will probably find much that is enigmatic here.

Sun Yat-sen (1866 to 1925), beloved founder of the Chinese Republic (1911), lived here with his wife, Soong Ching-ling, from June 1918 to November 1924, when the address would have been No. 29, Rue de Moliere. Here, Sun's wife later met with such literary stars as Lu Xun and George Bernard Shaw (at the same dinner party) and political leaders including Vietnam's Ho Chi Minh (in 1933). Visitors enter through the kitchen on the way to the dining room, passing a photo of Sun and his wife with the first airplane ever assembled in China (1923). A recording in English, played by a resident guide, describes some of the rooms. Upstairs is Sun's study, complete with ink stone, brushes, maps drawn by Sun, and a library of 2,700 volumes. The bedroom contains an embroidery of a cat with extraordinary eyes that follow visitors, while the drawing room has an original "Zhongshan" suit, similar to the later Mao suit. The backyard has a charming garden.

Zhou En-lai's Former Residence (Zhou Gong Guan). 73 Sinan Lu, Luwan District. ☎ **021/6473-0420.** Admission 2RMB (25¢). Daily 9–11:30am and 1–5pm. Located 2 blocks south of Fuxing Zhong Lu, east side, directly south of the Sun Yat-sen residence.

China's most revered leader during the Mao years, Premier Zhou En-lai (1898 to 1976) moved to this house in 1946. His old black Buick is still parked in the garage. The backyard has a small courtyard garden, where there's a statue of Zhou. Inside are numerous photographs of Zhou, although all explanatory signs are in Chinese only. The house was used more as an office than residence, and it served before the revolution as the Communist party's Shanghai office. Zhou kept a spartan room on the first floor (his threadbare blankets are neatly folded on the bed), newspapers were produced on the second floor, and a dorm was maintained in the attic.

8 Additional Attractions

Many of Shanghai's top attractions aren't easily categorized. The city's many Children's Palaces and the world's tallest hotel are examples of the many unusual sights one can view in Shanghai.

Children's Municipal Palace (Shi Shaonian Gong). 64 Yan'an Xi Lu, Jing An District. ☎ **021/6248-1850.** Free admission. Usually open Sat; call ahead for schedule and appointments. Located near Huashan Lu intersection, north of Hilton Hotel.

Children's Palaces offer after-school programs geared to enrich high-achieving children with advanced instruction in music, art, science, sports, and computers. The idea was forwarded by China's honorary president, Soong Ching-ling, who lived in Shanghai, which is where Children's Palaces are most common. Of the two dozen in the city, this one is perhaps the largest and certainly the most visited. The huge building was actually once the Kadoorie Mansion, known in colonial Shanghai as the Marble Hall. One of the pleasures in touring a Children's Palace in Shanghai, in addition to meeting children and peeking in on their classes-in-progress, is the setting: these European-style mansions are very little changed from the 1920s and 1930s. In order to tour a Children's Palace, usually in the company of one or two of the children who are practicing their English, you need to call ahead for an appointment or make arrangements through CITS or your hotel concierge.

Another charming Children's Palace open to visitors is at 75 Wuxing Lu, a block west of Hengshan Lu in a very trendy neighborhood of the Xuhui District.

Grand Theatre (Da Ju Yuan). 300 Renmin Da Dao, People's Square, Huangpu District. ☎ **021/6372-8701** or 021/6372-3833. Admission 50RMB ($6). Tours daily 9am and 1pm. Located on west side of People's Square, north of the Shanghai Museum, west of the People's Plaza Station (Metro Lines 1 and 2).

Boasting the largest stage in the world, Shanghai's Grand Theatre is a space-age complex with three theaters, the largest seating 1,800. It has quickly become the city's premier venue for international performances, dramas, and concerts. Back-stage tours (conducted in English and Chinese), which last over 2 hours, can be booked at the theater's ticket office or through your hotel.

✪ Huxinting Teahouse (Huxinting Chashi). 257 Yu Yuan Lu, Nanshi District. ☎ **021/6373-6950.** Free admission. Daily 8:30am–10pm. In the center of the Old Town Bazaar.

China's quintessential teahouse has floated atop the lake at the heart of Old Town, in front of Yu Gardens, since 1784, built by area cotton-cloth merchants as a brokerage hall. Tea drinking inside was forbidden for almost a century, until the late 1800s, when it became what it is today. Many visitors believe it was the original model for Blue Willow tableware; at the very least, it certainly looks the part. Huxinting (meaning "mid-lake pavilion") is reached via the traditional Bridge of Nine Turnings, so designed to deflect evil spirits who are said to travel only in straight lines. The five-sided, two-story pavilion with uplifted eaves and turrets has served everyone from visiting heads of state to local laborers. It's the place in Shanghai to idle over a cup of green tea, seated in front of the open windows. The first floor is a tea shop, the second a cafe.

Jin Mao Tower (Jin Mao Ta). 2 Shiji Da Dao, Pudong New Area. Admission 50RMB ($6). Daily 9am–10pm. Located 3 blocks southeast of the Pearl of the Orient TV Tower, across from Lujiazui Station (Metro Line 2).

This is the tallest building in China, and it looks it. Jin Mao also has a public observation deck at the top with views to rival those of the nearby Pearl of the Orient TV

Tower (and its admission charge is only half as much). Currently the third-highest building in the world at 1,379 feet (420.5m), the Jin Mao Tower, completed in 1998, boasts 88 floors (the upper stories encasing the world's highest hotel, the Grand Hyatt). Built on a former river delta, engineers had to drive pilings 328 feet (100m) down to reach bedrock. The tower's exterior, that of a tapered skyscraper, is meant to evoke the first Chinese skyscrapers—the ancient pagodas. This modern pagoda consists of 13 distinct, tapering segments. The high-tech steel bands that bind the glass like an exoskeleton represent bands of bamboo. The building is serviced by 60 elevators and 19 escalators. Tourists enter on the east side, pass through the Food Live food court (with nine international open kitchens), and are directed to the two high-speed elevators on Level B1, which take just 45 seconds to rocket to the top. The view from here is almost too high, but exquisite on a clear day. Vertigo sufferers, be reassured: even the strongest winds have caused a sway at the top of no more than 29 inches (75cm).

✪ **Peace Hotel (Heping Fandian).** 20 Nanjing Dong Lu, Huangpu District. ☎ **021/ 6321-6888.** Located on the Bund.

Shanghai's number-one architectural landmark, this is an Art Deco palace, with a lobby, suites, ballroom, and rooftop that define romantic colonial Shanghai. It began as the Sassoon House in 1929, the private residence of Ellice Victor Sassoon, heir to the family's Shanghai real-estate fortune, and became the Cathay Hotel, one of the world's finest international hotels in the 1930s. Take a stroll through the wings of the old lobby, then ride the elevator to the top to see the "Nine Nations" suites, usually open for viewing and each decorated in a national style (American, Chinese, English, French, German, Indian, Italian, Spanish, Turkish). Walk from here up to the roof and the new garden bar for a superb view of the Bund, Nanjing Road, the hotel's famous pyramid roof, and the Huangpu River (the same view enjoyed by the world's celebrities in the 1930s).

✪ **Pearl of the Orient TV Tower (Dongfang Mingzhu Dianshi Tai).** 2 Lujiazui Lu, Pudong New Area. ☎ **021/5879-1888.** Admission 100RMB ($12). Daily 8am–9pm. Located 2 blocks east of the Huangpu River, 1 block west of Lujiazui Station (Metro Line 2).

Asia's tallest structure, this high-tech tower with its rising spheres (known locally as "twin dragons playing with pearls") affords startling panoramic views of all of Shanghai. Handbags must be checked near the ticket booth before entering the high-speed elevators; the elevator attendant recites TV tower statistics in English and Chinese during the rapid quarter-mile (0.4km) ascent. The tower's lower spheres contain shopping areas, restaurants, and even a hotel. The circular observation deck at the top (elevation 1,550 feet/468m) is equipped with telescopes.

Shanghai Arts and Crafts Research Institute (Shanghai Gongyi Meishu Yanjiusuo Jiugong Yipin Xiufu Bu). 79 Fenyang Lu, Luwan District. ☎ **021/6437-3454.** Free admission. Daily 8:30am–4:30pm. Located on the east side of the Yueyang/Taojiang intersection, southeast of Chang Shu Station (Metro Line 1).

This French Concession mansion, owned by a French general, and former residence of Chen Yi, Shanghai's first mayor after Liberation (1949), gives a fine, unretouched picture of how the colonials lived in old Shanghai. At the same time, its many rooms have been converted to workshops in which you can watch craftspeople produce traditional handicrafts and art works, including paper cuts and embroidery. A salesroom is attached.

Colonial Shanghai, 21st-Century Style

The new Shanghai, it appears, has its own "foreign concessions," just as old colonial Shanghai did a century earlier. Only this time, the neighborhood is not carved out of the city by force of arms or international treaty, but by economics, the new world order, and savvy real-estate developers. The result is **Gubei New Town,** a semi-planned community designed to house and service expatriate businesspeople and their families in style and comfort. It's located in Changning District, near the zoo and Hongqiao Airport, in a subdivision bounded by Hongqiao Lu, Hong Xu Lu, Gubei Lu, and Guyang Lu. You can see the results by taking a stroll on **Shui Cheng Lu,** the main street that runs due south from the Gubei Gate on busy Hongqiao Lu. On either side are gated and fenced condominium-like towers bearing names like "Rotterdam Garden," "Golden Lion," "Mandarine City," and "Rome Garden." There's plenty of neo-Greek and -Roman white-plaster statuary to match these grand European images. The housing here would not be out of place on the Las Vegas strip.

The stores, shops, plazas, and restaurants are decidedly upscale and international, too. Walking the length of the main street (less than a mile), you'll pass a Manabe coffeehouse (with picture menus), the swank new New Yorker Café, a McDonald's, a Gino Cafe, a Linhua Supermarket, and a giant Carrefour international megastore. The main shopping squares, **Vanke Plaza** and **Golden Lion Plaza,** contain Mexican restaurants, French cafes, beauty salons, foreign-language bookstores, pizza joints, ice-cream shops, loads of Japanese restaurants, furniture stores, and mall kiosks selling arts and crafts and "folk" snacks. This could be a subdivision in any well-to-do suburb in the West, except for the occasional bicycle-powered delivery vehicle in the streets (fighting for space with a chauffeur-driven Mercedes) and the sign posted at the entrance to the Vanke Plaza's pedestrian courtyard that reads in English ON THE WALKING SQUARE, RIDING BIKES AND MOTHS ARE FORBIDDEN.

Shanghai Library (Shanghai Tushuguan). 1557 Huaihai Zhong Lu, Xuhui District. ☎ **021/6445-5555.** Free admission. Daily 8:30am–8:30pm. Located between Wulumuqi Zhong Lu and Hunan Lu, 6 blocks west of Chang Shu Lu Station (Metro Line 1), past the American consulate.

Opened in 1996, the new city library is a state-of-the-art facility with many modern reading rooms, including one devoted to foreign periodicals. The collection includes almost two million rare scrolls, manuscripts, and books that can be viewed upon request. Downstairs, west of the main entrance, is an Internet room, popular with local students.

Shanghai Stock Exchange (Shanghai Zhengquan Jiaoyisuo). 528 Pudong Nan Lu, Pudong New Area. ☎ **021/6880-8888.** Mon–Fri 9–11:30am and 1–4pm. Located in the Shanghai Securities Exchange Building, south of the Lujiazui Central Green and Metro Line 2 station.

Opened in 1992, the Shanghai Stock Exchange is China's largest. It recently moved to this new building in the heart of Pudong, Shanghai's Wall Street. While visitors aren't permitted on the trading floor, a tour of the exchange can be arranged through your hotel desk.

9 Especially for Kids

In a country known for the emphasis it places on the family, attractions for children are commonplace. Some attractions listed elsewhere in this chapter, such as the Pearl of the Orient TV Tower, the Jin Mao Tower, and the Shanghai Arts and Crafts Research Institute, will amuse the kids. The following are some that should appeal particularly to younger foreign travelers (and often their parents, too).

Aquaria 21. 451 Daduhe Lu, Changning District. ☎ **021/5281-8888.** Admission 80RMB ($10) adults, 60RMB ($7) children under 55 inches (1.4m), free for children under 39 inches (1m). Daily 9am–6pm. Located west of the Inner Ring Road in Chang Feng Park (entrance at Gate 4).

Shanghai's best aquarium (designed by a New Zealand company) features a "touch pool" so kids can mingle with the sea life (crabs, starfish, urchins, shrimp). The main tank, built under Yinchu Lake, is stocked with sea horses, tuna, turtles, and patrolling sharks (who are fed daily by keepers in diving suits). There's also an arena of penguins from Peru and Chile. In fact, you can journey through a series of ocean habitats, from the Amazon River to Antarctica, highlighted by a trip through the all-encompassing shark tunnel.

Dino Beach. 78 Xin Zhen Lu, Minghang District. ☎ **021/6478-3333.** Admission RMB40 ($4.80) Mon–Fri, 60RMB ($7) Sat–Sun; children under 59 inches (1.5m) half price; free for toddlers. June–Sept daily 9am–9pm. Located in southwest Shanghai's Qibao Town, off the Shanghai–Hangzhou Highway; regular shuttle buses from Shanghai Stadium and the Hongmei Lu and Xin Zhuang Metro Stations.

The best water park in Shanghai, this is the place to go for water-slide and "beach-wave" enthusiasts. Scenery consists of model snowcapped mountain peaks and plastic dinosaurs. The wave pool covers 2 acres, Asia's largest; the longest of the eight water slides is almost 500 feet (150m). There are also three swimming pools for kids, a mile-long river with rapids, and organized beach volleyball and water-polo games. Add six fast-food outlets, including a branch of Church's Chicken from Atlanta, and this is the closest thing to an American-style water park you'll find in China.

✪ Great World (Da Shi Jie). 1 Xizang Nan Lu, Huangpu District. ☎ **021/6326-3760,** ext. 40, or 021/6374-6703. Admission 25RMB ($3). Daily 9am–9:30pm. Located southeast of People's Square at corner of Yan'an Dong Lu.

This infamous gambling and vice den of the 1920s and 1930s has been converted into an entertainment center for the entire family, its rooms and floors now stuffed with dozens of attractions, from bumper cars to fortune tellers. There's a Guinness Book of World Records gallery and video-game salon on the third floor; folk-dancing performances and movies on the fourth floor; and a Children's Palace on the fifth floor. The live performances run all day from 9am to 6pm. Evening shows start at 7:30pm, when acrobatic and martial-arts troupes perform on the outdoor stage in back while opera and comedy mime teams perform on the second-floor stage indoors. This distinct baroque tower with its wedding-cake tiers of white columns was built in 1915 by Huang Chujiu for the entertainment of the rich.

Jin Jiang Amusement Park. 201 Hongmei Lu, Xuhui District. ☎ **021/6436-4956.** Admission 40RMB ($4.80); includes 5 rides. Daily 8:30am–9pm. Located on the northwest side of Huming Lu, near Gongmei Lu Station (Metro Line 1).

Shanghai's most complete modern amusement park, the Jin Jiang has rides such as a loop-the-loop roller coaster, merry-go-round, and bumper cars, as well as a haunted house. There's a special playground for preschoolers, too. The "Gorge Drifting Waterland" is a park within the park, a water-sports area requiring a separate additional admission (30RMB/$3.60) and maintaining separate hours, daily from 10am to 4:30pm.

Ocean World. 666 Tian Yao Qiao Lu, Xuhui District. ☎ **021/6426-6068.** Admission 40RMB ($4.80) Mon–Fri, 50RMB ($6) Sat–Sun. Mon–Fri 1–9pm, Sat–Sun 10am–9pm. Located inside Shanghai Stadium at Shanghai Stadium Station (Metro Line 1).

This water world is entirely indoors and particularly geared toward preschoolers. Most pools are shallow enough for nonswimmers, and lifeguards are always on duty. There's a wading stream with Jacuzzi-jet seats, a wave beach, slides, fountains, and seesaws. For lunch, the Regal International East Asia Hotel's Top of the World Café is also in the stadium complex.

⭐ **Shanghai Circus World.** 2266 Gong He Xin Lu, Zhabei District. ☎ **021/5665-3646** or 021/6652-2395. Tickets 50RMB–150RMB ($6–$18); "VIP" seats 280RMB ($34). Performances Tues, Fri, Sat 7:30pm; Sun 2pm. Located north of the Railway Station and the Inner Ring Rd. (Zhongshan Bei Lu), near Zhabei Park.

This glittering new arena, opened in the northern suburbs in 1999, supplies Shanghai with a much needed world-class venue for acrobatic and circus performances. The large gold-and-green superdome, fashioned from an aluminum-titanium alloy, houses a circus theater with computer-controlled lighting and state-of-the-art acoustics that seats 1,672. The motorized revolving stage, covering 1,300 square feet (120m²), is equipped for elaborate sets and special lighting effects. The complex also includes a 16,577-square-foot (1,540m²) animal house with rooms for elephants, tigers, lions, chimps, horses, and pandas. The celebrated Shanghai Acrobatic Troupe inaugurated the new arena with 2 months of sold-out 20-act performances. Check with your hotel for the current performers, schedules, and tickets.

Shanghai Natural History Museum (Shanghai Ziran Bowuguan). 260 Yan'an Dong Lu. ☎ **021/ 6321-3548.** Admission 5RMB–16RMB (60¢–$1.90), depending on age. Daily 9–4:30pm. Located on the north side of the Yan'an Lu overpass, just east of Henan Nan Lu.

Built in 1956 and showing its age, this museum's highlights are its collections of animals, mummies, and fossils, including, in the central atrium, a complete specimen of a 140-million-year-old dinosaur skeleton from Sichuan Province. From here, head upstairs to the aquarium and, on the top floor, a gallery of stuffed creatures.

Shanghai Wild Animal Park. San Zao Township, Nanhui County, Pudong New Area. ☎ **021/5803-6000.** Admission 70RMB ($8) adults, 35RMB ($4.20) children under 47 inches (1.2m). Daily 8am–5pm. Located in east Pudong on the way to the new international airport.

Shanghai's only drive-through safari is located far to the east in Pudong, well beyond the new financial district. At least the tigers, lions, zebras, giraffes, camels, bears, elephants, and flamingos have some legroom here. Buses transport visitors through the grounds, home to 5,000 animals (130 species). The Children's Garden has a petting zoo.

Shanghai Zoo (Shanghai Dongwu Yuan). 2831 Hongqiao Lu, Changning District. ☎ **021/6268-7775.** Admission 24RMB ($2.90). Nov–Feb daily 7am–4:30pm; Mar and Oct daily 7am–5pm; Apr–May daily 6:30am–5pm; June–Sept daily 6:30am–5:30pm. Located a mile (1.6km) west of the Hongqiao Airport.

The zoo, one of China's best, is improving, but it still has a long way to go to rival the best preserves in the West. It was originally a private estate of the Sassoon

An American Nightmare

When the **American Dream Park** opened in Shanghai in 1997, it was a smash hit, but daily attendance rapidly dwindled down to a few dozen. Lowering ticket prices from 100RMB ($12) to just 20RMB ($2.40) just didn't help. The American dream became the Shanghai nightmare. This former theme park, located in the northern Shanghai suburb of Jiading, at 4498 Cao An Lu, cost $6 million to build, but lacked an operating budget. The toilets reeked and it seems the rides stank, too. "Although it provides Western-style atmosphere," one Shanghai parkgoer told the local press, "it does not provide Western-style excitement." The five theme areas (Main Street USA, USA Today, Children's Treasure Island, American Heritage Area, The Wild West) failed to compensate for the lack of green spaces and scenic sights that Shanghai city dwellers crave. This American theme park was really just a big parking lot; by 2000, after just 3 years in operation, the park closed, and the American Dream had become a ghost town.

family, and then a city golf course, before its conversion to a zoo in 1954. There are plenty of open spaces for children to play and adults to picnic or feed the pigeons, but the spaces for animals are quite confined. The tigers and other big cats are penned in old-fashioned concrete canyons; the panda center, a 20-minute stroll northwest from the entrance, has small indoor and outdoor areas. Altogether, the zoo is home to about 6,000 specimens (600 species), as well as a children's zoo and recreation center with playground equipment.

10 Organized Tours

Most Shanghai hotels have tour desks that can arrange a variety of day tours for guests. These tour desks are often extensions of **China International Travel Service (CITS),** with its head offices near the Bund at 2 Jinling Dong Lu (☎ 021/6321-7200), and its best branch for independent travelers located near Shanghai Centre at 1277 Beijing Xi Lu (☎ 021/6289-7827 or 021/6289-8899). CITS operates most of the English-language group tours in Shanghai, even those you book through your hotel. The only reason to go directly to the CITS office is to arrange a special tour, perhaps of sites not offered on the regular group-tour list, or for a private tour with guide, driver, and car.

Group tours are inexpensive, convenient, and efficiently organized—ideal if you are new to the city and have little time. These tours cost about 250RMB to 400RMB ($30 to $48) per person. The **Jin Jiang Optional Tours Center,** located near the Jin Jiang and Garden hotels at 191 Changle Lu (☎ 021/6445-9525; fax 021/6472-0184), offers a typical group tour of Shanghai by bus, with English-speaking guide and lunch, for 250RMB ($30); sites include Yu Garden, the Bund, Jin Mao Tower, Jade Buddha Temple, and People's Square. Jin Jiang offers similar 1-day group tours to Suzhou (350RMB/$42), Zhou Zhuang water village (350RMB/$42), and Hangzhou (500RMB/$60). Hotel desks have a wider range of group-tour itineraries to select from, but at higher prices than those offered by the Jin Jiang Optional Tours Center.

Group tours aren't for everyone. They are rushed, and at major sites, group-tour participants are shown only a fraction of what's there. A good guide can outline the history and culture of a place, but you'll usually get no more than an hour to see a major site. Most of the commentary is delivered during the bus ride. If you want additional commentary at a particular site, it's a good idea to stick close to the guide.

CITS and other travel agencies can arrange in-depth **private tours,** customized to fit your itinerary or interest (such as education, art, food, or the martial arts). These tours include an English-speaking guide, driver, and private car for the day. The Jin Jiang Optional Tours Center, for example, offers a full-day private tour of the city, including door-to-door service, air-conditioned company car, English-speaking guide, and lunch, at a cost of 950RMB ($114) for one person, 550RMB ($66) each for two people, or 480RMB ($58) each for three or four people.

Travel agencies and hotel tour desks can act as ticketing agents for nighttime entertainment, too, such as acrobatics, the opera, the circus, the Peace Hotel Jazz Bar, and Huangpu River cruises.

In addition to CITS and Jin Jiang, another proven private travel agency providing group day tours, private tours, tickets, and hotel bookings to international clients is the **Shanghai Spring International Travel Service,** 1556 Dingxi Lu (☎ **021/6251-5777;** fax 021/6252-3734; www.china-sss.com), which also maintains a 24-hour **Tourist Information Line** (☎ **021/6252-0000**).

11 Outdoor Pursuits

Most visitors to Shanghai do not come intending to pursue outdoor recreation or sports, but there is a wide range of such activities. Hotels provide exercise equipment and limited court sports, routinely offering exercise machines, weights, aerobics and workout areas, swimming pools, locker rooms, and, less often, tennis and squash courts, all at little or no charge to their guests. It is possible to use the fitness facilities and courts of some hotels on a daily basis, too, even if you are not a guest (although the fees can be steep).

Some pursuits, such as jogging, require little in the way of facilities. Runners and joggers in Shanghai can always take to the early-morning streets (before the crowds block them), but the public parks are much nicer places for a run. No one bats an eye at runners these days; Shanghai, after all, has its own annual international marathon, the Toray Cup (in mid-Nov).

Golf, bowling, and billiards have become the three most popular recreational sports in Shanghai, pursued by well-to-do locals, foreign residents, and overseas visitors. Kite flying, traditional tai ji quan, and even go-cart racing can also be enjoyed if time and energy allow.

Spectator sports, on the other hand, are more limited and less to Western tastes, although professional basketball, interleague soccer, and international badminton and volleyball matches draw large crowds to Shanghai Stadium.

BOWLING Bowling experienced a boom in China during the 1990s, when more than 15,000 alleys were built, many of them in Shanghai. There are good alleys in the Cypress, Equatorial, Hua Ting, Jin Jiang, Nikko Pudong, Novotel, Radisson SAS Lansheng, Regal International East Asia, and other hotels. The **Buckingham Bowling Hall** (☎ **021/5681-9988**) on Dingxi Lu, across from the Westin Crowne Plaza Hotel, is popular with foreign residents. Rates run from 10RMB to 30RMB ($1.20 to $3.60) at Shanghai bowling halls, depending on the quality of the facility and the time of day (the later, the more expensive); shoe rentals toe the line at 5RMB to 10RMB (60¢ to $1.20).

CLIMBING Climbers should check out the **Mastermind Climbing Club,** located in Hongkou Stadium at 444 Dongjiangwan Lu, Hongkou District

(☎ 021/5696-6657). The six walls are available daily from 10am to 10pm at a cost of 40RMB ($4.80) per day, with all equipment (except shoes) provided.

EXTREME SPORTS   Those interested in bungee jumping from the ceiling of Shanghai Stadium can now do so through the **Extreme Sports Center,** Suite 2303, 666 Tian Yao Qiao Lu, Xuhui District (☎ 021/6426-5535), open daily from 1 to 9pm. One jump (230 ft./70m) costs 180RMB ($22); a reverse jump, from the ground to the sky, 150RMB ($18); and "sky gliding," just RMB100 ($12). The center hopes to add a skateboard park and a rock-climbing wall to its facilities.

GO-CARTING   The best tracks to take a Formula One drive in miniature are the **Shanghai Fushida Racing Car Club,** 880 Zhongshan Bei Yi Lu (☎ 021/6531-6800), and **SSC Karting Club,** in Shanghai Stadium, 666 Tian Yao Qiao Lu (☎ 021/6426-5116), which is open daily from 10am to 3am. At the SSC Karting Club, drivers receive printouts of their times; cost is 40RMB ($4.80) for 8 minutes on the track until 7pm, when the price goes up to 50RMB ($6) for 8 minutes in the fast lane.

GOLF (GAOERFU)   Greens fees at Shanghai's dozen or more golf courses run from 250RMB to 830RMB ($30 to $100) Monday to Friday, from 625RMB to 1,250RMB ($75 to $150) on Saturday and Sunday. Caddies cost 85RMB to 170RMB ($10 to $20) and club rental 250RMB to 330RMB ($30 to $40). All courses require advance reservations; summer weekends are particularly crowded.

Two courses located an hour west of Shanghai in Qingpu County are the **Sun-Island Golf Club,** Shenxiang Town (☎ 021/5983-1863 or 021/5983-0888, ext. 8033), open daily from 8:30am to 4:30pm; and the world-class, Robert Trent Jones–designed **Shanghai International Golf and Country Club,** Xinyang Village, Zhujiajiao Town (☎ 021/5972-8111), open Wednesday to Monday from 9am to 5pm.

Two courses located an hour northwest of Shanghai in Jiading County are the **Shanghai Riviera Golf Resort,** 277 Yangzi Lu, Nanxiang Town (☎ 021/5912-6888), a Bobby J. Martin–designed course with a driving range and year-round night golfing, open Tuesday to Friday from 9am to 10pm and Saturday and Sunday from 8am to 10pm; and the **Shanghai Golf Club,** Shuangtang Village, Tanghang Town (☎ 021/5995-0111), open Tuesday to Friday from 8am to 5pm, Saturday and Sunday from 7am to 5pm.

The Pudong New Area has three good courses: the 18-hole Jack Nicklaus–designed **Shanghai Links Golf and Country Club,** 1600 Lingbai Lu (☎ 021/5897-3068), open Tuesday to Sunday from 8am to 4pm; the **Tomson Golf Club,** 1 Longdong Lu, open Monday from 1 to 10pm and Tuesday to Sunday from 8am to 10pm, with reservations through the New Asia Tomson Hotel (☎ 021/5831-8888); and Shanghai's only 54-hole course, the **Shanghai Binhai Golf Club,** Binhai, Nanhui (☎ 021/5805-8888), near the new airport (call for hours).

A convenient driving range in the French Concession is the **Shanghai East Asia Golf Practicing Club,** 135 Jianguo Xi Lu, Luwan District (☎ 021/6433-1198), open Monday to Saturday from 6 to 11pm, Sunday from 1 to 11pm.

HEALTH CLUBS   Some hotels offer day rates to nonguests. The **Hilton Hotel** (☎ 021/6248-0000) charges 250RMB ($30) per day to outsiders, for example, while the **Cypress Hotel's Longbai Club** (☎ 021/6268-8868) charges 150RMB ($18) per day. The most complete range of fitness facilities is offered by the **Shanghai International Tennis Centre Club,** attached to the Regal International East Asia Hotel, 516 Hengshan Lu, Xuhui District (☎ 021/6415-5588), with its

---

The Race to the Top

The ninth day of the ninth month on the Chinese lunar calendar is traditionally observed with a festival devoted to mountains and mountain climbing. In Shanghai, not noted for its peaks, the day was recently marked by a race to the top of the city's (and Asia's) highest skyscraper, the 88-story Jin Mao Tower. While some runners required oxygen infusions, the winner, Hua Xiao, made the 1,400-foot climb in under 15 minutes. You can post your own time (during the annual Shanghai Tourism Festival in late Oct) when a "climbing contest" is held here, or simply take the stairs rather than the 45-second elevator to Shanghai's highest indoor summit.

25-meter indoor lap pool, aerobics rooms, exercise machines, and superb indoor and outdoor tennis and squash courts (open daily from 6:30am to 11:30pm). Among private fitness clubs, two of the best (also two of the newest) are **CITIGYM,** Shui On Plaza, 8th floor, 333 Huaihai Zhong Lu, Luwan District (☎ 021/ 5306-6868), and **Gold's Gym,** near Shanghai Centre at 258 Tongren Lu, Jing An District (☎ 021/6279-2000). CITIGYM, open Monday to Saturday from 6:30am to 10:30pm and Sunday from 10am to 6:30pm, has plenty of exercise equipment and regular aerobics classes (RMB75/$9 per class). Gold's, open 24 hours a day, offers exercise machines, weights, aerobics rooms, and personal trainers.

KITE FLYING   Chinese have been flying their invention for more than 2,000 years. The best places to buy and to fly local Shanghai kites are in the public parks and in People's Square in front of the Shanghai Museum.

TAI CHI (TAI JI QUAN)   These venerable and graceful "shadow-boxing" exercises, which tens of thousands of Shanghainese practice every morning before work, and Wu Shu, the martial-arts forms developed in China, can be learned at the **Shanghai Wushu Center,** 595 Nanjing Xi Lu, Huangpu District (☎ 021/ 6215-3599).

SPECTATOR SPORTS

Check local listings or your hotel desk for current sports in town. The **Chinese National Basketball League (CNBL)** has been building a strong following across China since its inception in 1994. Each team is allowed to hire two foreign players (usually Americans). The Shanghai team plays most of its home basketball games November through April in the Luwan Gymnasium, 128 Jiaozhabang Lu (☎ 021/ 6427-8673).

Shanghai Stadium, 666 Tianyaoqiao Lu, Xuhui District (☎ 021/6426-6666 or 021/6426-6888, ext. 8268), is the usual venue for big sporting events (soccer, track and field). **Shanghai Zhabei Stadium,** 2100 Gonghexin Lu, Changning District (☎ 021/5665-7626), is a popular venue for rugby tournaments.

Shanghai Strolls

7

Despite its immense and dense population, Shanghai is one of China's great cities to stroll. Much of the street-level fascination comes from the European architecture left over from colonial days (1842 to 1949), when Shanghai was sliced up by the Western powers into foreign concessions. Shanghai's present cityscape is an amalgam of Art Deco mansions from that colonial period, *longtangs* (walled brick town-house rows) with distinctive *shikumen* (stone gates) from the local Chinese tradition, and malls of towering glass and steel from international modernism.

Walking Shanghai involves a few obstacles. Street signs are sometimes difficult to spot and interpret, addresses are omitted from buildings, and the sidewalks are crowded not only with other pedestrians, but also with bicycle parking lots, construction sites, vendors and their carts, card players, laundry strung between doors and trees, cars brazenly parked on walkways, and motorcycles and bicycles zooming up and down the sidewalks as though they were extensions of the streets. This is heads-up walking, exhilarating but tiring. Half a day's walk is often plenty. You may return to your room feeling not so much exhausted as bruised—bruised by the polluted air and dust, the raw odors, the jarring sounds, the slamming crowds, the grinding obstacle course.

The strolls described in this chapter are rewarding but require vigilance. Remember that cars have the right of way even when they shouldn't. The basic rule of survival on foot: *Cars always have the right of way, even when you have a green light, so look both ways and always be prepared to yield.* Adjust to the flow of Shanghai residents. They know how and when to proceed across the intersections. Follow, don't lead; slow down; and savor these walks through China's biggest, most densely packed city, where the past and the future, and the East and West, meet at every corner. Despite these warnings, the best way to see Shanghai is on foot.

Walking Tour 1: Nanjing Road

Start: Shanghai Centre (subway: Jing An).
Finish: Peace Hotel, the Bund (subway: Huangpu).
Time: 3 to 4 hours (to cover 4¹/₂ miles/7km).
Best times: Any weekday starting at 9:30am or at 2:30pm to avoid the midday crowds.

Worst times: Sunday is quite crowded, and Saturday isn't much better. Most stores aren't open before 9:30am, but they stay open late, often until 10pm.

Nanjing Road is the most famous shopping avenue in China, long celebrated for its large department stores, silk shops, and fashionable clothing stores. Nanjing Road West was known in colonial Shanghai as Bubbling Well Road, the domain of carpet salesmen and clairvoyants; Nanjing Road East, built largely as a pathway to successive horse-race tracks, became dominated with silk shops, luxury hotels, and huge department stores. It still has remnants of its past retail glories, but the department stores have been modernized and Western-style boutiques are rapidly cornering the fashion trade. There are still plenty of colonial period structures sandwiched in along the avenue (hotels, offices, department stores). **People's Park** is the halfway point, dividing **Nanjing Xi Lu** (the western portion of the avenue) from **Nanjing Dong Lu** (the avenue east to the Bund and Huangpu River). If you want to save your legs, begin your stroll at People's Park and head east for the river. The new, easy-to-stroll **Nanjing Road Pedestrian Mall** begins just east of People's Park at Xizang Zhong Lu and continues to within 2 blocks of the Bund at Henan Zhong Lu. You can walk either the east or west half of Nanjing Road in an hour or less, if you don't stop—but you will.

To begin, take a taxi or walk straight east from the Jing An subway station down Nanjing Xi Lu to:

1. **Shanghai Centre (Shanghai Shangcheng),** the premier office complex in Shanghai (at no. 1376, north side), with the Hard Rock Cafe on the west, the plush Shanghai Centre in the middle, and the 42-story Portman Ritz-Carlton Hotel towering over everything. This Western-style city-within-a-city contains expensive residential apartments (mostly for the families of foreign businesspeople), an American school, the city's top business center, and a raft of upscale boutiques. If you need a latte and bagel, grab one here at Espresso Americano.

Straight across the street is the:

2. **Shanghai Exhibition Centre (Shanghai Zhanlan Zhongxin),** 1000 Yan'an Lu, built in 1955 with help from the Soviet Union (then a staunch Communist ally). It displaced the 26-acre Hardoon Gardens, a colonial-era fantasy estate erected by a millionaire from Persia. The present somber yet grandiose monument to socialist realism is yet another chapter in Shanghai's history of foreign architecture, one that is best observed from afar. If you have plenty of time, however, you might enjoy crossing the street and inspecting its immense, decaying interiors, where a large but poorly organized arts-and-crafts store now presides.

Otherwise, head east along Nanjing Xi Lu past the new Plaza 66/Hanson Garden shopping plaza and cross the street south at Shaanxi Bei Lu to:

3. **Shanghai Jingdezhen Porcelain Artware** (no. 1185), on the corner, which carries a nicely displayed array of classic Chinese pottery and porcelain, much of it from factories and artisans in Jingdezhen, one of China's most celebrated pottery centers (located up the Yangzi River from Shanghai).

As you continue east along the south side of Nanjing Xi Lu, you'll pass some of the small shops that are changing the face of Shanghai shopping, including an ATM (no. 1141), a New Balance shoe store (no. 1131), and the improbable-but-true Playboy store (selling bunny-logo merchandise, not the magazine).

In the next block, across the street, is:

4. **Westgate Mall** (no. 1038), an upscale mall whose tenants include KFC, Burberry's, Watson's Drugstore, and Isetan department store. This is also the location of one of Shanghai's most famous local restaurants, Meilongzhen. In the

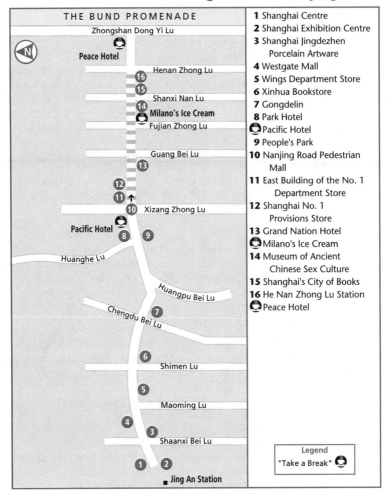

THE BUND PROMENADE

Zhongshan Dong Yi Lu

Peace Hotel

Henan Zhong Lu

16

15

Shanxi Nan Lu

14 Milano's Ice Cream

Fujian Zhong Lu

Guang Bei Lu

13

12

11 ↑

10

Xizang Zhong Lu

Pacific Hotel

8   **9**

Huanghe Lu

Huangpu Bei Lu

Chengdu Bei Lu

7

6

Shimen Lu

5

Maoming Lu

4

3

Shaanxi Bei Lu

1   **2**

Jing An Station

1 Shanghai Centre
2 Shanghai Exhibition Centre
3 Shanghai Jingdezhen Porcelain Artware
4 Westgate Mall
5 Wings Department Store
6 Xinhua Bookstore
7 Gongdelin
8 Park Hotel
Pacific Hotel
9 People's Park
10 Nanjing Road Pedestrian Mall
11 East Building of the No. 1 Department Store
12 Shanghai No. 1 Provisions Store
13 Grand Nation Hotel
Milano's Ice Cream
14 Museum of Ancient Chinese Sex Culture
15 Shanghai's City of Books
16 He Nan Zhong Lu Station
Peace Hotel

Legend
"Take a Break"

next block is a convenient entrance to the Shi Men Yi subway station, part of the new Metro Line 2 that runs under Nanjing Road.

The next 2 blocks are lined with red paper lanterns in the trees and many buildings from the 1920s and 1930s, although the street-level facades are up-to-date, including those on the:

5. **Wings Department Store** (no. 869), which is newly remodeled inside, and **Silk Fabrics King** (no. 819, open daily from 10am to 8:30pm), which is a typical and friendly Nanjing Road fabric store. Across the street, under the Shimen Yi Lu pedestrian overpass, is the **Marco Polo** bakery (no. 772), advertising "Bread from the Oven."

Beyond here, stay on the south side of the street to reach:

6. **Xinhua Bookstore** (no. 777), a state-run book dealer that offers a few English-language titles, and the **Lei Yun Pharmacy** (no. 719), a Chinese apothecary that claims to have been business since 1662. On the next corner, believe it or not, there's another KFC (15 Wunjian Lu), and then up ahead another skyscraper

complex, as big as its name, the **Shanghai Broadcasting & Television International News Exchange Centre.**

You're now ready to cross Chengdu Bei Lu, where there are two contrasting restaurants on the south side:

7. **Gongdelin** (no. 445), Shanghai's top vegetarian restaurant, with a take-out counter just inside the main entrance, and yet another **KFC** (no. 135), a two-story model, open daily from 9am to 11pm. Your time might be better spent on the other side of the street, at the **Shanghai Arts & Crafts Shopping Center** (no. 190), although the prices and selection are not stunning.

The next block skirts the entrance to People's Park on the south, but keep on the north side as you cross Huanghe Lu for a detour through the lobby of:

8. **Park Hotel (Guoji Fandian),** no. 170, with its finely restored Art Deco interiors. This is the hotel, built in 1934, that Chairman Mao favored. There's a Bank of China branch next door (no. 146) with an ATM that accepts major credit cards, followed by another historic hotel that's worth a peek.

🍵 **TAKE A BREAK** Stop for a cup of tea in the romantic lobby of the **Pacific Hotel (Jinmen Dajiudian),** no. 108, where there's yet another splendid Art Deco lobby of coffered ceilings and carved columns to admire. This lovely nine-story building was constructed in 1926, serving first as the China United Assurance Company, then as the Overseas Chinese Hotel. If you'd rather have a more familiar repast, immediately next door are two foreign fast-food outlets, a McDonald's (no. 90) and a Pizza Hut (no. 88).

If window shopping has worn you down, cross the street to the entrance of:

9. **People's Park (Renmin Gongyuan),** no. 231, the city's biggest downtown green, which together with People's Square covers what in colonial days was the Shanghai Racetrack.

People's Park is the halfway point. At the Xizang Zhong Lu Overpass, Nanjing Xi Lu becomes Nanjing Dong Lu and the wide vehicle-free:

10. ❂ **Nanjing Road Pedestrian Mall.** From here east to Henan Zhong Lu, 2 blocks from the Bund and the river, strollers can enjoy the new pedestrian-only mall, paved in red brick and marble, designed by Arle Jean Marie Carpentier and Associates (France), and opened on September 20, 1999. New buildings dwarf the colonial-period landmarks of Nanjing Road here, but there's still plenty of history along the way. *Caution:* Although this is a pedestrian mall, the cross streets (north-south) still permit vehicular traffic, so look both ways at controlled intersections.

The circular overpass at Xizang Zhong Lu is an excellent place to pause for an overview (and snapshots) of Nanjing Road and the **Mu'en Church** to the south. The overpass connects the modern **Nanjiren Department Store** and **New World City** (the former Shanghai No. 1 Department Store, at 830 Nanjing Dong Lu) on the northwest corner to the:

11. **East Building of the No. 1 Department Store** (no. 800) on the northeast corner of the pedestrian mall. In the old days, this emporium was known as **The Sun,** one of Nanjing Road's "Big Four" department stores. The Sun's building was designed by Chinese architects, opened its doors in 1934, and was the first store in China to use an escalator. Later, renamed the No. 1 Department Store complex, it attracted more than 150,000 shoppers daily; these days, it may doing more business than ever with the addition of the 22-story tower on its East Building, its first 11 floors devoted to retailing. Women's wear occupies the first three floors, men's wear is on the fourth floor, gifts and books on the fifth floor, house-wares on the sixth floor, and computer items on the ninth floor.

In the same block on the north side is the:

12. Shanghai No. 1 Provisions Store (no. 729), still in its old building, where it opened in 1926. It was formerly known as Sun Sun, one of Shanghai's "Big Four" department stores.

On the south side of the mall, half a block further east, is the brand-new:

13. Grand Nation Hotel (no. 700), with the most elegant European lobby in Shang-hai, worth a detour, followed by the **Hualian Department Store** (no. 635), for-merly the No. 10 Department Store and before that, in colonial days, the famous **Wing On** (a department-store chain transplanted to Hong Kong after 1949). Gold tinted glass now frames its entrance, part of a recent $24-million renova-tion. After opening in 1918, it became the first in town to use large display showcases.

At this point, the mall crosses a vast square at the busy intersection with Zhe-jiang Zhong Lu and Hubei Lu, site of an old hotel on the south corner, now known as the Seventh Heaven Hotel. On the north side of this block is an **Itokin** department store, followed by an underground **McDonald's** (no. 588) and an underground **KFC** (no. 558), but the best place for a break or lunch is farther east, across Fujian Zhong Lu, in the 30-story **Hotel Sofitel Hyland** (no. 505).

☕ **TAKE A BREAK**   Pause over coffee, tea, or ice cream in **Milano's Ice Cream,** located on the ground floor of the Hotel Sofitel Hyland, behind the huge picture windows right on the mall. For a more substantial meal and beer brewed on the premises, try the second-story **Brauhaus,** a Bavarian-style pub and eating hall with a fine view through a wall of windows on the Nanjing Road pedestrian mall.

The next big building to the east is the old **Sincere** department store (no. 479), one of Nanjing Road's original "Big Four" emporiums, now the unlikely site of:

14. The Museum of Ancient Chinese Sex Culture (no. 479, south street-side entrance, 8th floor, Sincere Building), China's first sex museum. Open daily from 10am to 9pm (50RMB/$6 admission), it contains more than 1,200 erotic arti-facts from Chinese history. At the end of this same block is yet another new mod-ern shopping mall, **Shanghai Landmark Plaza** (no. 409), on the south side, and an interesting smaller shop, **Ao Feng Xiang Jewelers** (no. 438), on the north side.

Across Shaanxi Nan Lu looms **Europe City,** an upscale department store spe-cializing in Western goods, and:

15. Shanghai's City of Books (no. 345), the city's glittery new answer to the mega-bookstores sweeping Western nations, complete with its own music-and-video gallery and coffee bar.

The eastern end of the mall looms ahead at Henan Zhong Lu, site of a plaque commemorating the building of the mall and of life-size wrought-iron statues of families shopping. Here you'll also find:

16. He Nan Zhong Lu Station, one of several new subway stations on **Metro Line 2,** which runs under Nanjing Road to the west and under the Huangpu River east to the Pudong New Area. The station is equipped with rest rooms and an elevator. Beside it you can also buy tickets for the **sightseeing trolley,** a three-car electric train that weaves its way up and down the length of the pedestrian mall; tickets, purchased from the roving conductor, cost just 1RMB (12¢).

The Shanghainese were inordinately proud of Nanking Road, not only because of its shops overflowing with goods, but because there was truly nothing like it in the rest of China. It was so modern, and nothing enthralled the Shanghainese more than modernity. While the rest of the nation was still sunk in rusticity, here were young girls clacking about on Italian heels, photographic studios, department stores, special offers and seasonal sales, and publicity gimmicks which called for bands to play and even a dwarf got up in a top-hat to cry "Fantastic value! Fantastic value!" outside the shop.

—Pan Ling, *In Search of Old Shanghai,* 1982

WINDING DOWN   From Henan Zhong Lu, the eastern terminus of the pedestrian mall, you can continue two more blocks along Nanjing Dong Lu to the Bund. This pinched, grimy, fragrant strip gives you an idea of what Nanjing Road was like before the mall was in place. Roving vendors may approach you here selling fake Rolex watches and laptop computers. The sidewalk is so narrow and crowded, you may have to walk in the street (but watch out for vehicles if you do). The reward at the end of this final strip of Shanghai window shopping is the glorious Art Deco lobby and rooftop bar of the incomparable colonial-style **Peace Hotel** (no. 20).

Walking Tour 2: The Bund

Start: Waibaidu Bridge, Suzhou Creek (subway: He Nan Zhong Lu, Metro Line 2).
Finish: Yan'an Dong Lu, south Bund.
Time: 2 hours.
Best times: Weekday mornings or late afternoons.
Worst times: Weekends bring out the crowds on the Bund promenade. Evenings are pretty, with the lights on the Bund buildings and the river, but the architecture cannot be viewed well after dark.

The Bund (Wai Tan) refers to both sides of the wide avenue (Zhongshan Dong Yi Lu) that runs north and south along the western shore of the Huangpu River, defining the eastern boundary of downtown Shanghai. The **Bund promenade** now occupies the east side of the street, affording terrific pedestrian-only walks along the river shore. This stroll concentrates, however, on the other side of the street, on the remarkable wall of colonial-era European-style architecture that is the singular landmark of old Shanghai.

The colonial era began in Shanghai after the Treaty of Nanjing ended the First Opium War in 1842; the British and other Western nations opened up the city (by force as well as negotiation) to trade, establishing foreign enclaves (concessions) within Shanghai. The Bund became the chief shipping, trading, and financial district of the colonialists. The Bund (which means embankment) consisted of mudflats and streams that were drained. Bungalows with spacious verandas served as the first foreign offices. Trade was in silk, tea, and opium, and Shanghai had a worldwide monopoly on these commodities in the late 19th century. Shanghai's foreign population grew from 10,000 in 1910 to 60,000 by 1940 with the increasing wealth from trade along the Bund, and it was during this period that the great buildings that still line the river avenue were built. Foreign banks, the Customs House, luxury hotels, private clubs, and embassies dominated the skyline.

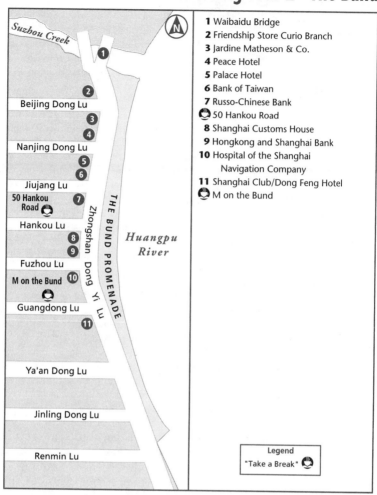

1 Waibaidu Bridge
2 Friendship Store Curio Branch
3 Jardine Matheson & Co.
4 Peace Hotel
5 Palace Hotel
6 Bank of Taiwan
7 Russo-Chinese Bank
50 Hankou Road
8 Shanghai Customs House
9 Hongkong and Shanghai Bank
10 Hospital of the Shanghai Navigation Company
11 Shanghai Club/Dong Feng Hotel
M on the Bund

Legend
"Take a Break"

War with Japan signaled the end to the Bund's colonial heyday, the first bomb dropping on the Bund's Peace Hotel on August 14, 1937. In January 1943, the foreign concessions of Shanghai were ended and the Japanese occupied the city. Shortly after the Communist triumph and the declaration of the People's Republic of China in 1949, the last of the foreign trading houses abandoned the Bund. In the decades since, the great buildings have been occupied sporadically by local banks, organizations, and businesses, but in the late 1990s, there was a concerted effort to restore the Bund's architectural grandeur, to refurbish the colonial interiors, and to open them to a curious public. This has created a fascinating walking tour.

Begin at the northern end of the Bund (Zhongshan Dong Yi Lu) on the southern shore of Suzhou Creek at:

1. **Waibaidu Bridge,** the steel span built in 1907 to replace the wooden Garden Bridge that once connected the American Settlement and International Concession to the Bund. On the north side of the bridge, you can still see a number of

colonial towers: to the left, the former **Broadway Mansions** (now Shanghai Mansions), a redbrick Art Deco apartment house built in 1934; to the right, the old **Astor House,** built in 1860 and reconstructed in 1910, with its palm garden and tearoom (today the one-star Pujiang, serving foreign budget travelers); and next door to it, the former and again current **Russian Consulate,** built in 1917, which served as the Seagull Hotel in intervening years.

Our stroll heads south from here, on the west side of the Bund, beginning with the:

2. **Friendship Store Curio Branch** (no. 31), an intriguing little antiques shop built of stone and related to the big Friendship Store (located at 40 Beijing Dong Lu, a block west). This is part of the building that once housed the offices of the NYK Line. The Friendship Store itself used to occupy the old British Consulate located here, too, a lovely wooden bungalow dating from the 1870s that was torn down in the 1980s.

In the first block of the old Bund, south of the curio store, there are two large colonial-period buildings: the former **Banque de L'Indo-Chine** (no. 29, now the Everbright Bank), a French classic structure built in 1914, and the **Glen Line Building** (no. 28, now empty), built in 1922 as the largest German bank in Shanghai.

Crossing Beijing Dong Lu, you come to:

3. **Jardine Matheson & Co.** (no. 27, now the Wai Mao Da Building), erected in 1927. This was one of the first and most powerful foreign trading companies to take root in Shanghai. Next door is the former **Yangtze Insurance Building** (no. 26, now the Agricultural Bank), built in 1916 and possessed of a nicely restored lobby, worth a quick peek to whet your appetite for the splendors that lie ahead. The building at no. 25 Zhongshan Dong Yi Lu is currently empty, but the **Bank of China,** at no. 23, is still the Bank of China, as it has been ever since the tall, squarish structure with its Chinese windows and eaves was erected in 1937 under Chiang Kai-shek's Nationalist government.

Next door, on the corner of Nanjing Road, is a Bund landmark, the:

4. ✪ **Peace Hotel** (no. 20), built in 1929 as both the private residence of the Sassoon family and as a grand hotel, the **Cathay.** This is where Noël Coward wrote a play in 1930 and where Steven Spielberg later filmed part of *Empire of the Sun* (based on J. G. Ballard's memoir of growing up as an expatriate during the Japanese occupation). It is a living museum of Art Deco, capped by its famous pyramid roof. Walk through its romantic lobby and check out its rooftop views of the Bund (11th floor). You should even be able to talk one of the staff into giving you a tour of its quaint suites.

Immediately across the street is the hotel's older sister, the:

5. **Palace Hotel** (no. 19), built in 1906 by the Sassoons. The white brick of each story is crisscrossed by red brickwork, yielding a checkerboard effect. Its interiors are less extravagant than those of the Peace Hotel, but also less restored; the undiluted decay of the decades gives them a rich patina.

There are three more historic buildings in this first block south of Nanjing Road. The former **Chartered Bank of India, America, and China** (no. 18), with its two baroque stone columns, built in 1923, is unoccupied now, but it has been designated a "Municipal Preserved Building," meaning it is slated for renovation and occupancy. The former **North China Daily News Building** (no. 17, now the AIA Building) next door, built in 1921, also has the official preservation designation, but there is nothing so far to attract visitors inside (although the two towers on its high veranda would offer great views).

Of more interest is the last building in this block, the:

6. Bank of Taiwan Building (no. 16, now the China Merchants Bank). It was rebuilt in 1924 in Japanese/Western style and was actually a Japanese bank, despite its name. The four massive columns in front are original.

In the next block of the Bund, across Jiujiang Lu, are two contrasting buildings, the:

7. Russo-Chinese Bank Building (no. 15, now the China Foreign Exchange Trade System Building), built in 1901, a wide and squat edifice and the first tile-faced construction in Shanghai, and, next door, the modernistic, soaring **Bank of Communications Building** (no. 14, now the Bank of Shanghai), built in 1940, its large entrance framed in copper sheets. Between these buildings is currently one of the few retail shops remaining, the curiously named **Three Gun Monopoly Shop.** This is a branch of China's largest underwear manufacturer, founded in 1937 by Gan Tinghui. Gan had won renown as a marksman, winning three titles and receiving a gun each time as a prize.

☕ **TAKE A BREAK**   Stop for lunch, coffee, or a drink at **50 Hankou Road,** located just around the corner (and west) on Hankou Road. Occupying an old bank building with brick floors, it offers superb, inexpensive set lunches from its Western and Southeast Asian menu, prepared by Hong Kong chefs. Pull up a wicker chair, relax, and enjoy the Indonesian decor.

Then cross Hankou Lu and return to the Bund. On the corner is a venerable landmark, the:

8. Shanghai Customs House (no. 13). Built in 1927, the Renaissance-style Customs House is fronted by four massive granite Roman columns and topped by a rising bell tower (known as "Bing Ching"), its clock face visible up and down the river. It is still the Customs House for Shanghai, but it is no longer in the hands of foreigners.

Next door is the even more spectacular:

9. ✪ Hongkong and Shanghai Bank (no. 12, now the Pudong Development Bank). Built in 1923 of granite and other stone, it is a classic European Renaissance building (designed by G. L. Wilson) with exterior columns and archways, capped by a huge Greek dome. Inside the massive revolving doors, the restored dome and lobby are the most magnificent on the Bund. The dome, supported by eight marble columns, is decorated with an eight-panel gold-trimmed mosaic, each panel a salute, in heroic Greek style, to one of the world's financial capitals (these being Bangkok, Hong Kong, Tokyo, New York, London, Paris, Calcutta, and, of course, Shanghai). The bank's lobby is also stunning, restored in leather and carved wood. This Shanghai interior feels like it could be in Vienna or old London (as it must have for the colonists who lived here in the 1920s and earlier). The English hailed it as the most spectacular building ever erected between the Suez Canal and the Bering Strait.

When you are satiated with this splendid interior, proceed south across Fuzhou Lu to view the four buildings in the next block. The building at no. 9 is currently empty, but next to it stands the former:

10. Hospital of the Shanghai Navigation Company (no. 7, now the Bangkok Bank and the Thai Consulate). This is one of the oldest buildings on the Bund, built in 1907; but next door is an even older, more stately edifice, the **China Merchants Bank** (no. 6, now empty and under renovation). This bank was the first established in China during the Republican era, but the building, erected in 1897, served earlier as the Municipal City Hall. Its English Gothic style with

Baroque pillars and Gothic windows makes it one of the most graceful to survive from the colonial period. The narrower building next to it on the corner of Guangong Lu is the former headquarters of the **Nishin Navigation Company** (no. 5, now the Huaxia Bank). Another modernistic, Western-style building, it was constructed by its Japanese owners in 1925.

Three more historic buildings remain on the Bund in the next block south, beginning with the former **Union Insurance Company Building** (no. 4, now empty), erected in 1922. It is a fine Renaissance-style corner structure, topped by a spire.

Next door is one of the most famous buildings on the Bund, the former:

11. Shanghai Club (no. 2), which for much of the late 20th century was the **Dong Feng Hotel.** Built in 1910, it was the city's most extravagant private club, an English Renaissance structure with elaborate white columns and baroque attic windows. It housed the famous black-and-white granite **Long Bar,** at over 100 feet reputedly the longest bar in the world; this was the watering hole for the "old boys' club" that ruled colonial Shanghai. Today, it is closed and gutted, awaiting yet another transformation.

The last building on the tour, at the corner of Yan'an Dong Lu, is the former **Asiatic Petroleum Building,** also known as the **McBain Building** (no. 1, now the China Pacific Insurance Company), built in 1916. This substantial but blocky specimen employs the ubiquitous baroque pillars, Roman stone archway, and Greek columns.

WINDING DOWN   You have the option of taking the pedestrian walkway across Zhongshan Dong Yi Lu to the Bund promenade, where you can view the magnificent facades of the colonial skyline you've just seen close up. But if walking north for nearly 2 miles (3km) back up the Bund seems daunting, don't cross over to the Bund promenade. Simply retrace your steps to Guangdong Lu (1 block north), go left (west) for half a block, and on the north side of this side street find the elevator entrance for **M on the Bund** (7th floor, 20 Guangdong Lu). M has a splendid lounge, serves world-class Mediterranean cuisine, and offers a spacious balcony overlooking the Bund and the Huangpu River atop the Huaxia Bank Building, which has been ensconced at no. 5 on the Bund since the 1920s. This is a perfect place to look down on and admire your jaunt through Shanghai's museum of colonial architecture. M is open from noon to 3pm and 5 to 10pm.

Walking Tour 3: Old Town Bazaar

Start: Shanghai Old Street, Nanshi District
Finish: Renmin Lu, Nanshi District
Time: 2 to 4 hours.
Best times: Weekday mornings or early Sunday morning (for the Temple of the Town God antiques market).
Worst times: Weekends are packed with tourists and shoppers. If you can't go on a weekday, head out early in the day.

Shanghai's Old Town (today's Nanshi District, just southwest of the Bund), was the main Chinese district of downtown Shanghai during the colonial era (1842 to 1949), when the Westerners had their own enclaves (called concessions) nearby. It was encircled by a wall (which followed the course of today's little ring road of

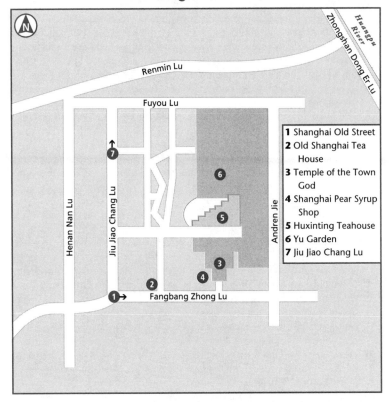

1 Shanghai Old Street
2 Old Shanghai Tea House
3 Temple of the Town God
4 Shanghai Pear Syrup Shop
5 Huxinting Teahouse
6 Yu Garden
7 Jiu Jiao Chang Lu

Renmin and Zhonghua sts.) that came down when the last dynasty fell, in 1911. The old city wall, 27 feet (8m) high and 3 miles (5km) round, dated from the 16th century, when it served as a barrier against Japanese pirates. It is considered the oldest district of Shanghai; its shops, the most traditional; its steamed dumplings, the best. Within this former walled city, the Old Town Bazaar (bounded by Renmin Lu, Henan Nan Lu, Fangbang Zhong Lu, and Zhonghua Lu) is now a large pedestrian mall and alleyway labyrinth that draws as many as 200,000 visitors daily. Within its bounds are some marvelous attractions, including Yu Garden, the Huxinting Teahouse, the Bridge of Nine Turnings, the Temple of the Town Gods, the new Shanghai Old Street (Fangbang Zhong Lu), and hundreds of traditional Chinese shops (as well as many new stores). Since motor vehicles aren't permitted within the Bazaar area, it is an ideal location for a walking tour of old Chinese Shanghai.

There are many entry points into the maze of the Old Town Bazaar, and many ways to become disoriented here. Renmin Lu, just off the lower Bund area, forms the northern border; the teahouse is at the center of the maze; and Shanghai Old Street (Fangbang Zhong Lu) marks the southern border. Most tour buses enter from the north, but to avoid the congestion, begin your stroll at the intersection of Henan Nan Lu and Fangbang Zhong Lu on the southwest side of the Old Town Bazaar.

Here you'll see a traditional-style Chinese gate; pass through it, walking east, and enter:

1. ✪ **Shanghai Old Street (Shanghai Lao Jie),** an 899-yard (825m) stretch of Fangbang Zhong Lu that was renovated in 1999 as an Old Town theme street.

Here the traditional shophouses, selling antiques, collectibles, crafts, and tea, display the architectural and cultural evolution of Shanghai as you walk east, from the Ming Dynasty through the Qing Dynasty into the Chinese Republican era. There's a large, irresistible courtyard stuffed with antiques and junk immediately on your left and a series of quaint crafts and jewelry shops on your right.

In the second block, after the Houjia Lu intersection, watch on your right (north) for the:

2. **Old Shanghai Tea House** (385 Fangbang Zhong Lu). This two-story shophouse has a number of fine historical photos of old Shanghai and a few relics. Upstairs is a teahouse, with windows open to the street.

Continue zigzagging your way east on Old Shanghai Street, just past the large new **Hua Bao Building** (265 Fangbang Zhong Lu), with antiques on sale in the basement, to the stone arch entrance of the:

3. **Temple of the Town God (Chenghuang Miao),** at 1 Yicheng Lu, which is also the southern entrance to the Old Town Bazaar. A Daoist Temple since 1726, it can be quickly toured from 8:30am to 4pm daily (5RMB/60¢ admission). Its courtyard was the setting for large temple fairs and trade markets, a tradition recently revived with an outdoor antiques market held every Sunday morning.

Turn back east from the temple courtyard and follow the road 1 block to the:

4. **Shanghai Pear Syrup Shop,** old China's answer to cough drops. Here you can either turn north along a twisting lane or continue east into a large shopping square that contains two large statues of lions on its southern shop front. If you continue east, you'll eventually want to bear north and then west. Your goal is to come out at the teahouse and lake, which is a few blocks northwest of the Temple of the Town God. Don't worry if you get lost on your way; you'll eventually solve the maze and reach the teahouse at its center. Meanwhile, enjoy the array of little shops selling everything from chopsticks to folk toys.

When the teahouse floating on the lake finally comes into view, you'll know where you are. Near the rickshaws for hire, take the **Bridge of Nine Turnings** to the celebrated:

5. **Huxinting (Mid-Lake Pavilion) Teahouse** (257 Yu Yuan Lu), China's most famous place to drink tea. Step inside, take a look at the teas for sale on the first floor, and head upstairs for a cup and a Shanghai snack.

🍵 **TAKE A BREAK**   Sip tea and nibble on Shanghai "crumpets" (steamed pastries) by an open window in the 200-year-old **Huxinting Teahouse** (open daily from 8:30am to 10pm). For a more substantial repast, lunch on a variety of Shanghai dumplings and noodle dishes at the **Nanxiang Restaurant** that sits on the west shore of the lake.

The north side of the lake at the heart of the Old Town Bazaar is the location of the main entrance to its single most beautiful attraction:

6. ✪ **Yu Garden (Yu Yuan),** 218 Anren Lu. Completed in 1577, this magnificent private classical garden is exceedingly charming. It, too, is a maze, but you'll come out fine if you explore its pavilions, ponds, bridges, and rockeries in a clockwise direction, heading north, then turning east and south. The garden is open daily from 8:30am to 5pm and is usually quite crowded (admission 20RMB/$2.40). You can exit at the southern Inner Garden and find your way back to the Huxinting Teahouse by walking west a block on Yu Yuan Lu.

Now's your last chance to wander and window-shop. The lanes on the west side of the lake and Yu Garden are the most interesting in the Bazaar. Here you'll come across pottery shops, jewelers, fan makers, traditional Chinese apothecaries, chopstick stores, scissors shops, and silk emporiums. One way out of the maze is via Bailing Lu (which runs straight west from the Bridge of Nine Turnings) to Old Town Bazaar's western border:

7. **Jiu Jiao Chang Lu.** This shopping street heads south back to Shanghai Old Street, where you began this stroll; but if you take it north, you'll see plenty of pottery and crafts outlets, shophouses, and, near Renmin Lu, a forest of vendors' stalls offering a bit of everything, including Western-style sports clothing. There are also several major jewelry and antiques stores along this street. The **Lucky Gold/Zijin Building** (81 Jiu Jiao Chang Lu) houses three floors of jewelry and gem counters; across the street, **Chenghuan Jewelry** (88 Jiu Jiao Chang Lu) has an ATM at the entrance and antiques and curios on the third floor. **Lishui Gate** (Lishuimen) at Renmin Lu marks the north end of the Old Town Bazaar.

WINDING DOWN   If you have shopping energy left, Huaihai Zhong Lu, the favorite modern shopping street of today's Shanghainese, is a long stroll directly west from here; to the southwest, about 30 minutes by foot, is the newly refurbished Temple of Confucius; and the Bund Promenade is about 5 blocks to the northeast. But perhaps a 10-minute taxi uptown to the **Peace Hotel**'s rooftop bar packs the most appeal. It offers sure cures for whatever "shopping shock" you may be suffering after getting lost and found in very old Shanghai.

Walking Tour 4: French Concession

Start: Huaihai Lu, Luwan District (subway: Huangpi)
Finish: Hengshan Lu, Xuhui District (subway: Hengshan)
Time: 4 to 6 hours.
Best times: Weekday mornings and midafternoons.
Worst times: On weekends (especially Sun) and evenings, many of these streets are quite crowded with local shoppers and visitors. Lunchtime (from 11:30am to 2pm) also brings out big crowds.

Shanghai's French Concession, consisting of a corridor running from the lower Bund between today's Yan'an Lu and the Chinese Old Town west along Huaihai Lu, contains many of the city's most picturesque colonial mansions, parks, hotels, and town houses. The French arrived in 1846 and leased land just south of the British Concession's holdings downtown. They established a series of fine residential neighborhoods west across today's Luwan District, branching off Huaihai Lu, the main avenue known in colonial times as Avenue Joffre. Its northern border, today's Yan'an Lu, was then known as Avenue Edouard VII. The streets in the long, sprawling settlement were lined with plane trees; the buildings, with their mansard roofs and shutters, resembled those of French towns of the time.

These neighborhoods, most now dating from the first 3 decades of the 1900s, remain much intact, although the modern construction boom has laid waste considerable clusters of the French legacy. Still, especially in recent years, a concerted effort has been made to preserve and spruce up many charming blocks of the original French residences, open historic houses, and convert some of the surviving mansions and estates to fine restaurants and retail shops—all making for a delightful, if spread out, stroll through colonial Shanghai. The French Concession refused to join the International Concession formed in 1863 by the British and Americans, providing its own electric power, bus system, and legal system to its 4-square-mile (10km^2) quarter. It was a quarter that attracted not only the French, but also international adventurers, Chinese gangsters, White Russian refugees, pimps and prostitutes, and Communist revolutionaries. By the 1930s, the French were vastly outnumbered here, but their sense of style has endured.

Our walking tour begins west of Old Town, the Chinese settlement near the south end of the Bund, and winds for several miles west, taking in many of the relics of French colonial days.

It starts, however, firmly in the 21st century, on one of Shanghai's most modern shopping avenues, at Huangpi Nan Lu Station (Metro Line 1), on:

1. **Huaihai Zhong Lu.** The former Avenue Joffre, this was the main street of the old French Concession, stocked with fashions from Paris. It still has its boutiques and fashionable shops; the locals prefer it to Nanjing Road for shopping. Recent years have brought an influx of modern shopping malls and department stores, eliminating much of the old Shanghai flavor. Unlike Nanjing Road, this is no pedestrian mall. You may have to shoulder your way along the crowded sidewalk. On the south side of the wide, busy avenue are the Shui On Center (no. 333) at the subway entrance and—as you near the massive Chengdu Bei Lu/Chongqing Nan Lu overpass—the Central Plaza (no. 381) with its Delifrance baguette and coffee shop.

   Use the pedestrian overpass here, descend, and take the first major left, south on:

2. **Yandang Lu,** yet another brand-new (1999) cobblestone pedestrian food street lined with small cafes, bars, and shops in colonial-style buildings. If you need a cup of coffee or tea, take your pick here (they all have English-language menus). The Island Café Bar (no. 6), Lisa (no. 62), and Travelers Salon (no. 71) are all friendly.

   Continue down Yandang 2 blocks to the entrance of:

3. **Fuxing Park** (on Nanchang Lu). Since the French established it as their park in 1909, it has been known locally as **French Park,** and it is still one of Shanghai's loveliest urban green spots, famous for its rose gardens. At the statues of Karl Marx and Friedrich Engels (a favorite point for Shanghai's ballroom dancers to practice), bear right (west) for the upscale **Park 97** restaurant and exit here on Gaolan Lu (the former Rue Corneille).

   Cross Sinan Lu and continue 1 more block on Gaolan Lu to a decidedly strange sight at the:

4. **Ashanti Restaurant** (16 Gaolan Lu), strange because this little French restaurant with the South African wine list shares with the Good Luck Hotel the interior of a former Russian Orthodox church, testimony to the former presence of White Russians in the French quarter. The icons, stained glass, and religious murals are still inside, too, although the exterior of the dome has the greatest incongruity of all, a portrait of Chairman Mao.

   After a gawk, retrace your steps east along this pretty lane, back to Sinan Lu (the old Rue Masenet), and go 1 block south to Xiangshan Lu (Rue de Moliere), where you can enter:

5. **Sun Yat-sen's Former Residence** (7 Xiangshan Lu). The founder of the Chinese Republic, Sun lived here with his famous wife, Soong Ching-ling, from 1918 to 1924, the year before his death. You can tour the house, portico, and rear garden daily from 9am to 4:30pm. This is a typical small mansion of the French era.

   Continue south 1 block down tree-lined Sinan Lu, cross busy Fuxing Lu, and walk another block south to:

6. **Zhou En-lai's Former Residence** (no. 73 Sinan Lu), on the east side of the street. Premier Zhou was next in power to Chairman Mao. As head of the

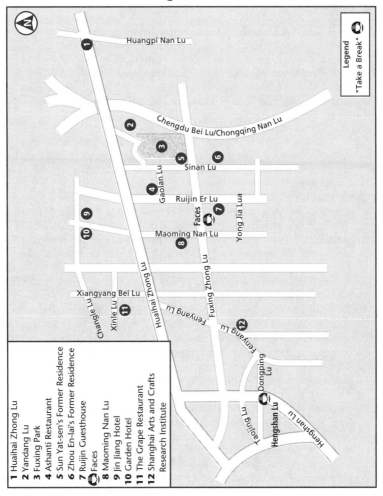

Huangpi Nan Lu

Chengdu Bei Lu/Chongqing Nan Lu

Sinan Lu

Gaolan Lu

Ruijin Er Lu

Yong Jia Lua

Faces

Maoming Nan Lu

Fuxing Zhong Lu

Xiangyang Bei Lu

Changle Lu

Xinle Lu

Huaihai Zhong Lu

Fenyang Lu

Fenyang Lu

Dongping Lu

Taojiang Lu

Hengshan Lu

Hengshan Lu

Legend
"Take a Break"

1 Huaihai Zhong Lu
2 Yandang Lu
3 Fuxing Park
4 Ashanti Restaurant
5 Sun Yat-sen's Former Residence
6 Zhou En-lai's Former Residence
7 Ruijin Guesthouse
8 Faces
8 Maoming Nan Lu
9 Jin Jiang Hotel
10 Garden Hotel
11 The Grape Restaurant
12 Shanghai Arts and Crafts
　　Research Institute

Communist party, he lived modestly in this fine French Concession house starting in 1946, conducting secret party business before Liberation (1949).

Return to Fuxing Zhong Lu (1 block north) and take it west to Ruijin Er Lu, the next major street. Turn left (south) on Ruijin Er Lu (the former Route Pere Robert) and take it a block or so to the:

7. **✪ Ruijin Guest House** (118 Ruijin Er Lu, west side of the street). This beautiful estate, now the grounds for a hotel and restaurant, incorporated the **Morriss Villas** in colonial times. The owner of the villas that still stand in these spacious gardens built his fortune by running the *North China Daily News,* then the main English-language newspaper in Shanghai; he also owned the dog track (the 50,000-seat Canidrome) just to the west (today's Cultural Square); and he died in the gatekeeper's house when the Communists took over Shanghai in 1949. The wide green lawns and ornate villas with stained-glass windows are exquisite relics of the privileged life wealthy foreigners led in old Shanghai. The grand villa on the northwest edge of the property now houses a bar (Faces) and two superb restaurants (one Thai, one Indian), which you must visit, even if only to stare.

☕ **TAKE A BREAK**   No place better to relax, have a drink, or enjoy a fine Asian meal than at **Faces,** on the Ruijin Guest House estate (59 Maoming Lu). Faces is the lounge on the main floor; down the hall is an excellent Indian restaurant, **Hazara;** and upstairs, a superb Thai restaurant, **Lan Na Thai.** The setting is a 1930s mansion that is said to have housed the Soong family and, on occasion, Chairman Mao himself. The decor is strictly 1930s colonial; the courtyard dining area features a large manicured lawn fit for a croquet match.

Retrace your steps through the Ruijin/Morriss estate to the entrance on Ruijin Er Lu, turn right (south) 1 block to Yongjia Lu (formerly Route Herve de Sieyes), and proceed to the corner, where you can cut through the **Yongjia Flower Market** as you turn north on:

8. ✪ **Maoming Nan Lu.** The most famous side street in the French Concession these days, Maoming Lu was known in colonial days as Route Cardinal Mercier. Take it north, viewing the cafes, bars, and tiny shops on either side of this pinched but pretty tree-lined lane. Although this street is filled with tourists, its architecture and many of its little cafes (such as the 1931 Café at 112 Maoming Nan Lu) retain the quaint flavor of the French Concession.

North up Maoming, you'll cross Fuxing Lu, Nanchang Lu, and finally Huaihai Lu, ultimately coming to another landmark, the:

9. **Jin Jiang Hotel** (59 Maoming Nan Lu), the massive old hotel complex on the right (east) side of the street. It consists of several Art Deco buildings. The steel-and-brick high-rise on the north end, built in 1929 in the modern Western style, became Shanghai's classiest apartment site. After becoming a hotel in 1951, the Jin Jiang was Shanghai's top hotel for decades, up to the time when Richard Nixon came here to sign the Shanghai Communiqué in 1972, which opened China to the West for the first time since World War II. The Jin Jiang structures have been modernized recently, gaining in luxury but losing in character. The Jin Jiang shopping lane (just inside the gate, parallel to Maoming Lu) is worth a stop. It has excellent restaurants, bars, and gift shops; its **bookstore** is one of the best in the city, geared to foreign shoppers, and worth a thorough look.

Reemerging on Maoming Lu and walking north to the corner, you can see the old **Lyceum Theatre,** built in 1931 by the British Consul for the Amateur Dramatic Society, across Changle Lu (formerly Rue Bourgeat). It still serves as a theater for performing groups. Another recreational relic is concealed directly across Maoming Lu from the Jin Jiang Hotel in the:

10. **Garden Hotel** (58 Maoming Nan Lu). Cross Maoming Nan Lu at the Changle Lu intersection, turn left, and walk half a block back south to the driveway entrance. The towering Garden Hotel, a Japanese-managed five-star property, opened in 1989 on the site of the 1926 **Cercle Sportif Francaise** (later known as the Jin Jiang Club). Once the most luxurious private club in the French quarter, with its grand ballroom, swimming pool, lounges, and wicker sofas, it has been displaced but not utterly destroyed. Enter the hotel lobby and turn right. Go down the hall, past the lavish business center (which was one of the Jin Jiang Club's old French-style rooms), to the atrium. This is the original entrance to the Cercle Sportif's ballroom, complete with marble stairways and colonnades, Art Deco fixtures, stained glass, ornate ceiling, lobby, and arched entrance. It can take your breath away.

Outside, head back north up Maoming Nan Lu to the corner, turn left on Chengle Lu and walk 2 blocks west, then turn left (south) on Xiangyang Bei Lu.

Xiangyang Bei Lu, the former Rue L. Lorton, comes to a major intersection at Xinle Lu. Cross Xinle Lu and take it west (to your right) a few paces to:

11. **The Grape Restaurant** (55 Xinle Lu). This is a popular, inexpensive place to eat Shanghai cooking, popular with expatriates—but the real attraction is the setting. Here is another restaurant ensconced in a wing of an abandoned Russian Orthodox church. Built in 1934 of cement and yellow sand, the church's domes are painted a sharp peacock blue. Strangest of all, perhaps, is what's inside the main sanctuary, under the big green onion dome. You can see it from the street through the large entryway: a stock exchange, with an electronic trading board lit full tilt.

   Walk back to Xiangyang Lu and take it south a block to Huaihai Zhong Lu. Xiangyang Park, on the east side of the street, was a private garden in French Concession days, famous for its cherry trees. Cross the street and jog to the right (west), then turn left and southwest down the slanting street of Fenyang Lu (the old Route Pichon). Keep on Fenyang Lu after it crosses Fuxing Lu (or Route Lafayette, as it was once known) until you come to a mansion surrounded by a 10-foot-high wall on the south side of the street. A sign in English will point you to the entrance of the:

12. ☻ **Shanghai Arts and Crafts Research Institute** (79 Fenyang Lu). This marvelous old marble-and-stone mansion (open daily from 8:30am to 4:30pm) is in the grand French Renaissance style; it served as the private estate of the Director of the French Municipal Council, a French general, and finally the first mayor of Communist Shanghai, Chen Yi, before becoming the open workshops of some of China's most skilled artisans. This survivor of colonial Shanghai packs a double punch: first, as a place to watch traditional arts and crafts being fashioned; second, as an architectural masterpiece, resplendent with its unaltered interiors, sculptures, and marble fountains in its garden.

   ☕ **WINDING DOWN**   The trendiest avenue in Shanghai, **Hengshan Lu,** is just west of here. Continue along Fenyang Lu (bearing right), past the huge yellow courtyard building of Paulaner Brauhaus (150 Fenyang Lu) to the **Puxijin Monument,** located in a tiny island in the middle of a chaotic intersection (consisting of Fenyang Lu, Taojiang Lu, Dongping Lu, and south-running Yueyang Lu). Take either of the west-running roads (Taojiang or Dongping) another block to Hengshan Lu, the big tree-lined avenue with the orange-tile sidewalks, wrought-iron railings and light poles, and ivy-covered mansions. The English-style villa with the yellow walls at 9 Dongping Lu was the "palace away from the palace," where President Chiang Kai-shek stayed when he visited Shanghai before 1949.

   You could stroll the Hengshan area for hours admiring the architecture old and new, but why resist the wonderful food and drink, served up in splendid colonial French settings, that's so near at hand? If you fancy fine Continental dishes, including fondues, presented in a 1920s Soong-family mansion, try **Sasha's** (House 11, 9 Dongping Lu at Hengshan Lu). If you prefer Irish ale, live Irish music, and Irish stew, served in an old courtyard house, turn into **O'Malley's** (42 Taojiang, west 1 block off Hengshan Lu). If something lighter, or just a leisurely cup of latte or tea, would hit the spot, the "fragrant camphor" teahouse of **Harn Sheh** (10 Hengshan Lu at Taojiang Lu) is the perfect place to end a stroll through colonial Shanghai.

8 Shopping

Even before economic reforms took hold in China in the 1980s and kicked into high gear in the 1990s, Shanghai was a shopper's city. All across the country, the mainlanders dreamed of making one visit to the great port, not to sightsee, but to shop. Anything made and sold in Shanghai, it seems, had to be the best; non-Shanghai goods were by definition inferior—and this reputation for the best goods and great shopping persists today. The focus of many travelers is on uniquely Chinese products and on international brand names at wholesale prices; both are widely available at department stores and shops, at sidewalk stalls, and in open-air free markets where bargaining and caution are the bywords. The Shanghainese enjoy shopping immensely, and they are known as careful buyers, master sellers, and connoisseurs of fashion and style. Expect to find elbow-to-elbow shopping at some sites, and head into the fray with your commercial wits sharpened. Language won't be a problem; shopping is universal.

1 The Shopping Scene

Shanghai has long been an oasis of international shopping, so it is no surprise that Western-style malls are replacing traditional shop fronts, Chinese department stores, and alley markets across Shanghai. Privately run shops are nearly always versions of the boutiques and specialty outlets familiar to shoppers in the West. Yet you can still find open-air markets and street-side vendors offering more traditional arts and crafts, collectibles, and clothing at low prices. If you're looking for souvenirs or Chinese treasures, check out the cost and selection at hotel shops, the Friendship Store, and modern shopping malls first; then, see what's available in the streets and at markets.

SHANGHAI'S BEST BUYS

Shanghai is known for selection and low prices in **silk** (both off the bolt and in finished garments). The market in **antiques** is also nearly synonymous with Shanghai. A red wax seal must be attached to any item created between 1795 and 1949 that is taken out of China; older items cannot be exported. Many hotel shops and modern department stores will send purchases to your home, and the Friendship Store has a highly efficient shipping department. **Furniture,** old or new in traditional Chinese styles, can be purchased or custom ordered at several antiques stores, and the prices are good, although shipping can add considerably to the bill.

TIMBUKTU   KALAMAZOO

AT&T Direct® Service

The easy way to call home from anywhere.

Global
connection
with the AT&T
Network

AT&T
direct
service

Buyer Beware

One note of caution: The open-air markets that line the entrances to major tourist sites generally charge extravagant prices and offer mass-produced kitsch of shoddy quality, including outright fakes. **Jade** is particularly difficult to evaluate and prone to being fake, so buy only what you like and don't pay much.

Jewelry can also be a bargain, particularly **jade, gold, silver,** and **freshwater pearls,** but bargaining and a critical eye are required. **Electronics, cameras,** and other high-tech goods are not particularly good buys, although **small appliances** such as razors can be found in department stores for low prices. Fashionable **clothing** in cotton, wool, and silk is common in Shanghai; prices are low.

Among arts and crafts, Shanghai is renowned for its **ceramics.** There are also especially good buys in hand-stitched **embroideries, teapots, painted fans,** and **chopsticks.** These are often sold in markets and on the sidewalks by itinerant vendors. Collectibles include **Mao buttons** and posters, old Chinese **coins,** small religious **statues, woodcarvings,** and **screens**—all priced lowest at markets and stands. Other popular crafts made in Shanghai are **carpets, lacquerware, painted eggs, peasant paintings,** and **artificial flowers.** Prices vary considerably. The best rule is to find something you truly like, then consider how much it is worth to you.

Designer-label **sportswear** and **stuffed toys** (such as Beanie Babies) are abundant in department stores and street markets alike. One of the most popular gifts is a **chop** (also called a seal), which is a small, stone custom-engraved stamp with your name (in English, Chinese, or both), used with an ink pad to print your "signature" on paper. Chops can be created the same day or overnight, sometimes even while you wait. Prices depend on the stone you select and the skill of the engraver.

THE ART OF BARGAINING

It helps to know the going prices for items you're interested in. The Friendship Store is worth scoping out with prices in mind, since it sets the standard price for most items. Also check the prices in hotel shops and at the new megamalls. This will give you a notion of the high-end. Then see if you can beat the price elsewhere.

The street markets usually have the lowest prices. Here, for example, you can buy porcelain chopstick rests for 5RMB (60¢), painted fans for 10RMB ($1.20), silk shirts for 100RMB ($12), quilts for 150RMB ($18), and ecru tablecloths for 200RMB ($24).

Haggling is not done at government-run stores, most hotel stalls, and modern shops, but it is expected on the street and in small private stores. A good rule of thumb is to offer no more than a quarter of the quoted price and to not accept the first counteroffer. Try to reach a compromise (no more than half the quoted price). Walking away with a firm but polite "no" often brings about a more favorable price. Remember that locals are demon shoppers who scrutinize each potential purchase and exercise mountains of patience before making a buy.

Shopping Hours

Most stores are open daily from about 10am to 9pm (even later in the summer). Weekends (especially Sun) are the most hectic days to shop, since most Shanghainese make their purchases then and tens of thousands spend these days window-shopping.

One-Stop Gift Shopping at the Friendship Store

It's easier to shop for gifts, souvenirs, and Chinese treasures at the Friendship Store than anywhere else in Shanghai. The merchandise is targeted at foreign travelers, the selection is good, and the prices (no bargaining allowed) are high enough to ensure quality, while generally lower than in the high-end hotel shops and megamalls. Start here to get an overview of what's available in Shanghai at a fair price, shop the streets and malls, then return to make those last-minute purchases.

Friendship stores began as outlets exclusively for foreigners in China (at one time, no local Chinese were allowed inside), but they now compete freely with department stores, shopping plazas, private shops, and street vendors. Beyond its wide selection, quality goods, and convenience, the Shanghai Friendship Store provides a currency-exchange counter and honors credit cards. It also has an overseas shipping department to handle those big purchases.

Opened in 1958 in a building of the former British Consulate on the Bund (since demolished), the Shanghai Friendship Store now has six floors of shopping and more than 1,000 employees. It sells just about everything, from musical instruments to home appliances, in its new building (remodeled in 1994 and located behind the Peace Hotel, just off the Bund). There are Chinese kites, folk paper cuts, teas, medicines, watches, porcelains, English-language books, magazines, international newspapers, clothing for adults and children (silks, brocades, woolens, cotton sportswear), shoes, coats, leather jackets, toys, scrolls and paintings, lacquerware, jade, silver and gold jewelry, carved screens, and opera masks—over 50,000 items in all. You'll also find a separate supermarket, a carpet store, an antiques shop, and a Chinese-furniture showroom.

In other words, you can find most of the items that foreigners coming to China dream of buying. A frequent stop for group tours and hotel shuttle buses, the Friendship Store is located at 40 Beijing Dong Lu (☎ **021/5308-0600;** fax 021/5308-8200), and is open daily from 9:30am to 10pm.

SHANGHAI'S TOP SHOPPING AREAS

Shanghai's top street to shop has always been **Nanjing Road,** especially the new **Nanjing Road Pedestrian Mall** on Nanjing Dong Lu downtown (described in chapter 7, "Shanghai Strolls"), where the most modern and the most traditional modes of retailing commingle.

Even more popular among locals is **Huaihai Zhong Lu,** the wide avenue south of Nanjing Road and parallel to it. The Huaihai shopping tends to run far west across the city, from the Huangpi Nan Lu subway station to the Changshu Station. The modern shopping malls here have better prices than you'll find on Nanjing Road, and there are plenty of boutiques featuring fashions and silks. Some of the best shopping in the French Concession is concentrated in the **Maoming Lu** area, just north off Huaihai Lu.

Another major shopping street is **Hengshan Lu,** which continues at the western end of Huaihai Lu and runs south to the **Xu Jia Hui** intersection and subway stop, where one of the city's largest new shopping centers has just opened.

Shanghai's **Old Town Bazaar** (see chapter 7, "Shanghai Strolls") is a fine place to shop for local arts and crafts and antiques. In Pudong, the shopping is concentrated well east of the riverfront and south of the Pearl of the Orient TV Tower in the downtown malls anchored by the massive **Yaohan/Nextage** department store on Zhangyang Lu.

2 Markets & Bazaars

Some of Shanghai's most interesting shopping experiences are found in its street markets and alley bazaars. Curios, crafts, collectibles, antiques, jewelry, and coins are all here for those who are willing to bargain hard. Most of these markets are outdoor affairs where the vendors pitch their stalls and awnings in a courtyard or on both sides of a narrow passageway. Perhaps the most common item you'll find in the markets these days is not silk, souvenirs, or crafts, but designer-label clothing, much of it knockoffs (copies) with the upscale labels sewn in. Some items may be factory seconds or overruns (sometimes smuggled out of legitimate brand-name factories and sold on the side). Many of the markets also sell fresh produce, seafood, spices, and other foodstuffs to locals, along with snacks and drinks. These markets and bazaars are quite colorful and the prices can be low, but they are also attractive to pickpockets, so don't bring a purse or wallet. Keep all your valuables in a concealed pouch or money belt. And, speaking of valuables, these market vendors are seldom if ever equipped to deal with credit cards; Chinese currency is the sole means of exchange.

BIRD & FLOWER MARKET   Located on Jiangyin Lu, a narrow lane running west off Huangpi Lu and parallel to (but south of) Nanjing Xi Lu, just west of the Grand Theatre and People's Square, this market doesn't have too many birds or flowers, but it does offer goldfish, ceramic teapots, wood carvings, flower pots, birdcages of cane, pets, and carvers of stone chops (personal seals) in abundance. This lane is one of the more colorful in downtown Shanghai. There are hundreds of sidewalk vendors here, most without stalls, and plenty of vendors selling snacks as well. As autumn nears, singing crickets in tiny rattan cages are sold here, too.

DONGTAI ANTIQUES MARKET   You'll find hundreds of stalls and a few permanent shops on Dongtai Lu and Liuhe Lu, 1 block west of Xizang Nan Lu, Luwan District, about 3 blocks south of Huaihai Lu. Dealers specialize in antiques, curios, porcelain, furniture, jewelry, baskets, and bric-a-brac (especially Mao memorabilia). There are also stalls dealing in birds, flowers, goldfish, and crickets. When it rains, most stalls are closed. Open daily from 9am to 5pm.

✪ GHOST MARKET   Also called the **Fuyou Market,** 457 Fangbang Zhong Lu at Henan Nan Lu (the western entrance to Shanghai Old Street in the Old Town

What to Know Before You Go

The customs services of many nations frown on the importation of knockoffs on trademark goods. The U.S. Customs Service allows U.S. residents to return with one trademark-protected item of each type, that is, one counterfeit watch, one knockoff purse, one camera with a questionable trademark, and so on. For instance, you may not bring back a dozen "Polo" shirts as gifts for friends. Even if the brand name is legitimate, you are not a licensed importer. In addition, copyrighted products like CD-ROMs and books must have been manufactured under the copyright owner's authorization; otherwise, tourists may not import even one of these items—they are considered pirated goods. The U.S. Customs Service booklet *Know Before You Go* and the U.S. Customs Web site (**www.customs.ustreas.gov**) provide further guidelines.

The Pearls of China

In the Chinese tradition, pearls are the gems of love. Ground into a powder, in fact, they are the essential ingredient in Nanzhung tablets, a Chinese aphrodisiac. These days, they are also a hot commodity with visitors, who purchase them for beauty while hoping to snare a bargain.

China's oyster beds remain among the world's most fertile grounds for pearls, of both the saltwater and freshwater variety. Cultured (farmed) pearls are the most widely sold, but the problem is how to determine quality and a fair price.

Seawater pearls are usually more expensive than the freshwater gems, but in both cases, the qualities to look for are roundness, luster, and size. The bigger, rounder, and shinier the pearl, the better (and the more expensive).

Fakes can be detected by nicking the surface of the pearl with a sharp blade (the color is uniform within and without); rubbing the pearl along your teeth (to feel or hear a grating sound, since a real pearl's surface is actually scored and minutely cratered); scraping the pearl on glass (pearls leave a mark); or passing the pearl through a flame (fakes turn black, real pearls don't).

Try to pick a string of pearls that are of the same size, shape, and color. Here's a rough pricing guide, based on what's generally charged in Shanghai:

10RMB to 20RMB ($1.20 to $2.40) for a string of small rice-shaped pearls

20RMB to 40RMB ($2.40 to $4.80) for a string of larger pearls of mixed or low luster

50RMB to 100RMB ($6 to $12) for a string of larger pearls of different colors

A string of very large, perfectly round pearls of the same color sells for considerably more, 10,000RMB to 20,000RMB ($1,200 to $2,400) and more. Tassels of odd-shaped pearls can also fetch higher prices, selling for 100RMB to 1,000RMB ($12 to $120).

Bazaar, Nanshi District), this is the best place for weekend antique and curio hunting. It's called a ghost market because the traders—up to 800 of them—set out their wares before sunrise (when only ghosts can see what's for sale). There are vendors in the courtyard of the market building on the north side of Fangbang Lu at the entrance, but many of the goods are inside the building. Come as near to dawn as possible on Saturday or Sunday morning. The goods are various and few are polished up; many of the items are from the attic or the farm. Porcelain, old jade pendants, used furniture, Qing Dynasty coins, Chairman Mao buttons and little red books, Buddhist statues, snuff bottles, and carved wooden screens are just a few of the treasures here, none with price tags. Three floors of the market building are open daily from 9am to 5pm; the weekend market runs from 5am to 6pm, but tapers off by 11am.

HUATING CLOTHING MARKET   The lane (Huating Lu) 1 block east of Changshu Lu, across from the Changshu Lu subway station, on the north side of Huaihai Zhong Lu, Xuhui District, is stuffed with clothing stalls selling Western brand-name and designer-label attire (jeans, shirts, coats, shoes, handbags) for a fraction of the retail prices in the West. Be careful, though, because the labels may not be genuine (and that silk tie or scarf may prove to be synthetic). Open daily from 8am to 5pm.

TEMPLE OF THE TOWN GOD MARKET   This market starts out in the basement of the Huabao Building, 265 Fangbang Lu, Old Town Bazaar, Nanshi District, but on weekends it spills over into the courtyards of the temple and nearby Yu Garden pedestrian mall. It offers hundreds of vendors and hundreds of chances to bargain for curios, collectibles, and an occasional museum-quality relic. Open daily from 8:30am to 9pm.

ZHONGHUA XIN LU FLEA MARKET   Situated at Zhonghua Xin Lu and Hengfeng Lu, Zhabei District, a few blocks north of the Shanghai Railway Station, this is Shanghai's biggest market. It consists largely of tiny storefronts filled with everything from opium pipes and old radios to bike parts and Cultural Revolution posters, any collectible, castoff, or attic treasure that might possibly ever find a buyer. Open daily from sunrise to sundown.

3 Shopping A to Z

ANTIQUES & FURNITURE

The markets and bazaars (listed above) are a primary source of antiques, collectibles, and Chinese furniture and furnishings, as are some hotel shops, but there are also several private antiques stores worth checking out. Shanghai is no Hong Kong, but it offers some of the best antique shopping in mainland China.

Annly's Antique Warehouse. 1255 Wu Zhong Lu, Changning District. ☎ **021/6406-0242.**

Annly Chan provides custom-made sofas, chairs, draperies, and cushions; picture framing; and good antique furniture. Open daily from 9am to 6pm.

Antique Alley. 1438 Hongqiao Lu, Changning District. ☎ **021/6219-9229.**

This row of warehouses, workshops, and factory-outlet shops on the way to the Hongqiao Airport offers new and old furniture and furnishings. Among the shops here are **Shugu Yingmu,** which has Ming Dynasty–style chairs, Qing Dynasty beds, and old cradles; and **Hongmei,** which carries furniture from the 1930s. Open daily from 9am to 6pm.

Antique Market. 457 Fangbang Lu (at Henan Lu), Nanshi District.

This is where the Ghost Market (also called the Fuyou Market) runs every Saturday and Sunday morning in Old Town (see above). The rest of the week, the first three floors do plenty of business in every imaginable antique and collectible, from Buddhist statuary to Qing Dynasty coins. Open daily from 9am to 5pm.

Chine Antiques. Shop: 38 Liuhe Lu (at Dongtai Lu), Luwan District. ☎ **021/6387-4100.** Warehouse: 1660 Hongqiao Lu, Changning District. ☎ **021/5914-4424** or 021/6270-1023.

Here you'll find high-end (and high-priced) antiques, mainly wooden pieces from the Qing Dynasty. Overseas shipping is available. The shop in the Dongtai Market has pictures of what you can find in the warehouse showroom near the Hongqiao Airport. Open daily from 9am to 5pm.

Dragon Era. 477 Hua Xiang Lu (near Hu Qing Ping Hwy.), Changning District. ☎ **021/6421-0218** or 021/6421-9841, ext. 8008.

This combination showroom, pottery studio, and warehouse features classical Chinese furniture and reproductions, antiques and curios, ceramics and chinaware, and a pottery studio where you can learn to make or paint your own pieces (50RMB/$6 per session). It's located southwest of the Hongqiao Airport. Open daily from 9am to 6pm.

G-E-Tang Antique Co. Ltd. 2nd floor, No. 50, Liuhekou Lu (west of Xizang Nan Lu), Luwan District. ☎ **021/6384-6388.**

Located in the antiques market west of Old Town, G-E-Tang sells top-of-the-line antique furniture, with overseas shipping available. Furniture finishes here tend to be lighter than in most shops. New pieces are made from parts of old pieces. The warehouse is southwest of the Hongqiao Airport (at 7 Hu Qing Ping Hwy.). Open daily from 9am to 6pm.

Hua Bao Building. 265 Fangbang Zhong Lu, Old Town, Nanshi District. ☎ **021/6355-2272** or 021/6355-9999.

The basement of this shopping center on "Shanghai Old Street" near the Temple of the Town God and Yu Garden has plenty of antiques and collectibles for sale, as does much of the pedestrian lane here. The 250 booths sell embroidery, calligraphy, jade, carvings, and porcelain pieces. Open daily from 8:30am to 9pm.

Ming Qing Antique Furniture. 360 Hong Xu Lu (between Yan'an Xi Lu and Wu Zhong Lu), Changning District. ☎ **021/6406-8364.**

Qing and Ming Dynasty pieces and handcrafted reproductions are the specialty here. Overseas shipping can be arranged. The showroom and workshop are open daily from 9am to 6pm.

Shanghai Antique and Curio Store. 192-246 Guangdong Lu, Huangpu District. ☎ **021/6321-4697** or 021/6321-2864.

The owners hope to make Guangdong Lu, which runs west off the south end of the Bund, into something of an antiques row for shoppers. Under their umbrella so far are three high-end specialty galleries: Mo Yuan Hall, dealing in calligraphy and art supplies; Yi Gu House, old jades and porcelain; and Cui Zhen Pavilion, antique furniture, wood carvings, embroidery, and tapestries. Open daily from 9am to 8pm.

BOOKS

Hotel kiosks and shops are often the best place to find English-language guides to Shanghai attractions and books about China, but there are several bookstores with decent selections.

Chinese Classics Bookstore. 424 Fuzhou Lu, Huangpu District. ☎ **021/6351-7745** or 021/6322-4984.

This antiquarian-book dealer on Shanghai's book row (Fuzhou Lu) specializes in old books published in or written about China. Most of the books are in Chinese. It also sells calligraphy supplies, including fine paper. Open daily from 10am to 9pm.

Foreign Language Bookstore. 390 Fuzhou Lu (east of Fujian Lu), Huangpu District. ☎ **021/6322-3200.**

The city's largest selection of English-language books and magazines (along with some maps, tapes, and CDs) is contained in this big government-run store. English-language books are on the fourth floor. It accepts credit cards and will ship books overseas. Open daily from 9am to 6pm.

✪ **Jin Jiang Bookstore.** 59 Maoming Nan Lu, Luwan District. ☎ **021/6472-1273.**

This is the best single selection in town of English-language books on Shanghai and Chinese travel and culture—boasting everything from coffee-table books to city maps, plus friendly expert clerks. It's located in the shopping mall just inside the Jin Jiang Hotel's southwest gate. Open daily from 10am to 9pm.

✪ **Old China Hand Reading Room.** 27 Shaoxing Lu (between Ruijin Er Lu and Shaanxi Nan Lu), Luwan District. ☎ **021/6473-2526.**

Shanghai's most charming coffeehouse, opened in 1996 by photographer Deke Erh, is also a bookstore, with hundreds of old and new, obscure and popular books and magazines on its shelves. Relax at a Qing Dynasty antique table by the window as you peruse your possible purchases over green tea or cappuccino. Open daily from 10am to 11pm.

Shanghai Museum. 201 Renmin Da Dao (People's Square), Huangpu District. ☎ **021/6372-3500.**

The main gift shop on the first floor and the small shops on the floors above carry a good selection of English-language books on art, history, and culture, including coffee-table volumes. Open Sunday to Friday from 9am to 5pm, Saturday from 9am to 10pm.

✪ **Shanghai's City of Books.** 345 Nanjing Dong Lu (east of Shaanxi Nan Lu) and 465 Fuzhou Lu, Huangpu District. ☎ **021/6352-2222.**

Shanghai's state-of-the-art megamall for book lovers, this new store has eight floors of books, music, and even its own Internet cafe and Web site (**www.bookmall. com.cn**). Open daily from 9:30am to 10pm.

Xinhua Bookstore. 777 Nanjing Xi Lu (at Shimen Yi Lu) and 701 Huaihai Lu, Huangpu District. ☎ **021/6327-1914** or 021/6358-2464.

This state-run bookstore, Shanghai's largest, has some English-language books, maps, and travel guides near the entrance. Open daily from 10am to 9pm.

CARPETS

Check over carpets carefully, with an eye to faded colors. Colors should be bright and the threads fine. A 6-by-8-foot silk carpet, tightly woven (300 to 400 stitches per inch) can cost 50,000RMB ($6,000) or more.

Bokhara Carpets. 679 Xian Xia Lu (off Yan'an Xi Lu), Changning District. ☎ **021/6273-7745** or 021/6467-5658.

Excellent choice of new and old carpets from Iran, Pakistan, Afghanistan, India, and Uzbekistan. Open daily from 10am to 6:30pm.

Peace Silk Carpet Shop. 3rd floor, Yuyuan Bazaar Building, Yu Yuan Lu, Nanshi District. ☎ **021/6355-1842.**

Photography Needs

Kodak, Fuji, and other imported camera films can be purchased all over Shanghai, at hotel kiosks, megamalls and shopping plazas, and camera stores. Prices are about on par with those in the West. One-hour and next-day film-processing outlets can be found in hotels and shopping centers, too. The new **Kodak Image Center** in the Carrefour supermarket, 560 Quyang Lu, Gubei New Town, Changning District, develops film and carries new products. For repairs, try **Guanlong Photographic Equipment Company,** 180 Nanjing Dong Lu, Huangpu District (☎ **021/6329-0414**), a reputable firm on the Nanjing Road Pedestrian Mall (open daily from 9:30am to 9pm).

Hundreds of handwoven silk carpets in the Chinese style. Open daily from 9am to 9pm.

CRAFTS & GIFTS

Jingdezhen Ceramics Shanghai Art Centre. 1253 Daduhe Lu (west side of Changfeng Park), Changning District. ☎ **021/6385-6238,** 021/6245-3834, or 021/5281-4431.

It's a long ride from downtown Shanghai, but this is the largest porcelain shop in the city. The first floor has an assortment of ceramics (including purple sand porcelain) for both daily use and display. The second floor is an exhibition hall with 60,000 pieces of pottery by master craftspeople from the porcelain regions of Jingdezhen and Yixing. Pottery-making demonstrations are put on for tourists, who are sometimes invited to make their own pieces. Open daily from 9am to 5pm.

✪ **Shanghai Arts and Crafts Research Institute.** 79 Fenyang Lu (south of Fuxing Zhong Lu), Xuhui District. ☎ **021/6437-0509.**

What you see made in the many workshops of this French Concession mansion is for sale in the factory-outlet shop, from embroideries to snuff bottles and kites. Open daily from 8:30am to 4:30pm.

Shanghai Arts & Crafts Shopping Center. 190 Nanjing Xi Lu (at Huanghe Lu), Huangpu District. ☎ **021/6327-5299** or 021/6327-6530.

A one-stop emporium for ceramics, Chinese arts and crafts, and souvenirs, it has a good selection of gifts (jewelry, chops, clothing, silk, carpets, furniture), but high prices. Jewelry is on the first floor; gifts and souvenirs on the second; garments, tablecloths, and bedspreads on the third; and household decorations are on the fourth floor. Open daily from 10am to 10pm.

Shanghai Exhibition Centre. 1000 Yan'an Zhong Lu (west of Shaanxi Nan Lu), Jing An District. ☎ **021/6247-4781.**

Shopping in this state-run souvenir-and-gift gallery (officially known as the Shanghai Arts and Crafts Trading Corporation) is a bit on the grim side. The selection of Chinese arts and crafts, clothing, jewelry, and antiques isn't bad, but prices are a bit steep, there's no bargaining, and service can be slow. Open daily from 9am to 6pm.

Shanghai Jingdezhen Porcelain Artware. 1185 Nanjing Xi Lu (at Shaanxi Bei Lu), Jing An District. ☎ **021/6253-3178.**

An excellent selection of some of China's most prized ceramic creations, produced by factories and artisans in nearby Jingdezhen. Vases, plates, cups, and artware are expensive here, but the quality is high. Open daily from 9am to 9pm.

DEPARTMENT STORES

Shanghai has a large number of new, Western-style department stores that have almost completely replaced the traditional (but shoddy) Chinese version. Most of them are joint ventures with overseas retailing chains.

✪ **Friendship Store.** 40 Beijing Dong Lu, Huangpu District. ☎ **021/5308-0600.**

For visitors, this is the ultimate one-stop shop, containing a generous sampling of nearly everything worth hauling home: arts and crafts, jewelry, silk, books, souvenirs, antiques (see "One-Stop Gift Shopping at the Friendship Store," above). Make this your first and last shopping stop. Open daily from 9:30am to 10pm.

Hualian Department Store. 635 Nanjing Dong Lu (at Jinhua Lu), Huangpu District. ☎ **021/6322-4466.**

Shanghai's second-largest locally run department store, the former No. 10 Department Store was extensively remodeled in 1994, and it fits in nicely with the remodeled pedestrian mall. A supermarket was added in 1997. Open daily from 9:30am to 10pm.

Isetan. 527 Huaihai Zhong Lu (at Chengdu Lu), Luwan District. ☎ **021/5306-1111.**

A Japanese department store with high prices on exceptional goods and fashions, it offers its own bakery and an Esprit boutique in the heart of Huaihai Lu's most upscale shopping area. There's also a branch at the Westgate Shopping Mall on Nanjing Xi Lu (☎ **021/6375-1111**). Open daily from 10am to 9pm.

Jin Jiang Dickson Centre. 400 Changle Lu (at Maoming Nan Lu), Luwan District. ☎ **021/6472-7663,** 021/6472-6888, or 021/6472-0626.

Luxury clothing and housewares (as found in Hong Kong's best stores), offered here in the heart of the French Concession next door to the five-star Jin Jiang and Garden hotels. This is the place to shop for Ralph Lauren (although why you've come all the way to Shanghai to do so is a bit of a mystery). Open daily from 11am to 9pm.

Maison Mode. 1312 Huaihai Zhong Lu (at Changshu Lu), Xuhui District. ☎ **021/6437-5970.**

Here's an upscale Western department store with a touch of French fashion, across the street (north) from the Changshu subway station. It contains a Dunhill boutique and the city's first Elizabeth Arden Beauty Salon. Open daily from 10am to 9:30pm.

New World Department Store (Nanjiren). 2-68 Nanjing Xi Lu (at Xizang Zhong Lu), Huangpu District. ☎ **021/6358-8888.**

Located on the northwest side of the intersection where Nanjing Road East and the pedestrian shopping mall begins, this flashy seven-story emporium is highlighted by name-brand Western fashions and cosmetics. It is connected on the second floor to the intersection overpass and the new East Building of the No. 1 Department Store. Open daily from 10am to 10pm.

Parkson. 918 Huaihai Zhong Lu (at Shaanxi Lu), Luwan District. ☎ **021/6415-6384.**

On the north side of the street, this Malaysian-based department store is yet another upscale emporium of Western fashions and cosmetics, with a McDonald's next door. Prices are lower than on Nanjing Road. Open daily from 10am to 10pm.

Printemps-Shanghai. 939-947 Huaihai Zhong Lu (at Shaanxi Lu), Luwan District. ☎ **021/6431-0118.**

Carrying on the French Concession image of yesteryear, the Printemps is furnished in high Art Nouveau style (modeled after the 19th-century mother store in Paris), down to its designer-label boutiques and Parisian cafes. Open daily from 10am to 10pm.

✪ **Shanghai No. 1 Department Store, East Building.** 800-830 Nanjing Dong Lu (at Xizang Zhong Lu), Huangpu District. ☎ **021/6322-3344.**

Shanghai's most famous department store, opened in 1934, has been thoroughly updated with the incorporation of a 22-story tower. The first 11 floors are devoted to retailing, with women's shoes and cosmetics on the first floor; women's casual wear and lingerie on the second floor; women's business wear, cheong-sams, and children's wear on the third floor; menswear and shoes on the fourth floor; gifts, books, watches, toys, and musical instruments on the fifth floor; housewares on the sixth floor; sports equipment and sportswear on the seventh floor; snack shops on the eighth floor; and computer items on the ninth floor. Exhibitions and offices occupy the rest of the tower. Open daily from 10am to 10pm.

Wings Department Store. 869 Nanjing Xi Lu (at Taixing Lu), Jing An District. ☎ **021/6255-1111.**

Recently remodeled, this department store carries a variety of both Western and Chinese goods at fairly reasonable prices. Open daily from 10am to 10pm.

✪ **Yaohan/Nextage Department Store.** 501 Zhangyang Lu (at Pudong Nan Lu), Pudong New Area. ☎ **021/5830-1111.**

Touted as the second-largest department store on Earth (surpassed only by Macy's in New York), this Japanese-owned mega-store is only 10 stories tall, but a square block wide, and it's chock-full of everything department stores ever carry (and some they don't, such as automobiles on the ground floor and a roller coaster on the top floor). Directly across the street (south) is yet another big shopping mall, Times Square (☎ **021/5836-8888**)—as if another were needed. Open daily from 9:30am to 10pm.

Zhongsi Itokin. 592 Nanjing Dong Lu (at Hubei Lu), Huangpu District. ☎ **021/6352-3668.**

Eight floors of upscale shopping with a Japanese touch on the new Nanjing Road Pedestrian Mall. Open daily from 10am to 10pm.

JEWELRY

Angel Pearls. 17-D Maoshang Mansion, 1051 Xinzha Lu (at Shaanxi Lu), Jing An District. ☎ **021/6215-5031.**

The best place to shop for pearls (freshwater, South Sea pearls, Japanese cultured pearls). It also carries silk carpets and embroideries. Open daily from 10am to 6pm.

Lao Feng Xiang Jewelers. 438 Nanjing Dong Lu (at Shaanxi Nan Lu), Huangpu District. ☎ **021/6322-0033.**

Located on the north side of the Nanjing Road Pedestrian Mall, this jewelry store has long specialized in jade, pearls, and fine silver and gold ornaments. Open daily from 9am to 9pm.

Shanghai Li Ya Jewelry & Antiques. 369 Huashan Lu, Jing An District. ☎ **021/6249-8576.**

This shop offers finely crafted jewelry and art objects in jade, silver, gold, ivory, stone, and wood. Open daily from 10am to 6pm.

Drugstores

East meets West at **Shanghai Number One Dispensary,** 616 Nanjing Dong Lu (at Zhejiang Lu), Huangpu District (☎ **021/6322-4567**). This apothecary on the pedestrian mall carries a considerable number of foreign medicines. It's open daily from 9am to 10pm. If you just need a large, Western-style drugstore, try **Watson's,** 1376 Nanjing Lu, Shanghai Centre, Jing An District (☎ **021/6279-8381**), the only such store in Shanghai, with a fairly wide range of imported beauty and health aids, from cosmetics to toothpaste. There are two other branches, one in the nearby Westgate Mall and a second at 789 Huaihai Zhong Lu (☎ **021/6474-4775**). Open daily from 9:30am to 10pm.

Shanghai Qing Xiang Jade Factory. 33 Caobao Lu (west off Caoxi Lu), Xuhui District. ☎ **021/6436-0126.**

Start with a factory tour of handcrafted jade-carving workshops, followed by shopping for carved jade, ivory, and cloisonné giftware and jewelry. Popular with tour groups, this place has a fairly decent Mongolian barbecue buffet restaurant with a fresh-salad bar. Open daily from 9:30am to 9pm.

MALLS & SHOPPING PLAZAS

Shanghai has plenty of mammoth new shopping plazas (consisting of scores of independent brand-name and designer-label outlets selling international merchandise under one roof), particularly along Huaihai Zhong Lu.

Grand Gateway Plaza. 1 Hongqiao Lu (at Huashan Lu), Xuhui District. ☎ **021/6404-0111.**

When it opened on December 28, 1999, this claimed to be the biggest shopping mall in China with 245 shops. It is certainly big—and new and flashy. There are 30 restaurants alone on the fifth and sixth floors. Open daily from 10am to midnight.

Hongqiao Friendship Shopping Centre. 6 Zunyi Nan Lu (north off Yan'an Xi Lu), Hongqiao Development Zone, Changning District. ☎ **021/6270-0000.**

An excellent modern department store and specialty shops across the street from the Westin and the New World Marriott in the Hongqiao Development Zone of west Shanghai. Gucci, Clarins, and Christian Dior headline the international offerings. There's also a grocery, bakery, coffee shop, ice-cream counter, arts-and-crafts gallery, electronics shop, and book dealer, as well as a currency-exchange center. Open daily from 9:30am to 10pm.

✪ **Shanghai Centre.** 1376 Nanjing Xi Lu, Jing An District. ☎ **021/6279-8600.** www.shanghai-centre.com.

Just like never leaving home, this ark of the Western world has one or two of everything, from a Hard Rock Cafe to an espresso bar, from a drugstore (Watson's) to a supermarket (The Market). That's not to mention a deluxe hotel (Portman Ritz-Carlton Hotel), a medical and dental clinic, a theater, two apartment towers, an international school, and offices (DHL, American Express, half a dozen international airlines)—all in the same complex. The shopping is the most upscale in Shanghai, with outlets for Cerruti, Louis Vuitton, a. testoni, Stefano Ricci, and Cartier. Shop and office hours vary, but many are open daily from 10am to 10pm.

Shanghai Orient Shopping Center. 8 Caoxi Bei Lu (at Xujia Hui Station), Xuhui District. ☎ **021/6487-0000.**

Here you'll find everything under one high-tech roof, from an international wine gallery to the latest in women's international fashions. This is a four-story Hong Kong joint venture, complete with a marble lobby. Open daily from 10am to midnight.

Westgate Mall. 1038 Nanjing Xi Lu (at Jiangning Lu), Jing An District. ☎ **021/6218-7878.**

Called *Meilongzhen* in Chinese (after the famous restaurant that's adjacent), this is one of Shanghai's top Western-style malls. Among its most useful outlets are a florist, a Watson's drugstore, and a Park 'N Shop supermarket. On the 10th floor is Studio City, a multiplex cinema with six theaters, popcorn, and nice seats (☎ **021/6218-2173**). The anchor is Isetan department store (☎ **021/6272-1111**). The mall is open daily from 9:30am to 10pm.

SILKS & OTHER FABRICS

Golden Dragon Silk & Wool. 816 Huaihai Zhong Lu, Luwan District. ☎ **021/ 6473-6691.**

Golden Dragon carries a large selection of silk and wool yardage, as well as some blouses, suits, and dresses. Open daily from 10am to 9pm.

Silk Fabrics King. 819 Nanjing Xi Lu (near Shimen Yi Lu), Jing An District. ☎ **021/ 6215-3114.**

Silk yardage and a good selection of shirts, blouses, ties, sheets, and other finished silk goods are on offer here. A favorite stop for visiting heads of state and other VIPs, it features the local "Qifang" brand of silk garments. There is a second store at 139 Tianping Lu, Xuhui District (☎ **021/6282-5025**). Open daily from 10am to 8:30pm.

SUPERMARKETS

Many of Shanghai's hotels have a small shop with some Western snacks and bottled water, but for a broad range of familiar groceries, try one of the large-scale supermarkets listed below.

Carrefour. 268 Shuicheng Nan Lu, Gubei New Town, Changning District. ☎ **021/ 6270-6829.**

This French commodities giant offers the most extensive range of imported Western groceries in Shanghai. There's also a store at 560 Quyang Lu in the Hongkou District. Open daily from 8:30am to 10pm.

Friendship Supermarket. 40 Beijing Dong Lu (behind the Peace Hotel), Huangpu District. ☎ **021/6323-1419** or 021/5308-0600.

The Friendship Supermarket has a fair selection of Western foods and drinks. The entrance is near the back of the Friendship Store. Open daily from 9:30am to 10pm.

Lianhua Supermarket. 268 Shuicheng Lu, Gubei New Town, Changning District. ☎ **021/ 6278-3354.**

This is just one of the newest outlets of a huge modern Chinese grocery chain in Shanghai. There are more than 100 groceries in every section of the city and, seemingly, on every street. Lianhua carries plenty of local produce and Chinese brands, along with some imported goods at very reasonable prices. Clean, bright, and thoroughly up-to-date facilities make this the best local chain. Open daily from 8am to 9pm.

The Market. 1376 Nanjing Xi Lu (at Shanghai Centre), Jing An District. ☎ **021/ 6279-8018.**

Best place in town to pick up those Western foodstuffs you've been missing. It can be pricey, but there's a nice selection, with a fine deli in the back. This was the former **Wellcome Grocery Store.** Open daily from 8am to 10pm.

Park 'N Shop. 242 Julu Lu, Jing An District. ☎ **021/6253-3397.**

The emphasis here is on Western imports, including cheese and dairy products, wines, bakery goods, and soft drinks. Open daily from 8am to 10pm.

TAILORS

Other cities in Asia offer more extensive tailoring of suits, shirts, blouses, and dresses. Shanghai does have reliable and reasonably priced tailors, but most work out of tiny workshops. Check with your hotel desk for a reliable tailor.

Dave's Custom Tailoring. 8th floor, Jiu An Plaza, 258 Tongren Lu, Jing An District. ☎ **021/6247-4417.**

One popular choice, located near Shanghai Centre, is Dave's. It specializes in suits, shirts, and blouses from cotton and wool fabrics. Call for an appointment.

TEA
Huangshan Tea Company. 2nd floor, 853 Huaihai Zhong Lu, Luwan District. ☎ **021/6473-8101** or 021/6473-7627.

This store carries a nice assortment of classic Yixing teapots (made in the province next door) and loose Chinese teas sold by weight. There are additional retail outlets at 362 Huaihai Zhong Lu; 133 Xian Xia Lu (Hongqiao Development Zone); 218 Tainmu Xi Lu (in the Jusco Store); 1038 Nanjing Xi Lu (Westgate Mall); and 321 Changshu Lu (Gubei New Town). Open daily from 10am to 9pm.

9

Shanghai After Dark

Less than a century ago, Shanghai was the most notorious city in Asia, the fleshpot of China, with a nightlife that rivaled that of Paris. Old Shanghai had its gangsters and gambling dens, but it also had its tycoons and movie companies. After the Communists came to power in 1949 and set up the People's Republic of China, Shanghai was cleaned up overnight: drugs and prostitution were ended by decree; and entertainment was reduced to a few politically acceptable plays and dances. Well into the 1990s, visitors retired to their hotels after dark, unless they were part of a group tour that had arranged an evening's outing to see the Shanghai acrobats. Recently, however, the possibilities for an evening on the town have multiplied. Shanghai is not in the same late-night league as Hong Kong or Paris quite yet, but it is gaining ground.

On the one hand, Shanghai offers large-scale performances of acrobatics, opera, theater, dance, magic, and traditional music by China's premier artists. On the other, Shanghai has experienced an explosion of Western-style entertainment. Small cafe bars are booming. More than mere watering holes, these restaurants-by-day become music clubs by night, featuring live rock and jazz until the wee hours. There's even a Shanghai branch of the Hard Rock Cafe. Discos are popular, too, and, like the cafe bars, have become mixing bowls for locals and foreigners.

Shanghai is not quite the city it was in the romantic 1920s and 1930s (which may be a blessing since the colonial era had a very dark underside), but it is converting some of its newly won wealth into venues for culture and entertainment, enough so to tempt a traveler from turning in early.

1 The Performing Arts

Shanghai acrobatics are world-renowned, and a performance by one of the local troupes makes for a diverting evening. Classical music (both Eastern and Western) is regularly featured in the capital's theaters, hotels, and concert halls, as are Chinese opera, traditional music, and puppet and magic shows.

ACROBATICS
For 2000 years, the Chinese have been perfecting their acrobatic skills. These days, the juggling, contortionism, unicycling, chair

How to Find Out What's On

Check the entertainment listings in *Shanghai Daily* or the free English-language monthly papers for tourists and expatriates such as *that's Shanghai, Shanghai Now,* or *Shanghai Talk.* Your hotel tour desk or concierge may be able to secure tickets. The **Jin Jiang Optional Tours Center,** 191 Changle Lu, in the French Concession (☎ **021/6445-9525** or 021/6466-2828, ext. 231; fax 021/6472-0184), secures tickets for the Peace Hotel Jazz Bar and acrobatics and other performances at a number of theaters and concert halls. You can also go to individual ticket offices yourself. Locations of theaters, concert halls, teahouses, cafe bars, movie theaters, and other entertainment sites are listed in this chapter.

stacking, and plate spinning have entered the age of modern staging; performances are beginning to resemble the high-tech shows of a Las Vegas–style variety act. That's exactly what you'll see at the new Shanghai Circus World, a circus of many acts, headlined by acrobats. The **Shanghai Acrobatic Troupe,** certainly one of the world's best, tours the stages of the world, but it can often be found performing here at home. Acrobatic shows receive high marks from foreign tourists. Local acrobatic stages include the following.

Great World (Da Shi Jie). 1 Xizang Nan Lu (near People's Square), Huangpu District. ☎ **021/6326-3760,** ext. 40, or 021/6374-6703. Tickets 25RMB ($3). Performances nightly at 7:30pm.

This infamous vice den of the 1930s has been converted into an entertainment center for the entire family, with evening shows of acrobatics and martial arts on the outdoor stage in back, and opera and comedy mime teams on the second-floor stage indoors.

✪ **Shanghai Centre Theatre.** 1376 Nanjing Xi Lu, Jing An District. ☎ **021/6279-8663** or 021/6279-7132. Tickets 30RMB–60RMB ($3.60–$7). Performances most nights at 7pm.

This luxurious 1,000-seat modern auditorium at Shanghai Centre is equipped for a variety of performances, from movies to plays, but specializes in performances by the Shanghai Acrobatic Theater, which almost nightly gives a 2-hour variety show featuring about 30 standard and inventive acts, from plate spinning and tightrope walking to clowns and magic. A favorite with foreign tour groups.

✪ **Shanghai Circus World.** 2266 Gong He Xin Lu (near Zhabei Park), Zhabei District. ☎ **021/5665-3646** or 021/6652-2395. Tickets 50RMB–150RMB ($6–$18); "VIP" seats 280RMB ($34). Performances Tues, Fri, Sat at 7:30pm; Sun at 2pm.

This glittering new arena in the northern suburbs supplies Shanghai with a much-needed world-class venue for acrobatic performances. The large gold-and-green superdome, fashioned from an aluminum-titanium alloy, houses a circus theater with computer-controlled lighting and state-of-the-art acoustics that seats 1,672. The motorized revolving stage, covering 1,300 square feet (120m^2), is equipped for elaborate sets and special lighting effects. The celebrated Shanghai Acrobatic Troupe inaugurated the new arena with 2 months of sold-out 20-act performances. Check with your hotel for the current schedule and tickets.

OPERA

Shanghai has its own troupe that performs Beijing opera (*Jing Ju*) regularly at the Yifu Theatre. Beijing opera is derived from 8 centuries of touring song-and-dance troupes, but became institutionalized in its present form in the 1700s under the Qing Dynasty. The stylized singing, costumes, acrobatics, music, and choreography set Chinese opera quite apart from Western opera. It usually strikes foreigners as garish, screechy, and incomprehensible. It helps to know the plot (usually a historical drama with a tragic outcome), and English subtitles are sometimes provided. Songs are performed on a five-note scale (not the eight-note scale familiar in the West). The gongs, cymbals, and string and wind instruments punctuate (often jarringly) the action on the stage. Faces are painted with colors symbolizing qualities such as valor or villainy, and masks and costumes announce the performer's role in society, from emperor to peasant. Most Beijing opera these days consists of abridgments, lasting 2 hours or less (as opposed to 5 hours or more in the old days), and with the martial-arts choreography, the spirited acrobatics, and the brilliant costumes, these performances can be a delight even to the unaccustomed, untrained eye. Regional operas, including the Kunju form, are also performed in Shanghai. Regular venues include the following.

Kunju Opera House. 9 Shaoxing Lu (south of Fuxing Lu), Luwan District. ☎ **021/ 6437-1012.** Tickets 20RMB–30RMB ($2.40–$3.60). Performances Sat at 1:30pm and 7:15pm.

Kunju is the oldest form of opera in China, and this is China's leading troupe. Kunju opera was born near Shanghai in the old city of Kunshan. This style of opera uses traditional stories and characters, as does Beijing opera, but is known for being more melodic.

Majestic Theater (Mei Qi). 66 Jiang Ning Lu (at Beijing Xi Lu), Jing An District. ☎ **021/ 6217-4409.** Tickets 30RMB–60RMB ($3.60–$7). Performances as scheduled at 7:15pm.

Opera in Chinese, performed by local and touring groups, are staged in one of Shanghai's oldest and most ornate theaters. Worth attending just for the traditional atmosphere.

Shanghai Chinese Opera School. 1551 Zhongshan Xi Lu, Changning District. ☎ **021/ 6438-0820** or 021/6438-4277, ext. 2. Tickets 30RMB ($3.60). Performances Tues and Fri at 9am.

The Shanghai Chinese Opera School is where the region's best young students perfect the many skills required of top opera performers. Visitors can tour the facility and watch the students learn and perform scenes from classic opera every Tuesday and Friday morning.

✪ Yifu Theatre. 701 Fuzhou Lu, Huangpu District. ☎ **021/6351-4668.** Tickets 10RMB–40RMB ($1.20–$4.80). Performances most nights at 7:15pm; occasional matinees on weekends.

This is the premier venue for Shanghai's opera companies, accompanied by live opera orchestras and featuring dazzling acrobatics and martial arts to punctuate the singing and acting. The Shanghai Peking Opera House Troupe, featuring some of China's greatest opera stars, performs here regularly, as do the Shanghai Kunju Opera Troupe and such visiting companies as the Hangzhou Xiao Bai Hua Yueju Opera Troupe.

PUPPETS & MAGIC

Puppet shows (*mu ou xi*) have been performed in China since the Han Dynasty (206 B.C. to A.D. 220). Shadow puppets, hand puppets, and string puppets (marionettes) all take part in a typical show. Magic performances also have a long

Symphony Enters Its Third Century

The Shanghai Symphony was founded in 1879 to entertain the colonialists, taipans, and other Westerns in the city's International Settlement and French Concession. Known then as the Shanghai Municipal Band, it was the first such music group in China. The Shanghainese have embraced it over the decades, and Shanghai has produced many world-class classical musicians. After 1900, its conductor was the German Rudolf Buck; after World War I, the Italian Mario Paci took over. During World War II, the symphony suspended operations; in 1956, performances resumed; in 1990, it performed in Carnegie Hall. Over the last 44 years, it has held some 3,000 concerts, produced many recordings, and performed across Europe and North America. On October 9, 1999, its 100 musicians, under the baton of Chen Xieyang, celebrated its 120th birthday with a concert at the Shanghai Grand Theatre. The program featured two symphonies, one by Zhu Jian'er (his No. 10) and the other by Beethoven (his No. 9). The Shanghai Symphony is generally judged the best in China.

tradition in China. Neither art has a regular venue in Shanghai, but chances are you will find puppets, magic, or traditional comedy performed in the French Concession at the historic **Lyceum Theatre (Lan Xin),** 57 Maoming Nan Lu, Luwan District (☎ 021/6217-8530), built by the British as a drama theater. Shows begin at 7:30pm; tickets are usually 30RMB to 60RMB ($3.60 to $7).

OTHER PERFORMING-ARTS VENUES

Shanghai is the site of major national and international music, drama, and dance performances nearly every day of the year. The most frequent venues are listed here. In addition, local dramatic productions are often mounted at the **Shanghai Drama Arts Centre,** 201 Anfu Lu, Xuhui District (☎ 021/6433-5133), in a delightful old villa, and at the **Shanghai Theatre Academy,** 630 Huashan Lu, Jing An District (☎ 021/6248-5600 or 021/6248-2920, ext. 3040), where experimental plays are sometimes presented.

✪ **Grand Theatre (Da Ju Yuan).** 300 Renmin Da Dao, People's Square, Huangpu District. ☎ 021/6372-8701 or 021/6372-3833. Tickets and times vary depending on performance.

Boasting the largest stage in the world, Shanghai's Grand Theatre is a space-age complex with three theaters (the largest seating 1,800). It has quickly become the city's premier venue for international performers and concerts. Prices are usually 83RMB ($10) or more, and can top 1,250RMB ($150) for the best seats to world-class popular concert performers. Tickets can now be booked online at **www.thatsShanghai.com** and paid for at the box office the evening of the performance.

Jing An Hotel. 370 Huashan Lu, Jiang An District. ☎ 021/6248-1888, ext. 687. Tickets 20RMB ($2.40). Performances Fri at 8pm.

In the San Diego Room of this historic Art Deco hotel, there are weekly chamber concerts featuring performers from the Shanghai Symphony.

Shanghai Concert Hall. 523 Yan'an Dong Lu (south of People's Square), Huangpu District. ☎ 021/6460-4699 or 021/6318-3197. Ticket prices and times vary depending on performance.

This is where the Shanghai Symphony, the Shanghai Broadcasting Symphony, and the Shanghai Chinese Music Orchestra most often perform. Tickets can often be booked at the Shanghai Centre ticket office.

2 Jazz Bars

Shanghai was China's jazz city in the pre-revolutionary days (before 1949), and the place to meet over drinks to that sound was the Peace Hotel bar—a tradition that continues to this day (see below). The colonial legacy in jazz has been revived for the 21st century, too. Jazz is heard nightly in a number of Shanghai lounges, bars, and clubs. The preeminent venue is provided by the **Shanghai International Jazz Concert Series,** a spillover from the Beijing Jazz Festival that has been held during the second week of November each year since 1996. Headline groups from North America, Europe, Japan, and Australia perform at various venues. Visitors can hear year-round live jazz across Shanghai at the following nightspots.

Full House 2. 4 Hengshan Lu, Xuhui District. ☎ **021/6473-1181.** No cover.

This snazzy little bar is home to local Shanghai jazz bands who perform most nights from 9 to 11pm. The cafe bar is open daily from 10:30am to 2am.

✪ **Peace Hotel Old Jazz Bar.** 20 Nanjing Dong Lu, Peace Hotel (on the Bund), Huangpu District. ☎ **021/6321-6888.** Cover 50RMB ($6) at door, 80RMB ($10) in advance (assuring a table).

This place is an institution, with nearly continuous performances since the 1930s—and several of the band members claim to have played before Liberation (1949). The drinks are expensive and the music (old New Orleans standards) isn't always super, but the atmosphere is sheer nostalgia, and no evening could be more Old Shanghai than this. Heads of state have dropped in to hear Shanghai renditions of all the old standards. Performances start nightly at 8pm in the historic Art Deco jazz bar at the rear of the main lobby; closing time is 2am.

Portman Ritz-Carlton Hotel. 2nd floor, 1376 Nanjing Xi Lu (at Shanghai Centre), Jing An District. ☎ **021/6279-8888.** No cover.

Smooth, easy-listening jazz is performed by international combos Tuesday to Sunday evenings. There is no cover and the sofa seating is comfortable, but drinks and cigars are expensive.

Bells on the Bund

It's a two-story hike above the last elevator stop to the 11th-story roof garden of the Peace Hotel, but worth it for the view, the atmosphere, and the bells—the ancient chime bells of the fabled Kingdom of Chu. The bells were recently unearthed, and although no music from the period 2,400 years ago survives, some historically sound scores have been re-created. The elaborate and gorgeous set of bells played on the roof of the Peace Hotel is an exact copy of the priceless museum set, and the sounds are stunning. Chime-bell performances are held nightly from 7 to 10pm at the **Peace Hotel's Shanghai Night Bar,** 20 Nanjing Dong Lu (on the Bund), Huangpu District (☎ **021/6321-6888,** ext. 6248). There's a cover of 50RMB ($6).

Octoberfest in Shanghai

It may not require 6,000,000 liters of beer and 200,000 sausages, as in Germany, but Shanghai's Octoberfest can be quite Bavarian these days. A notable beer-garden celebration at **Paulaner Brauhaus,** 150 Fenyang Lu, Xuhui District (☎ **021/6474-5700**), runs for 10 nights starting in mid-October, featuring beer, games, and a brass band direct from Munich. One year (1999), even the mayor of Munich himself showed up here to kick things off. Still, the best fest is at the **Yangtze New World Hotel Marriott,** 2099 Yan'an Xi Lu, Changning District (☎ **021/6275-0000,** ext. 2369), where for 12 straight days (in late Sept; check for exact dates at the hotel), a large blue-and-white tent is pitched in the parking lot, long tables with German tablecloths are set up, an exceptional German buffet with barbecue opens, and a four-piece band from Munich performs polkas and jokes well into the night. The 138RMB ($17) admission includes plenty of music, lucky draws, a beer-drinking competition, all you can eat, and three huge glasses of beer. Hours are 6:30 to 11pm. On weekends, there's even an Octoberfest Family Brunch from 11:30am to 2:30pm; it costs 138RMB ($17) for adults and RMB8 (95¢) plus the child's age for kids 6 to 12.

3 Dance Clubs & Discos

Shanghai has some of the most sophisticated and elaborate dance clubs and discos in China. The bar scene is lively, too (see section 4, below), but clubs and discos are for those who really want to party on the dance floor as well as at the bar—or at least for those who want to observe Shanghai nightlife at a pitch it hasn't reached since the 1930s. What follows is a list of the top venues, which like all trends is subject to overnight revisions.

Cotton Club. 1428 Huaihai Zhong Lu, Luwan District. ☎ **021/6437-7110.** No cover.

This is the best place for live jazz and blues in the city, as the standing-room-only crowds on weekends make abundantly clear. There's no band on Monday; Tuesday is open-mike night. It's open nightly from 7:30pm to 3am; happy hour runs from 7:30 to 9:30pm. Credit cards are accepted.

D.Ds. 2nd floor, 322 Huashan Lu, Jing An District. ☎ **021/6248-2251.** No cover.

Opened in a new location late in 1999, this is a supper club with Southeast Asian dishes that features a special Latin dance night on Thursdays. The dance-floor action starts at 8pm every night, with no set closing hours.

Dkd. 172 Maoming Nan Lu, Luwan District. ☎ **021/6415-2688.** No cover.

With steel walls and silver counter, this is a hard-rock disco for those who like to dance. Women get two-for-one drinks on Friday and Saturday nights. The dance action starts at 8pm nightly.

George V. 1 Wulumuqi Nan Lu, Xuhui District. ☎ **021/6466-7878.** No cover.

You'd think you were in a colonial mansion, but this is actually a modern reproduction, with a stage and bar stools on the first floor and a mezzanine with seating above. There's live jazz during the week and heavy blues on the weekends. The music starts at 7:30pm nightly.

Pu-Js Puts Pudong on the Entertainment Map

The Pudong New Area on the east side of the Huangpu River, across from the Bund, has been the poor stepsister of old Shanghai when it comes to entertainment, but this late-night Cinderella suddenly stepped into the glass slipper with the opening of **Pu-J's Entertainment Centre**—Shanghai's newest, most stunning nightspot—in the Grand Hyatt Hotel. Located on Podium 3 at the base of the 88-story Jin Mao Tower, the world's third-tallest building, Pu-J's is the most upscale club in Shanghai. Designed by Tokyo's Super Potato, it is divided into four continuous action zones. There's a music sector devoted to live jazz performances, defined by a long bar with bottles and cigars displayed in 10 floor-to-ceiling glass columns; a tapas bar with Mediterranean snacks arranged on the counter; a lounge area that is lined with a ravine of granite slabs and its own waterfall; and the "Dance Zone," a raised disco stage encircled by glass bar stools on the floor and a white alabaster mezzanine bar above. Lively, sophisticated, and comfortable, Pu-J's has enough action and ambiance to keep visitors on this side of the river the entire night. Open Monday to Thursday from 7pm to 1am and Friday and Saturday from 7pm to 2am, Pu-J's exacts a 100RMB ($12) cover at the entrance (Podium 3, Jin Mao Tower/Grand Hyatt Shanghai, 2 Shiji Da Dao, Pudong New Area; ☎ **021/5049-1234,** ext. 8731).

✪ **Hard Rock Cafe.** 1376 Nanjing Xi Lu, Shanghai Centre, Jing An District. ☎ **021/ 6279-8133.** No cover.

American dining and the logo shop are downstairs; the band and dance floor are upstairs. There's live music Monday to Saturday beginning at 7:30pm. Credit cards are accepted. Open daily from 11:30am to 2am.

✪ **Judy's Too.** 176 Maoming Nan Lu, Luwan District. ☎ **021/6473-1417.** No cover.

An extremely popular dance spot with expatriates, the drinking and dancing here on the weekends often spills out into the streets. Live bands perform rock music. Doors open at 6pm, but the action doesn't start until much later (and seems to never end).

MGM. 141 Shaanxi Nan Lu, Luwan District. ☎ **021/6467-3353.** Cover 40RMB ($4.80) Sun–Thurs, 60RMB ($7) Fri–Sat.

One of Shanghai's most popular discos, at least with the local "beautiful people," MGM has a circular bar and a small, crowded dance floor at its heart. The dancing seldom gets going until 10pm. Open daily from 8pm to 5am.

New York New York. 146 Huqiu Lu (near the Bund), Huangpu District. ☎ **021/ 6321-6097.** Cover 50RMB ($6), free Wed–Thurs, free for women.

This started out as the hippest disco in Shanghai, but it's no longer quite the "in" spot that it once was. Open daily from 8:30pm to 3am.

Real Love. 10 Hengshan Lu, Xuhui District. ☎ **021/6474-6830.** Cover 30RMB ($3.60) Sun–Thurs, 50RMB ($6) Fri–Sat.

Located on the second floor over a bowling alley and packed nearly every night, this is currently the hottest disco spot in Shanghai. There are just enough red velvet sofas to go around. Open nightly from 8:30pm to 4am.

Rojam. 4th floor, Hong Kong Plaza, 283 Huaihai Zhong Lu, Luwan District. ☎ **021/ 6390-7181.** Cover 38RMB ($4.55) Sun–Thurs, 60RMB ($7) Fri–Sat.

Currently the hottest venue in town for disco. It opens nightly at 8pm and runs until almost dawn.

✪ **Tropicana.** 8th floor, 261 Sichuan Lu (at Hankou Lu), Huangpu District. ☎ **021/ 6329-2472.** No cover.

Shanghai's first salsa club recently opened a block off the Bund in a 1920s bank building. The eighth floor offers international chow (including caviar), the dance floor, stylish outdoor balconies, and a stage for live Latin bands. One story up, the rooftop bar has great downtown views and is perfect for those who fancy the Cuban cigars. Open nightly from 8pm.

YYs. 125 Nanchang Lu, Luwan District. ☎ **021/6431-2668.** No cover.

It used to have the stiffest cover charge among Shanghai's dozens of discos, but YYs, also known as Yin Yang, dropped the cover. It still has an exclusive feel. The dancing downstairs doesn't go into high gear until after 1am, although the doors open at 10pm. Upstairs is a lounge for chilling out. This place seldom closes much before sunrise.

4 The Lounge & Bar Scene

The big hotels often have elegant lounges on their top floors and some of Shanghai's best bars in their lobbies. These after-dark haunts are particularly popular with tourists and foreign business travelers. Outside the hotels, there's now no shortage of bars where foreign travelers are welcome to relax and enjoy a drink, listen to music, or dance into the wee hours. These independent spots run the gamut from upscale to down-and-dirty, but those listed below are frequented by a goodly number of English-speaking foreigners (residents and tourists alike) in addition to hip, well-to-do Shanghainese. Expect the drink prices, especially for imports, to be the same as you'd pay in the bars of a large city in the West. Tipping is not necessary, although it does make the bartenders happy. The greatest concentrations of late-night bars and lounges are in three adjacent areas west of the Bund: on Julu Lu (see below), in the upper Hengshan Lu area, and along Maoming Lu and Ruijin Lu in the heart of the French Concession.

Bar Twist. 53rd floor, Grand Hyatt Hotel (Jin Mao Tower), 2 Shiji Da Dao, Pudong New Area. ☎ **021/5049-1234,** ext. 8762.

This contemporary bar with its 22-foot (7m) lighted onyx counter doubles as a martini bar and a brew pub. The specialty beers (Shanghai's best selection) are displayed behind the bar and are illuminated from below by fiber-optic lights. Furnishings include tall mahjong tables and chairs with woven leather seats. Open nightly from 5pm to 1am; happy hour runs from 5 to 7pm. Credit cards are accepted.

B.A.T.S. Basement, Shangri-La Pudong Hotel, 33 Fucheng Lu, Pudong New Area. ☎ **021/ 6882-8888.**

This is a lively spot for drinking, dancing, and listening to live international bands (Latin sounds, Top 40). The dance floor has plenty of disco lights. B.A.T.S. stands for Bar At The Shangri-La. Open nightly from 5pm to 1am (until 3am Fri–Sat). The music starts at about 9:30pm. Credit cards are accepted.

Charlie's Bar. 400 Panyu Lu, Holiday Inn Crowne Plaza (in the lobby), Changning District. ☎ **021/6280-8888,** ext. 11010.

Often voted by international business travel magazines as one of Shanghai's top bars, Charlie's bills itself as a "fun pub" and comes equipped with dart boards, pin-ball machines, and monitors tuned to TV sports. Foreign bands play pop tunes Monday to Saturday nights. It boasts one of the longest happy hours in Shanghai: daily from 3 to 9pm. Open daily from 11am to 2am. Credit cards are accepted.

✪ **Cloud Nine and the Sky Lounge.** 87th floor, Grand Hyatt Hotel (Jin Mao Tower), 2 Shiji Da Dao, Pudong New Area. ☎ **021/5049-1234,** ext. 8098.

A top reason to spend the evening on the other side of the river, this lounge is the Art Deco crown of Shanghai's 21st-century glass-and-steel pagoda. It is also the highest hotel lounge in Asia. It takes three elevators just to reach Cloud Nine on the 87th floor; you can then walk up yet another flight to the intimate Sky Lounge on the 88th. Extraordinary panoramas abound, and the spring rolls, roving magician, and champagnes shouldn't be missed either. Open nightly from 5pm to 1am. Credit cards are accepted.

Dublin Exchange. 101 Yin Cheng Dong Lu (2nd floor, Senmao Building, east of the Pearl of the Orient TV Tower), Pudong New Area. ☎ **021/6841-2052.**

Sister bar to the popular O'Malley's, the Dublin Exchange is more upscale, with its stunning dark-wood Irish interior and fine, mostly European menu. Even the bar snacks are special (the "Pick O' Plenty," a mix of bacon, sausage, and chicken wings with deep-fried cheese and potato wedges, is a meal in itself). On tap are Guinness and Kilkenny. Live Irish music is played some nights, starting at 8pm, but the bar has yet to attract a large crowd from across the river for late evenings and weekends. Open Monday to Friday from 11am to midnight. Credit cards are accepted.

Face. Building 4, Ruijin Guest House, 118 Ruijin Er Lu, Luwan District. ☎ **021/6466-4328.**

The fading elegance of an old Shanghai villa is perfectly preserved in this romantic, relaxing, very colonial lounge with its cozy curving bar and tables. Face serves the two superb restaurants in the mansion (Lan Na Thai and Hazara) and anyone who wants to muse and sip. Open daily from 11am to 11pm. Credit cards are accepted.

Fest Brew House. 11 Hankou Lu, Huangpu District. ☎ **021/6323-0965.**

Shanghai's first true microbrew pub, Fest is still making its own good ales on the premises. It has a superb location, half a block off the Bund, and a happy hour that runs from 11am to 5pm. Open daily from 11am to 2am. Credit cards are accepted.

Flannagan's Pub. 899 Dongfang Lu (beside the Holiday Inn Pudong), Pudong New Area. ☎ **021/5830-6666,** ext. 70136.

A new, upscale pub in rich dark woods with some Irish touches, this is a popular spot with foreign businesspeople in the area for evening drinks and conversation. Open nightly from 5pm to 1 am. Credit cards are accepted.

Graffiti Bar. 2099 Yan'an Xi Lu, Yangtze Renaissance (Marriott) Hotel, Changning District. ☎ **021/6275-0000.**

Located just off the elegant hotel lobby, this bar's interior can be a shock, with its wildly painted walls and wildly shaped furniture, but it sets the tone for world beat and heavy metal music played live here Tuesday to Sunday nights. A trendy bar. Open nightly from 8pm to 3am. Credit cards are accepted.

K.M. Bar. 513 Haifang Lu (at Xikang Lu), Jing An District. ☎ **021/6256-4209.**

A discrete alternative bar, opened in 1998, that is favored by gay men. Open daily from 7pm to 2am.

Long Bar. 2nd floor, Shanghai Centre, 1376 Nanjing Xi Lu, Jing An District. ☎ **021/6279-8268.**

This lounge, popular with foreign residents, does have a fairly long bar. It also puts on fashion shows every Tuesday and Thursday at 9:30pm, and happy hours every day from 5 to 8pm. The pizzas and the jukebox are also worth a whirl. Open daily from noon to 3am. Credit cards are accepted.

M-Box. 3rd floor, Peregrine Plaza, 1325 Huaihai Zhong Lu (near Changshu Lu), Xuhui District. ☎ **021/6445-1777.**

Live local rock bands kick things off at 9pm nightly. Meals (Western and Asian) and drinks are served from 11am to 1am Sunday through Thursday, until 2:30am Friday and Saturday. Credit cards are accepted.

Malone's. 255 Tongren Lu (just northwest of Shanghai Centre), Jing An District. ☎ **021/6247-2400.**

The favorite sports bar of foreign residents in the area, Malone's is an American-style pub and restaurant with a dartboard, two pool tables, and 12 TV screens beaming down Western sports events. Most Friday and Saturday nights around 10:30pm, local rock bands take over the place. Open daily from 11:30am to 1am (until 2am Fri and Sat). Credit cards are accepted.

✪ **O'Malley's Irish Pub.** 42 Taojiang Lu (1 block west of Hengshan Lu), Jing An District. ☎ **021/6474-4533.**

Tucked away in a two-story colonial villa, this very comfortable pub is extremely popular with Shanghai's foreign residents (especially with its secluded front-garden seating in the summer). The Kilkenny and Guinness on tap are as good as Irish ale gets in China, and the Irish barkeepers are tops. So is the live Irish music that gets cranking around 8:30pm most nights. Open daily from 11am to 2am. Credit cards are accepted.

Penthouse Bar. 43rd floor, Hilton Hotel, 250 Huashan Lu, Jing An District. ☎ **021/6248-0000,** ext. 1880.

There's an incredibly romantic view of the city lights spreading all the way to the Bund from this richly furnished lounge where the lights shimmer like candles. Service and drinks are first-rate, as are the booths by the picture windows. Live music spices things up Monday to Saturday evenings at 8pm. Open nightly from 6pm to 1am. Credit cards are accepted.

Piano Bar. 53rd floor, Grand Hyatt Hotel (Jin Mao Tower), 2 Shiji Da Dao, Pudong New Area. ☎ **021/5049-1234,** ext. 8762.

Best described as luxurious, luxurious, luxurious, this lounge with the grand view has a spacious feel, oversize suede couches, contemporary opium beds, and crackled-glass Chinese tables discreetly spread out. The walls are lined in leather, and there's a baby grand. The bar specializes in single-malt Scotches from boutique distillers, cognacs, and cigars. Open nightly from 5pm to 1am. Credit cards are accepted.

Raise the Red Lantern. 5 Changshu Lu (south of the Hilton), Jing An District. ☎ **021/6247-1025.**

Shanghai's Bar Street (Julu Lu)

The liveliest, most compact strip of late-night bars in Shanghai these days is along Julu Lu, the city's unofficial bar street (*Shanghai Jiuba Jie*), located a few blocks southeast of the Hilton Hotel at the Changshu Lu intersection (Jing An District). Some of the cafe bars here barely survive a summer season, while others have been on Julu Lu for years. It's a popular place to stroll by day for inexpensive Western lunches and dinners, then barhop after the sun sets, although beyond midnight it attracts more than its share of drunken businessmen and Shanghai's ladies of the night. The street is gorgeous in the sunlight, especially the north side with its old plane trees and colonial villas. After dark, the neon takes over and the bars, mostly on the south side of the avenue, come alive and keep filling up until almost dawn.

Manhattan Bar, 905 Julu Lu (☎ 021/6247-7787), anchors the bar scene, opening its doors at 8pm, but not becoming packed with revelers until after midnight. It doesn't officially close until 7am. Manhattan is the oldest expat bar on the street and one of the oldest of its kind in Shanghai, dating back to 1988. It's flanked on the west side by **Goodfella's,** 907 Julu Lu (☎ 021/6467-0775), which pulls in a younger crowd than Manhattan's with its sound system. Opening up at 7pm, it may not close until dawn; its neon sign advertises BARFLIES & ALCOHOL & ROCK 'N ROLL.

On the east side of the Manhattan Bar is the new **Kinko Pub,** 903 Julu Lu (☎ 021/6279-2635), a fairly quiet, friendly place for a drink and popcorn at the bar in the rear (opens daily at 7:30pm). Kinko's sign promises NO FADE INSIDE . . . YOU WILL BE CONTENT . . . GO VENTURE. Eastward down the street are several eateries, including the venerable **Badlands,** 895 Julu Lu (☎ 021/6466-7788, ext. 8003), which serves decent, inexpensive Mexican grub in the back garden and holds a happy hour daily from 5 to 8pm; and **Yellow Submarine,** 911 Julu Lu (☎ 021/6415-1666), a favorite for pizzas.

Other popular watering holes within a 2-block crawl are the **H.J.H. Club,** 878 Julu Lu (☎ 021/6249-5537), and the **Woodstock Bar,** 893 Julu Lu (☎ 021/6466-7788, ext. 8001), where 1960s rock-and-protest music still lives into the wee hours.

The red lanterns are suspended over the sidewalk, and the red Chinese doors look ravishing. Inside is a big restaurant bar with plenty of snacks, coffees, drinks, and more than 5,000 songs on CDs. A new favorite of young, hip locals, it gives out free Internet use with each drink. The red lanterns are raised nightly at 5pm. Open daily from 10am to 5am.

Ritz-Carlton Bar. Mezzanine, Portman Ritz-Carlton Hotel, 1376 Nanjing Xi Lu (Shanghai Centre), Jing An District. ☎ 021/6279-8888.

Relaxed, sophisticated, and now outfitted with Shanghai's first walk-in humidor, this is a fine place to enjoy live jazz under the soothing effect of fiber-optic lighting. Open daily from 5pm to 1am. All credit cards are accepted.

Shanghai Sally's. 5 Xiangshan Lu (at Sinan Lu), Luwan District. ☎ 021/5382-0738.

Located in a fine old colonial mansion on the corner, opposite the Sun Yat-sen residence near Fuxing Park, Sally's was one of the first Shanghai bars to cater to foreigners.

Upstairs is an English pub; downstairs, you'll find a pool table and live rock music Monday to Saturday nights. Open Monday to Saturday from 5:30pm to 2am, Sunday from 2pm to 1am. Credit cards are accepted.

Soho Gallery Bar. 32 Maoming Nan Lu, Luwan District. ☎ **021/6217-9533.**

Drink mixes with art and music in this small, stylish gallery. The paintings on the walls, by local and international artists, are for sale, and the live music is traditional Chinese. Happy hour is always from 5 to 8pm. Open daily from 1pm to 2am.

Van Gogh Wine Bar. 207 Maoming Nan Lu, Luwan District. ☎ **021/6445-1146.**

This is a sweet, simple, pretty little two-story bar on the south end of the French Concession where the chief attraction is a quiet drink. Open daily from 5pm to 1am.

5 Cinema

Old Shanghai was the Hollywood of China. Many of the country's films were produced in Shanghai studios during the 1930s and 1940s. An aspiring actress with the stage name "Lan Ping" was among thousands who never achieved a starring role then, but later, after meeting and marrying the young revolutionary who would become Chairman Mao, she had her revenge. Known throughout the new Communist China after 1949 as Jiang Ching (and later punished as the leader of the Gang of Four), Madame Mao helped dictate the nature of politically correct cinema, drama, and other arts during the 1950s, 1960s, and 1970s. She was a star on the political stage for decades, but her real dream remained Hollywood.

Even today, China limits the release of new Hollywood films to just 10 a year, all dubbed into Mandarin. Chinese directors produced some of the best films in the world during the 1980s and 1990s, but some of these still can't be shown in China. Yet non-Chinese-speaking visitors hungering for a night at the pictures do have some outlets these days, particularly during the last 10 days of October, when the **Shanghai International Film Festival** comes to town (during odd-numbered years only). Originated in 1993, when Oliver Stone chaired the jury, the festival initially attracted 300,000 viewers to the screenings. The second festival, in 1995, drew an even larger audience, although there was a drop-off in numbers at the third festival, in 1997. The fourth festival, in 1999, signaled an upsurge. Four hundred films applied; those which were political in nature, addressed controversial topics, or contained sex scenes were dropped; and a final 19 were chosen. The good news for filmgoers is that many additional movies are shown "on the fringe" at select theaters during the festival. This biannual festival's next appearance will be in late October 2001.

In the meantime, the following are the best venues for flicks in Shanghai, which still has a long road to travel to regain its reputation as China's Hollywood. Tickets are generally just 20RMB to 30RMB ($2.40 to $3.60), unless otherwise noted.

Golden Cinema (Haixing). 4th floor, Haixing Plaza, 1 Ruijin Nan Lu, Luwan District. ☎ **021/6418-7034** or 021/6418-7031, ext. 122.

This big multiplex with four large screens, DTS and Dolby sound systems, and all the up-to-date conveniences often shows Hollywood and foreign films.

Guotai (Cathay) Theatre. 870 Huaihai Zhong Lu (at Maoming Nan Lu), Luwan District. ☎ **021/6473-2980** or 021/6473-0415.

Chinese and Hollywood movies are screened in this old Art Deco theater for the amazing price of just 5RMB (60¢).

Judy's Too. 176 Maoming Nan Lu, Luwan District. ☎ **021/6473-1417.**

This bar, restaurant, and disco club, a favorite with expatriates, shows many foreign movies (new and old) on Sunday nights at 7pm (during Judy's happy hour) and 9pm.

Paradise Theatre (Yong Le Gong). 308 Anfu Lu, Xuhui District. ☎ **021/6431-2961.**

Many English-language films with Chinese subtitles are screened here at the Shanghai Drama Arts Centre complex.

Shanghai Film Art Center. 160 Xinhua Lu (next to the Holiday Inn Crowne Plaza), Changning District. ☎ **021/6280-4088.**

The leading venue during the biannual Shanghai International Film Festival, this modern cinema complex with five spacious theaters features Hollywood releases on the big screen. Movies in the morning are just 5RMB (60¢) per ticket.

Studio City. 10th floor, Westgate Mall, 1038 Nanjing Xi Lu, Jing An District. ☎ **021/6218-2173.**

Shanghai's top multiplex theater with six cinemas, it features all the comforts of a movie complex at home: Dolby surround-sound system, seats with built-in cup holders, and popcorn from the concession in the lobby.

Yang's Kitchen. No. 3, Lane 9, Hengshan Lu, Jing An District. ☎ **021/6431-3028.**

Old films, including many Hollywood classics, are screened at this popular restaurant every Friday and Saturday at 10pm.

Suzhou, Hangzhou & Other Side Trips from Shanghai

Within an easy day trip of Shanghai are three superb destinations that should not be missed. To the north is Suzhou, the "Venice of China," with China's foremost gardens and canals. To the south is Hangzhou, renowned for beautiful West Lake and the surrounding tea plantations. To the east is Zhou Zhuang, the classic water village of the Yangzi River delta, with its arched bridges, narrow canals, and Chinese gondolas. Most travelers to Suzhou, Hangzhou, or Zhou Zhuang book a group tour with an English-speaking guide to smooth the way. The main drawback to such an arrangement is that you will have but a short time to explore the sites, the duration dictated by the tour company's schedule rather than your interest (or lack of it) at any point. Alternatives are to hire a driver and car yourself, with the assistance of your hotel concierge, or to use public buses (the cheapest but most grueling way to make the trip). Whatever means you choose, seeing these very different towns outside Shanghai will open up three more windows to Old Cathay.

1 Zhou Zhuang Water Village

The 900-year-old water village of Zhou Zhuang (Zhou's Town), 50 miles (80km) southwest of Shanghai, provides a superb opportunity to see something of rural China and the traditions that have been erased in a modern metropolis. On the way to the water village, you'll see the flat delta lands that surround Shanghai and the farms and factories that help fuel the port's booming economy. You can stop along the shores of **Lake Dianshan,** one of the largest in China, for a tour of **Grand View Garden (Da Guan Yuan),** a modern theme park that re-creates the setting of a classic 18th-century novel, *The Dream of the Red Chamber.* Zhou Zhuang Village is the real highlight, a town of canals and old mansions where you can take a ride on a gondola.

ESSENTIALS

Check with your hotel tour desk to book a bus tour of Zhou Zhuang. The **Jin Jiang Optional Tours Center,** 191 Changle Lu, near the Garden and Jin Jiang hotels (☎ **021/6445-9525**), offers a convenient group bus tour with an English-speaking guide and village lunch every Saturday, departing at 8am and returning in the late afternoon. The price is 350RMB ($42) for adults, 175RMB

($21) for children 2 to 11, and free for children under 2. The same operator can also arrange a private tour (on any day) with a guide, air-conditioned car, lunch, and door-to-door service (1,200RMB/$144 for one person; 650RMB/$78 each for two people; 550RMB/$66 each for three or four people; 450RMB/$54 each for five to seven people).

Independent travelers can also book a taxi for the day through their hotel or venture here completely on their own by using the **Qiangsheng Sightseeing Bus,** which departs from the corner of Jinling Lu and Yandang Lu four times a day (90-min. ride, 12RMB/$1.45 one-way). A public bus (the no. 4 Qingpu County sight-seeing bus) leaves from Shanghai Stadium every 45 minutes daily beginning at 8:30am with service to Zhou Zhuang (for more information, call ☎ **021/5605-2581**).

EXPLORING GRAND VIEW GARDEN

Even if you haven't read the classic Qing Dynasty soap opera of life and love on a vast estate (*The Dream of the Red Chamber,* by Cao Xueqin), you will enjoy a stroll through this garden theme park on the shores of Lake Dianshan, 37 miles (59km) from Shanghai. The grounds consist of a series of pavilions, courtyards, ponds, lanes, and scenic spots reconstructed to correspond to the lavish settings described in the novel. Local musicians entertain visitors in several of the courtyards, performers in costume reenact traditional Chinese marriages, and the scenery is splendid. Grand View Garden is open daily from 8am to 4:30pm (☎ **0520/6926-6629** or 0520/6926-6831). Admission is 40RMB ($4.80), and boat cruises on Dianshan Lake can be booked here for 50RMB to 100RMB ($6 to $12).

EXPLORING THE WATER VILLAGE

The water village of Zhou Zhuang resembles a scene from an antique blue-willow dinner plate, complete with canals, stone arched bridges, narrow lanes, and tile-roofed wooden houses. The town dates back 900 years, and many of its surviving mansions have roots in the Ming and Qing dynasties. It is quaint and cute and demands a few hours for strolling along the canal banks, exploring the tiny shops, touring several of the courtyard mansions, stopping for lunch, and above all, taking a gondola ride.

Surrounded by an ugly new town, the heart of the village is south, beyond the big public parking lot and the five-story Quanfu Pagoda. (At 100 feet high, it looks authentic, but was actually built in 1987.) An "ancient memorial archway" (also of recent vintage) leads to the first old canal. Follow the canal east (to your left) to the Double Bridge, and then turn south (to your right) along the main canal, which is bordered on both sides by old houses, restaurants, shops, and narrow lanes. Even today the town depends on canal traffic, although there's as much traffic in throngs of tourists as in sacks of rice. In the old days, these waterways (fed by the Baixian River and linked to the Grand Canal) were the chief means of moving rice, silk, handicrafts, and pottery to the port of Shanghai. Zhou Zhuang is one of thousands of water villages that once dotted the delta; it is one of the very few that still preserves its original landscape and canal system. These days, it caters to tourists who flood the town, especially on weekends, and clog the narrow lanes on either side of the main canal.

Of the 14 bridges that cross the town's waterways, nearly all date from dynastic times. The most celebrated is the **Double Bridge,** consisting of two arched bridges (Shi De and Yong An) built during the Ming Dynasty and linked to form an image

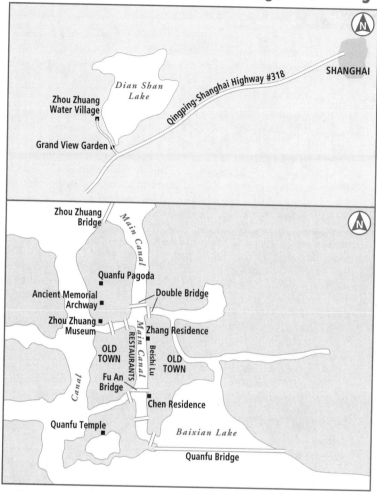

resembling that of an ancient Chinese key. These bridges lead to several mansions, built by village chiefs over the last 400 years, which are open to visitors (with welcome signs in English posted at their entrances). Roughly 600 of the 1,000 houses in the village date from the Yuan, Ming, and Qing dynasties.

Today, the **Zhang Residence** (just southeast of the Double Bridge, on Beishi Lu) is the oldest open to the public. Built between 1436 and 1449, it consists of six courtyards and more than 70 rooms. The Ruojing River runs beside it, and in ancient times it was said that while one might enter this house by a sedan chair, one could leave it by boat. In fact, beside the main hall (Yu Yan Hall), with its old carved wooden columns, there's a square pond where riverboats can stop and turn around. The Ming Dynasty interiors of the Zhang Residence are cool and mysterious, but rather plain and dark when compared to the brighter, more elaborately decorated interiors of the Qing Dynasty homes in the village.

Insider Tip

To escape the press of the crowds in the Zhou Zhuang water village, follow the main canal south to where it empties into Baixian Lake. Here, you can walk on the long Quanfu Bridge, watch the village fishermen row or sail in and out, and get a glimpse of the smaller courtyard houses of ordinary village families today.

The **Chen Residence** is the most fascinating of the houses dating from the Qing Dynasty (A.D. 1644 to 1911). Located south of the Zhang house near the Fu An Bridge, it was built in 1742. This wooden complex, which consists of a series of two-story halls separated by seven courtyards, occupies both sides of the lane. The canal side consists of a water gate and a wharf for mooring barges. The other side of the lane includes a Tea Hall and the main building (Song Mao Hall) with its elaborately carved beams and pillars, which served as a reception room and chamber for both weddings and funerals. One of the subsequent halls was reserved for men only; following it is a separate hall for women of the clan. At the rear of the courtyard estate are the bedrooms of the family and the workshops of craftsmen employed by the clan. Altogether, the residence has more than 100 rooms. The two-story buildings on the shore are joined to the two-story halls across the lane (Nanshi Lu) by an early Chinese versions of the skywalk. The Chen Residence is also stuffed with Qing Dynasty furniture; there's a statue of the clan founder, Mr. Chen himself, in the ancestral shrine; and there are even rumors that a restaurant will open soon.

The main canal is lined not only with crafts and antiques shops run by villagers, but also by art students from Shanghai who set up their easels along the shore and draw or paint the idyllic vistas that are the chief charm of the town. The main canal is also the site of dozens of simple dining halls, each with their shutters wide open to the busy canal traffic. Lunch here consists of simple rice-and-vegetable dishes, highlighted by river fish and the local specialty, a slow-cooked pork leg with a sweet, salty soup (known locally as Wansan Pig's Upper Leg). The Shanghainese usually purchase slabs of this roasted treat to take home. More adventurous diners partake of dishes cooked to order on the canal by floating kitchens (small open boats equipped with charcoal stoves and the catch of the day).

The canal **gondolas** are irresistible. Driven and propelled by local peasant women who deftly row the waters using only the long tillers mounted on the stern, they provide visitors with a quiet, relaxing sail up and down the long canal, passing under the old arched bridges and anchoring uptown near the Zhou Zhuang Museum. The gondolas, canals, shops, and mansions make for something of a poor man's Venice, distinctly rural and Chinese. The city museum is modest, too, without English signage, housing a pretty collection of 300-year-old pottery produced here. While the whole village is like a living-history museum of country life on the Yangzi River delta, and crowded now with tour groups, it retains its rustic charms, making for a fascinating break from the modern urban maze of busy Shanghai.

There is no charge for entry to the town. The mansions and museums exact a small charge (5RMB/60¢ to 10RMB/$1.20), lunch is well under 83RMB ($10), and the gondolas, which hold up to eight people, can be hired for about 60RMB ($7). Weekdays are the least crowded times to visit. Current information is available by calling ☎ 520/721-1643 or 520/721-1655. The township's high-tech Web site is at **www.zhouzhuang.net**.

2 Suzhou, City of Gardens

50 miles NW of Shanghai

Suzhou's interlocking canals, which have led it to be called the "Venice of the East," its classic gardens, and its embroidery and silk factories are the chief surviving elements of a cultural capital that dominated China's artistic scene for long periods during the Ming and Qing dynasties. Despite modernization, Suzhou remains one of the most beautiful cities in China.

ESSENTIALS

Check with your hotel tour desk to book a bus tour of Suzhou. The **Jin Jiang Optional Tours Center,** 191 Changle Lu, near the Garden and Jin Jiang hotels (☎ **021/6445-9525**), offers a convenient 1-day group bus tour with an English-speaking guide and lunch, departing at 8am every Monday, Wednesday, Friday, Saturday, and Sunday, and returning in the late afternoon. The price is 350RMB ($42) for adults, 175RMB ($21) for children 2 to 11, and free for children under 2. The same tour operator can also arrange a private tour (on any day) with a guide, air-conditioned car, lunch, and door-to-door service (1,400RMB/$168 for one person, 800RMB/$96 each for two people, 600RMB/$72 each for three or four people, 500RMB/$60 each for five to seven people).

Independent travelers can also book a taxi for the day through their hotel or venture here completely on their own by frequent trains (25RMB/$3) from Shanghai. The train trip takes less than 90 minutes. **China International Travel Service (CITS),** with headquarters in the Suzhou Hotel, 115 Shiquan Jie (☎ **0512/ 522-3175;** fax 0512/523-3593), can arrange tours of the city with English-speaking guides. A daylong "Panda Car Tour" of the city costs 260RMB ($31), with lunch included.

EXPLORING SUZHOU

Central Suzhou, surrounded by remnants of a moat and canals linked to the Grand Canal, has become a protected historical district, 2 by 3 miles (3km by 5km) across, in which little tampering and no skyscrapers are allowed. Here the outlines of old Suzhou are still clearly imprinted on its chessboard of canals and bridges. More than 170 bridges arch over the 20 miles of slim waterways within the moated city. The poetic private gardens number about 70, with a dozen of the finest open to public view. No other Chinese city contains such a concentration of canals and gardens.

CLASSIC GARDENS

Suzhou's magnificent collection of formerly private gardens, the finest surviving examples of the classic tradition, are small, exquisite jewels of landscaping art, often choked with visitors, making a slow, meditative tour difficult. Designed on different principles than those of the West, a Chinese garden fuses landscape painting and literary composition to create an art of its own in which nature is shaped but not tamed. These private classic gardens are Suzhou's most prized possessions. Among those worth visiting are the gardens listed below.

FOREST OF LIONS GARDEN (SHI ZI LIN YUAN)   Founded in 1336 by a Buddhist monk and last owned by relatives of renowned American architect I. M. Pei, this garden consists of four small lakes, a multitude of buildings, and random swirls of tortured rockeries that resemble the manes of lions. These rocks and rockeries, a standard feature of Chinese gardens, evoke the mountains of the natural world, just as the ponds evoke lakes or seas. The finest of the expressionistic rock slabs in the Forest of Lions Garden come from nearby Lake Tai (Tai Hu). Since the Tang Dynasty (A.D. 618 to 907), connoisseurs have been selecting the best "Tai Hu" rocks for the gardens of emperors, high officials, and rich estate owners. During the Song Dynasty (A.D. 960 to 1126), rock appreciation reached such extremes that the expense in hauling stones from Lake Tai to the capital is said to have bankrupted the empire. Since the Forest of Lions Garden was designed to emphasize the role of mountains in nature, it is not surprising that it contains the largest rocks and most elaborate rockeries of any garden in Suzhou. The garden is located at 23 Yulin Lu (☎ **0512/727-2428**). It's open daily from 7:30am to 5pm; admission is 10RMB ($1.20).

LINGERING GARDEN (LIU YUAN)   This garden is the setting for the finest Tai Hu rock in China, a 20-foot-high, 5-ton contorted castle of stone called Crown of Clouds Peak. Lingering Garden is also notable for its viewing pavilions, particularly its **Mandarin Duck Hall,** which is divided into two sides: an ornate southern chamber for men and a plain northern chamber for women. Suzhou's contemporary painters maintain a sales gallery in this garden, which is planted in osmanthus and willow. These varieties are not known for their brilliant flowerings, in keeping with a traditional prejudice for plain, unshowy vegetation. Lingering Garden is at 80 Liuyuan Lu (☎ **0512/533-7940**). Hours are daily from 8:30am to 5pm; admission is 20RMB ($2.40).

HUMBLE ADMINISTRATOR'S GARDEN (ZHOU ZHENG YUAN)   Usually translated as "Humble Administrator's Garden," but also translatable as "Garden of the Stupid Officials," Zhou Zheng Garden, which dates from the 16th century, makes complex use of the element of water. The maze of connected pools and islands seems endless, and the creation of multiple vistas and the dividing of spaces into distinct segments are the garden artist's means to expand the compressed spaces of the estate. As visitors stroll through a small garden, new spaces and vistas **826-7737**). It's open daily from 7:30am to 5pm; admission is 30RMB ($3.60).

✪ MASTER OF THE NETS GARDEN (WANG SHI YUAN)   The most perfect of Suzhou's gardens**,** the Master of the Nets Garden is a masterpiece of landscape compression. Hidden at the end of a blind alley, its tiny grounds have been cleverly expanded by the placement of innumerable walls, screens, and pavilion halls, producing a maze that seems endless. The eastern sector of the garden is a cluster of three interlinked buildings, the residence of the former owner and his family. At the center of the garden is a pond, just one mu square (about 2,700 sq. ft.), encircled by verandas, pavilions, and covered corridors, crossed by two arched stone bridges. Set back from this watery "mirror of heaven," with its proportionate rockeries and bamboo, is a complex of halls and inner courtyards: a garden within a garden. The halls invite rest and meditation.

The most lavish hall, **Dianchun Cottage,** furnished in palace lanterns, dark chairs and tables, and hanging scrolls, served as the model for Mingxuan Garden, the Astor Chinese Garden Court, and Ming Furniture Room constructed in 1980 at the Metropolitan Museum of Art in New York City. The original, owing to its setting, has a much more open feel than its museum version.

Master of the Nets Garden is at 11 Kuotao Xiang, off Shiquan Jie (☎ **0512/ 522-3550**). Hours are daily from 8am to 4:30pm; admission is 10RMB ($1.20). In the summer, performances by traditional music and dance troupes are staged in the garden daily at 7:30pm (60RMB/$7).

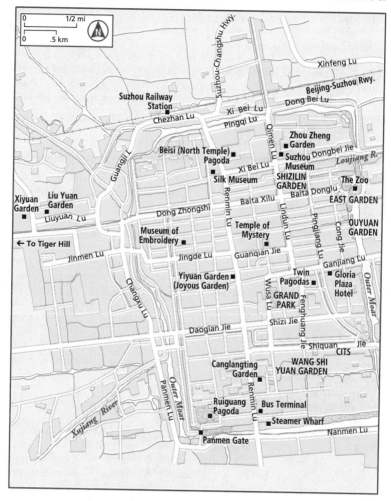

Map of Suzhou showing: Suzhou-Changshu Hwy., Xinfeng Lu, Beijing-Suzhou Rwy., Suzhou Railway Station, Chezhan Lu, Xi Bei Lu, Pingqi Lu, Dong Bei Lu, Qimen Lu, Zhou Zheng Garden, Dongbei Jie, Loujiang R., Beisi (North Temple) Pagoda, Suzhou Museum, Silk Museum, Xi Bei Lu, SHIZILIN GARDEN, Baita Donglu, The Zoo, EAST GARDEN, Xiyuan Garden, Liu Yuan Garden, Guangji L, Liuyuan Lu, Dong Zhongshi, Baita Xilu, Rennin Lu, Lindun Lu, Pinghang Lu, Cong Jie, OUYUAN GARDEN, ← To Tiger Hill, Museum of Embroidery, Temple of Mystery, Jinmen Lu, Jingde Lu, Guanqian Jie, Ganjiang Lu, Changxu Lu, Yiyuan Garden (Joyous Garden), Wusa Lu, Twin Pagodas, Gloria Plaza Hotel, GRAND PARK, Fenghuang Jie, Outer Moat, Daogian Jie, Shizi Jie, Shiquan Jie, CITS, Canglangting Garden, WANG SHI YUAN GARDEN, Panmen Lu, Outer Moat, Renmin Lu, Ruiguang Pagoda, Bus Terminal, Steamer Wharf, Nanmen Lu, Panmen Gate, Xujiang River

✪ **TIGER HILL (HU QIU SHAN)**   Suzhou's best park contains not only gardens in the classic style, but also a famous pagoda and theme-park robotic figures as well. These modern additions have jazzed up the place and appeal to young children and their parents, it seems, but they are really just so much garish frosting.

A new path from the entrance passes by a number of the park's historic sights, including Han Spring (used since A.D. 500, when it cured a monk of blindness) and several mythic rocks. At the very top of Tiger Hill is the remarkable leaning pagoda **Yunyan Ta (Cloud Rock Pagoda),** a seven-story work dating from A.D. 961, now safely shored up by modern engineering, although it still leans. Under the pagoda is the legendary grave of Suzhou's founder, He Lu, a 6th-century B.C. leader whose arsenal of 3,000 swords is also said to be buried in the park and protected by a white tiger. The artificial hill on which the pagoda stands was once an island. To one side is a stone tablet engraved by Qing emperor Qianlong, as well as the plain Great Hall Temple. Down below is a large bonsai garden with more than 600 specimens and a big tree said to be over 500 years old.

The most remarkable site at the foot of the Tiger Hill pagoda is a natural ledge, the **Ten Thousand People Rock,** where, according to legend, a rebel delivered an oratory so fiery that the rocks lined up to listen. A deep stone cleavage, the **Pool of Swords (Jianchi),** runs along one side of it, reputedly the remnants of a pit dug by order of the First Emperor (Qin Shi Huang) 2,000 years ago in search of the 3,000 swords.

Tiger Hill is located 2 miles (3km) northwest of the city at 8 Huqiu Shan (☎ 0512/826-7737). It's open daily from 8am to 5pm; admission is 25RMB ($3).

WATER GATES & CANALS

Suzhou is the city of canals as well as of gardens. **Panmen Gate,** at 2 Dong Da Lu (☎ 0512/826-7737), once operated as a water gate and fortress when the Grand Canal was the most important route linking Suzhou to the rest of China. Built in A.D. 1351, Panmen is the only major piece of the Suzhou city wall to survive. It's open daily from 8am to 5pm. Nearby is a large arched bridge, **Wumen Qiao,** over the Grand Canal—the finest place to view the ever-changing traffic—and a small arched bridge over a feeder canal that connects to Panmen. Panmen also has excellent vistas of the old city, including a view of Ruiguang Ta, a 122-foot pagoda built in A.D. 1119. The keepers of this gate now levy an admission fee (15RMB/$1.80), which includes a ticket to an uninteresting, recently restored royal mansion and a new, uninspiring amusement park adjacent.

The Panmen district and the southern streets of old Suzhou are excellent places to walk at one's leisure. Traditional shophouses predominate, the streets are narrow and shaded by trees, interesting galleries abound, and there are bridges and lanes where you can watch the canal traffic, an endless stream of barges propelled by poles as well as motors. Near Panmen, the old city moat widens and the water traffic thickens.

Uptown, Suzhou is laced by narrow canals. The backs of the white houses are still open to the water, and quite a bit of commerce is conducted here. The gondoliers of Suzhou evoke little of the romance of vanished dynasties, but they do reveal the rough-edged world of handwork that hundreds of millions of Chinese do each day. And there is something beautiful still in the canal scene of Suzhou when the arched bridges and simple stucco houses and floating barges line up just right.

SILK FACTORIES

Suzhou is synonymous not only with gardens and canals, but also with silk. Its silk fabrics have been among the most prized in China for centuries, and the art of silk embroidery is still practiced at the highest levels. Perhaps more than any other product, silk made Suzhou a city of importance in China. When the Song Dynasty rulers moved the political capital to nearby Hangzhou, Suzhou became China's cultural capital.

The **Museum of Suzhou Embroidery,** 262 Jingde Lu (☎ 0512/522-2403), is both a factory and a sales outlet, containing the most accomplished silk embroideries you'll find in China. The artists working upstairs stitch by hand, depending only on natural light, without magnifying lenses or other aids. Thinning the filaments of silk thread down to almost invisible lines, they work 2-hour stretches and take 10-minute tea breaks. The embroidery factory also produces double-sided embroideries on a canvas of thin silk gauze, a technique developed here in which two different figures, front and reverse, are stitched using two needles simultaneously—what the factory guide calls "a secret technique." The finished embroidery is mounted in a mahogany frame carved in Ming or Qing Dynasty style. The museum is open daily from 9am to 5pm; admission is free.

A less commercial display of Suzhou's silk industry is offered by the **Suzhou No. 1 Silk Mill,** 94 Nan Men Lu (☎ 0512/525-1047), open daily from 9am to 6pm with free admission. This is the site of a 60-year-old silk factory where you can still see the old looms in operation. The complete history of silk and the process of its manufacture is explained by English-speaking guides. An extensive sales room offers silk clothing and souvenirs.

WHERE TO STAY & DINE

If you plan to spend the night in Suzhou, the top hotel is the five-star **Sheraton Suzhou Hotel & Tower (Kailai Dajiudian),** 388 Xin Shi Lu, near Pan Men, southwest Suzhou (☎ 800/325-3535 in the U.S. and Canada, or 0512/510-3388; fax 0512/510-0888). With 328 rooms each going for 1,435RMB ($175) double, this hotel receives rave reviews from most visitors. Another good choice is the 300-unit **Gloria Plaza Hotel Suzhou (Kailai Dajiudian),** east of city center at 535 Ganjiang Dong Lu (☎ 0512/521-8855; fax 0512/521-8533). A double costs 1,230RMB ($150) here.

Hotel restaurants offer the best food in town and accept credit cards. The best local fare is at the **Songhelou (Pine and Crane Restaurant),** 141 Guanqian Jie (☎ 0512/727-7006), a downtown establishment that claims to have been in business since Emperor Qianlong visited Suzhou in the 18th century. The menu is strictly Suzhou, with braised eel, sea cucumber, and duck and pork dishes. Prices are 30RMB to 120RMB ($3.60 to $14) per dish; it's open daily from 8am to 9pm.

3 Hangzhou & West Lake

115 miles SW of Shanghai

Seven centuries ago, Marco Polo pronounced Hangzhou "the finest, most splendid city in the world . . . where so many pleasures may be found that one fancies oneself to be in Paradise." Today, Hangzhou's claim to paradise does not lie in its streets, which are ordinary, but in its shoreline and the surrounding countryside, where strolling and biking are the best you'll find in the Middle Kingdom.

The focus of Hangzhou's exceptional beauty is **West Lake (Xi Hu).** It's a small lake, about 3 miles (5km) across and 9 miles (14km) around. You can walk the circumference in under 4 hours—longer if you linger at a temple, pavilion, cafe, or park. Two causeways—one running on the north shore, the other on the west shore—vary and shorten the journey. The islets and temples, pavilions and gardens, causeways and arched bridges of this jadelike lake have constituted the supreme example of lakeside beauty in China ever since Hangzhou served as China's capital during the Southern Song Dynasty (A.D. 1127 to 1279). The shallow waters of West Lake are sufficient to fill and beguile the eye's compass, but not to overwhelm it. Hangzhou's West Lake remains to this day what one 12th-century visitor proclaimed it: "a landscape composed by a painter."

ESSENTIALS

Check with your hotel tour desk to book a bus tour of Hangzhou. The **Jin Jiang Optional Tours Center,** 191 Changle Lu, near the Garden and Jin Jiang hotels (☎ 021/6445-9525), offers a convenient 1-day group bus tour with an

Hangzhou

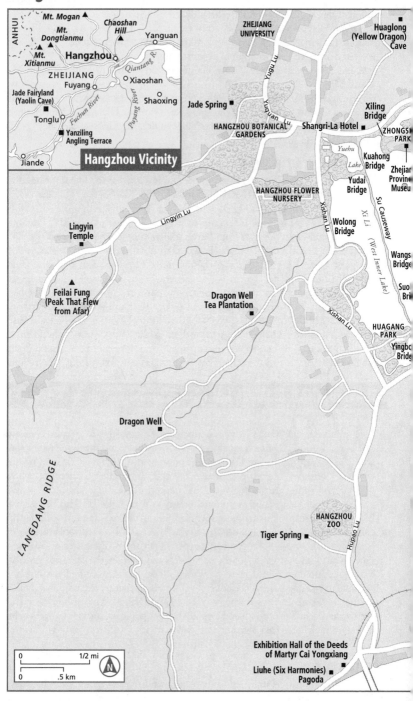

Mt. Mogan ▲

Chaoshan Hill ▲

ANHUI

Mt. Dongtianmu ▲

Yanguan ○

Mt. Xitianmu ▲

Hangzhou ○

ZHEJIANG

Fuyang ○

Qiantang R.

Xiaoshan ○

Jade Fairyland (Yaolin Cave) ●

Fuchun River

Shaoxing ○

Puyang River

Tonglu ○

Yanziling Angling Terrace ▲

Jiande ○

Hangzhou Vicinity

ZHEJIANG UNIVERSITY

Huaglong (Yellow Dragon) Cave ■

Yugang Lu

Jade Spring ■

Yuquan Lu

Xiling Bridge

HANGZHOU BOTANICAL GARDENS

Shangri-La Hotel ■

ZHONGS PARK

Yuehu Lake

Kuahong Bridge

Zhejian Provin Museu

HANGZHOU FLOWER NURSERY

Yudai Bridge

Lingyin Lu

Xishan Lu

Wolong Bridge

Su Causeway

Xi Li (West Inner Lake)

Lingyin Temple ■

Wangs Bridge

Feilai Fung (Peak That Flew from Afar) ▲

Dragon Well Tea Plantation ■

Suo Bri

Xishan Lu

HUAGANG PARK

Yingbo Bridge

Dragon Well ■

LANGDANG RIDGE

HANGZHOU ZOO

Hupao Lu

Tiger Spring ■

Exhibition Hall of the Deeds of Martyr Cai Yongxiang ■

Liuhe (Six Harmonies) Pagoda ■

0   1/2 mi
0   .5 km

N

186

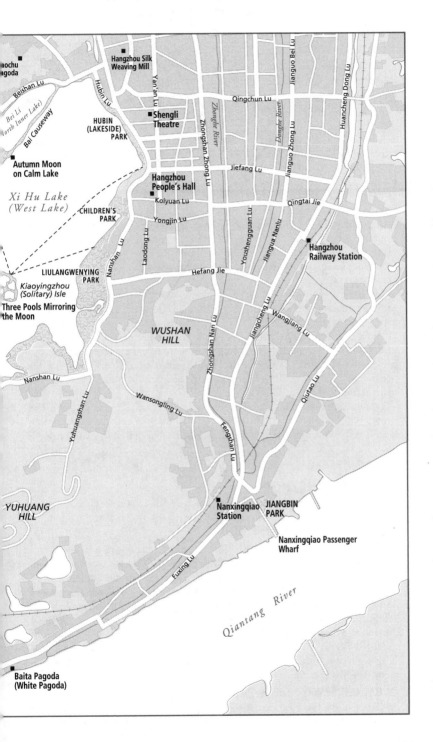

Hangzhou Silk Weaving Mill

iochu
agoda

Beishan Lu

Bei Li
North Inner Lake)

Bai Causeway

HUBIN
(LAKESIDE)
PARK

Autumn Moon
on Calm Lake

Xi Hu Lake
(West Lake)

CHILDREN'S
PARK

LIULANGWENYING
PARK

Kiaoyingzhou
(Solitary) Isle

Three Pools Mirroring
the Moon

Hubin Lu

Yan'an Lu

Shengli
Theatre

Hangzhou
People's Hall

Koiyuan Lu

Yongjin Lu

Nanshan Lu

Laodong Lu

Zhongshan Zhong Lu

Zhonghe River

Qingchun Lu

Jiefang Lu

Hefang Jie

Youshengguan Lu

Jianguo Zhong Lu

Dinghe River

Jianguo Bei Lu

Huancheng Dong Lu

Qingtai Jie

Jianhua Nanlu

Hangzhou
Railway Station

WUSHAN
HILL

Nanshan Lu

Yuhuangshan Lu

Wansongling Lu

Zhongshan Nan Lu

Fengshan Lu

Jiangcheng Lu

Wangjiang Lu

Qiutao Lu

YUHUANG
HILL

Nanxingqiao
Station

JIANGBIN
PARK

Nanxingqiao Passenger
Wharf

Fuxing Lu

Qiantang River

Baita Pagoda
(White Pagoda)

English-speaking guide and lunch, departing at 8am every Tuesday, Thursday, and Saturday, and returning in the late afternoon. The price is 500RMB ($60) for adults, 250RMB ($30) for children 2 to 11, and free for children under 2. This tour can be extended to include overnight accommodations and a train back to Shanghai for an extra 350RMB ($42) for adults and 175RMB ($21) for children 2 to 11. The same tour operator can also arrange a private day tour (on any day) with a guide, air-conditioned car, lunch, and door-to-door service (2,000RMB/$240 for one person; 1,200RMB/$144 each for two people; 850RMB/$102 each for three or four people; 700RMB/$84 each for five to seven people); the 2-day overnight private tour with hotel costs 3,300RMB ($396) for one, 1,800RMB ($216) each for two, 1,400RMB ($168) each for three or four, 1,150RMB ($138) each for five to seven people.

Independent travelers can book a taxi for the day through their Shanghai hotel (Hangzhou is a 2- to 3-hour ride via the new Hu Hang Expressway) or venture here completely on their own via frequent trains (2-hr. trip, 35RMB/$4.20). In Hangzhou, **China International Travel Service (CITS),** Shihan Lu (☎ **0571/ 515-2888;** fax 0571/515-6576), can arrange tours of the city with English-speaking guides.

The business center in the Shangri-La Hotel's West Building also offers escorted half- and full-day tours of Hangzhou, conducted by local English-speaking guides, with the price based on the number of participants. Half-day tours cost 470RMB ($56) for one person, 300RMB ($36) each for two to five people, 200RMB ($24) each for six to nine, and 160RMB ($19) each for 10 or more people. Full-day tour rates are proportionate, costing 696RMB ($84) for one, 420RMB ($50) each for two to five, 320RMB ($38) each for six to nine, and 240RMB ($29) each for 10 or more people.

Various Chinese airlines connect Hangzhou to Shanghai, a 25-minute flight. The airport is 9 miles (14km) from downtown (50RMB/$6 taxi fare). For getting around Hangzhou, hire taxis or rent a bicycle at the Shangri-La Hotel (see below). Bikes go for 20RMB ($2.40) per hour, 50RMB ($6) per half day, or 100RMB ($12) per day.

EXPLORING HANGZHOU

The city surrounds the shores of West Lake, which is gorgeous. Strolling the lakeshore and its causeways and visiting the tiny islands by tour boat should not be missed. The top attractions are as follows.

SOLITARY ISLAND (GUSHAN) Situated on the lake's northwest shore, this big island is connected to shore by the **Xiling Bridge,** dedicated to poet Su Xiaoxiao, who was entombed here in A.D. 501. Here the dawn mists enwrap a willow-draped shoreline that resembles an old Chinese landscape. A roadway sweeps eastward across Solitary Island toward the city skyline, past monumental tile-roofed halls built in the style of Qing Dynasty palaces. One of these buildings is the **Zhejiang Provincial Museum** (☎ **0571/797-0017**), which contains the oldest grains of cultivated rice in the world (discovered 7,000 years ago in a nearby Hemudu village). The museum is open daily from 8:30am to noon and 2 to 5:30pm; admission is 10RMB ($1.20).

✪ BAI CAUSEWAY Solitary Island is connected to downtown Hangzhou by Baidi, one of the two great man-made causeways that divide West Lake into three parts. These two causeways are the finest stretches to walk on West Lake. Both are scenic and serene. The **Bai Causeway** is named after a Tang Dynasty poet, Bai Juyi, who served as prefectural governor here from A.D. 822 to 824 and saw to its construction. Composed of silt dredged from the lake, this causeway runs east for half a mile, rejoining the north shore road (Beishan Lu) at **Broken Bridge (Duan Qiao),** so named because when winter snows first melt, the bridge appears from a distance to be broken.

LAKESHORE PROMENADE   This combination walkway and roadway encircles West Lake. At Broken Bridge, it joins the Bai Causeway and runs parallel to the western edge of downtown Hangzhou. The downtown portion of the promenade is dotted with pavilions that are jammed at dawn with devotees of the latest recreational craze, Western ballroom dancing, as well as with practitioners of the more ancient form of exercise, tai ji quan (shadow boxing).

WEST LAKE CRUISING   All along the lakeshore, but particularly on Hubin Lu (Lakeside Avenue) downtown and near Solitary Island (northwest corner of West Lake), there are boats for hire, from heavy 10-foot wooden rowboats (where you take the oars) to small junks propelled by the owner's single oar to full-fledged ferries—flat-bottomed launches seating 20 under an awning. To tour the lake in a small junk, you have to bargain for the fare (usually about 40RMB/$4.80 for 2 hr. on the water). The passenger ferries sell tickets at roughly twice the price (80RMB/$10). The touts will find you if you don't get to a ticket booth first, but the easiest place to purchase your cruise ticket is at the dock across the street from the Shangri-La Hotel. Here many a fairly comfortable and sizable motorized launch, its bowsprit the head of a dragon, departs for a 2-hour lake tour, with stops at several of the islands.

✪ ISLAND OF LITTLE OCEANS (XIAO YING ZHOU)   Make sure your boat docks on this island, at the center of West Lake. The Island of Little Oceans was formed during a silt-dredging operation in 1607. As a Chinese saying goes, this is "an island within a lake, a lake within an island." Its form is that of a wheel with four spokes, its bridges and dikes creating four enclosed lotus-laden ponds. The main route into the hub of this wheel is the Bridge of Nine-Turnings, built in 1727. Occupying the center is the magnificent Flower and Bird Pavilion, an exceedingly graceful structure that is notable for its intricate wooden railings, lattices, and moon gates. It isn't an ancient work, dating only from 1959, but it's a superb rendition of the best in traditional Chinese architecture. It's open daily from 8am to 5pm; admission is 13RMB ($1.55).

THREE POOLS MIRRORING THE MOON   Located just off the southern shore of the Island of Little Oceans, this monument consists of three little water pagodas, each about 6 feet (2m) tall. They have "floated" like buoys on the surface of West Lake since 1621. Each pagoda has five openings. On evenings when the full moon shines on the lake, candles are placed inside; the effect is of four moons shimmering on the waters. Even by daylight, the three floating pagodas are a startling touch, the grand flourish of ancient engineers and scholar-administrators who shaped the lake into a work as artful as any classical garden.

The floating pagodas were the creation of Hangzhou's most famous governor, the poet Su Dongpu (A.D. 1036 to 1101), who placed the original trio of pagodas here, at the deepest point in the lake, to stake out an area where water plants were forbidden to grow. Lily, lotus, and a host of other plants had repeatedly strangled West Lake and still pose a threat today.

A voyage on this lake offers more refreshment and pleasure than any other experience on Earth. On one side it skirts the city so that your barge commands a distant view of all its grandeur and loveliness . . . . On the lake itself is an endless procession of barges thronged with pleasure seekers.

—Marco Polo

✪ **SU CAUSEWAY** The best view from land of the Three Pools Mirroring the Moon is from the Su Causeway (Sudi), the great dike that connects the north and south shores along the western side of West Lake. This pathway across West Lake has vistas as rewarding as those along the east-west Bai Causeway, but the Su Causeway is three times as long (running nearly 2 miles/3km). Lined with weeping willows, peach trees, and shady nooks, it crosses six arched stone bridges. Locals fish and picnic along its hems.

The Su Causeway begins on the north shore at a small park, **Lotus Stirred by the Breeze,** across from the patriotic **Monument to Yue Fei,** a 12th-century general. Favored by Emperor Kangxi, this park became the best spot for viewing lotus blossoms. Today, it is also popular with fanciers of gardens and koi (goldfish), especially at Jade Spring in the **Hangzhou Botanical Garden,** about a mile (1.6km) west of the Shangri-La Hotel (☎ **0571/702-5793;** open daily from 8am to 6pm; admission 10RMB/$1.20), and at **Huagang Yuan (Flower Harbor Park),** which is at the south end of the Su Causeway (☎ **0571/796-7386;** admission 12RMB/$1.45). Flower Harbor Park's pavilions and fishponds date back to the Qing Dynasty.

✪ **LINGYIN TEMPLE** Open from dawn to dusk (admission 25RMB/$3), this temple in the lush hills just west of West Lake is easily reachable by bicycle or taxi. Lingyin Temple (Temple of the Soul's Retreat) has been rebuilt a dozen times since its creation in A.D. 326. The entrance path is lined with attractions, including a sculpture garden on the left (Fei Lai Feng Zaoxiang) with reproductions of famous Buddhist statues from all over China.

The real attraction on the way to the temple is a limestone cliff, called the **Peak That Flew from Afar (Feilai Feng),** so named because it resembles a holy mountain in India seemingly transported to China. The peak, nearly 500 feet (150m) high, contains four caves and about 380 Buddhist rock carvings, most of them created more than 600 years ago during the Yuan Dynasty. The most famous carving here is of a Laughing Buddha, carved in the year A.D. 1000. This Buddha of the Future is laughing with joy at the ultimate glorious fate of the world, and he is laughing with amusement at the childish vanities of the unenlightened. Scholars have deemed these stone carvings the most important of their kind in southern China.

The small pagoda at the entrance to the first temple, built in 1590, is the burial marker for a monk named Huili, who founded Lingyun 16 centuries ago. The present buildings go back decades rather than centuries, but they are immense—some of the grandest temples in China. The Front Hall and the Great Hall beyond it have the typical Chinese Buddhist layout. The Front Hall contains the Four Guardians of the Four Directions, two on either side, protecting a rotund image of Maitreya (the Laughing Buddha). Lingyin's Maitreya dates from the 18th century, and behind this image is a statue in camphor wood of Skanda, another protector, which dates from the Southern Song Dynasty when Hangzhou was China's capital. The even larger Great Hall contains an image of Buddha crafted in 1956 from 24 sections of camphor and gilded with 104 ounces of gold—not a bad modern re-creation.

DRAGON WELL TEA VILLAGE   Another jaunt by bicycle or taxi west of West Lake is toward the village of Dragon Well, the capital of Hangzhou's famous **Longjing tea,** grown only on these hillsides and revered throughout China as cool and refreshing—a favorite summertime quencher. Longjing tea is said to be a supreme vintage with four special characteristics: its green color, smooth appearance, fragrant aroma, and sweet taste. The best tea at Dragon Well is still picked and processed by hand. A popular stop near the village is the **Dragon Well Tea Plantation (Cha Yuan Chun)** (☎ 0571/796-4112), open daily from 8:30am to 4:30pm; admission is 20RMB ($2.40). Here you can comb through extensive displays of Chinese teas, pots, cups, and ceremonial tea implements. The admission includes a tea sampling and demonstration of the Chinese tea ceremony in a private tearoom.

Dragon Well Village itself, a few miles beyond the Tea Plantation, is where the best tea is grown and processed. Plenty of local grandmas are on-hand to kidnap independent travelers, take them into their homes and kitchens, ply them with hand-picked tea, and sell them a few pounds at inflated prices. They can be resisted, but they can also be regarded as a special indulgence of this traditional Chinese paradise.

WHERE TO STAY & DINE

If you're spending the night, the best hotel is the five-star, 387-unit **Shangri-La Hotel Hangzhou (Hangzhou Xiangge Lila Fandian),** 78 Beishan Rd., on the north shore of West Lake (☎ 800/942-5050 in the U.S. and Canada, or 0571/797-7951; fax 0571/799-6637). A double with a hillside view goes for 1,517RMB ($185), while a room with a lakeside view costs 1,927RMB ($235). Another good choice is the 294-unit **Holiday Inn Hangzhou (Hangzhou Jiari Fandian),** Fengqi Lu and Jianguo Bei Lu, in the new central business district in northeast Hangzhou (☎ 800/465-4329 in the U.S. and Canada, or 0571/527-1188; fax 0571/527-1199), where a double is 902RMB ($110). A less expensive choice is the three-star **Lily Hotel,** 45 Shuguang Lu, northwest of West Lake (☎ 0571/799-1188; fax 0571/791-1166). Doubles in this 152-unit choice go for just 492RMB ($60).

For dining, try the traditional **Lou Wai Lou (Pavilion Beyond Pavilion),** 30 Gushan Lu (☎ 0571/796-9023; fax 0571/702-9023), on Solitary Hill Island, between the Xiling Seal Engraving Society and the Zhejiang Library. Hours are daily from 11:30am to 2pm and 5 to 8pm; meals cost around 150RMB ($18) and credit cards are not accepted. In the summer, the restaurant offers dinner cruises on West Lake.

The Shangri-La Hotel's signature restaurant, **Shang Palace** (☎ 0571/797-7951), is more elegant and also more expensive (100RMB/$12 to 210RMB/$25 and up).

Appendix A: Shanghai in Depth

1 Shanghai Today

No one knows quite how large China's largest city really is. The most recent official figures for Shanghai peg the population at nine million for the city proper and 14 million for the metropolitan area, ranking Shanghai as the sixth-largest city in the world. Its "floating population" of unregistered and uncounted residents (those who have moved in from the countryside) make the actual figures considerably higher. The United Nations estimates that Shanghai's population will stand at 23.4 million by the year 2015. When Shanghai's unique architectural legacy and its recent economic transformation are factored in, it is easy to see why 7 out of every 10 visitors to China come to Shanghai. This is China's commercial center, its largest city, and the heart of China's future. No other supercity in China, including Hong Kong and Beijing, is more vibrant or fascinating. It is only a slight exaggeration to call Shanghai the New York City of China.

Numbers tell an essential part of the story. While the city has just 1% of China's population, Shanghai accounts for 4% of China's gross domestic product (GDP), 11% of its financial services, and 12% of China's total industrial output. Textiles, steel, manufacturing, and shipbuilding dominate the city's economy, which reports double-digit growth year after year. Nearly half its workforce is involved in manufacturing. Its largest single steel plant, Baosteel, boasts a payroll of 176,000 workers and produces half of China's steel. Foreign investment in Shanghai is evident everywhere. Volkswagen and Buick maintain large auto plants here. Mary Kay has more than 10,000 beauty consultants at work in Shanghai (its China headquarters), and Amway counts 70,000 distributors in the city. Hallmark recently built a $5-million plant in the Pudong area to design and manufacture seasonal greeting cards. Coca-Cola, which opened its largest bottling plant outside of the United States in Shanghai in 1933, now bottles far more cases in the city than ever before. Not since colonial days (1846 to 1949), when Shanghai was dominated by Western companies, has the port produced such an array of international investments. Business, both domestic and foreign, has made Shanghai quite wealthy by Chinese standards. Per capita annual income (based on GDP) is now over $3,000, the highest in China.

While Shanghai has more than its share of overnight millionaires, ordinary Shanghainese must still be counted as residents of a developing rather than a developed nation. Living space is slim (under 140 sq. ft. per person) and many (including two million pensioners) must get by on less than the official minimum wage (set at just above U.S.$1 per day). Beggars congregate at tourist sites, temples, and avenues where visitors are likely to appear (as do touts hawking postcards and souvenirs). The unemployed, most arriving illegally without residence permits in Shanghai, can be sighted sleeping under bridges, awaiting work.

Nevertheless, Shanghai has an air of prosperity and aggressive optimism that it has carried with it since the heady days of the wealthy foreign concessions. There's plenty of disposable income, it seems, and as China's longtime center of shopping, plenty of upscale places to dispose of that income. Residents are not only forward-looking and business-oriented, but also fashionable. Shanghai is a city of boutiques, malls, and up-to-date department stores. Year by year, it is catching up with Hong Kong as one of Asia's paradises for shoppers. Shanghai not only is home to China's first and largest stock exchange, but also contains more than two dozen McDonald's, 50 KFCs, 2,000 Internet cafes, and one million mobile-phone users—not to mention the world's second-largest department store and the tallest hotel on Earth. With prosperity, even sales of the venerable bicycle, formerly the chief means of transport in the city, have declined (from one million sales in Shanghai in 1990 to half that today). Meanwhile, the streets are crowded with some 600,000 vehicles (including 40,000 taxis) and 280,000 motorcycles. Still, Shanghai is relatively easy to get around in, especially with the recent completion of elevated freeways and a second subway line across downtown to modern Pudong.

The economic boom has brought woes as well. Crime is on the rise (police arrested 5,000 pickpockets working just on buses in a recent 12-month period), prostitution is back in the bars and on the streets (after its complete eradication in the 1950s), and pollution is a major problem. But Shanghai is nothing if not ambitious. This is a city of big dreams. City planners promise that Shanghai will soon be not only China's financial and manufacturing capital, but also its "green" capital as well. Shanghai has converted Nanjing Road to a pedestrian mall, remodeled the Bund and its promenade, revitalized many avenues and villas in the old French Concession, and created 4,500 acres of greenway with trees and lawns (an area equivalent to 4,000 football fields). The city's 40,000 taxis are slated to be converted to natural gas as the primary fuel by 2002. The latest environmental project is a downtown forest park twice the size of People's Square at the intersection of two elevated freeways, part of a larger project to make Shanghai "China's garden city" by the year 2005. Shanghai now earmarks 3% of its GDP to anti-pollution efforts, the highest investment rate in China.

Indeed, the streets and buildings of Shanghai are already far cleaner today than a decade ago, even if the air remains smoggy much of the time. Fortunately, the dust is finally settling from the massive modernization and reconstruction of Shanghai (and creation of the Pudong New Area) initiated in the 1990s, which *New York Times* writer Ian Buruma hailed as "perhaps the greatest urban transformation since Baron Haussmann rebuilt Paris in the 19th century." Shanghai, with many of its 25,000 construction sites filled in at last, is again a very walkable city, its riversides and architecture, old and new, quite inviting (with still more skyscrapers popping up daily, even now). Its people—frank, efficient, and progressive, armed with their own proud dialect—are more open and friendly than the reserved Beijingers to the north, and they are more used to dealing with foreigners than Chinese anywhere else on the mainland. In the colonial 1930s, there was a saying that in Shanghai "everywhere within a radius of 10 miles, you'll see a foreign face." That international exposure was not wasted on the Shanghainese, who are now preserving their past as the "Paris of the Orient" as well as pushing forward to create China's most outward-looking, modern, brash, and progressive metropolis. Simply put, no city on Earth seems more optimistic about its future than Shanghai. It is that spirit of enterprise, arrogance, and adventure that gives the city and its people their indomitable character.

2 History 101

Dateline

- **4,000 B.C.** First evidence of settlements in the Shanghai area.
- **475–221 B.C.** Shanghai region is ruled by Chunshen, prime minister of the ancient Kingdom of Chu.
- **A.D. 751** During the Tang Dynasty, the Shanghai region is incorporated as the county of Huating.
- **1292** Shanghai township is created on the banks of Suzhou Creek, near the Huangpu River.
- **1553** City wall is built around what is today Shanghai's Old Town (Nanshi) as defense against Japanese pirates.
- **1559–1577** Yu Garden is built in the heart of Old Town by a wealthy official.
- **1664** By the end of the Ming Dynasty, Shanghai has become a major cotton and textile center; its population will soon reach 200,000.
- **1832** The British-based East India Company explores Shanghai and the Yangzi River as a potential trading center.
- **1842** Following the first Opium War, the British establish a consulate in Shanghai to promote international trade; city population reaches 500,000.
- **1845** Miss Fay, the first unmarried American woman in China, arrives to help establish the Protestant Episcopal Mission.

continues

Shanghai has a brief history by Chinese standards, although the general area has been occupied for about 6,000 years. Recent archaeological finds include 28 prehistoric sites and 1,540 ancient tombs, as well as some grains of rice that date back 6,000 years. Still, it is fair to say that Shanghai did not play an important role in China or become a large city until very recent times. In the 19th century, it became increasingly prominent as a trading center for the Yangzi River valley, and by the 1920s, Shanghai was the preeminent port for all of China, a position it has held ever since.

The name *Shanghai,* which means "above the sea," was not applied until after the Song Dynasty (A.D. 960 to 1279), in the year 1292. Before that, there was no Shanghai town or city; at most, there was just a county known as Hua Ting. Gradually, a small market town was established on the riverbanks and named Shanghai, but this small port did not reach the status of a county town until the late 13th century. Eventually, Shanghai's geographical position as a safe harbor between the silk- and tea-rich Yangzi River and the Pacific Ocean would make it one of China's key ports, especially for international trade. The Japanese were the first to benefit from trade with Shanghai, although by the 16th century, Japanese pirates were such a problem that Shanghai had to erect fortifications on the Huangpu River—a circular wall that surrounded today's Old Town (Nanshi) until 1912.

The 16th century also witnessed Shanghai's first contact with Christian missionaries. Xu Guangqi (1562 to 1633) had left Shanghai to serve the Imperial Court in Beijing, where he was baptized by a celebrated Italian Jesuit father, Matteo Ricci, in 1603. Taking the Christian name of Paul, Xu became the highest-ranking Chinese in the Empire to convert to Christianity. Some of his land in Shanghai was deeded to the Catholic Church, at what is now the site of Xujiahui Cathedral (*Xujiahui* meaning "Xu Family Village").

Foreign traders would come next to Shanghai's shores. The East India Company had its eye on the port as early as the mid-18th century, and one of its ships made an exploratory voyage up the Huangpu River in 1832, which was then thronged with junks, indicating that Shanghai had become one of China's major domestic ports. The British were eager to initiate international trade in tea, silk, and opium out of Shanghai, but local officials proudly refused. It took war to open Shanghai to the West. The First Opium War of 1842, in which British warships sailed past Shanghai up the Yangzi River in a show of force, led to the Treaty of Nanjing. The treaty mandated foreign trade and permitted British consuls and merchants, as well as their families, to live in any of five Chinese cities, including Shanghai. There, the British were excluded from residence within the walled city but were given control over the riverfront to the north, the present-day Bund and Nanjing Road area. The first British consul, Captain George Balfour, undertook the drainage and embankment of the muddy riverfront.

After the British established their own consulate court in Shanghai in 1842, foreign firms began to drift up from Canton (Guangzhou). The Americans moved into neighborhoods just north of the Bund, in today's Hongkou District, where Japanese merchants also settled. In 1863, the British and American districts formally merged, creating the International Settlement, which encompassed most foreign residences, businesses, and consulates, except for those of the French, who began arriving in Shanghai in 1846 and maintained their own concession west of the Bund. Throughout the remainder of the 19th century, foreign firms based in Shanghai controlled much of the world's supply of three key Chinese commodities: tea, silk, and opium. As wealth accumulated, the colonialists began to build a new Shanghai based on a European model. Nanjing Road was extended west of the Bund as a way to reach the new racetrack, where betting on horses became a major form of recreation. Both Catholics and Protestants set up missions and churches.

In 1853, the Chinese walled city within Shanghai was seized by the Small Swords Society, headquartered in Yu Garden. The Small Swords were a local branch of the Taiping rebels

- **1848** The foundation stone for the Catholic cathedral in Xujiahui District is laid.
- **1850** The first English-language newspaper in Shanghai, the *North China Herald*, is launched, serving fewer than 200 readers.
- **1854** Shanghai Municipal Council is formed to rule over the foreign concession areas.
- **1863** The International Settlement is created by the British and Americans in Shanghai; the French maintain their own independent sphere, the French Concession, established in 1847.
- **1871** The term *shanghai*, meaning to drug and forcibly kidnap hands for a departing ship, enters the English language; during this period, many sailors were literally "shanghaied," waking up at sea on clipper ships bound for China.
- **1883** A safe drinking-water system is introduced to the foreign settlements; a foreign police force, electricity, street lighting, and other modern services soon follow.
- **1912** The old city wall is demolished following the downfall of the last imperial dynasty (the Qing) and the establishment of the Republic of China under Sun Yat-sen, who lives from 1918 to 1924 in Shanghai.
- **1917** White Russians, fleeing the Russian Revolution, make Shanghai's international concessions their temporary home; by 1936, their population is 15,000.
- **1921** The Chinese Communist party is founded in Shanghai.
- **1925** A student protest on behalf of exploited Shanghai workers, known as the "May 30 Incident," paves the way for Communist revolutionaries in China.

continues

- **1927** Communist leaders are rounded up in Shanghai and executed by the government of Chiang Kai-shek, initiating a protracted civil war.
- **1928** A greyhound-race track (Canidrome) opens to 50,000 spectators in the French Concession.
- **1929** Shanghai millionaire Victor Sassoon opens the landmark Cathay Hotel (now the Peace Hotel) on the Bund.
- **1930** Noël Coward writes his play *Private Lives* in Shanghai.
- **1931** Triad godfather "Big-Eared" Du is elected to the Municipal Council in the French Concession.
- **1935** Population reaches nearly four million, including 60,000 foreigners.
- **1936** Lu Xun, China's best-known modern author, dies at his residence in Shanghai's Hongkou District.
- **1937** The Shanghai Municipal Council tallies 20,000 corpses of homeless people who have died in the streets during the year.
- **1937–1945** The Japanese gradually become the rulers of Shanghai, imprisoning all foreigners in 1943.
- **1949** Mao Tse-tung proclaims the creation of the People's Republic of China, ending civil war; Chen Yi becomes Shanghai's first Communist mayor.
- **1952** People's Park and People's Square are created on the former site of Shanghai's racetrack.
- **1966** The Cultural Revolution, led by the Shanghai-based "Gang of Four," which includes Mao's wife, a former Shanghai actress, isolates and immobilizes China.
- **1982** Shanghai opens the Hongqiao Development

continues

who were then attempting to overthrow the Qing Dynasty across China. The foreign militia assisted China's Imperial army in reclaiming Shanghai from the rebels in 1855. Just the year before, the Shanghai Municipal Council was founded by the British, French, and Americans, and it gave foreigners in Shanghai a powerful local government; the Chinese Maritime Customs, also initiated in 1854, gave them effective control over trade as well. The Second Opium War of 1856, followed by the Treaty of Tianjin in 1858, expanded the powers of the colonialists, opening ports up and down the Yangzi to foreigners and Christian missionaries.

The population of foreigners in Shanghai was never in proportion to the power the colonialists exercised. In the 1860s, the foreign population was less than 600; by 1910, it had reached 10,000. The largest influx of foreigners to Shanghai came during the prosperous 1920s through the 1940s, when the non-Chinese population topped 60,000 (still not many in a city that had swelled to several million inhabitants).

Concurrently, the development of the Bund's monumental European architecture picked up steam in the early 20th century. Most of the great surviving edifices, including the Customs House, the Peace Hotel, and the Hongkong and Shanghai Bank Building, date from this period, as does Shanghai's notorious reputation as the "Paris of the East" (or "the whore of Asia"). Shanghai was a libertine city of glitter and depravity, run not only by rich foreign companies and investors, but also by Chinese gangs known as Triads.

While much of the story of Shanghai has to do with trade and commerce, and colonialism and wealth, Shanghai also became a center of intense political rebellion in the early 20th century. The Chinese Communist party was founded in Shanghai in 1921, with Mao Tse-tung in attendance. Labor disputes led to violent protests in 1925, when Shanghai students marched to protest workers' exploitation by the Japanese, a historic event known throughout China as the May 30th Movement. In 1927, the Guomindang army, led by Chiang Kai-shek, the embattled president of the Chinese Republic, assisted by local Triad gangsters, rounded up and executed all the Communists they could find in Shanghai, initiating a civil war that the Communists would eventually win in 1949.

During World War II (known in China as the Anti-Japanese War, 1937 to 1945), Shanghai continued to prosper, but the Japanese gradually gained control of the city's political and commercial institutions. At the beginning of 1943, the British and Americans signed a treaty in Shanghai relinquishing their extraterritorial powers and the international concessions to the local Chinese, but this was immediately followed by the Japanese placing all foreign nationalists in concentration camps. Eight thousand foreigners were imprisoned in Shanghai, parts of the city were bombed, and the Japanese occupied Shanghai until the end of the war (1945).

Communist troops, representing the new People's Republic of China, entered Shanghai on May 25, 1949, without incident. Most of the colonialists and foreign companies pulled out within a year. For much of the next 40 years, Shanghai kept its role as China's chief port, manufacturing center, and shopping mecca, but the political power of the new nation had switched north to Beijing, where the rulers took much of Shanghai's wealth and invested it elsewhere. Shanghai achieved new prominence in the 1990s as economic reforms and new national leadership (headed by Jiang Zemin and Zhu Rongji, both former mayors of Shanghai) gave it freer rein and more autonomy, unleashing the entrepreneurial spirit that the

- Zone to attract foreign investors.
- **1990** China's first (and largest) stock market opens; development of the Pudong New Area on the east side of the Huangpu River begins.
- **1994** Metro Line 1, the second subway built in China, begins service.
- **1995** The Pearl of the Orient TV Tower in Pudong, the tallest structure in Asia, symbolizes the new Shanghai.
- **1996** The new Shanghai Museum, China's finest, opens on People's Square.
- **1997** Jiang Zemin, Shanghai's former leader, becomes China's paramount leader; Zhu Rongji, also a former Shanghai mayor, becomes the chief architect of China's economic revolution.
- **1999** Nanjing Road Pedestrian Mall, Pudong International Airport, and a second subway line open.
- **2000** Pedestrian tunnel under the Huangpu River connects the Bund with Pudong.

city had so cultivated during the colonial years. Beijing still receives more than half of Shanghai's tax revenue, but the city is riding the crest of the wave of an unprecedented economic boom. Building and modernization have swept across the city and into the new Pudong area on the east shore of the Huangpu River. Foreign investment, totaling more than $10 billion in some years, has fueled this transformation. Shanghai is now China's financial and commercial showcase, rather as it was a century earlier, and a startlingly modern metropolis has been reborn in the past decade, rivaling Hong Kong in wealth and power.

3 Chinese Ways & Manners

East is East and West is West, as the old adage goes—but in Shanghai the two meet and mingle. As visitors to China and guests of Shanghai, however, travelers should be aware of differing customs and make adjustments accordingly. Many Shanghainese are worldly, modern, and accustomed to Western behaviors. English-speaking tour guides, for example, have set answers to "embarrassing" questions that visitors sometimes ask. Uncomfortable topics include China's handling of political dissidents, the status of Tibet and Taiwan, restrictions on the media, abortion, prison labor, and the Tiananmen Square massacre—although many younger Shanghainese seem eager to tackle these topics head-on. The problem is that visitors can put their hosts—who may have government jobs—on the hot seat when posing politically sensitive questions. Feel free to ask the locals about anything, but remember that even in China's most international city, politics is often still taboo.

Recently, the government mandated a 5-day workweek. Most Chinese now work Monday to Friday. The workday begins about 9am, sometimes later, enabling thousands of Shanghainese to do their morning exercises. The parks and the Bund promenade fill up with locals performing traditional tai chi or chi gong, and sometimes even Western ballroom dancing. No one seems to mind being watched, and foreigners sometimes join in, but it is the most quiet and private time of the day. Lunch comes at the noon hour, although most shops no longer close down for afternoon siesta. Dinner is fairly early, usually around 6pm, followed by time at home with the family. Saturday and especially Sunday are spent shopping and enjoying the family in the parks and at other attractions.

This typical weekly schedule overlooks a fundamental difference in viewpoints between East and West. The Chinese tend to view the individual as part of greater wholes—of the family, foremost; of the workplace; and of the nation. The group has more power than the individual, and it must be consulted before decisions are made. In practical terms, this translates into a respect for hierarchies. Those of higher rank within any organization, be it a family or a business, hold the power over others and decide what those of lower rank may do. The individual often has far less autonomy and power in Chinese society than in Western societies—even when it comes to apparently insignificant matters.

In the days of dynasties and eunuchs, China's tiny upper class practiced a number of elaborate courtesies that have all but disappeared from the modern People's Republic. Shanghainese are not formal, nor do they have a set of enigmatic social rules that excludes outsiders. The Chinese do not bow (as the Japanese do), and they do not remove their shoes upon entering a house. Shanghainese tend to be frank, and they do not as a rule thank others for favors, except by later actions. They shake hands but seldom embrace or kiss in public. Until recently, spitting in public and smoking whenever and wherever one pleased were common habits, but in recent years in Shanghai, spitting has become unacceptable, and smoking in many public areas has become unlawful.

Shanghai residents are quite inquisitive and direct, asking some questions that are perfectly acceptable in China, if not in the West. Questions from locals you have just met can include details about your salary and the number of children in your family. You can answer such queries as you see fit, vaguely if you wish.

Among ancient customs that do endure in modern Shanghai are the respect for age, which is synonymous with wisdom and stature; the respect for higher education; and the respect for family matters, which are of more importance than those of work, politics, or world affairs. Among new customs, perhaps the most ubiquitous is an exaggerated respect for money: the millionaire now seems more respected than the scholar, a reversal of 2,000 years of Confucian thought, but something that Shanghai people, with their long history of conducting foreign business, are used to.

While women are equal to men by law and by Communist dogma, they are in fact often considered as they once were in traditional Chinese society: second best to men. Male children, who alone continue the family line, are still preferred over females by many couples. Even among foreigners, men are often treated with slightly more respect than women, although modern education and the influx of Western ideas has begun to erode such prejudices.

In social settings, the Chinese often take great pains to preserve "face," which involves maintaining one's self-respect while deferring important decisions to those of higher rank within a group. "Losing face" means to suffer embarrassment before others. To be criticized roughly by a visitor, for example, or to be asked to do something that is impossible puts a Chinese person in a dangerous position. "Saving face" is achieved by compromising, or sometimes by ignoring a problem altogether. Many Chinese will go to extremes to avoid settling a dispute or handling a complaint, since any loss of face in "kowtowing" to another could reflect badly upon their family and China, as well as upon themselves.

What visitors need to do when making requests or issuing complaints in Shanghai, then, is to control their tempers, avoid assigning personal blame, seek compromise when possible, and practice patience. A polite approach has a better chance of success than a more aggressive, brutally frank, or simply angry outburst. In a nation renowned for the size and inertia of its bureaucracy, some things are slow to be done, and some things are never done at all. It often helps to ask a person to relay your complaint or demand to a superior, remembering that a response may not be immediate.

A few other differences in customs are worth noting. The Chinese give their family names first, followed by their personal names, in the reverse order of most Western societies, and it is perfectly proper to refer to Chinese by their last names. Many Shanghainese use English first names that they have either chosen or received at school. Despite Shanghai's fascination with the latest Western fashions, it is still advisable for Westerners to dress conservatively and to wear less jewelry than usual, if for no other reason than to avoid broadcasting their wealth to shopkeepers, vendors, touts, and pickpockets. Finally, before snapping a close-up photo of a fascinating Chinese face, ask permission, by pantomime if necessary. Many Shanghainese do not want their photographs taken, although they usually give in when asked permission to take a picture of their children—whom the Chinese find as adorable as foreigners do.

One last caution: Remember that Shanghai residents drive on the right side of the road; they do not give pedestrians the right-of-way; and on a red light, vehicles seldom stop when making a right turn, whether pedestrians are in the crosswalk or not. Walking in Shanghai is rather like walking in downtown New York City, with the addition of millions of bicycles that also don't always give way.

4 Shanghai in Print & on the Silver Screen

RECOMMENDED BOOKS

At the top of the list is Pan Ling's nostalgic, romantic history of the city and its characters, *In Search of Old Shanghai.* Old Shanghai comes alive in Vickie Baum's novel *Shanghai '37,* and Andre Malraux's *Man's Fate* is a celebrated novel that evokes the rebellion and violence of Shanghai in the late 1920s. Shanghai of the 1930s is the setting for *The Blue Lotus,* one of the delightful Tintin adventures written by Herge. Far darker visions of Shanghai are powerfully evoked in J. G. Ballard's personal novel, *Empire of the Sun,* based on his imprisonment as a child during the Japanese occupation, and in Nien Cheng's

Life and Death in Shanghai, a memoir of her imprisonment during the Cultural Revolution. Anchee Min's *Red Azalea* recounts her extraordinary journey from revolutionary Red Guard to film star in Shanghai under the watchful eye of Madame Mao. For s spicy history of colonial Shanghai, try Stella Dong's *Shanghai: The Rise and Fall of a Decadent City, 1842–1949.*

Two of the best introductions to modern China are by former bureau chiefs of the *New York Times.* Fox Butterfield's classic account of the aftermath of the Cultural Revolution, *China: Alive in the Bitter Sea,* written in 1982, should be compared with the more optimistic vision of Nicholas Kristof and Sheryl Wudunn's study, *China Wakes: The Struggle for the Soul of a Rising Power,* written a scant 12 years later. These journalists seem to have covered completely different countries.

RECOMMENDED FILMS

Our cinematic image of Shanghai focuses on the romantic 1930s. For Western audiences, the classic is Josef von Sternberg's 1932 film *Shanghai Express,* starring Marlene Dietrich. A more recent film of suspense is *Shanghai Surprise,* starring Sean Penn and Madonna, made in 1986 but set in 1937 Shanghai. The Shanghai underworld of 1930s' gangsters and their molls is stylishly evoked in Zhang Yimou's 1995 film *Shanghai Triad,* starring China's best-known actress, Gong Li. Stephen Spielberg's 1987 film *Empire of the Sun,* based on English author J. G. Ballard's autobiographical novel, takes a look inside the concentration camps of Shanghai during the Japanese occupation; some of the most gripping scenes were filmed in the streets of Shanghai (using 15,000 local extras) and at the Peace Hotel on the Bund. A 1998 Austrian documentary by Joan Grossman and Paul Rosdy, *The Port of Last Resort,* tells the story of the Jews who fled Nazi Europe for Shanghai from 1937 to 1941.

Appendix B:
The Chinese Language

Speaking no Chinese is hardly an obstacle in Shanghai these days, particularly if you stick to big hotels, guided tours, Friendship Stores, tourist sights, and restaurants catering to foreigners. But once you venture out on your own and begin hailing taxis, shopping at local stores, buying admission tickets, getting lost on the streets, and ordering at out-of-the-way restaurants, then speaking English—no matter how loudly or clearly—isn't always enough. There are, however, measures a smart traveler can take when confronted with the baffling mysteries of the Chinese language, whether spoken or written.

The Chinese language is ancient, complex, and quite alien to those who know only the languages of the West. In Shanghai, educated residents speak the official dialect, called *putonghua* or Mandarin Chinese, which is similar to the Beijing dialect. This is the dialect that students throughout China learn to speak in school (where students are now taught English, too, although seldom in a thorough manner). Shanghai, however, has its own dialect, which most residents prefer to speak and which Chinese from other areas find baffling. Rather than try to learn the Shanghai dialect, which is only of use in the city, stick to practicing some Mandarin, the official dialect. Most Shanghainese understand and can use Mandarin. The rub is that even the rudiments of Mandarin can be difficult to grasp for those grounded in English or European languages. The four tones employed in pronouncing each syllable of Mandarin (each syllable generally equivalent to a word or a written Chinese character) are crucial to making yourself understood. Chinese is rife with homonyms—words that sound alike except for the tone.

Nevertheless, if you have time beforehand, it is fairly easy to learn a handful of useful basic spoken phrases. Correct pronunciation can be learned through careful listening as you go about in Shanghai. Since few travelers have time to take a Chinese-language course before visiting China, a **Mandarin phrase book,** especially one that has the words and phrases printed in Chinese characters, is essential. The written language is universal in China, regardless of local dialects.

In addition to a phrase book, an essential traveler's companion is a **trilingual map** (in English, Chinese characters, and pinyin) of Shanghai. If the map contains Chinese script in addition to English, helpful strangers on the street can consult it and point you in the right direction. Street signs, where they exist, can also be useful if they contain

Also helpful for travelers who don't speak Chinese are the small cards offered at most hotels that bear the name of the hotel and the name of your destination printed in Chinese characters. You can show the card to your taxi driver or to others along the way. These cards making getting to and returning from a site, a restaurant, or a shop quite easy.

pinyin as well as Chinese characters. **Pinyin** is the official transcription of Chinese into an alphabetical form. For example, a sign reading SHANGHAI BOWUGUAN means "Shanghai Museum." Street signs often have the name of the street in pinyin (such as NANJING) followed by the transcription of one of the words for street (such as LU).

The written form of Chinese is even more difficult to learn than the spoken form, since it does not employ an alphabetical system. Students must memorize the meaning (and pronunciation) of thousands of written characters, a time-consuming challenge even for native speakers. Travelers must rely again on phrase books, trilingual maps, and hotel staff to unravel these enigmatic signs, although many visitors quickly learn to recognize some of the simpler and more common characters as they travel. It can be particularly useful at times to recognize the difference between the symbols for male and female when approaching an otherwise unlabeled public toilet.

Even if your pronunciation is poor at first, it's worth making an attempt. Shanghai residents are not only amused but impressed when foreigners make a stab at using Chinese, the language they regard as supreme.

USEFUL PHRASES

English	Pinyin	Chinese
Hello	Ni hao	你好。
How are you?	Ni hao ma?	你好吗？
Good	Hen hao	很好。
Bad	Bu hao	不好。
I don't want ___	Wo bu yao ___	我不要_____。
Good bye	Zai jian	再见。
Thank you	Xie xie	谢谢。
Yes	Dui	对。
No	Bu dui	不对。
How's it going?	Ni chi le ma?	你吃了吗？
When?	Shenme shi hou?	什么时候？
Excuse me, I'm sorry	Dui bu qi	对不起。

How much does it cost?	Duo shao qian?	多少钱？
Too expensive	Tai gui le	太贵了。
It's broken	Huai le	坏了。
May I take a look?	Wo neng bu neng kan yi kan?	我能不能看一看？
Do you speak English?	Ni shuo Yingwen ma?	你说英文吗？
What's your name?	Ni gui xing?	你贵姓？
My name is ___	Wo xing ___	我姓_____。
I'm lost	Wo mi lou le	我迷路了。
I don't smoke	Wo bu chou yan	我不抽烟。
I'm ill	Wo sheng bing le	我生病了。
Bill, please!	Qing jiezhang!	请结帐。
I am vegetarian	Wo shi chisude	我是吃素的。
Can I take a photograph?	Wo keyi zhao ge xiang ma?	我可以照个相吗？
I can't speak Chinese	Wo buhui shuo Zhongwen	我不会说中文。
I don't understand	Wo ting bu dong	我听不懂。
It doesn't matter	Mei guanxi	没关系。
No problem	Mei wenti	没问题。
Do you have a ___?	Ni you mei you ___?	你有没有_____？
Do you know ___?	Ni zhi bu zhi dao ___?	你知不知道_____？
What do you call this?	Zhe jiao shenme?	这叫什么？
I want to go to ___	Wo xiang qu ___	我想去_____。
Where is ___?	___ zai nar?	_____在哪儿？
I want ___	Wo yao ___	我要_____。
Help!	Jiuming!	救命！
Police!	Jingcha!	警察！

USEFUL WORDS

English	Pinyin	Chinese
Airport	feji chang	飞机场
Bank	yinhang	银行
Beer	pijiu	啤酒
Bicycle	zixingche	自行车
Boiled water	kai shui	开水
Bus	gonggong qiche	公共汽车
Bus station	qiche zong zhan	汽车总站
Chinese "dollar"	(renminbi) yuan (kuai)	（人民币）元（块）
CITS	luxingshe	旅行社
Credit card	xinyong ka	信用卡
Hot water	re shui	热水
Hotel	binguan, dajiudian, fandian	宾馆、大酒店、饭店
Map	ditu	地图
Mineral water	kuangquan shui	矿泉水
Passport	hu zhao	护照
Restaurant	fanguan	饭馆
Soft drink	qi shui	汽水
Taxi	chuzu qiche	出租汽车
Telephone	dianhua	电话
Toilet	cesuo	厕所
Toilet paper	weisheng zhi	卫生纸
Train	huoche	火车
Train station	huoche zhan	火车站

The Chinese Language

COUNTRIES

English	Pinyin	Chinese
Where are you from?	Ni shi cong nar lai de?	你是从哪儿来的？
I am from ___	Wo shi ___ lai de	我是_____来的。
America	Meiguo	美国
Australia	Aodaliya	澳大利亚
Canada	Jia nada	加拿大
Denmark	Danmei	丹麦
England	Yingguo	英国
France	Faguo	法国
Germany	Deguo	德国
Holland	Helan	荷兰
Ireland	Aierlan	爱尔兰
Japan	Riben	日本
New Zealand	Xinxilan	新西兰
Norway	Nuowei	挪威
Scotland	Sugelan	苏格兰
South Africa	Nanfei	南非
Sweden	Ruidian	瑞典
Switzerland	Ruishi	瑞士
Wales	Weiershi	威尔士

NUMBERS

English	Pinyin	Chinese
Zero	ling	零
One	yi	一
Two	er	二

The Chinese Language

English	Pinyin	Chinese
Three	san	三
Four	si	四
Five	wu	五
Six	liu	六
Seven	qi	七
Eight	ba	八
Nine	jiu	九
Ten	shi	十
Eleven	shi yi	十一
Twelve	shi er	十二
Fifteen	shi wu	十五
Twenty	er shi	二十
Twenty-one	er shi yi (and so on)	二十一
Thirty	san shi	三十
Thirty-one	san shi yi (and so on)	三十一
One hundred	yi bai	一百
Two hundred	er bai	二百
Three hundred	san bai	三百
Four hundred	si bai (and so on)	四百
One thousand	yi qian	一千
Two thousand	er qian (and so on)	二千

The Chinese Language

DAYS OF THE WEEK

English	Pinyin	Chinese
Sunday	Xingqitian	星期天
Monday	Xingqi yi	星期一
Tuesday	Xingqi er	星期二
Wednesday	Xingqi san	星期三

Thursday	Xingqi si	星期四
Friday	Xingqi wu	星期五
Saturday	Xingqi liu	星期六
Yesterday	zuotian	昨天
Today	jintian	今天
Tomorrow	mingtian	明天

Appendix C: Chinese Translations

Below are Chinese translations (when available) of the establishments and attractions listed on the "Shanghai Accommodations" map in chapter 4, the "Shanghai Dining" map in chapter 5, the "Shanghai Attractions" map in chapter 6, and throughout chapter 10.

SHANGHAI ACCOMMODATIONS

See map on pp. 52–53.

City Hotel
城市酒店

Cypress Hotel
龙柏饭店

East China Hotel
华东大酒店

Garden Hotel
花园饭店

Grand Hyatt
上海金茂凯悦大酒店

Grand Nation Hotel
南新雅大酒店

Hilton Hotel
静安希尔顿酒店

Holiday Inn Crowne Plaza
上海银星皇冠假日酒店

Holiday Inn Pudong
浦东假日酒店

Hotel Equatorial
国际贵都大酒店

Hotel Nikko Longbai
上海日航龙柏

Hotel Nikko Pudong
上海中油日航大酒店

Hotel Sofitel Hyland
海仑宾馆

Hua Ting Hotel & Towers
华亭宾馆

Jianguo Hotel
上海建国宾馆

Jin Jiang Hotel
锦江饭店

Jin Jiang Tower
新锦江大酒店

Jingan Guest House
静安宾馆

M. P. (Man Po) Boutique Hotel
万宝大酒店

New Asia Tomson Hotel
上海新亚汤臣大酒店

Novotel Shanghai Yuan Lin
Hotel
上海园林宾馆

Pacific Hotel
金门大酒店

Park Hotel
国际饭店

Peace Hotel
和平饭店

Peace Palace Hotel
和平汇中饭店

Portman Ritz-Carlton Hotel
上海波特曼丽思卡尔顿饭店

Pudong Shangri-La Hotel
浦东香格里拉大酒店

Pujiang Hotel
浦江饭店

Radisson SAS Lansheng Hotel
兰生大酒店

Rainbow Hotel
虹桥宾馆

Regal International East Asia Hotel
富豪环球东亚酒店

Shanghai Hotel
上海宾馆

Shanghai International Airport Hotel
上海国际机场宾馆

Shanghai JC Mandarin
上海锦沧文华大酒店

Shanghai Worldfield Convention Hotel
上海世博会议酒店

Westin Tai Ping Yang
威斯汀太平洋大饭店

Yangtze Renaissance Hotel by Marriott
上海扬子江

YMCA (Qing Nian Hui) Hotel
青年会宾馆

SHANGHAI DINING

See map on pp. 76–77.

AD
AD餐厅

Ashanti
N/A

Badlands
露金酒家

Bi Feng Tang
避风塘

Big Fan
大风车

Blue Heaven Revolving Restaurant
新锦江饭店

Bourbon Street
波钵街

Brauhaus
海侨宾馆

Café 1931
1931酒吧

Canton
N/A

Casj
N/A

Chang An Dumpling
长安饺子楼

Cochinchina 1883
欧越年代

Delifrance
德意法兰西

Dragon and Phoenix Room
N/A

Dublin Exchange
N/A

Dynasty
扬子江饭店

El Popo's
波波墨西哥餐厅

Feng Zhe Lou
丰泽楼

50 Hankou Road
隆合美食有限公司

The Gap
锦亭

Gino Cafe
季偌

Giovanni's
太平扬大饭店

Gongdelin
功德林

Grand Café
浦东

The Grape
葡萄园酒家

Hai Yu Lan Ge
N/A

Hard Rock Cafe
硬石餐厅

Hazara
阿萨拉

Henry's
亨利餐厅

Irene's Thai
N/A

Itoya
伊藤家

JJ Mariachi
N/A

Judy's Too
杰迪酒吧

Jue Lin Shu Shi Chu
觉林素菜馆

Jurassic Pub
恐龙世界

Kathleen's
N/A

Lan Na Thai
兰纳泰国餐厅

Landhaus
N/A

Latina
锦江拉丁餐厅

Le Bouchon
N/A

Le Garcon Chinois
N/A

Lu Bo Lang
绿波廊

Lulu
鹭鹭酒家

M on the Bund
米氏西餐厅

Malone's
马龙美式酒楼

Mandy's
N/A

Maxim's de Paris
N/A

Meilongzhen
梅陇镇酒家

Mr. Stone
石板屋

O'Malley's
欧玛莉

Oxford's
N/A

Park 97
97复兴公园

Paulaner Brauhaus
宝莱纳餐厅

Sasha's
萨莎西餐厅

Shang Palace
N/A

Shanghai Drugstore
上海橘树岛食府

Soho
莎虹食府

Song Yue Lou
松月楼

Summer Pavilion
夏苑

Sumo Sushi
缘禄寿司

Tandoor
印度餐厅

Thousand Taste Noodle Shop
千味日本面

Tony Roma's
多利罗玛

Trattoria
N/A

1221
1221饭店

Yang's Kitchen
杨家厨房

Zips
N/A

SHANGHAI ATTRACTIONS

See map on pp. 100–101.

The Bund
外滩

Chenxiangge Temple
沉香阁

Children's Municipal Palace
上海市少年宫

Community Church
国际礼拜堂

Confucius Temple
孔庙

Fuxing Park
复兴公园

Grand Theatre
上海大剧院

Great World
大世界

Huangpu River
黄浦江

Huxinting Teahouse
湖心亭茶楼

Jade Buddha Temple
玉佛禅寺

Jin Mao Tower
金茂大厦

Jing An Temple
静安古寺

Longhua Temple
龙华寺

Lu Xun Park
鲁迅公园

Lujiazui Central Green
陆家嘴绿地

Mu'en Church
沐恩堂

Muller Mansion
马勒住宅

Ohel Moshe Synagogue
摩西会堂

Peace Hotel
和平饭店

Pearl of the Orient TV Tower
东方明珠广播电视塔

People's (Renmin) Park
人民公园

People's (Renmin) Square
人民广场

Riverside Promenade
泯江大道

Sex Museum
性博物馆

Shanghai Arts and Crafts Research Institute
上海工艺美术研究所

Shanghai Botanical Gardens
上海植物园

Shanghai History Museum
上海历史博物馆

Shanghai Library
上海图书馆

Shanghai Museum
上海博物馆

Shanghai Natural History Museum
上海自然博物馆

Shanghai Stock Exchange
上海证券大厦

Shanghai Urban Planning Exhibition Hall
N/A

Shanghai Zoo
上海动物园

Site of the First National Congress of the Communist Party
中国共产党第一次全国代表大会会址纪念馆

Small Peach Garden (Xiao Taoyuan) Mosque
小桃园清真寺

Soong Ching-ling's Former Residence
宋庆龄故居

Sun Yat-sen's Former Residence
孙中山故居

Chinese Translations

Temple of the City God
城隍庙

Waibaidu Bridge
外白渡桥

Wanguo International Cemetery
万国公墓

Xujiahui Cathedral
徐家汇天主教堂

Yu Garden
豫园

Zhou En-lai's Former Residence
周恩来故居

SIDE TRIPS FROM SHANGHAI

Dragon Well Tea Village
龙井村

Forest of Lions Garden
(Shi Zi Lin Yuan)
狮子林

Grand View Garden
大观园

Hangzhou
杭州

Humble Administrator's Garden
(Zhou Zheng Yuan)
拙政园

Lake Dianshan (Dianshan Hu)
淀山湖

Lingering Garden (Liu Yuan)
留园

Lingyin Temple
灵隐寺

Master of the Nets Garden
(Wang Shi Yuan)
网师园

Panmen Gate
盘门

Suzhou
苏州

Tiger Hill (Hu Qiu)
虎丘

West Lake (Xi Hu)
西湖

Zhou Zhuang Water Village
周庄镇

Index

See also Accommodations and Restaurant indexes, below.

ACCOMMODATIONS

FROMMER'S® COMPLETE TRAVEL GUIDES

Alaska
Amsterdam
Arizona
Atlanta
Australia
Austria
Bahamas
Barcelona, Madrid &
   Seville
Beijing
Belgium, Holland &
   Luxembourg
Bermuda
Boston
British Columbia & the
   Canadian Rockies
Budapest & the Best of
   Hungary
California
Canada
Cancún, Cozumel &
   the Yucatán
Cape Cod, Nantucket &
   Martha's Vineyard
Caribbean
Caribbean Cruises & Ports
   of Call
Caribbean Ports of Call
Carolinas & Georgia
Chicago
China
Colorado
Costa Rica
Denmark
Denver, Boulder & Colorado
   Springs
England
Europe

European Cruises & Ports
   of Call
Florida
France
Germany
Greece
Greek Islands
Hawaii
Hong Kong
Honolulu, Waikiki &
   Oahu
Ireland
Israel
Italy
Jamaica
Japan
Las Vegas
London
Los Angeles
Maryland & Delaware
Maui
Mexico
Miami & the Keys
Montana & Wyoming
Montréal & Québec City
Munich & the Bavarian
   Alps
Nashville & Memphis
Nepal
New England
New Mexico
New Orleans
New York City
New Zealand
Nova Scotia, New Brunswick
   & Prince Edward Island
Oregon
Paris

Philadelphia & the
   Amish Country
Portugal
Prague & the Best of the
   Czech Republic
Provence & the Riviera
Puerto Rico
Rome
San Antonio & Austin
San Diego
San Francisco
Santa Fe, Taos & Albuquerque
Scandinavia
Scotland
Seattle & Portland
Singapore & Malaysia
South Africa
Southeast Asia
South Pacific
Spain
Sweden
Switzerland
Thailand
Tokyo
Toronto
Tuscany & Umbria
USA
Utah
Vancouver & Victoria
Vermont, New Hampshire
   & Maine
Vienna & the Danube Valley
Virgin Islands
Virginia
Walt Disney World &
   Orlando
Washington, D.C.
Washington State

FROMMER'S® DOLLAR-A-DAY GUIDES

Australia from $50 a Day
California from $60 a Day
Caribbean from $70 a Day
England from $70 a Day
Europe from $60 a Day

Florida from $60 a Day
Hawaii from $70 a Day
Ireland from $60 a Day
Italy from $70 a Day
London from $85 a Day

New York from $80 a Day
Paris from $85 a Day
San Francisco from $60 a Day
Washington, D.C.,
   from $60 a Day

FROMMER'S® PORTABLE GUIDES

Acapulco, Ixtapa &
   Zihuatanejo
Alaska Cruises & Ports of Call
Bahamas
Baja & Los Cabos
Berlin
California Wine Country
Charleston & Savannah
Chicago

Dublin
Hawaii: The Big Island
Las Vegas
London
Maine Coast
Maui
New Orleans
New York City
Paris

Puerto Vallarta, Manzanillo
   & Guadalajara
San Diego
San Francisco
Sydney
Tampa & St. Petersburg
Venice
Washington, D.C.

FROMMER'S® NATIONAL PARK GUIDES

Family Vacations in the
   National Parks
Grand Canyon

National Parks of the
   American West
Rocky Mountain

Yellowstone & Grand Teton
Yosemite & Sequoia/
   Kings Canyon
Zion & Bryce Canyon

FROMMER'S® MEMORABLE WALKS

Chicago
London

New York
Paris

San Francisco
Washington, D.C.

FROMMER'S® GREAT OUTDOOR GUIDES

New England
Northern California

Southern California & Baja
Southern New England

Washington & Oregon

FROMMER'S® BORN TO SHOP GUIDES

Born to Shop: China
Born to Shop: France

Born to Shop: Italy
Born to Shop: London

Born to Shop: New York
Born to Shop: Paris

FROMMER'S® IRREVERENT GUIDES

Amsterdam
Boston
Chicago
Las Vegas

London
Los Angeles
Manhattan
New Orleans

Paris
San Francisco
Seattle & Portland
Vancouver

Walt Disney World
Washington, D.C.

FROMMER'S® BEST-LOVED DRIVING TOURS

America
Britain
California

Florida
France
Germany

Ireland
Italy
New England

Scotland
Spain
Western Europe

THE UNOFFICIAL GUIDES®

Bed & Breakfasts in
   California
Bed & Breakfasts in
   New England
Bed & Breakfasts in
   the Northwest
Beyond Disney
Branson, Missouri
California with Kids
Chicago

Cruises
Disneyland
Florida with Kids
Golf Vacations in the
   Eastern U.S.
The Great Smoky &
   Blue Ridge
   Mountains
Inside Disney

Hawaii
Las Vegas
London
Miami & the Keys
Mini Las Vegas
Mini-Mickey
New Orleans
New York City
Paris

Safaris
San Francisco
Skiing in the West
Walt Disney World
Walt Disney World
   for Grown-ups
Walt Disney World
   for Kids
Washington, D.C.

SPECIAL-INTEREST TITLES

Frommer's Britain's Best Bed & Breakfasts and
   Country Inns
Frommer's Britain's Best Bike Rides
The Civil War Trust's Official Guide
   to the Civil War Discovery Trail
Frommer's Caribbean Hideaways
Frommer's Food Lover's Companion to France
Frommer's Food Lover's Companion to Italy
Frommer's Gay & Lesbian Europe
Frommer's Exploring America by RV
Hanging Out in Europe
Israel Past & Present

Mad Monks' Guide to California
Mad Monks' Guide to New York City
Frommer's The Moon
Frommer's New York City with Kids
The New York Times' Unforgettable
   Weekends
Places Rated Almanac
Retirement Places Rated
Frommer's Road Atlas Britain
Frommer's Road Atlas Europe
Frommer's Washington, D.C., with Kids
Frommer's What the Airlines Never Tell Yo